How to Draw

Photorealistic

Animals

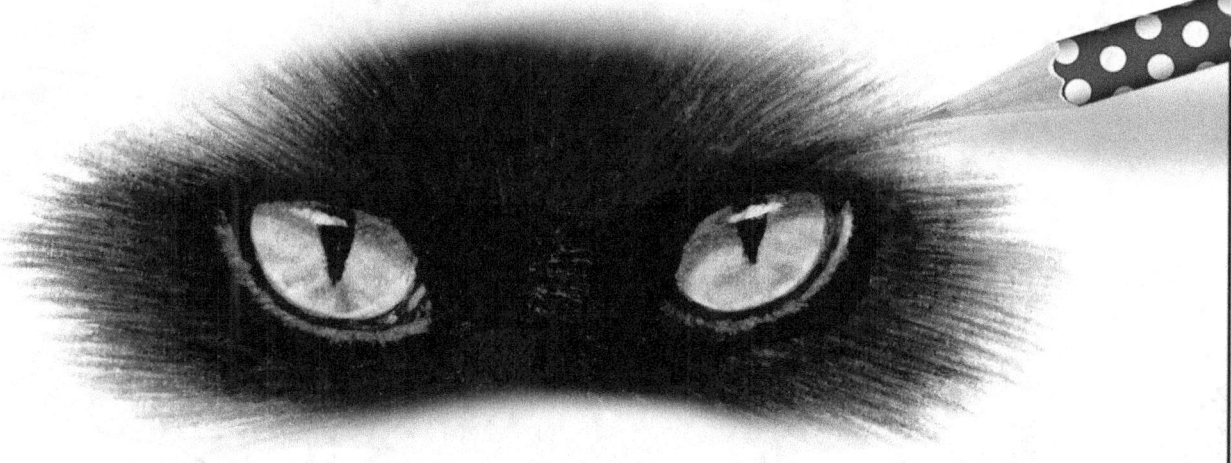

Drawing from Reference Photos
by Jasmina Susak

Inside the Book
A Collection of Drawings You'll Master

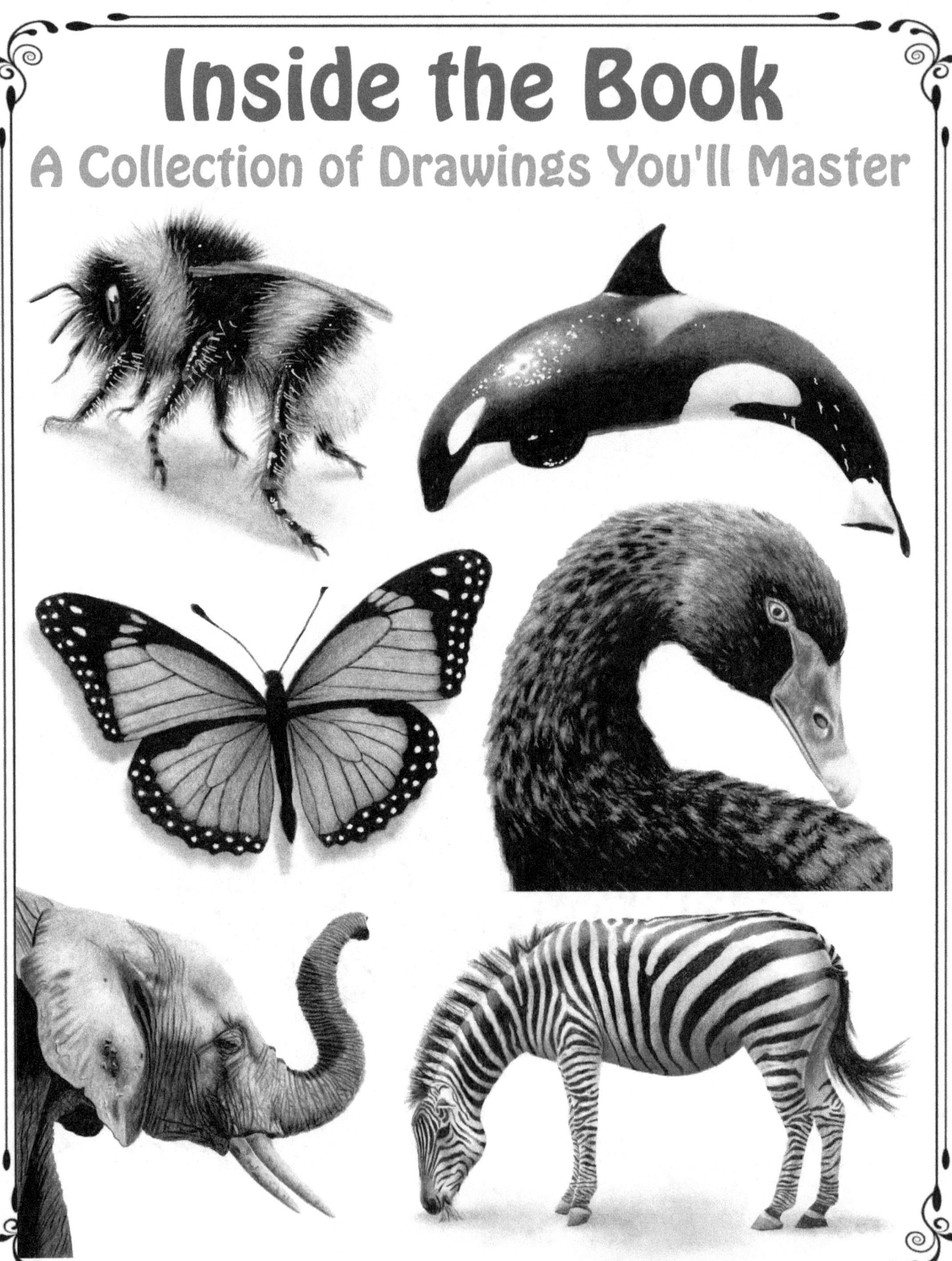

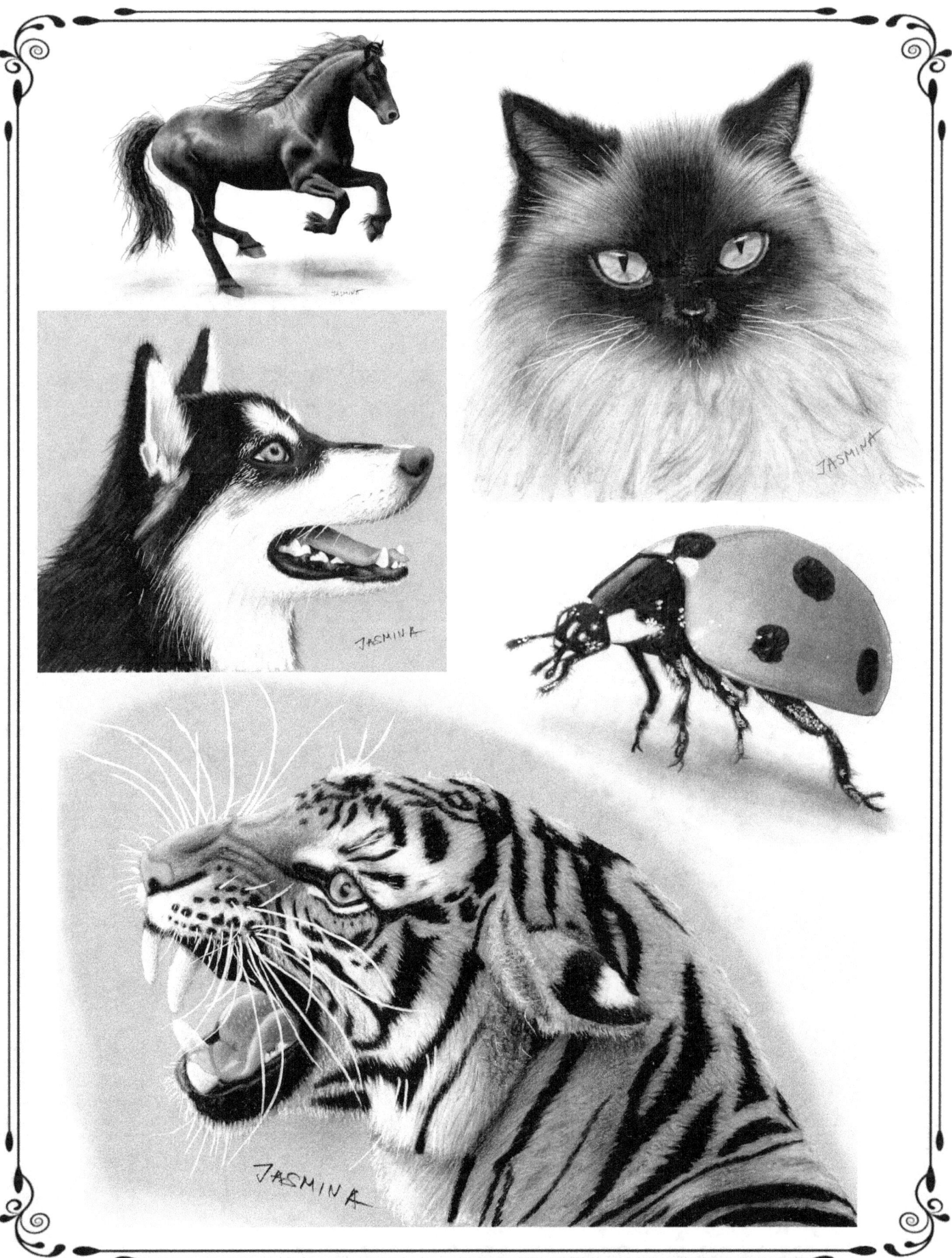

Copyright

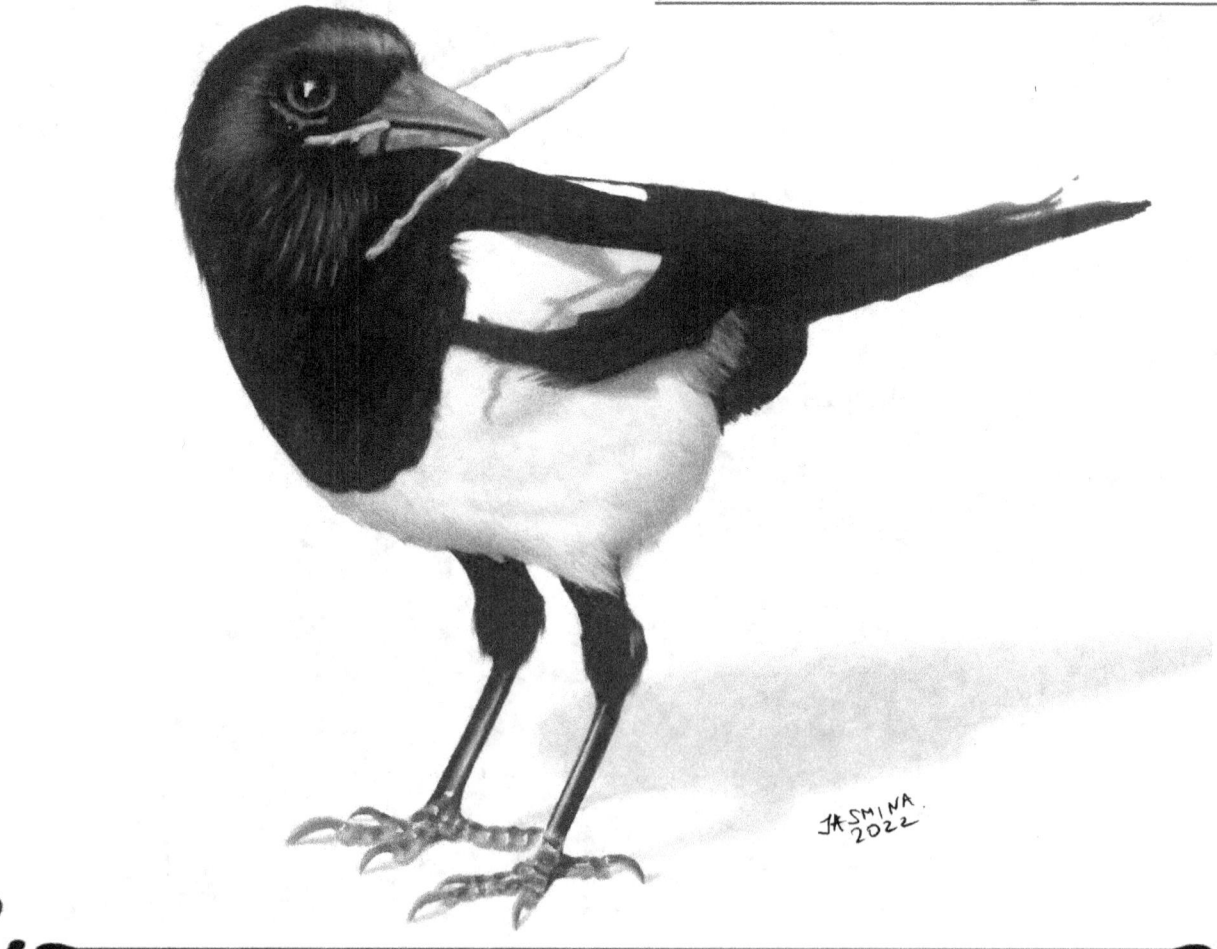

Dedication

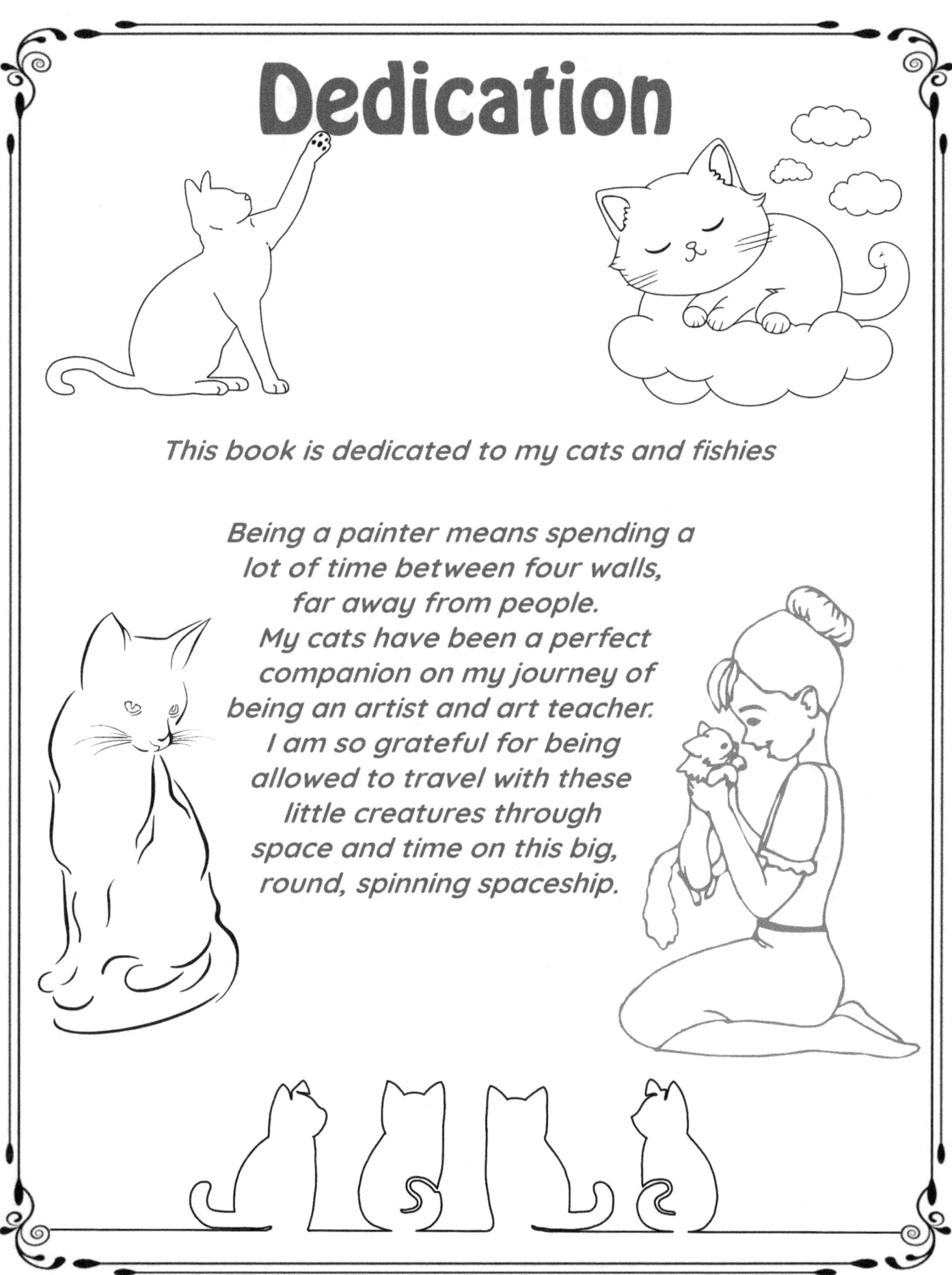

This book is dedicated to my cats and fishies

Being a painter means spending a
lot of time between four walls,
far away from people.
My cats have been a perfect
companion on my journey of
being an artist and art teacher.
I am so grateful for being
allowed to travel with these
little creatures through
space and time on this big,
round, spinning spaceship.

Table of Contents

Introduction

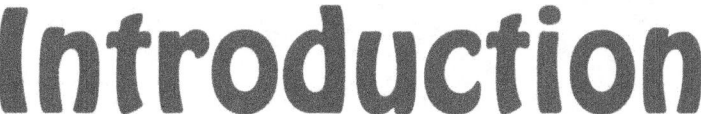

My ultimate aspiration has always been to create drawings that closely resemble photos. If you share this goal, then this book is specifically designed for you. I often come across the question, "Why not just take a photo?" My answer is simple: "Because that's easy, and we like to work hard!"
Drawing from reference photos is no easy task. Even with over a decade of experience in this field, I still find it challenging to replicate a photo with absolute precision, despite the appearance of effortlessness. I sincerely hope that you will embark on this exciting journey of learning a new process with enthusiasm and determination.

So, welcome to this guide, tailored to take your drawings to the next level. Assuming you have some prior drawing experience, this book aims to refine and enhance your existing skills. The focus here is to build upon your foundation, pushing beyond your comfort zone, and delving into more intricate and advanced techniques.

It is crucial to understand that achieving mastery in drawing is a gradual process. Your initial attempts may not be flawless, but it is important not to be discouraged. As you progress and compare your early works to your later ones, you will witness the remarkable improvement you have made. By persevering and consistently honing your skills, you will surpass your previous accomplishments. With time and practice, your skills will naturally progress, leading to remarkable growth.
To ensure a solid foundation, we will begin with simpler drawings as a warm-up before gradually advancing to more intricate and detailed projects. I urge you not to rush through the steps. Only move forward when you are content with the results of the previous stage, leaving no room for further improvement.

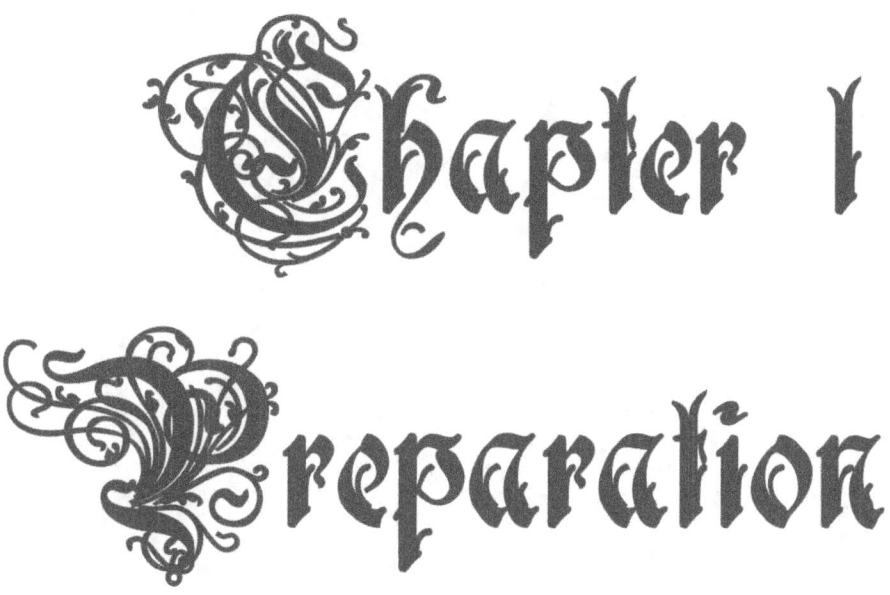

Chapter 1
Preparation

Essential Art Supplies

When it comes to drawing tools, there is no universal answer that suits everyone. Each artist has their own unique preferences and requirements. Depending on the specific outcomes you aim to achieve, a wide range of drawing supplies are available for you to choose from.

In this chapter, I aim to provide a comprehensive list of the tools and materials that will be utilized throughout the tutorials in this book. It is important to note that the mention of specific brands is purely based on personal preference and does not indicate superiority over other options.

I want to emphasize that I am not affiliated with nor sponsored by any of the mentioned brands. While I personally use and appreciate these particular brands, you are encouraged to explore and choose the brands that suit your own preferences. However, I recommend opting for established brands to ensure quality and durability.

Investing in slightly more expensive materials can enhance your overall artistic experience and yield better results compared to struggling with lower-quality tools. Remember, working with reliable and enjoyable materials can positively impact your creative process.

Graphite Pencils

First and foremost, I want to emphasize the flexibility and adaptability of the medium you choose for these tutorials. While graphite pencils are commonly used, feel free to explore other options such as charcoal or grey colored pencils. The key is to select the medium that resonates with you. Charcoal offers a rich and expressive texture, allowing for bold and dramatic effects. On the other hand, grey colored pencils provide a more controlled and precise approach while still offering a wide range of values.

So, whether you opt for charcoal, graphite pencils, or grey colored pencils, remember that the techniques and principles discussed in these tutorials can be applied across various mediums. Embrace the medium that speaks to you and encourages your artistic exploration.

For these tutorials, I personally favor and will be utilizing Pitt Graphite Matt pencils by Faber-Castell. These particular pencils offer a unique advantage in that they have a matte finish, eliminating any unwanted reflection of light.
This characteristic makes them ideal for artists who prefer a non-reflective surface.

What sets these pencils apart is that Faber-Castell has expanded their range to include even darker shades such as 10B, 12B, and 14B, surpassing the previous maximum darkness of 9B. This wider range allows for greater depth and intensity in your drawings.

The Pitt Graphite Matt pencils are available in eight degrees of hardness: HB, 2B, 4B, 6B, 8B, 10B, 12B, and 14B.
Since there are no lighter values lighter than HB, you can either use their regular pencils or an HB pencil and apply light pressure to achieve lighter tones. It is not necessary to purchase all eight pencils; acquiring a single HB, 2B, and 14B pencil will suffice.

By varying the pressure you apply while drawing, you can create a wide range of tones. I highly recommend practicing and experimenting with different pressures to familiarize yourself with the possibilities these pencils offer.

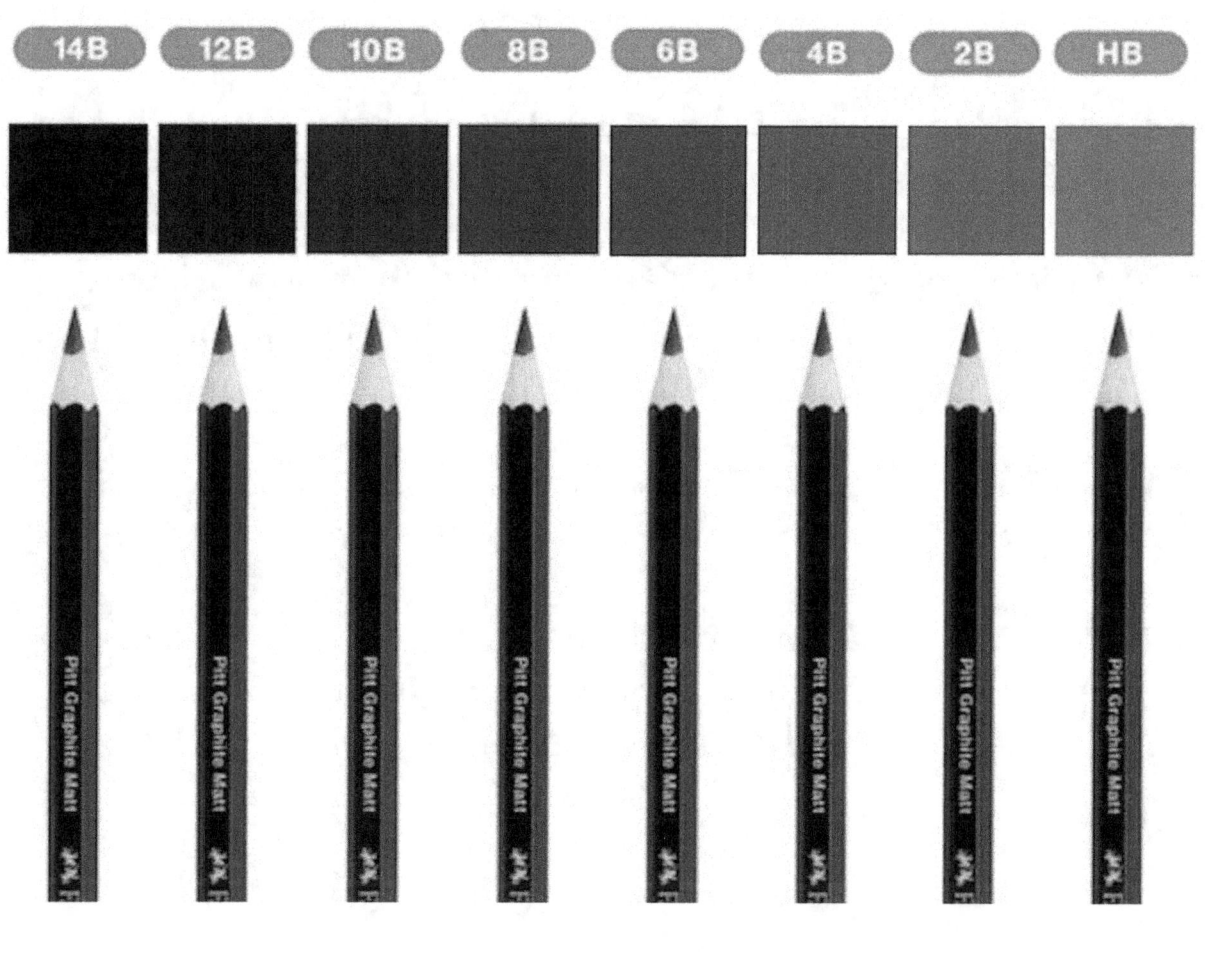

Paper

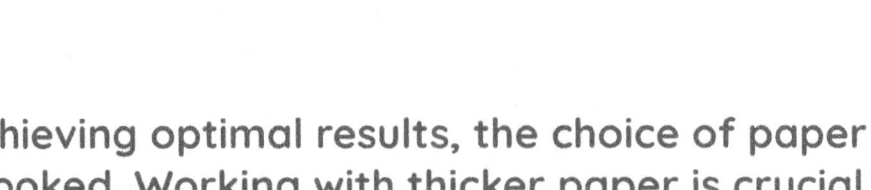

When it comes to achieving optimal results, the choice of paper should not be overlooked. Working with thicker paper is crucial to prevent wrinkling and tearing, which can be highly frustrating during the drawing process.

Over the past decade, I have consistently relied on Fabriano Bristol paper for both colored and graphite pencil drawings, and it has never disappointed. This paper boasts a weight of 250 g/m² or 145 lbs, making it exceptionally thick and sturdy. Its substantial weight has earned it the moniker of "illustration board" due to its thickness.

While some artists prefer textured or slightly yellowish paper, my personal preference lies in working on a smooth, pure white surface. This allows for precise control and a clean aesthetic in my drawings. Keep in mind that any bristol paper can serve as an excellent choice, as long as it meets your specific requirements.

As we progress through the drawings in this book, I will be utilizing the A4 paper format (210 x 297 mm or 8.3 x 11.7 in).

Remember, selecting the right paper sets the foundation for your artwork, ensuring a satisfying and enjoyable drawing experience.

Tools for Blending

When it comes to blending larger areas in my drawings, I find that a simple white tissue wrapped around my finger serves as a reliable tool. It's important to note that the tissue should be plain and free of any moisturizers, colors, or flavors. Opting for a basic, unadorned white tissue ensures a clean and effective blending process. When tackling smaller areas that require more precision, I turn to blending stumps or tortillons. These pencil-shaped tools, crafted from paper, are both affordable and highly efficient. They allow for controlled blending, making them ideal for achieving subtle transitions and softening edges in intricate details.

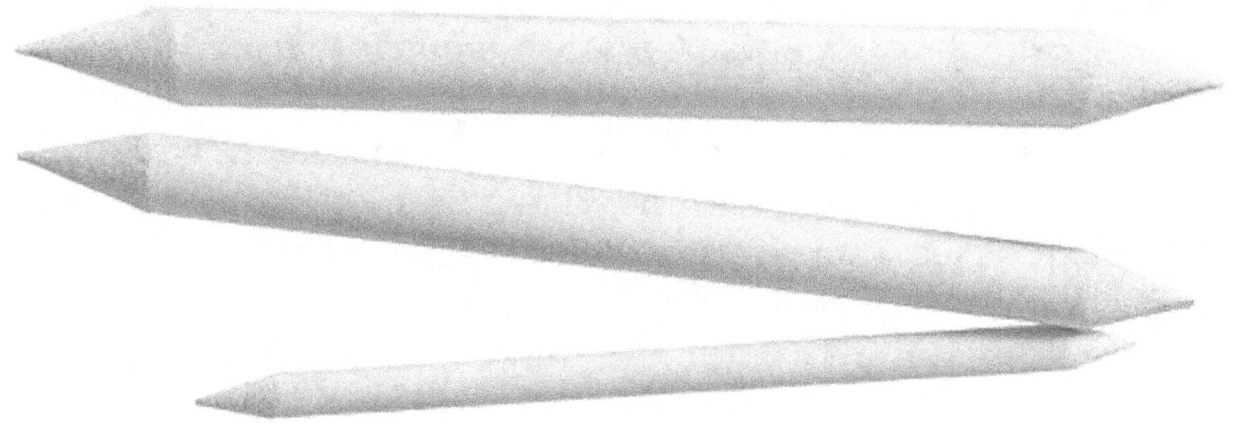

For instances where a balance between precision and broader coverage is needed, I rely on the versatility of Q-tips. These readily available cotton swabs provide a practical and accessible option for achieving intermediate blending effects.

I frequently use the Prismacolor Premier colorless blender pencil for graphite and colored pencil drawings. This versatile, wax-based tool effortlessly softens edges and achieves a fluffy appearance, as demonstrated in tutorials, including the one featuring a Ragdoll cat.

Erasers

Erasers play a vital role when working with graphite pencils, serving not only to correct mistakes but also to aid in the creation of highlights within shadowed areas. With a variety of erasers at my disposal, I am able to achieve different desired outcomes, making them an essential tool in my artistic process.

I rely on several types of erasers to achieve specific results and textures through the act of erasing graphite. My collection includes a simple eraser, a kneaded eraser, a mechanical eraser, and an electric eraser.

When confronted with the task of erasing a section within a particularly dark area, a kneaded eraser may prove ineffective. In such cases, I turn to the electric eraser, which excels at efficiently removing graphite, even from deep shadows. Its precision and thoroughness make it an invaluable tool.

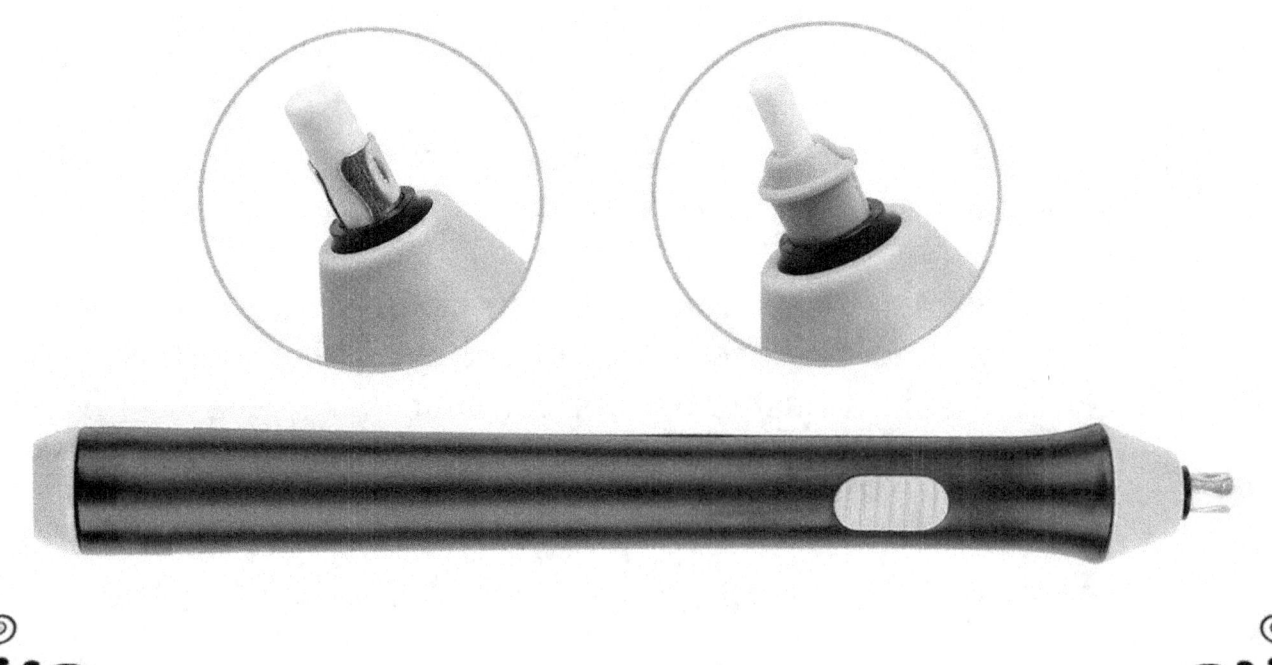

For lighter and more gradual erasing, especially when aiming for delicate details, the malleable nature of a kneaded eraser is ideal. Its ability to gently lift graphite allows for subtle adjustments without disturbing surrounding areas.

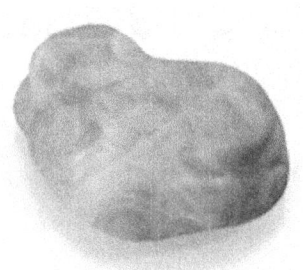

In instances where I seek a middle ground between precision and ease, the mechanical eraser emerges as the preferred option. Its retractable and precise nature enables me to selectively erase with control,
achieving the desired effect with ease.

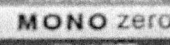

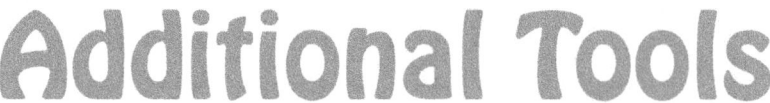

Additional Tools

In addition to the previously mentioned tools, a few other essentials greatly contribute to my drawing process:

Sharpener: A simple hand-held sharpener is a must-have for maintaining a fine point on my pencils.

Brush for Cleaning: To remove graphite powder and dust from my paper, I rely on a large makeup brush. Its soft bristles effectively eliminate unwanted residue without the risk of smudging or leaving fingerprints on the artwork. Regularly washing and properly drying the brush ensures its cleanliness and efficiency for future use.

Graphite Powder: For shading larger surfaces or creating atmospheric backgrounds, graphite powder is a valuable resource. It can be conveniently purchased or easily made by rubbing the tip of a graphite pencil against sandpaper. The resulting powder allows for smooth and versatile shading techniques, adding depth and dimension to the artwork.

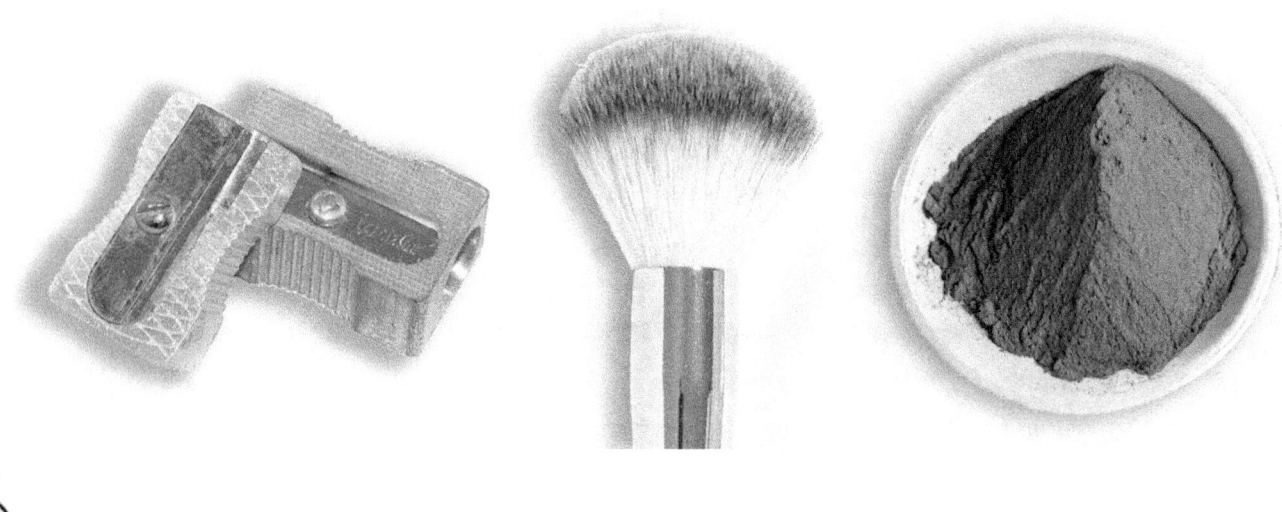

<u>Masking Tools:</u> When I want to preserve specific areas while shading or drawing, I rely on Frisket Masking Film. This film allows me to easily cover the desired regions and can be removed without causing any damage. While a regular masking tape or cut paper can serve the purpose, opting for a self-adhesive film specially designed for this task offers added convenience. This brand, well-regarded among artists, has proven to be reliable and highly recommended.

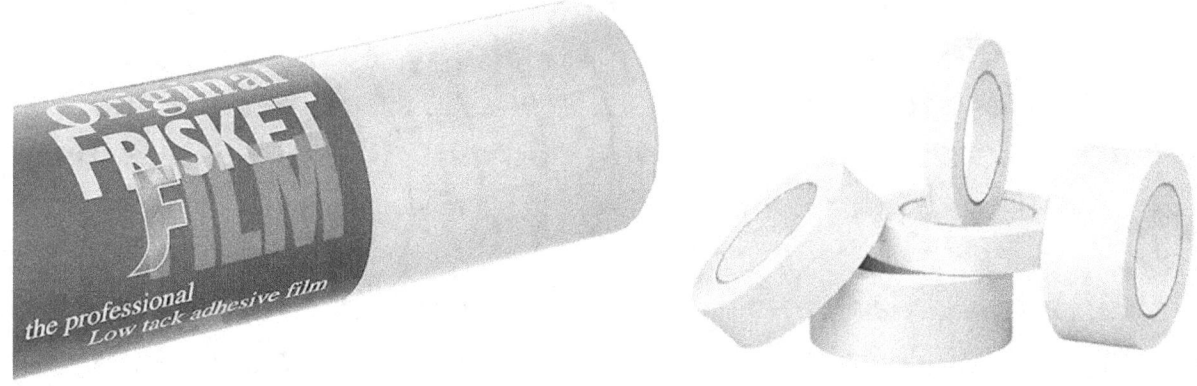

<u>White ink gel pen:</u> I often use a white ink gel pen or a white gelly roll for adding intricate white details to my drawings, especially when achieving pure white color is challenging. For instance, when drawing whiskers, I prefer using this pen instead of shading around tiny lines that must remain untouched until the end of the drawing to maintain their brightness. Erasers, on the other hand, can't create the precise lines needed for whiskers and may not remove enough graphite to achieve a truly white result. This versatile tool makes the process much easier and yields better results. If you don't have a white ink gel pen, any opaque white marker or even a correction fluid can serve the same purpose when applied over graphite or your chosen medium.

Sandpaper

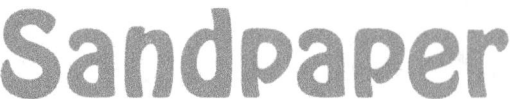

Sandpaper is a versatile tool that I always keep within reach during my artistic endeavors. It serves multiple purposes, including sharpening the tips of my pencils and cleaning both pencil tips and electric erasers.

Additionally, I rely on sandpaper to create a sharp point on my electric eraser. To accomplish it, I simply turn it on and run it at a 45-degree angle across the sandpaper. This technique ensures a crisp and precise tip, allowing for intricate erasing when working on detailed areas of my drawings.

To sharpen the tips of my pencils, I gently rotate them against the sandpaper, ensuring a precise and fine point. The abrasive surface of the sandpaper efficiently removes excess graphite and helps maintain the pencil's optimal performance.

Sandpaper can also serve as a tool for creating your own graphite powder.

Types of lines

Different textures require specific types of lines and shading techniques to achieve desired effects. Here, I will briefly introduce a few essential ones and provide accompanying example images.

<u>Hatching</u>

Hatching involves applying non-crossing, parallel lines next to each other to cover an area completely or partially. This technique is ideal for drawing curly human hair or long, shiny animal fur, such as a straight horse's mane.

To illustrate this technique, refer to the accompanying image.

In the first step (1), using a 2B pencil, draw lines towards the highlight of the curl, specifically targeting the middle section where the hair bends. Apply firm pressure on the left side at the darkest area and gradually move towards the highlight, releasing the pressure on the pencil.

Next, in step two (2), repeat the process on the opposite side. Begin with firm pressure and gradually lighten your touch as you near the area you've previously drawn. Leave some blank space in-between the lines. The size of the blank space determines the size and shine of the curls. For tiny curls, leave a small amount of blank space.

In the third step (3), add more shading by covering the end of the curl with a much darker shade, such as 8B. Apply firm pressure at the beginning and gradually release it as you draw the lines towards the highlight.

Finally, in step four (4), use a blending stump to blend the ends of the strokes over the highlight. To add more realism, create random flyaway hairs by erasing the graphite in various areas of the drawing. This technique will result in a shiny, curly lock of hair. It's important to note that in this case, we do not use cross-hatching or circulism, which I will discuss in more detail later on.

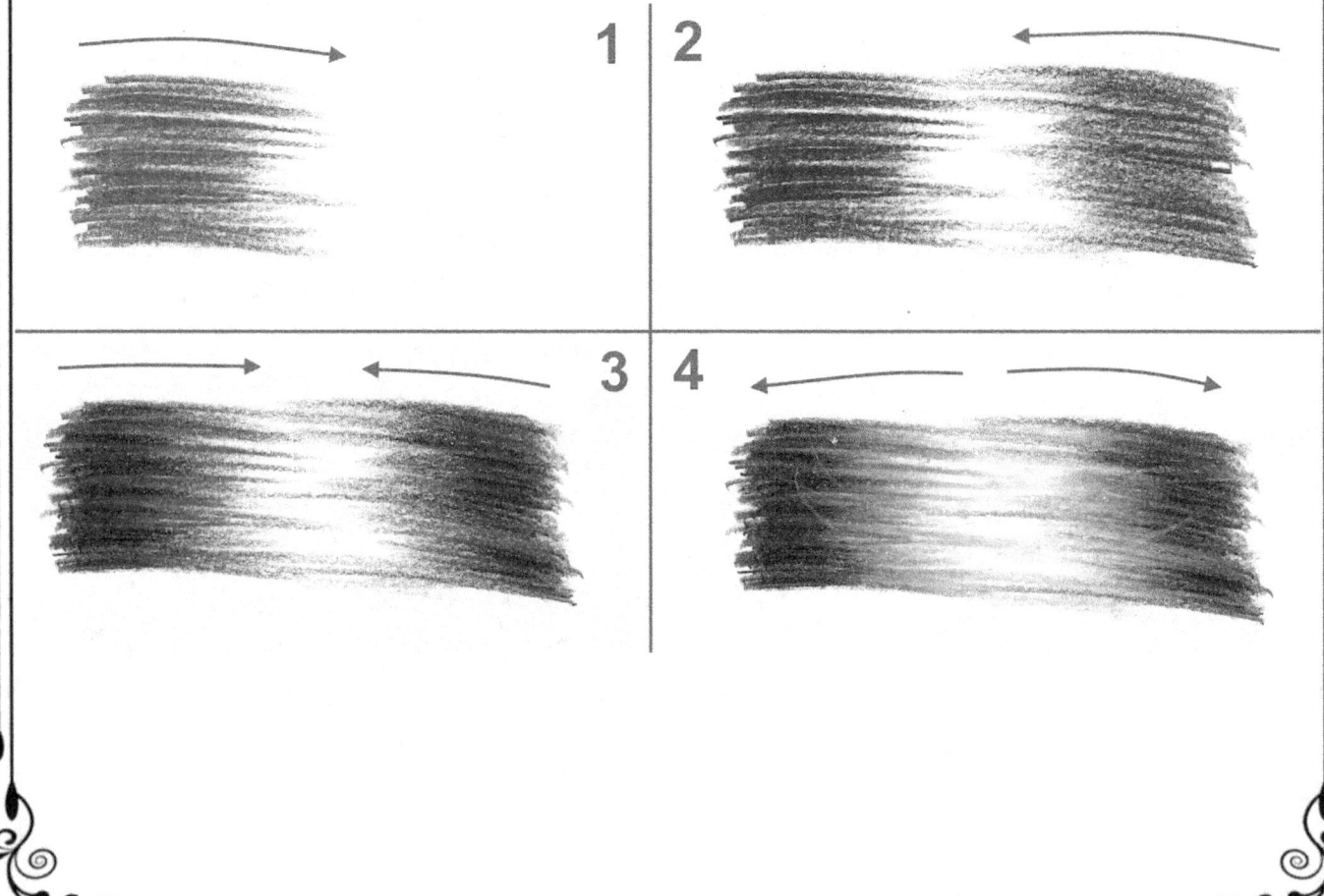

Crosshatching

Crosshatching is a valuable technique for creating a wide range of textures, particularly for fabrics and other intricate surfaces. To achieve this effect, start by applying parallel pencil strokes closely together in one direction. Then, layer another set of lines at a 90-degree angle, perpendicular to the initial strokes.

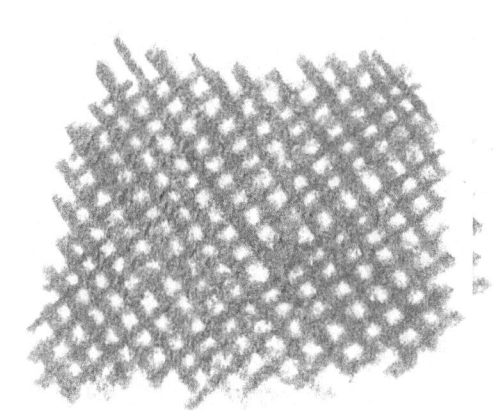

Stippling

Stippling is a technique that involves creating a pattern of numerous dots on the surface. Some artists even create entire artworks using only stippling. When using stippling to create shading, the dots are placed closer together in shadowed areas, while for highlights, the dots are spaced slightly further apart.

This technique is particularly useful when working with pencils that may not produce a smooth texture no matter how hard we press. Stippling allows us to even out the texture by applying more shade to lighter areas and achieving a gradual, controlled shading effect without making sudden progress or mistakes. It provides a methodical and precise approach to creating realistic textures and tones in our drawings. It is also crucial to consider the sharpness or dullness of the pencil tip when aiming for specific textures. A very sharp pencil tip can create precise and fine details, while an absolutely dull tip can produce broader and softer strokes. By adjusting the sharpness of the pencil tip, we have greater control over the textures we want to achieve in our drawings. This allows us to vary the level of detail and create different visual effects, enhancing the overall realism and expression of our artwork.

Scribbling

Scribbling is a technique that involves drawing lines in a random and unstructured manner to cover a specific area.

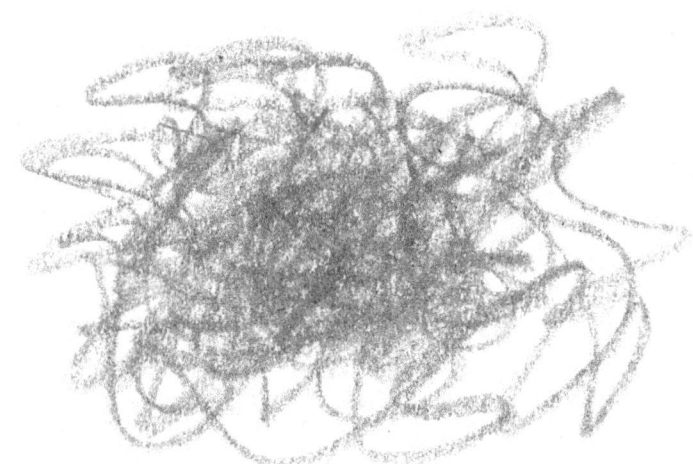

With scribbling, you have the freedom to let loose and create spontaneous marks. Once you have finished scribbling, you can blend the lines together using a tissue or a blending stump, resulting in a unique and textured effect. It can be particularly useful for creating certain textures in your artwork.

Circulism

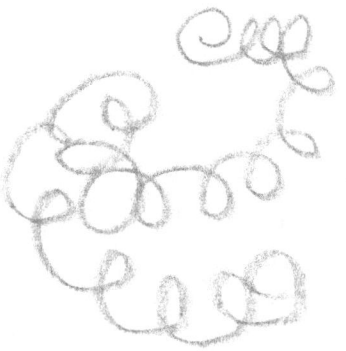

Circulism is a method that involves applying overlapping circles, as shown in the image on the left.
While the example provides a basic understanding, in practice, the circles should be much closer together and repeated until an even texture is achieved.

Now, let's draw the circles overlapping each other repeatedly. Take a look at the image on the right to see the final result. By drawing circles over one another, we can cover the paper completely and create a smooth texture, especially useful for drawing human skin and similar textures.

I personally use this technique and highly recommend it for achieving a seamless texture without visible lines. It's important to use a good quality, smooth, and thick paper that can handle multiple layers of hard-pressed coloring. Thin paper may crumble and tear when using a lot of overlapping circles.

A Smooth Gradient

In the realm of realistic drawings, mastering the art of creating a smooth gradient is paramount. This technique entails seamlessly connecting dark, mid, and highlighted tones without any visible edges between them. The shades should gracefully flow into one another, creating a seamless transition. Once you've mastered the smooth gradient, the possibilities for realistic drawing are limitless.

To practice this technique, I encourage you to shade a flat surface, as depicted in the accompanying image. Although I won't be delving into shading a sphere in this book, as it is a widely explored subject, I believe it's important to reinforce the significance of practicing the smooth gradient. It serves as the foundation for creating lifelike textures and volumes.

The key to achieving a smooth transition between different graphite grades lies in adjusting the pressure applied to your pencil. In the left image, you'll observe how I applied 2B, HB, H, 3H, and 5H pencils next to each other, maintaining a consistent pressure throughout. On the right side, I began with a 2B pencil, exerting firm pressure on the left side of the swatch. As I moved towards the lightest area on the right, I gradually released the pressure on my pencil.

Continuing with an HB pencil, I slightly overlapped the right side of the previously drawn 2B area, pressing harder to blend the shades, while easing the pressure as I shaded towards the right side. I repeated this process with an H and 3H pencil, and finally, I used a 5H pencil on the left side, applying very light pressure to allow the lightest shade to fade smoothly into the brightness of the paper. By revisiting the previously used pencils, we seamlessly blend them together, rendering the edges invisible.

2B HB H 3H 5H   2B HB H 3H 5H

Practicing this technique will refine your ability to create realistic gradients and develop a discerning eye for smooth transitions in your artwork.

How to Choose Reference Photos

When selecting a reference photo for your drawing, it's important to choose images that exhibit good contrast and avoid appearing flat. Even if the original photo lacks strong contrast, you can create it in your drawing by emphasizing highlights and shadows, as demonstrated in the zebra tutorial. Additionally, ensure that the subjects in the images are recognizable even as small thumbnails.

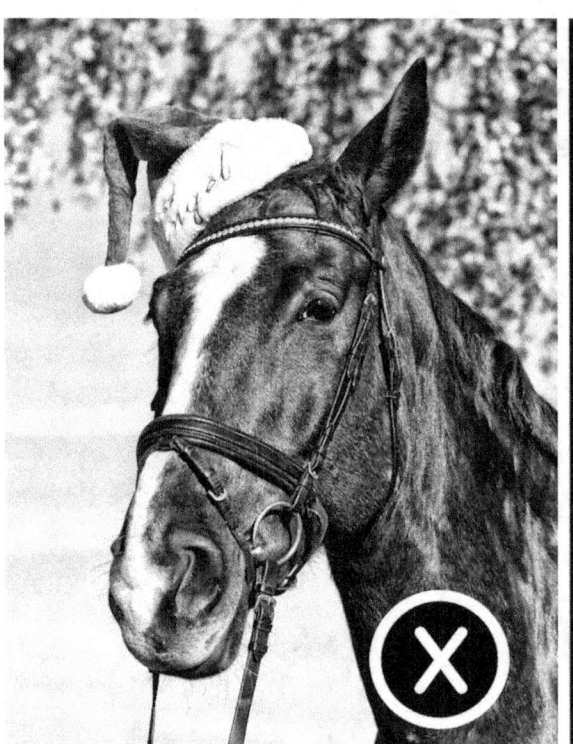 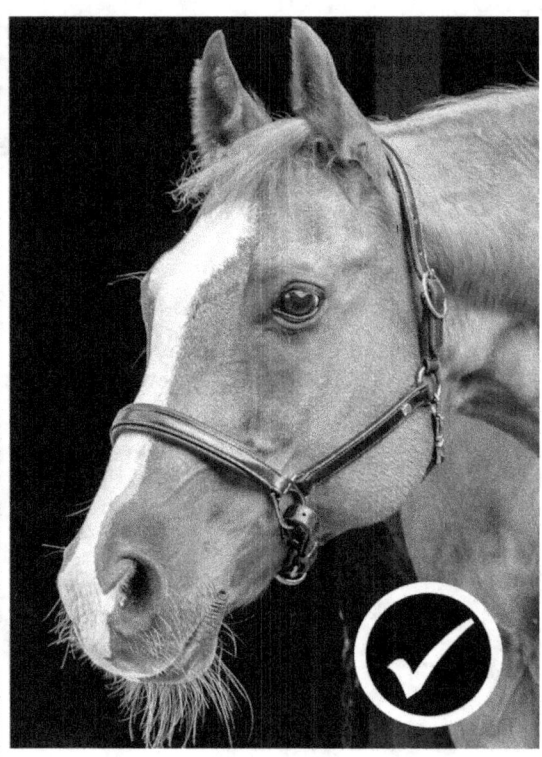

For improved clarity, you can consider coloring the background surrounding the animal with white or even black in image editing software. By simulating the white paper background, you can better assess the contrast, values, and overall composition of your subject. Removing the details in the background, the animal becomes the main focal point. This minimalist approach can result in a powerful and impactful composition, especially when the goal is to emphasize the animal and create a strong visual impact.

Throughout the tutorials in this book, I will delve further into the topic of choosing reference photos and provide you with valuable tips and advice to make the best selections for your artwork.

How to Choose the Right Pencils

You may wonder how to choose the right pencils for your future drawings when I won't be there to guide you like in these tutorials. The skill of choosing the right grade develops over time through practice and experience. I typically rely on my instincts and pick up the pencil that first comes to mind when I see the reference photo. However, this method can be challenging for beginners, as it's easy to select the wrong shade.

To assist you in the beginning, I have developed a helpful tool called the "Color Picker for Artists," available as both a mobile and desktop app. This tool allows you to upload your reference photo, select a specific area, and the app will suggest the closest match in terms of colored or graphite pencils. The desktop version even offers an accuracy feature, displaying the match in percentage. While these are paid apps, their cost is equivalent to just a few pencils, and they can save you valuable time in choosing the right pencils. For more information and links, visit our website at www.pen-pick.com

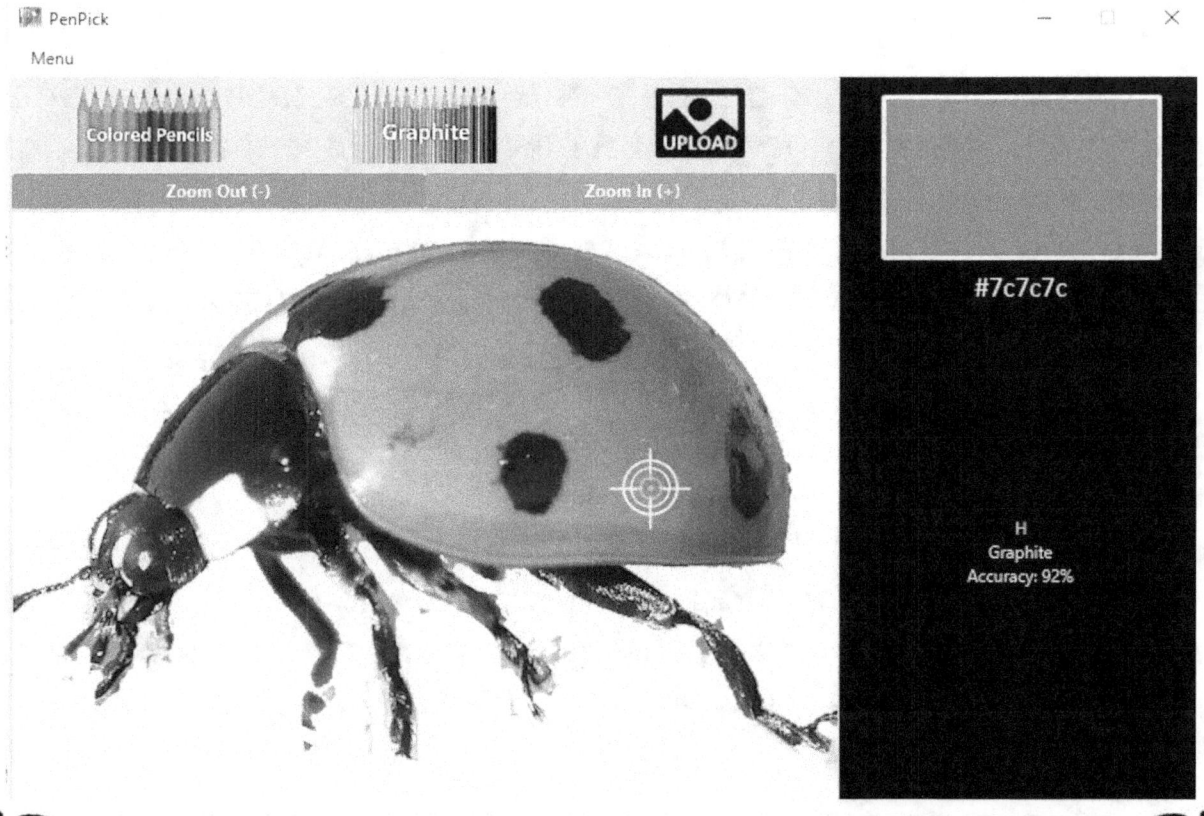

Proportional Sketching

When creating realistic drawings with graphite pencils, a solid foundation is crucial. The initial sketch must be both proportional and accurate since dark pencils are not easily erasable. However, sketching alone does not guarantee a realistic result. It is possible to have a perfect sketch but end up with a drawing lacking realism, just as a less perfect sketch can be transformed through shading and strategic value placement. While tracing may provide a quick solution, it hinders the development of freehand drawing skills and patience, and poses significant disadvantages in the long run. Additionally, on high-quality thick paper, tracing may be ineffective due to limited transparency, resulting in misplaced lines.

The Grid Method

The Grid Method is a simple and effective technique for accurately transferring the outlines of a reference photo onto your drawing surface. It involves dividing both the reference photo and the drawing area into a grid of equal-sized squares. By carefully observing the reference photo square by square and replicating the content in each corresponding square on your drawing surface, you can ensure accurate proportions and placement.

To develop freehand drawing skills, I highly recommend utilizing the grid method. Start by sketching the main lines freehand, resorting to the grid only if the proportions appear incorrect in your initial sketch. As you gain confidence, gradually increase the size of your grid squares, gradually relying less on the grid itself. Advanced artists may use just a few grid lines for reference, relying more on their "artistic eye".

The grid method has a rich history in the art world, dating back to the Middle Ages. One of the most renowned artists to employ this technique was Albrecht Dürer.

The accompanying image showcases Dürer's method of positioning his model within a framed grid, allowing him to sketch an accurate and faithful reproduction on paper.

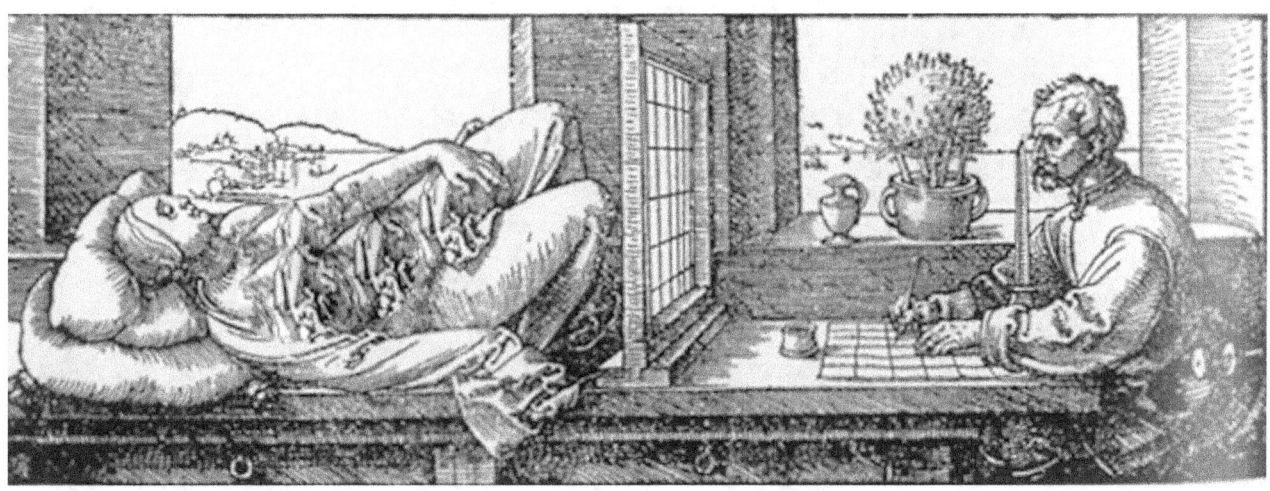

The Grid Method was also used by many other Renaissance artists, including the great Leonardo da Vinci. Even today, the Grid Method remains a valuable technique for artists seeking to break down complex subjects and maintain accuracy in their artwork.

How to Utilize the Grid Method

So, how to create a grid over your reference photo and your blank sheet of paper?

If you find it challenging to draw a grid over your reference photo by hand, there are digital tools available to assist you. One such tool is GriDraw, an app that I have developed. GriDraw offers a convenient grid drawing tool that can help you place grid lines on your reference photo. For more information about GriDraw and to make a purchase, please visit my website at www.gridraw.net

I highly recommend using square cells with a 1:1 aspect ratio instead of rectangular ones when drawing grids. This is because square cells are simpler and easier to work with, allowing for better accuracy and proportionality in your artwork.

1. Begin by deciding the desired number of columns and rows for your grid.

2. Draw a grid over your reference photo, labeling each cell with numbers or letters as shown in the accompanying image.

3. On a blank sheet of paper, draw the grid with matching rows and columns as your reference photo. Make sure to label the cells in the same manner. For optimal results, I recommend using an HB pencil and applying gentle pressure. Lighter (harder) pencils have a tendency to emboss lines into the paper, which can be undesirable when shading. It is unnecessary to use darker pencils as they may remain visible even after erasing.

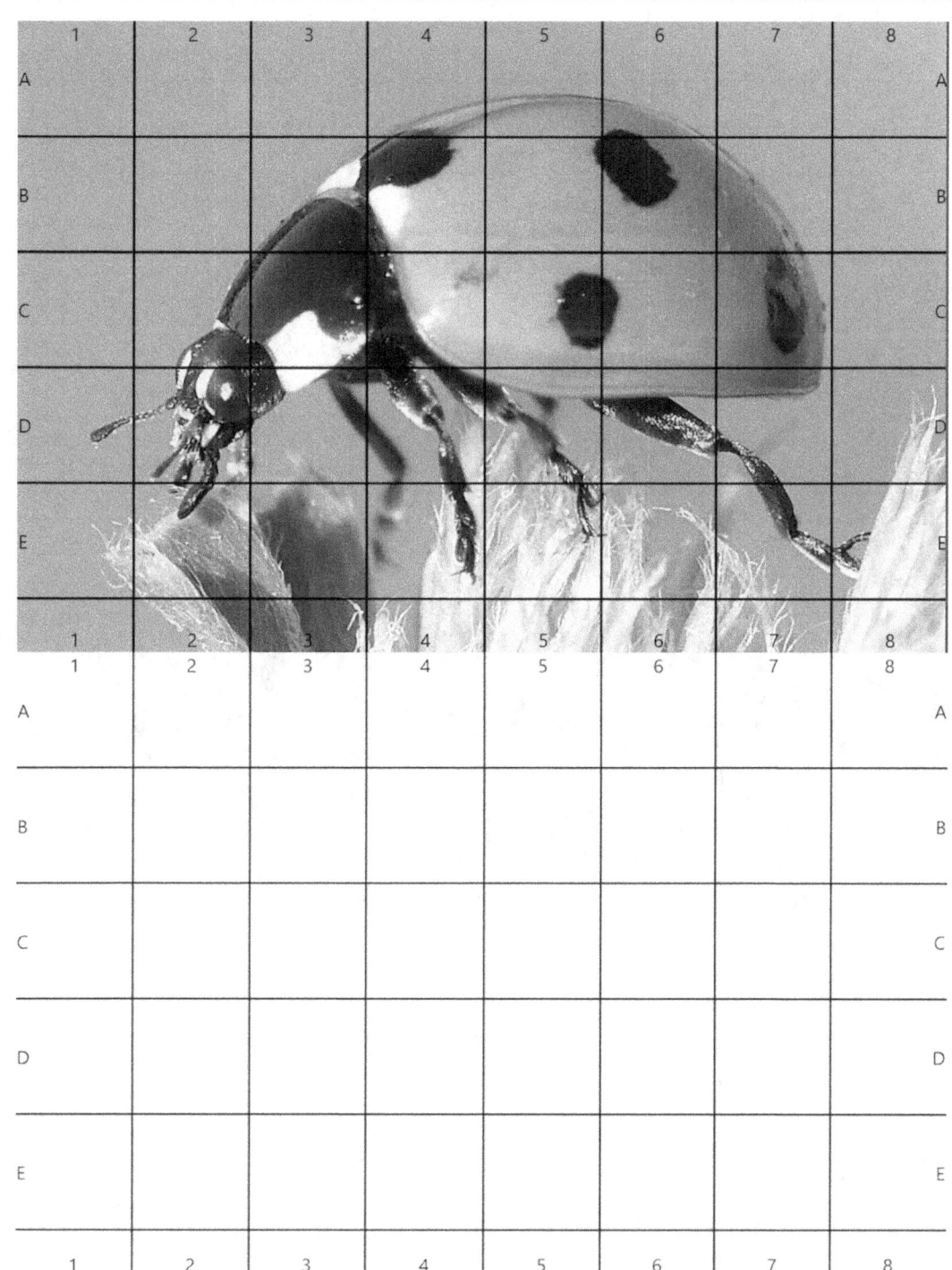

4. Now it's time to start sketching the lines you'll need for your drawing. These lines can be simple shapes or intricate details, depending on what you find most helpful from the reference photo. Choose a box on the grid as your starting point and

locate the corresponding box on your gridded paper or canvas. In the provided image, you can see that I began in box B7, drawing the curve of the ladybug's shell.

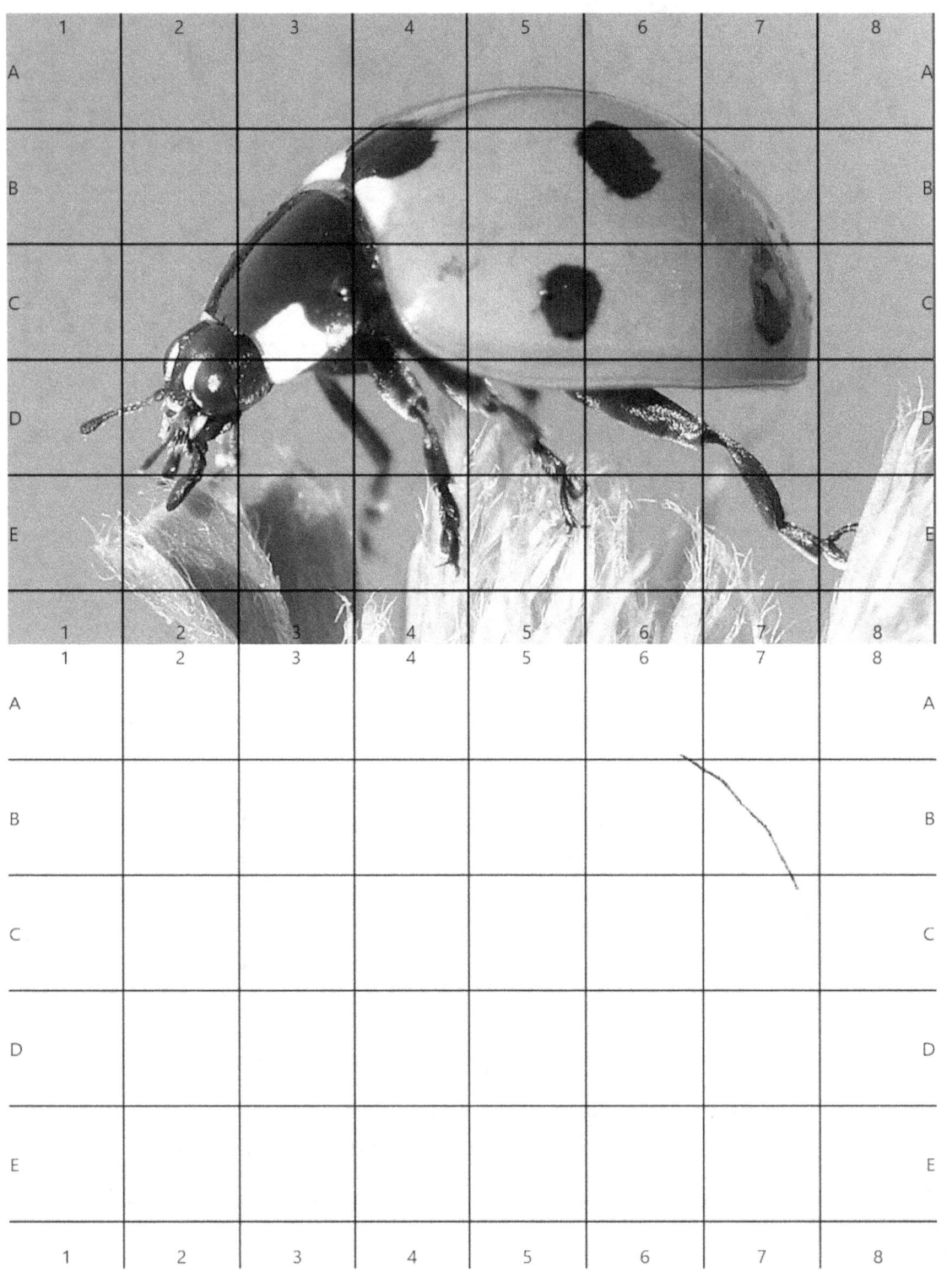

5. As you sketch, carefully follow the outline from one box to another, making sure to reference the marginal labels to keep track of your position. Pay close attention to where the outline begins and ends within each box, maintaining accuracy and capturing the desired shape

6. Take a moment to carefully review your sketch. Assess the overall accuracy and proportionality of the drawing, comparing it to the reference photo. Make any necessary adjustments to ensure that the proportions are correct and the details are accurately captured.

7. If you are satisfied with your sketch and confident in its accuracy, it's time to carefully erase the grid lines from your paper. Use a soft eraser and gentle strokes to remove the grid lines, ensuring that you don't smudge or damage any part of your drawing. Once the grid lines are erased, you'll have a clean drawing ready for the next stages of shading and detailing.

In the image provided, you can see the key sketch lines that I deemed important for my drawing.

To practice the grid method, use your pencil to recreate the sketch over the grid lines in the image I have provided after the step 4 in this chapter.

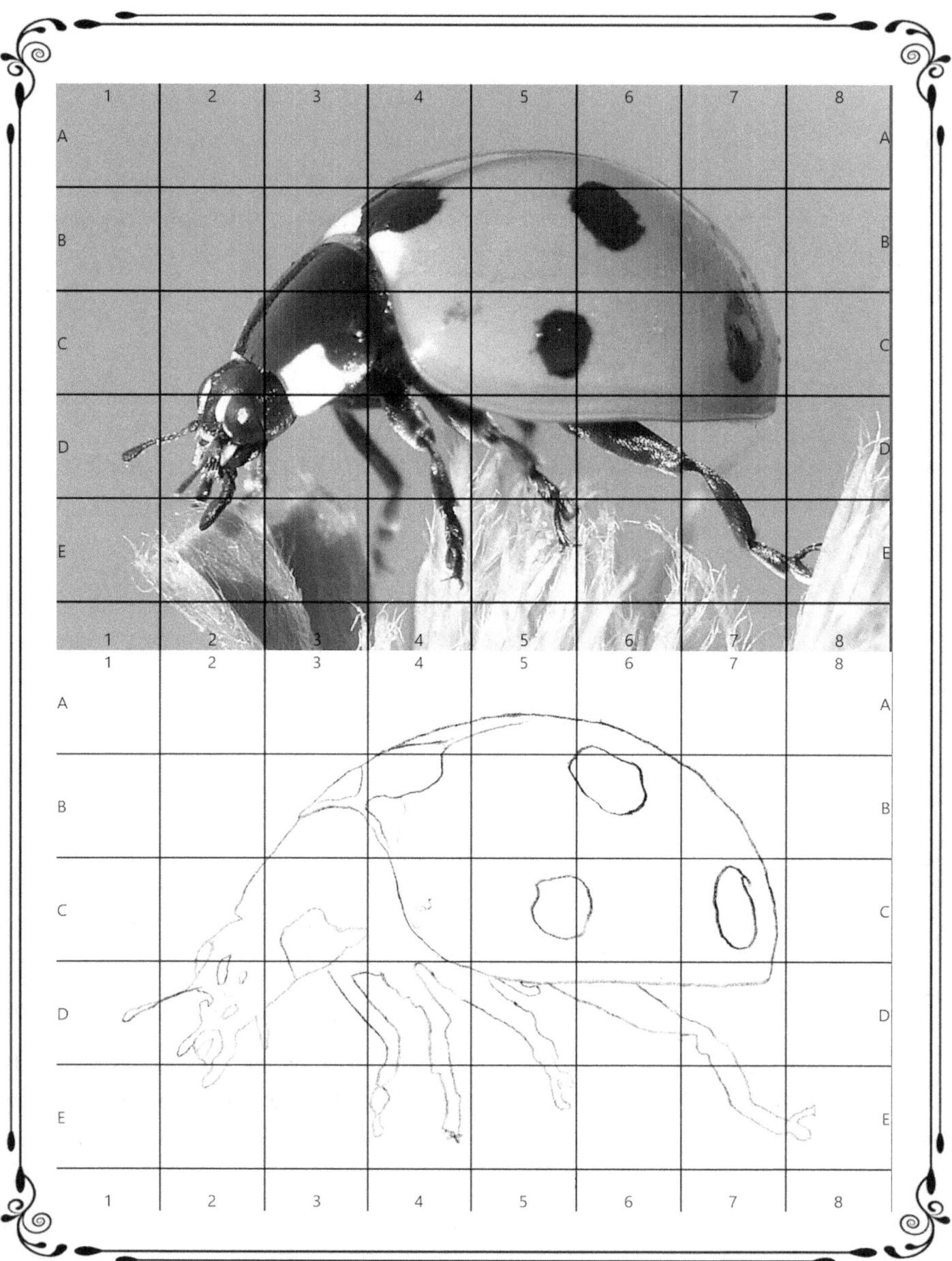

If you find it challenging to create the sketch using the grid method or if you simply prefer to have a pre-made sketch to work with, you can download all of the sketches featured in this book from my website www.jasminasusak.com/sketch

These sketches are provided in a compressed zip file for easy downloading. Once you have downloaded the file, you can decompress or unzip it to access the individual sketch images. From there, you can print the sketches onto your preferred paper and begin shading over the existing lines.
This can be a helpful option to save time and ensure accuracy in your drawings.

Here is another image for you to practice with:

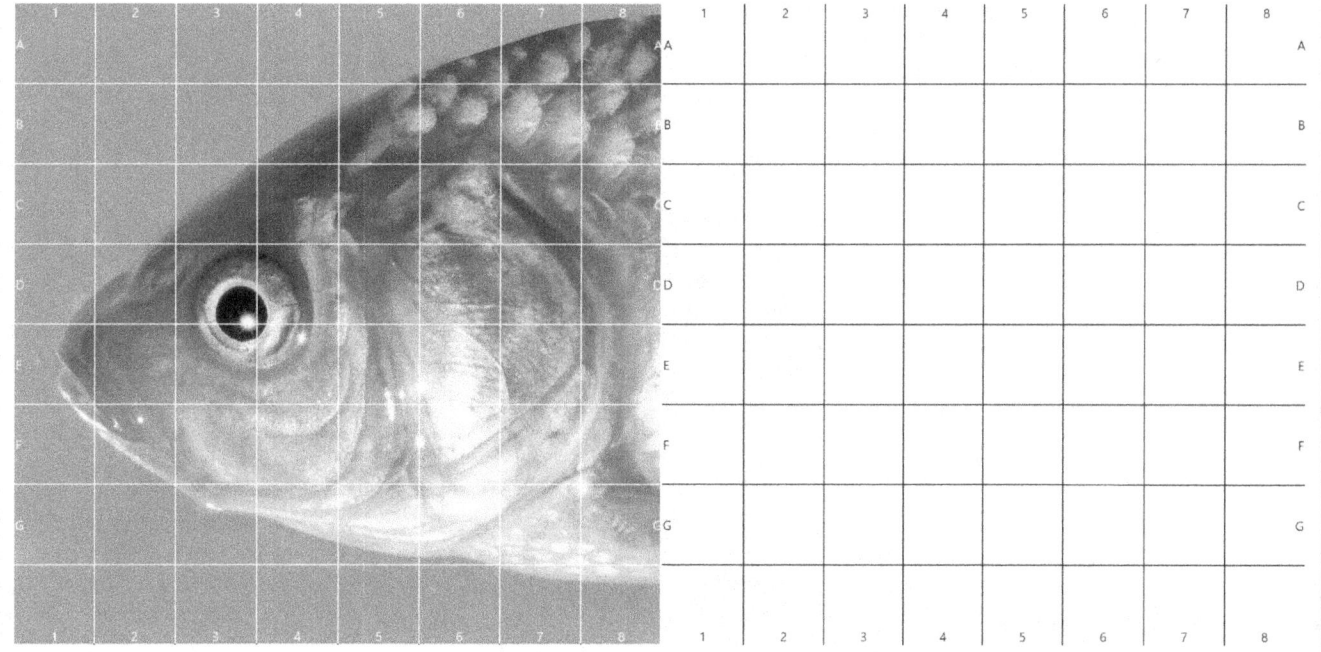

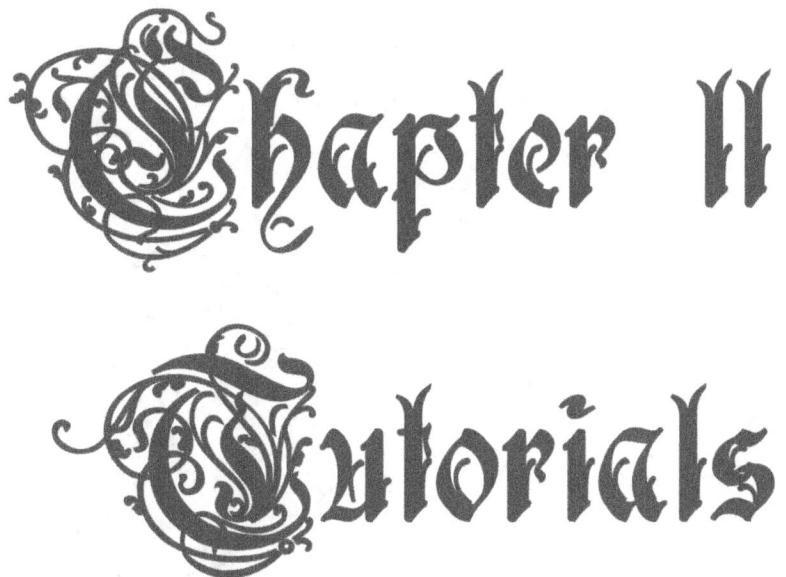

Chapter II

Tutorials

How to Draw a Butterfly

Drawing a butterfly can serve as a great starting point for beginners exploring graphite pencil techniques. It's relatively simple yet allows you to practice fundamental skills like sketching, shading, and capturing delicate details while creating a beautiful and recognizable subject.

As you progress, the skills learned in this simple tutorial will empower you to take on more complex and challenging subjects with confidence.

The Reference Photo

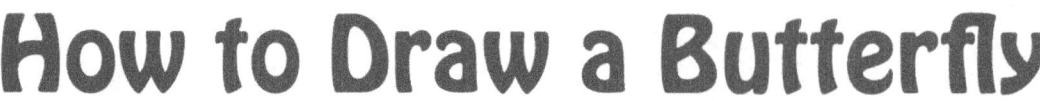

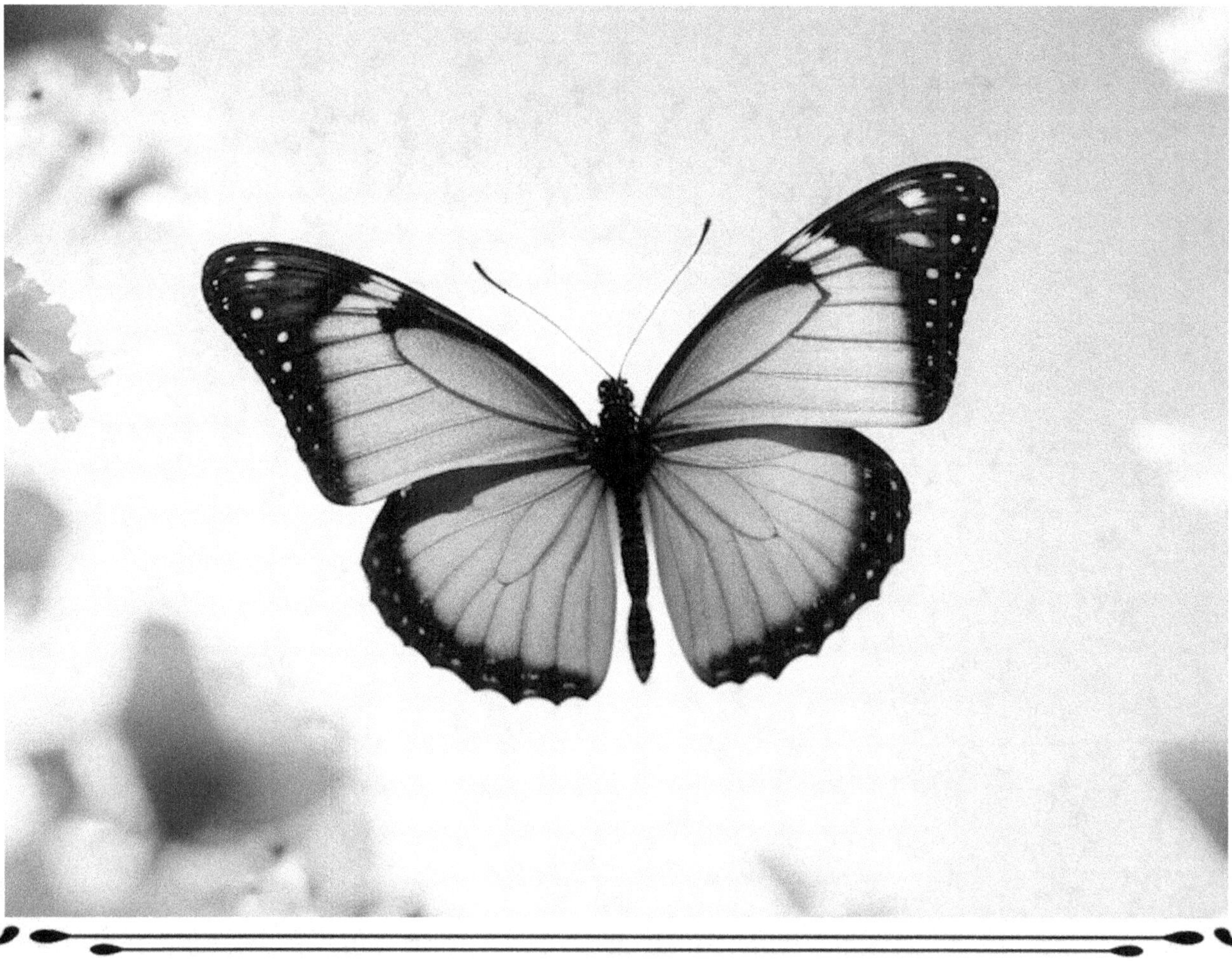

Sketching and Basic Shapes

I used an AI image generator to create this reference photo, ensuring that we won't encounter any copyright issues. I encourage fellow artists to embrace and utilize such innovations, as they open up endless possibilities to generate unique reference materials for our artwork.

In the image below, you'll find the main lines of my sketch. As you can observe, I've added additional dots along the edge compared to what's depicted in the reference photo.

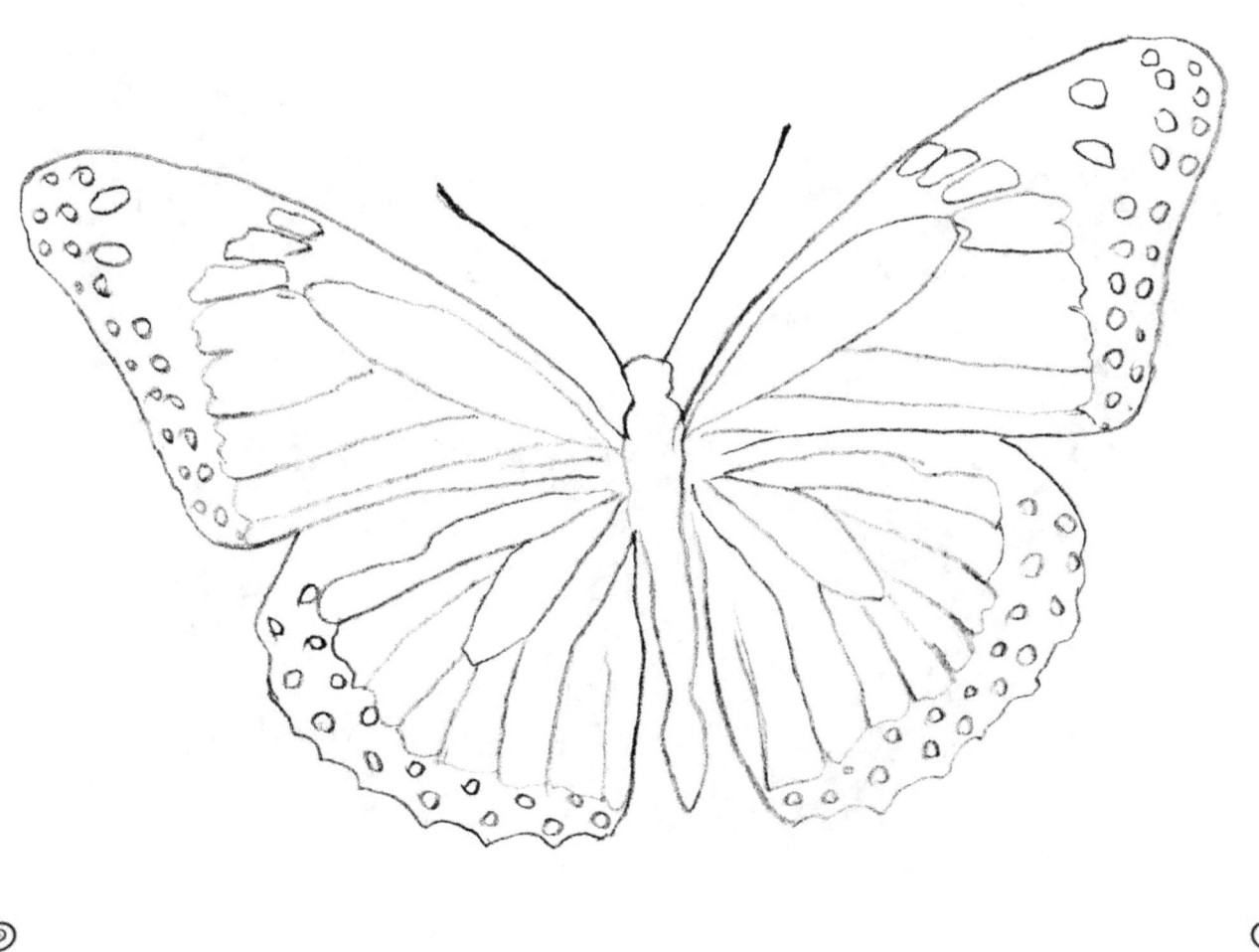

Creating the Deepest Shadows

Embark on the pivotal step that gives shape to almost the entire butterfly. Although not inherently challenging, this phase demands a substantial investment of time and precision. I employed a 14B pencil, exerting firm pressure to produce the profoundest shadows.

Regular pencil sharpening is essential for achieving crisp edges and delineating the lines within the pattern. Keep in mind that this soft pencil type wears down rapidly under strong pressure. I frequently need to restock on pencils darker than 2B, especially since I often rely on these deeper shades to achieve a photorealistic depth in my drawings.

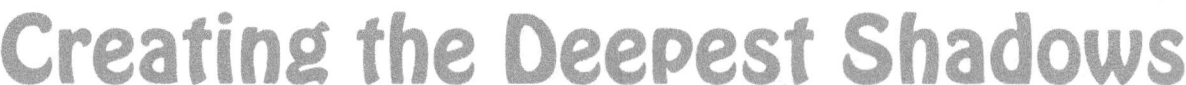

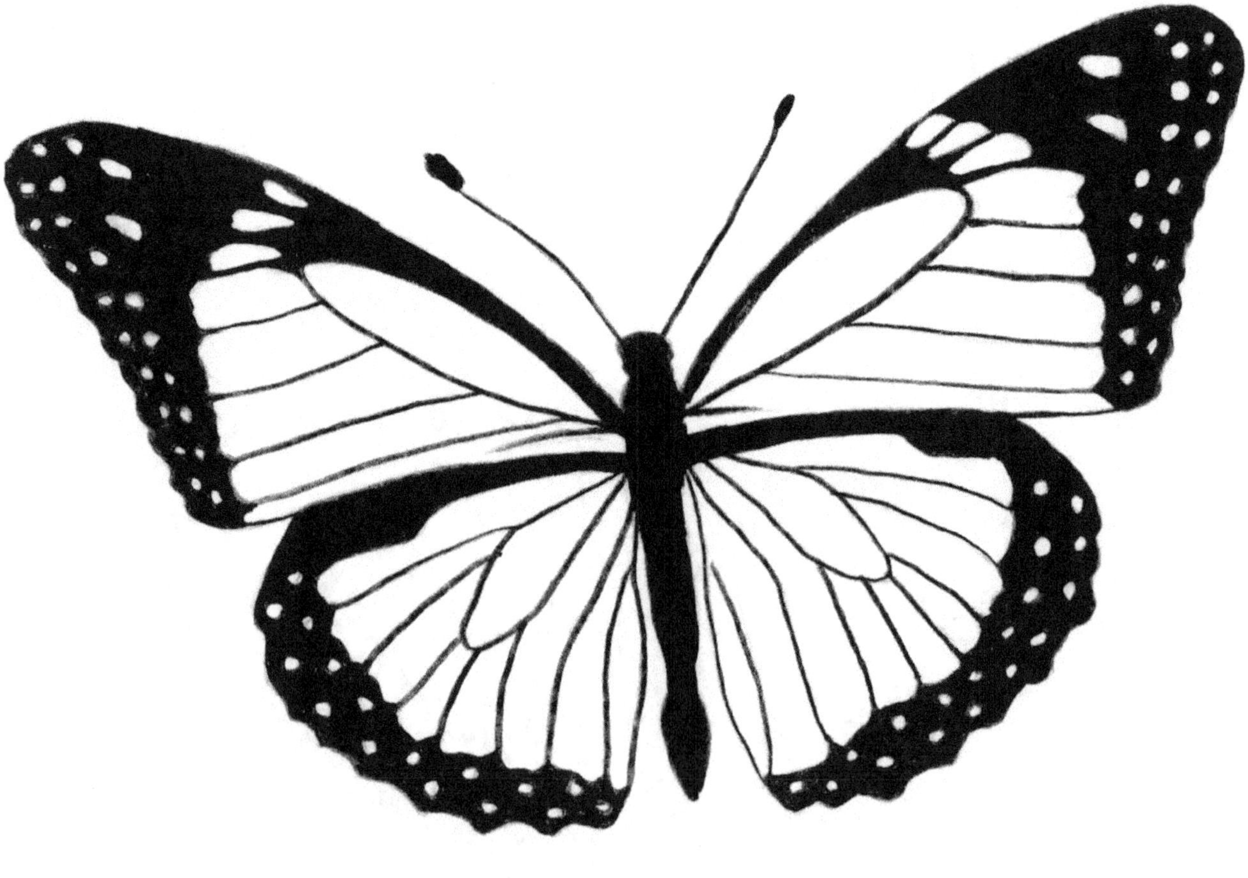

Initiating the Mid-Tone Process

Let's move on to shading the lighter values across the wings, preserving the whiteness exclusively for the small dots adjacent to the wing's edges. To maintain accuracy, ensure that your pencil strokes follow the pattern's direction.

Refer to the accompanying image, which is digitally marked with lines indicating the correct stroke direction. For this stage, refrain from utilizing cross-hatching or circulism techniques - focus solely on employing strokes along the designated directions.

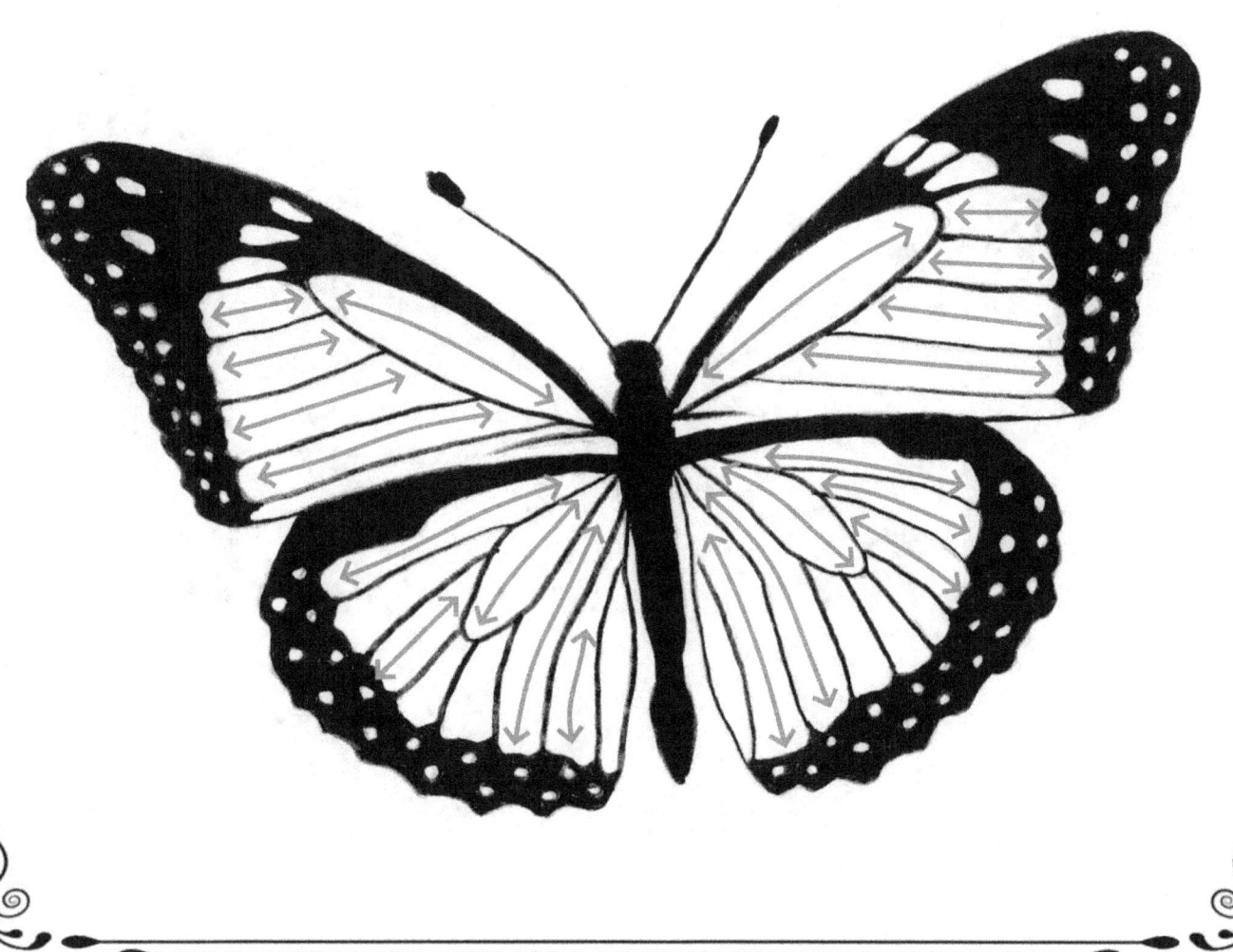

Sketching the Mid-Tone Sections

Now, using an HB pencil and referring to the indicated direction in the previous image, start sketching the strokes across the wing's patterns, aiming to completely cover the paper. It's essential to maintain consistent pressure throughout this process, as we will gradually add more depth later on.

My intention is to break down these steps into manageable stages, enhancing your understanding and guidance. Typically, when drawing for leisure, I often work on one area at a time, even with colored pencils. However, in this tutorial, I'm adopting a layer-by-layer approach, simplifying the process by focusing on one pencil at a time.

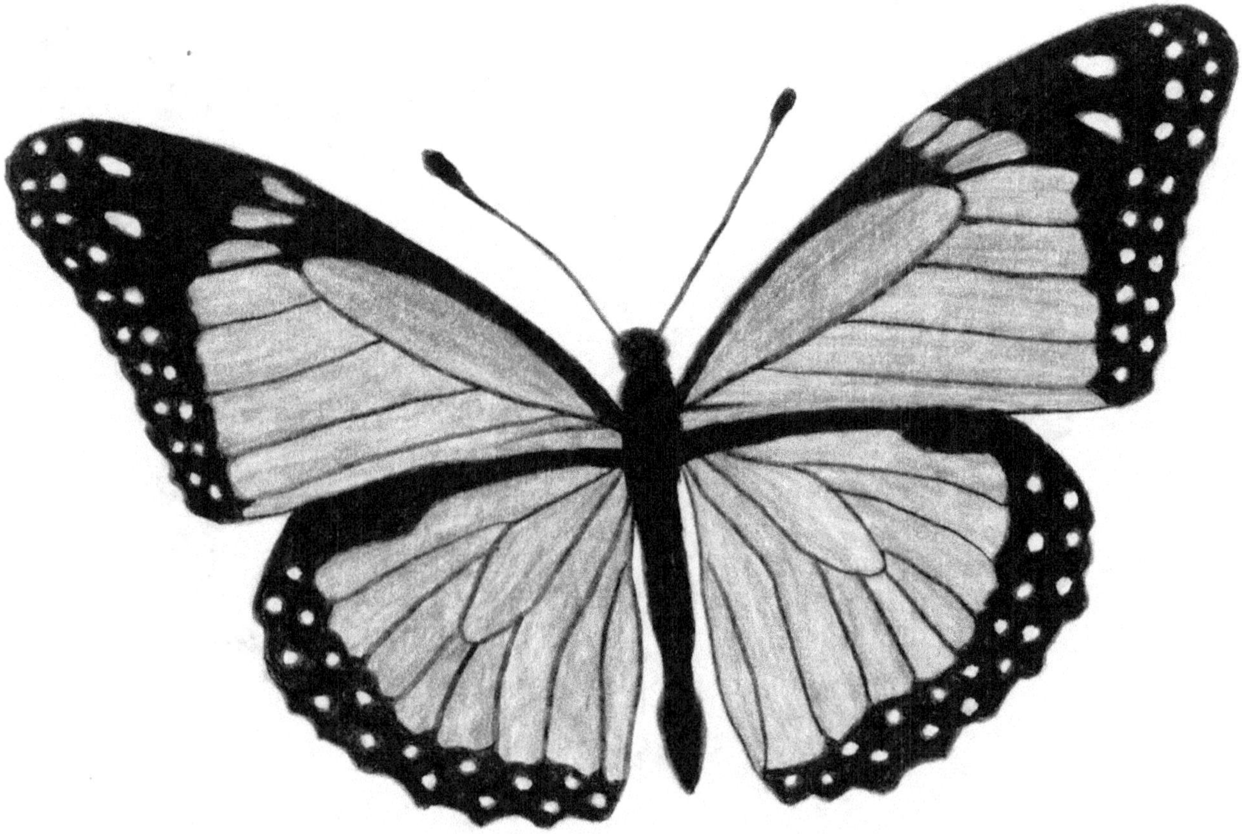

Understanding Pattern Flow

To combat the current flatness of the mid-tone areas, we need to introduce richer value variations. As evident in the reference image, these gray regions display significantly greater darkness adjacent to the butterfly's body and along the wing's edges. I've incorporated digital arrows in the previous image to indicate the direction in which you should draw.

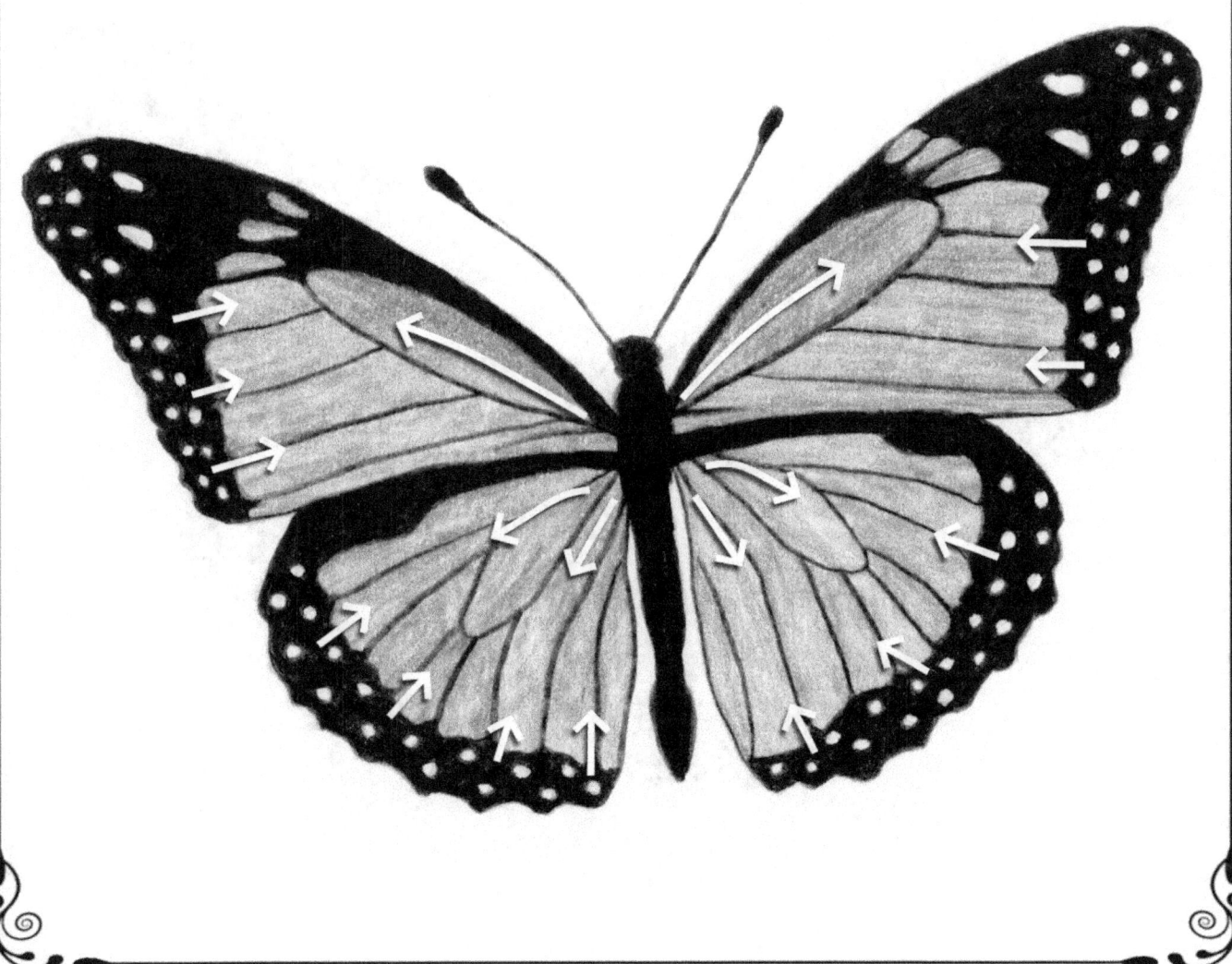

Enriching Mid-Tone Depth

With a 4B pencil, position the tip over the darker black areas and replicate the strokes in alignment with the arrows I provided. As you progress from the darker zones towards the mid-tones, gently release the pencil's pressure to ensure a seamless transition. Apply the same technique from the butterfly's body outward.

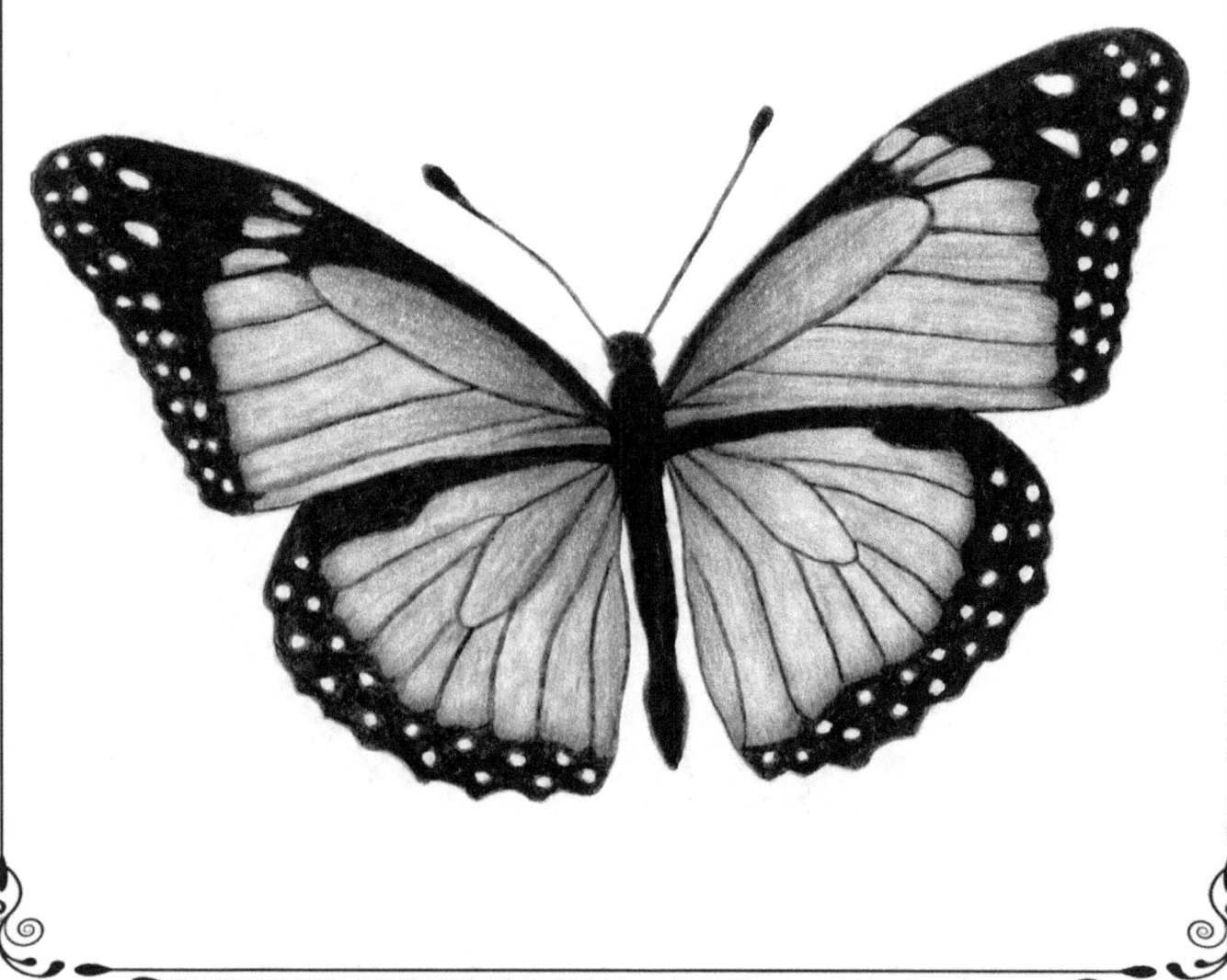

Smoothing Mid-Tones

Afterward, employ a blending stump or a Q-tip to delicately blend these regions. If the shaded sections appear lighter following blending, you can reapply the respective pencils. Conversely, if they appear darker, use a kneaded eraser to gently lighten the desired areas.

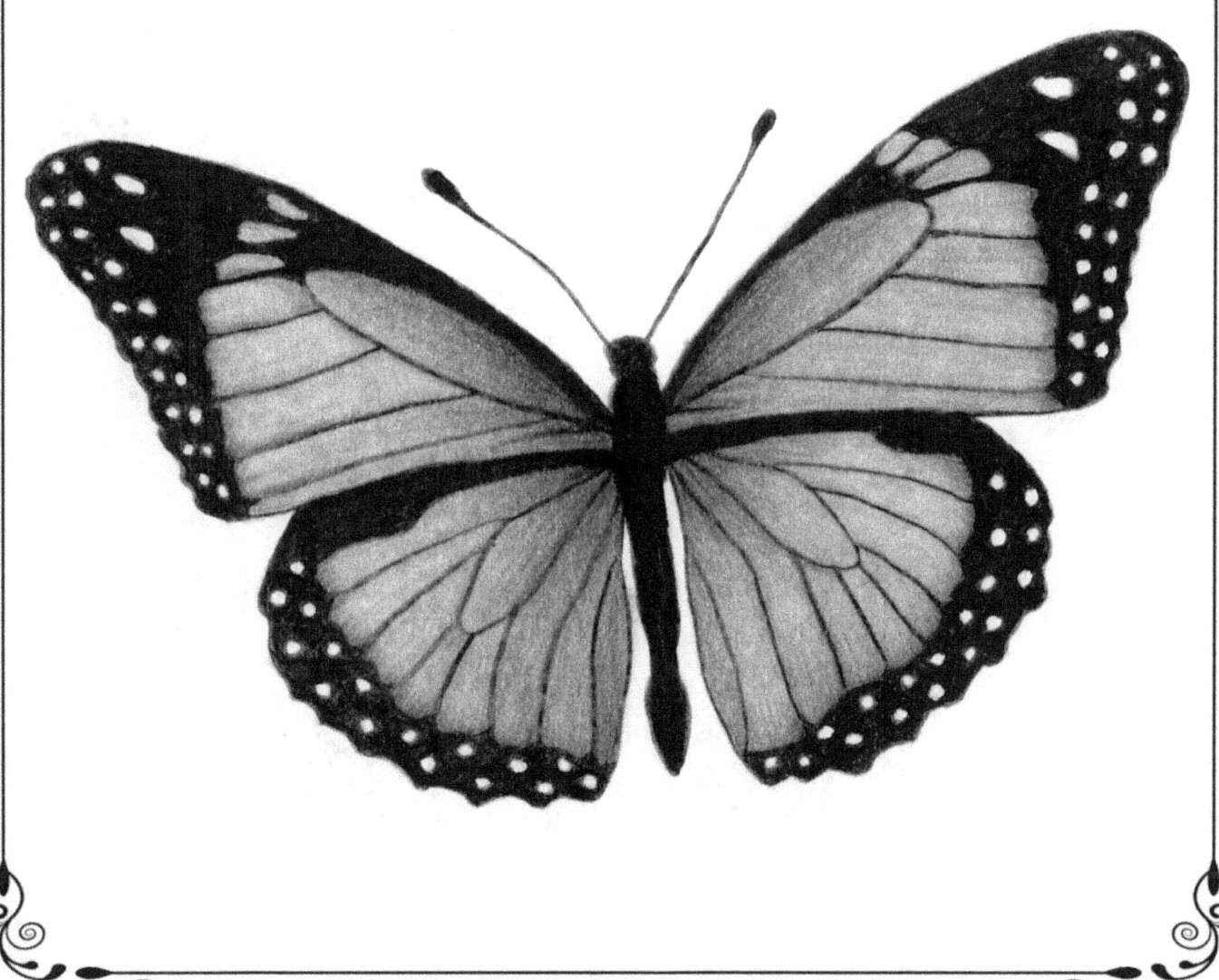

Crafting Cast Shadow

In order to lend a three-dimensional quality to the butterfly, let's introduce a shadow cast by the butterfly onto the hypothetical surface it rests upon, even though it differs from its position in the reference photo. I utilized a Q-tip to apply graphite powder for this cast shadow, as pencil strokes wouldn't yield the required smoothness for the desired effect. Simply, reproduce the lower shape of the butterfly using graphite powder while keeping the certain light source in mind. In my case, I envisioned the light source originating from the upper-right corner, and I shaded the area accordingly.

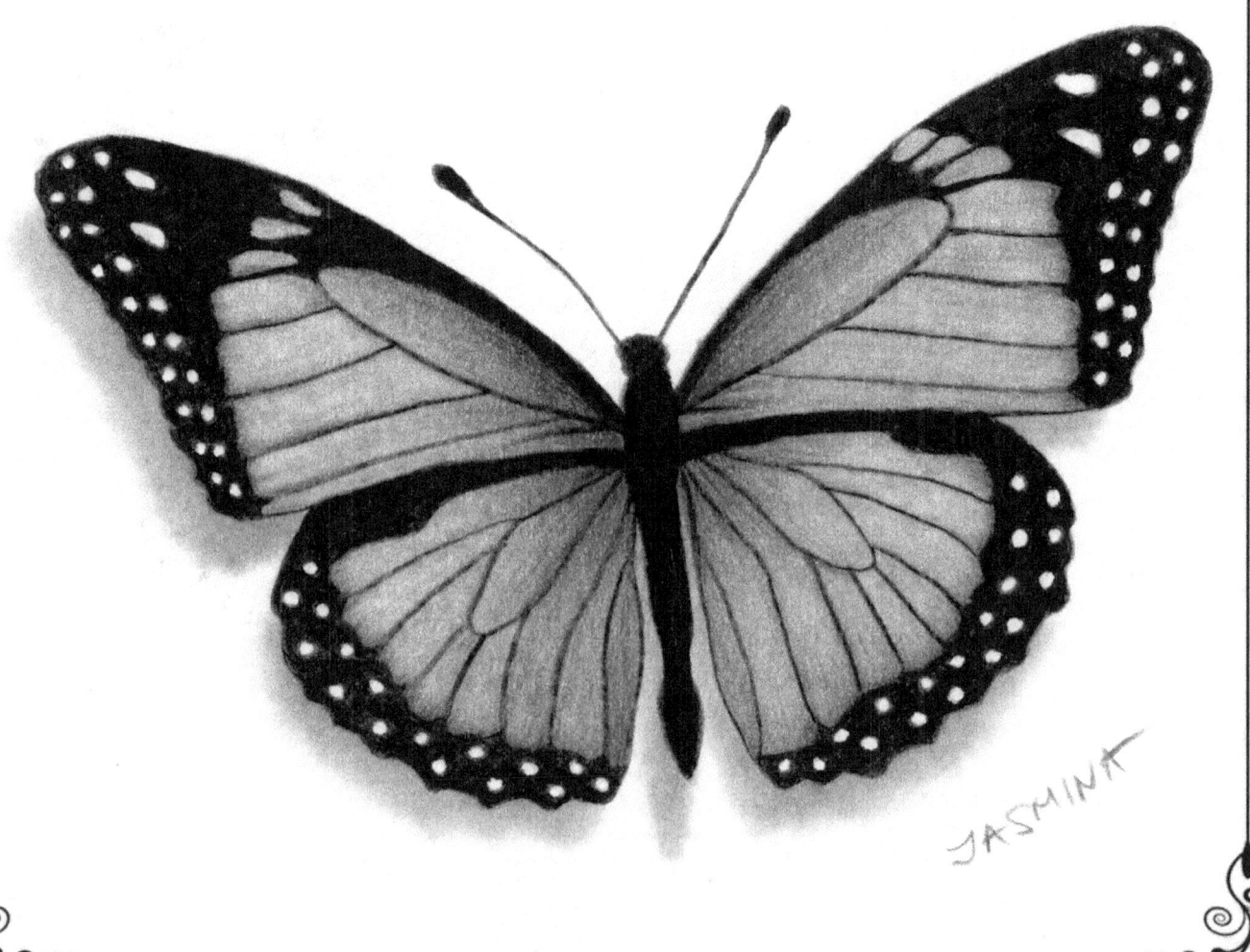

Drawing Interludes

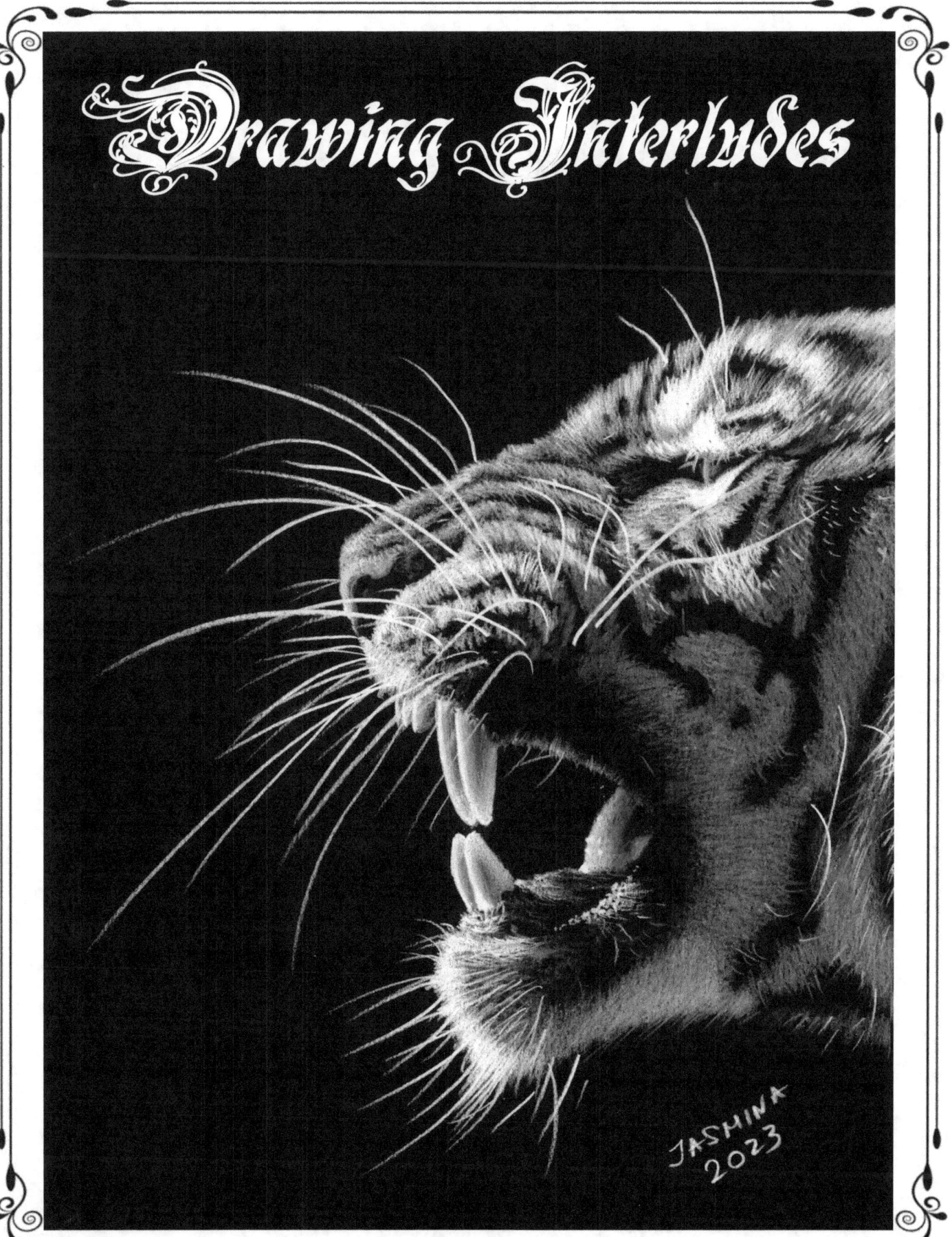

How to Draw an Orca

Drawing an Orca killer whale offers a captivating chance to embrace simplicity and create a striking piece of art with strong black and white contrast. By focusing on the whale's elegant and powerful form, artists can showcase the beauty of minimalism while honing their skills in capturing realistic textures and shading. The result is a captivating and visually impactful artwork that celebrates the magnificence of these remarkable marine creatures.

The Reference Photo

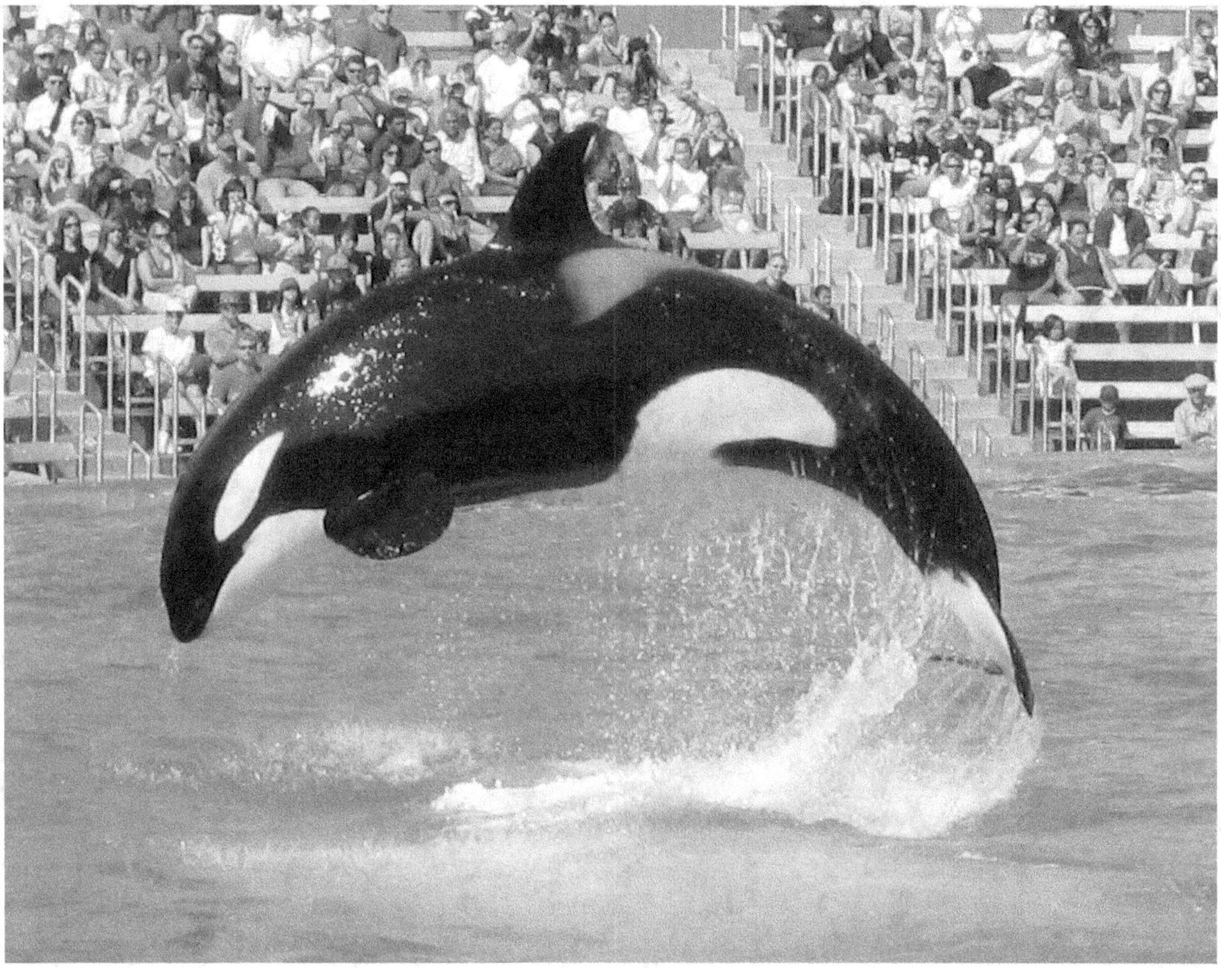

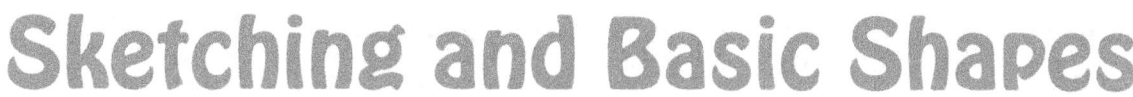

Sketching and Basic Shapes

In the image below, I have highlighted the crucial lines that play a significant role in guiding my shading process. These lines form the primary outline of the orca's body and help distinguish the boundaries between the contrasting black and white regions. As I progress, I'll be focusing on these key elements to ensure accurate shading and a realistic depiction.

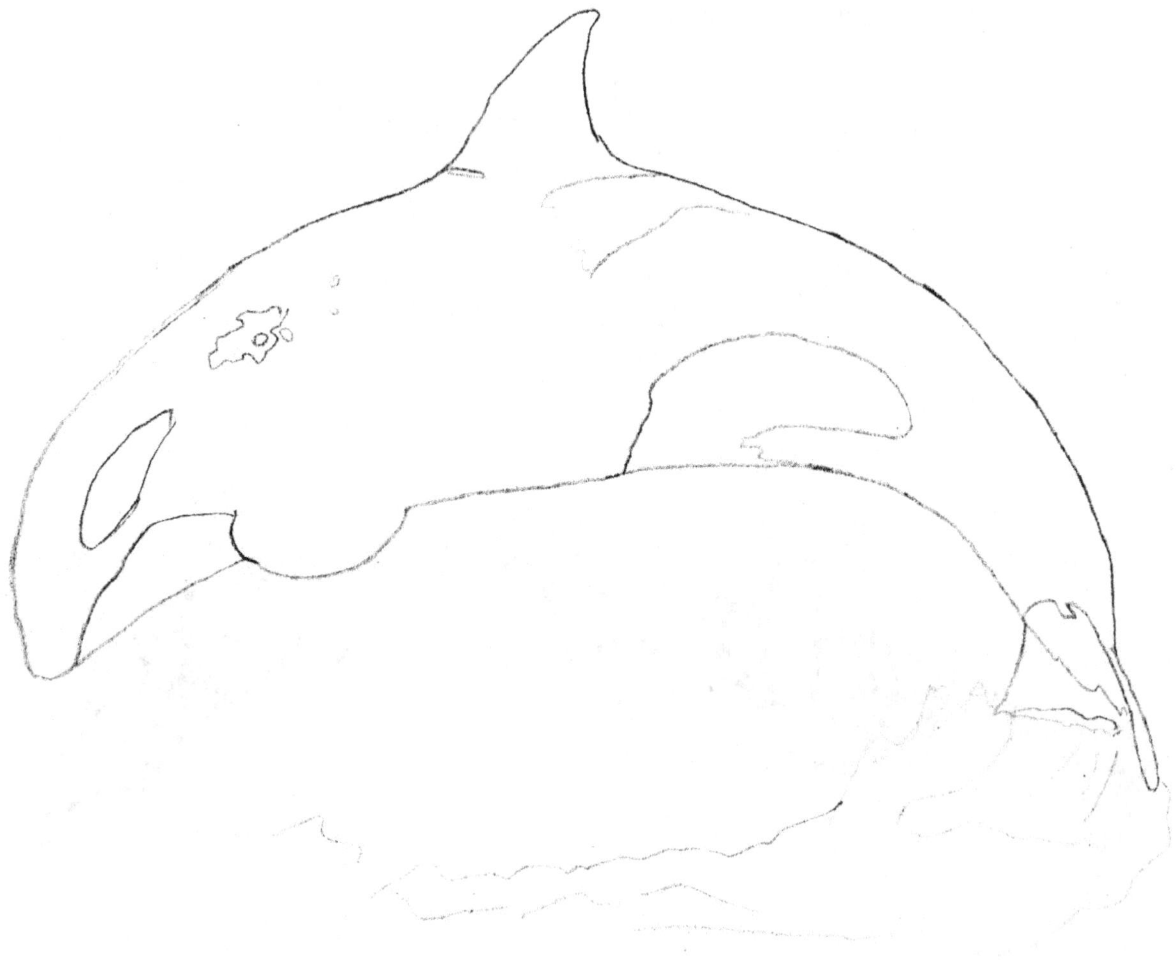

Drawing the Darkest Parts

As a common mistake among beginners, some might shy away from using black or dark colors in their drawings, fearing irreversibility. However, don't let that fear hold you back! Applying black hues can add a sense of depth and dimension to your artwork. Remember, if you make a mistake, you can always start anew. So, don't hesitate to begin with black shades.

In the case of this orca drawing, creating the deepest shade is essential. Utilizing a 9B or darker pencil, apply firm pressure to achieve the desired darkness. Observe the areas I've initially colored in this image. I applied slightly less pressure at the top of the dark regions in the middle of the body, as we want to preserve the space for highlighting.

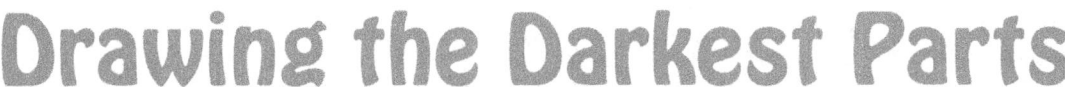

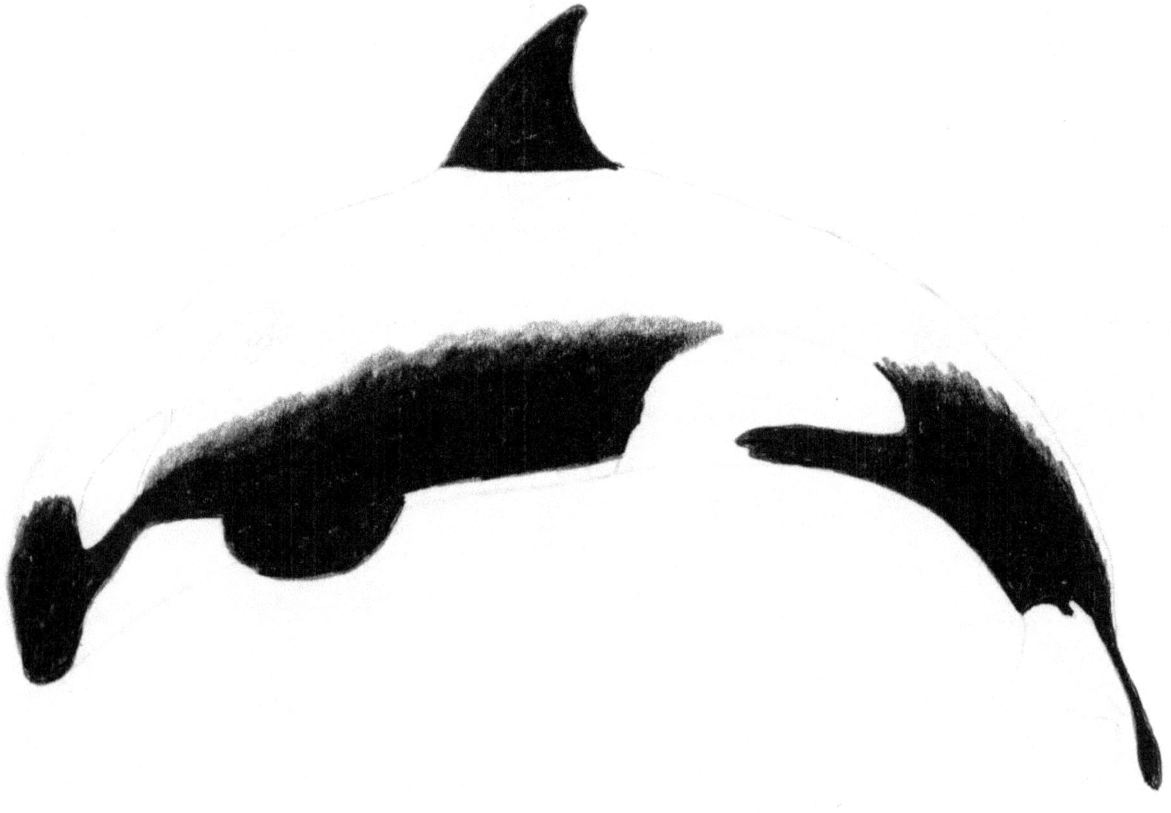

Shading Highlighted Areas

Now, progress with a 2B pencil, shading towards the top of the orca's body, focusing on achieving a smooth and even texture. Should you encounter any lighter spots, simply fill them in with the 2B or even a darker pencil if needed.

The key objective is to seamlessly blend the darkest parts with the highlighted areas, which are also quite dark, in order to craft a rounded and realistic form for the orca's body.

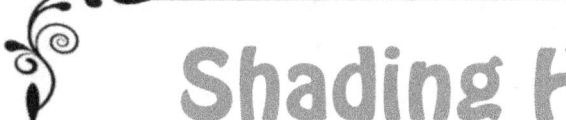

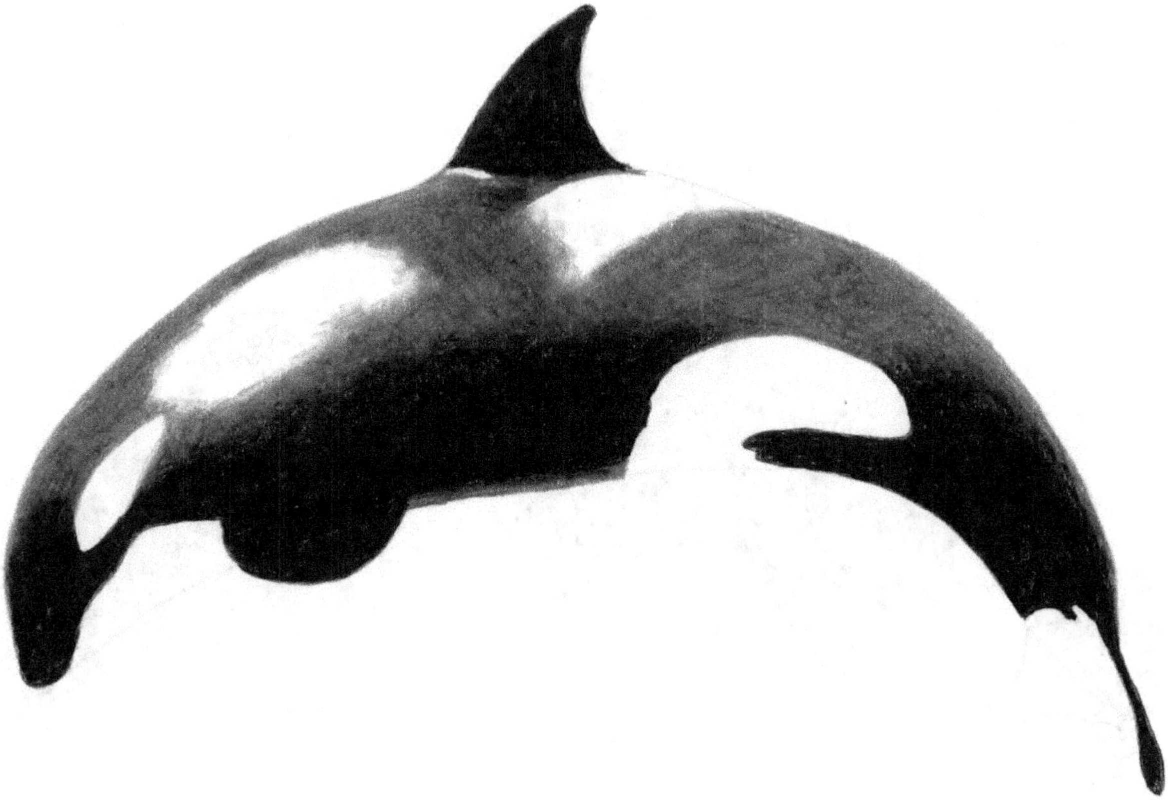

Creating Smooth Transition

To achieve a rounded and lifelike appearance for the orca's body, we need to focus on refining the transition between the highlighted and shaded areas. For this purpose, I recommend using an 8B pencil to delicately blend the values and create a more seamless gradient. As you shade upwards, try to reduce the pressure on your pencil or opt for a lighter shade like 6B to ensure a gradual shift in tones.

By carefully observing the changes I made in the previous image and comparing it to the current one, you'll notice how the new gradient enhances the contours of the orca's body, giving it a more realistic and three-dimensional look.

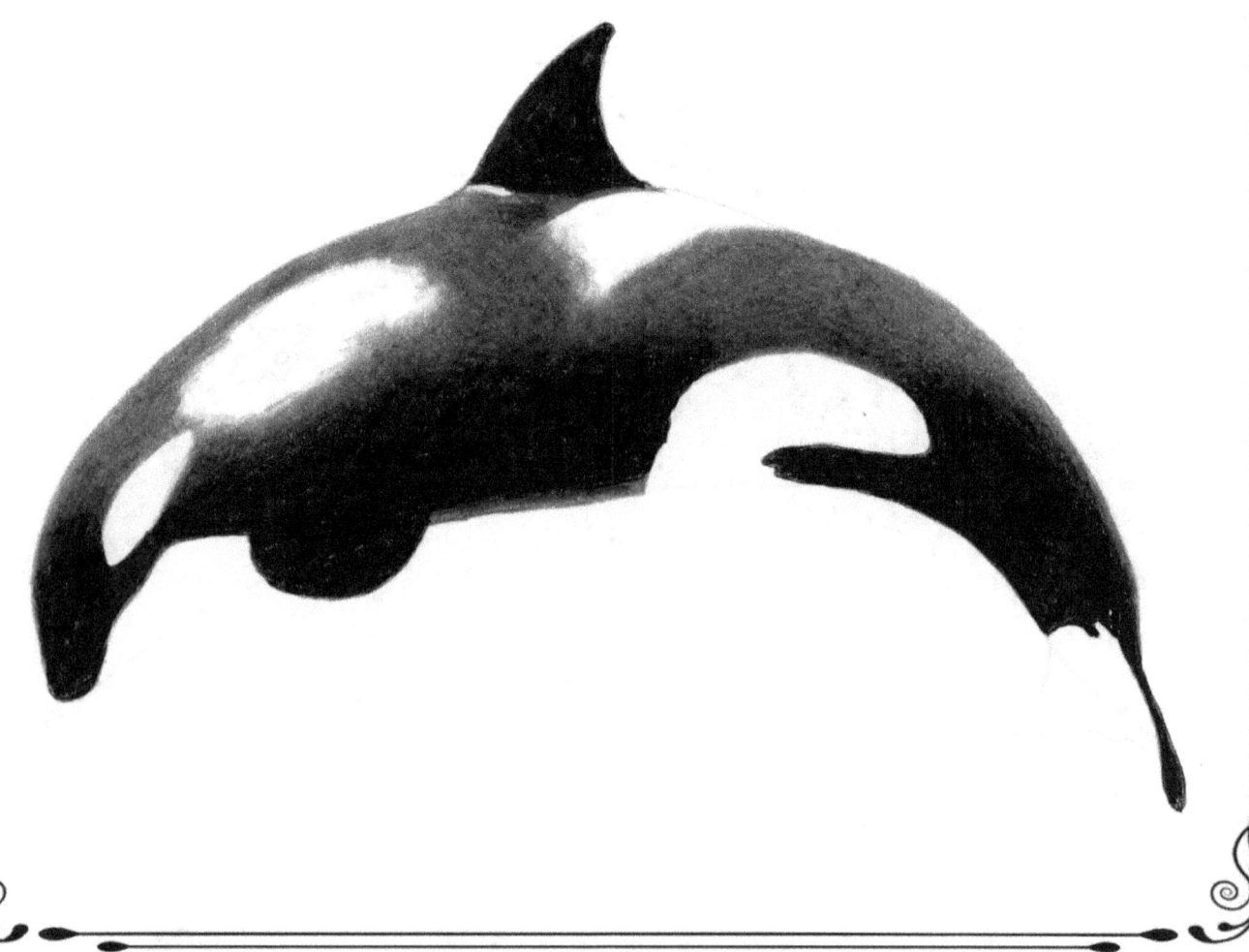

Shading the Illuminated Part

Now, let's focus on the area at the top of the orca's back that is highly illuminated. To achieve a smooth and realistic texture, I recommend using an HB pencil and applying the circulism technique. Begin by shading lightly and layering your strokes gradually to build up the desired effect. Remember, the key is to create a seamless texture, avoiding any visible lines over the orca's body, which is known for its smooth and sleek appearance, especially when wet, as depicted in the reference photo.

Take extra care to draw around the tiny area in the very center of the highlights, ensuring it remains absolutely white. This contrast with the surrounding shaded areas will add to the illusion of a shiny, illuminated surface. By skillfully incorporating three distinct values of highlights, you can achieve a striking effect that suggests both brightness and depth while still emphasizing the orca's black coloration.

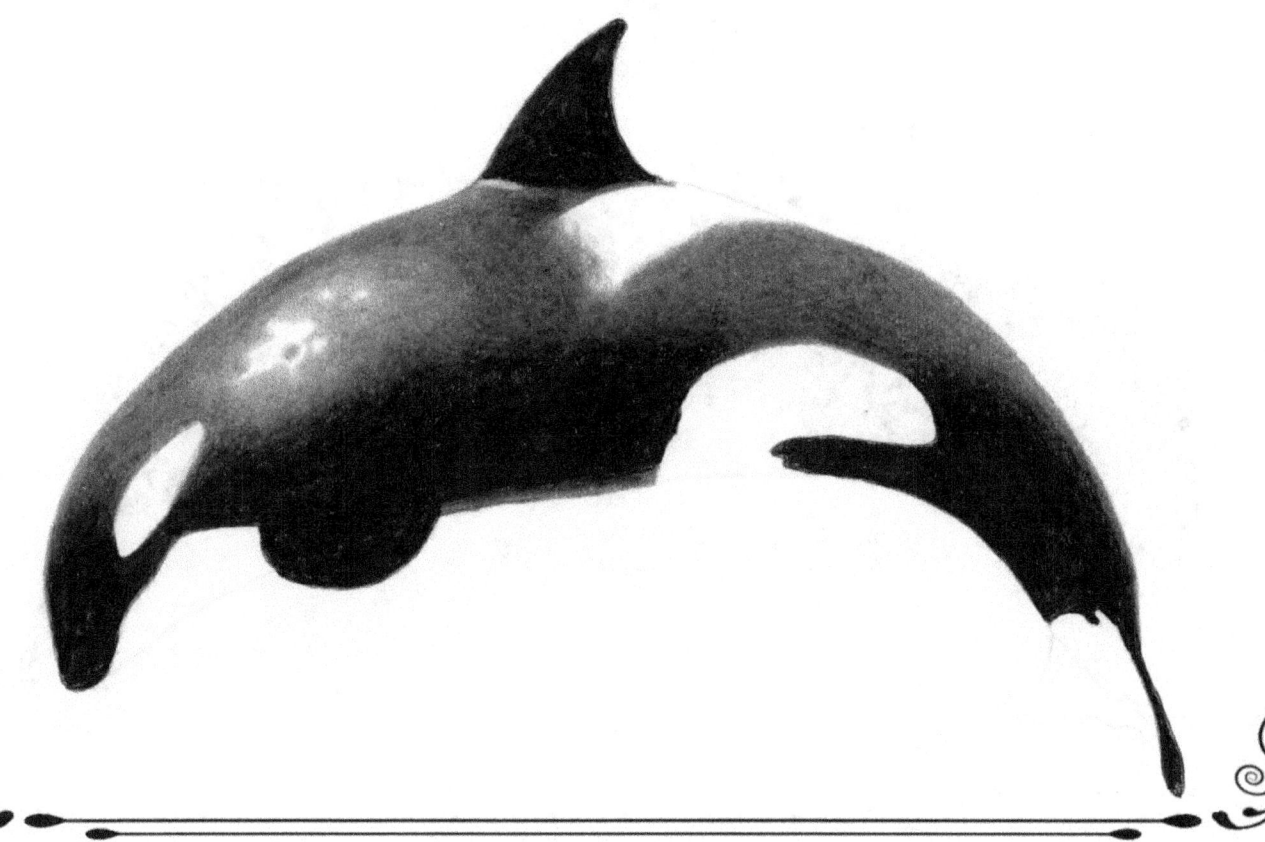

Shading the White Parts

To create depth and realism, it's essential to shade even the white parts of the orca's body, especially those in self-shadow. Imagine shading a sphere in a typical drawing tutorial, and apply a similar technique here. To achieve this, I suggest covering the background with masking tape or any suitable material to prevent unintentional shading, and then use a Q-tip to carefully shade the lower portions of the white areas.

Gradually decrease the pressure as you move upwards, blending the shading smoothly towards the illuminated white parts that should remain pristine. Don't forget to pay attention to the tail as well; study my step and the reference photo to ensure accuracy in your shading process.

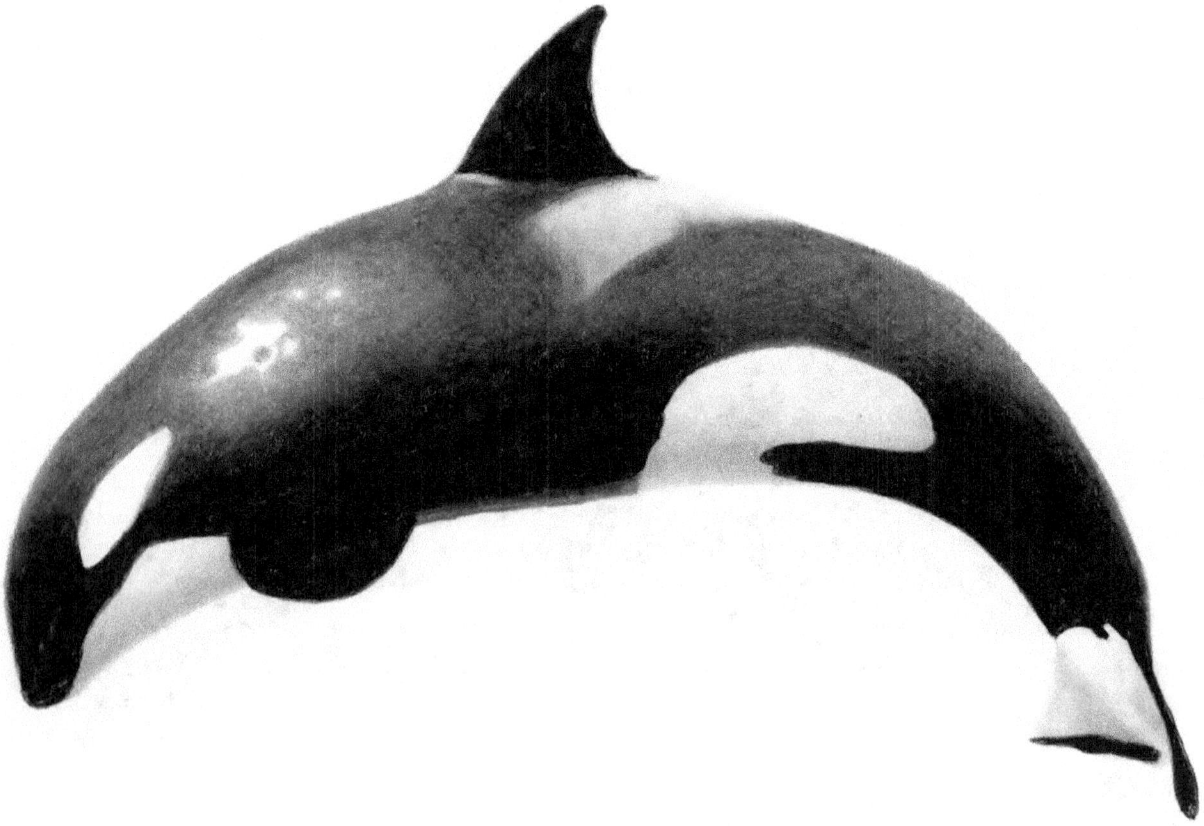

Creating a Wet Appearance

Now let's enhance the orca's glistening effect by adding tiny white dots around the highlighted back and other relevant areas. You can even create these dots using an electric eraser, but in my experience, using a white ink gel pen is much easier and produces better results. If you have both tools, feel free to try them out and see what works best for you. It's fascinating how these small details can truly bring out the watery look in the orca's depiction.

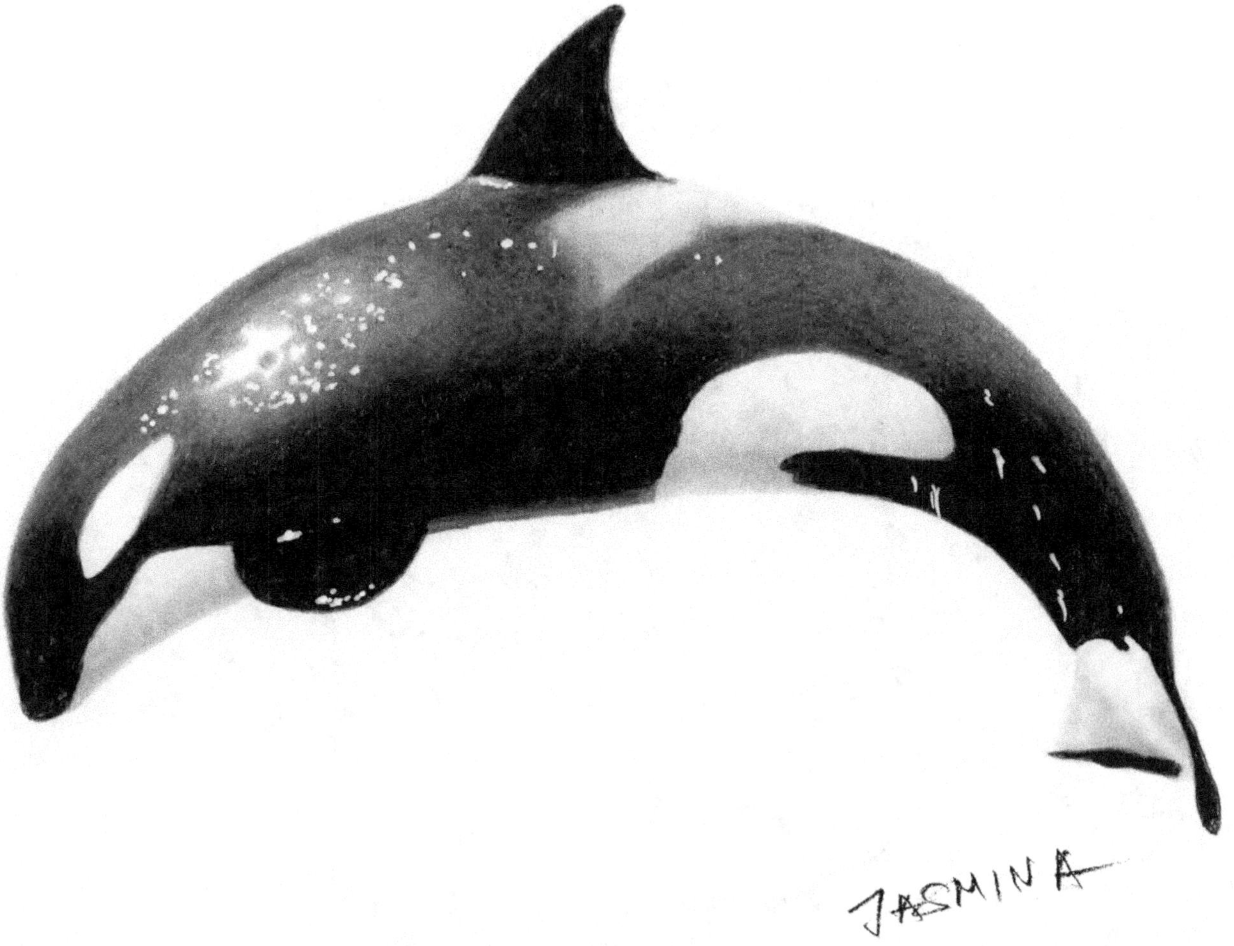

JASMINA

How to Draw a Ladybug

Drawing a ladybug provides an excellent opportunity to practice shading techniques, especially gradient transitions as discussed in the "Smooth Gradient" chapter.
These adorable insects not only bring joy but also play a vital role in maintaining ecosystem balance by devouring pests and contributing to the health of our bio gardens.
Let's capture their charm and beauty on paper while celebrating their beneficial presence in nature.

The Reference Photo

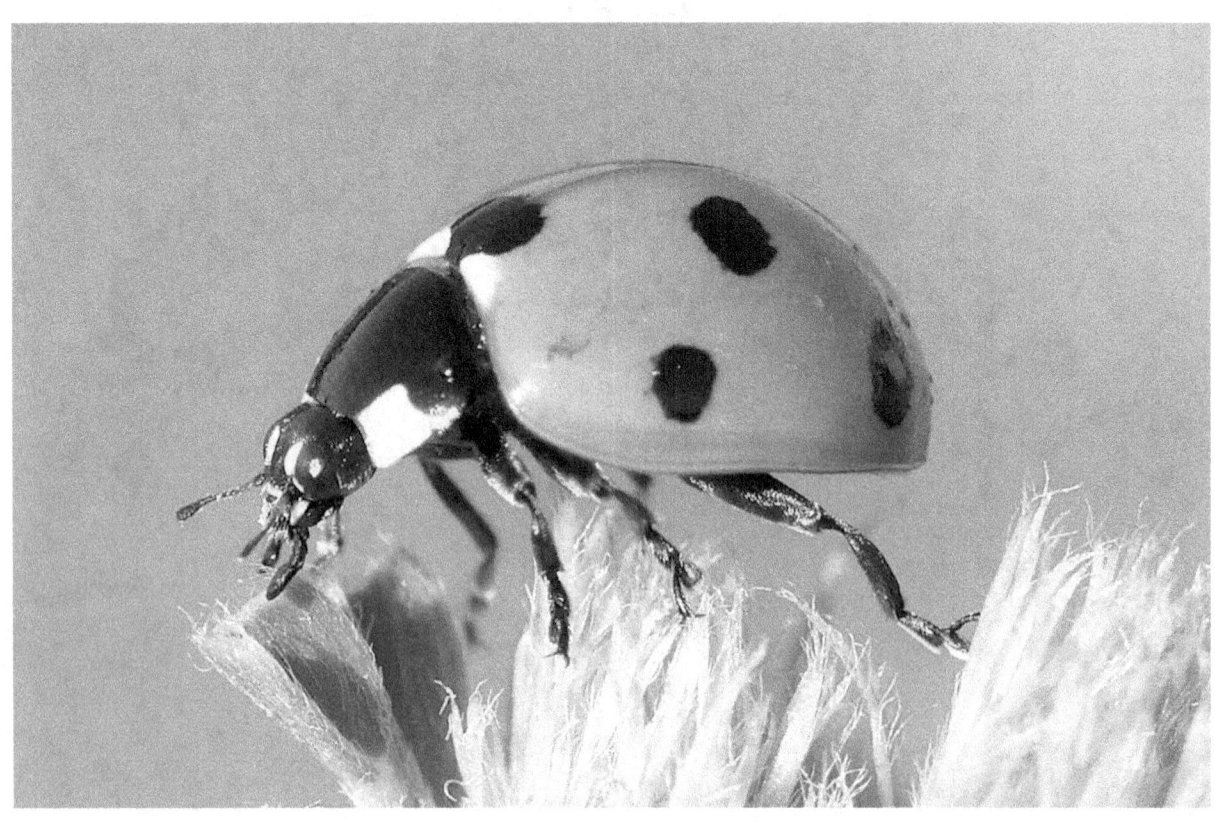

Sketching and Basic Shapes

To recreate this sketch, please refer to the "The Grid Method" chapter for detailed instructions and step-by-step guidance on the process.

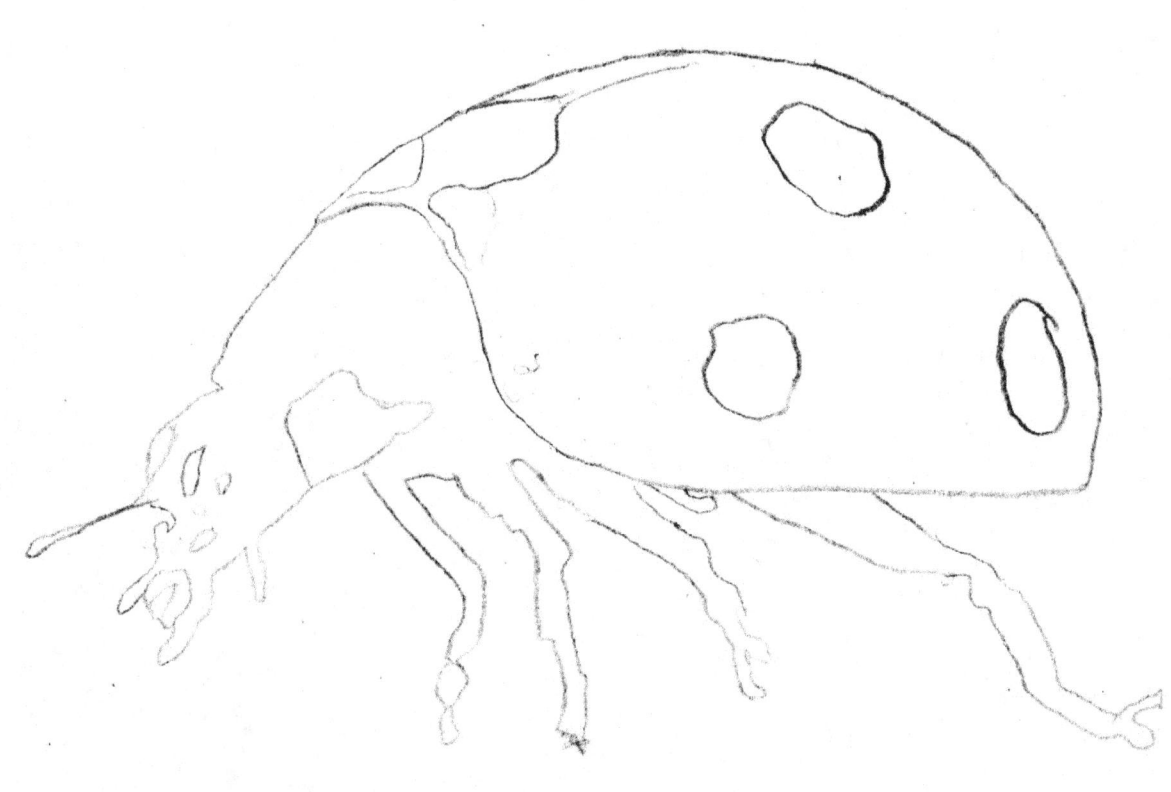

Masking the Background

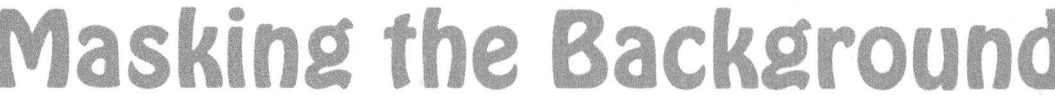

This time, I've chosen to shade using graphite powder applied with a tissue. To enhance the sketch lines of the black spots, strengthen them slightly to maintain their visibility beneath the layer of graphite shading. However, these spots don't need to be placed exactly in the same locations as in the reference photo. To block the background from shading and ensure clean and defined outer edges, I'm utilizing Frisket Masking Film. Using this product or a simple masking tape or a cut piece of paper is an effective technique to protect the surrounding area while working on specific details of the artwork. Using the masking film is essential because once the graphite is heavily impressed over the background, erasing it without leaving a trace would be virtually impossible.

This film can be easily stuck over the paper and removed without causing any damage. After placing the film over my sketch, I carefully cut around the edges of the ladybug with a precision knife, such as X-acto, leaving the shell accessible for shading while protecting the area around it.

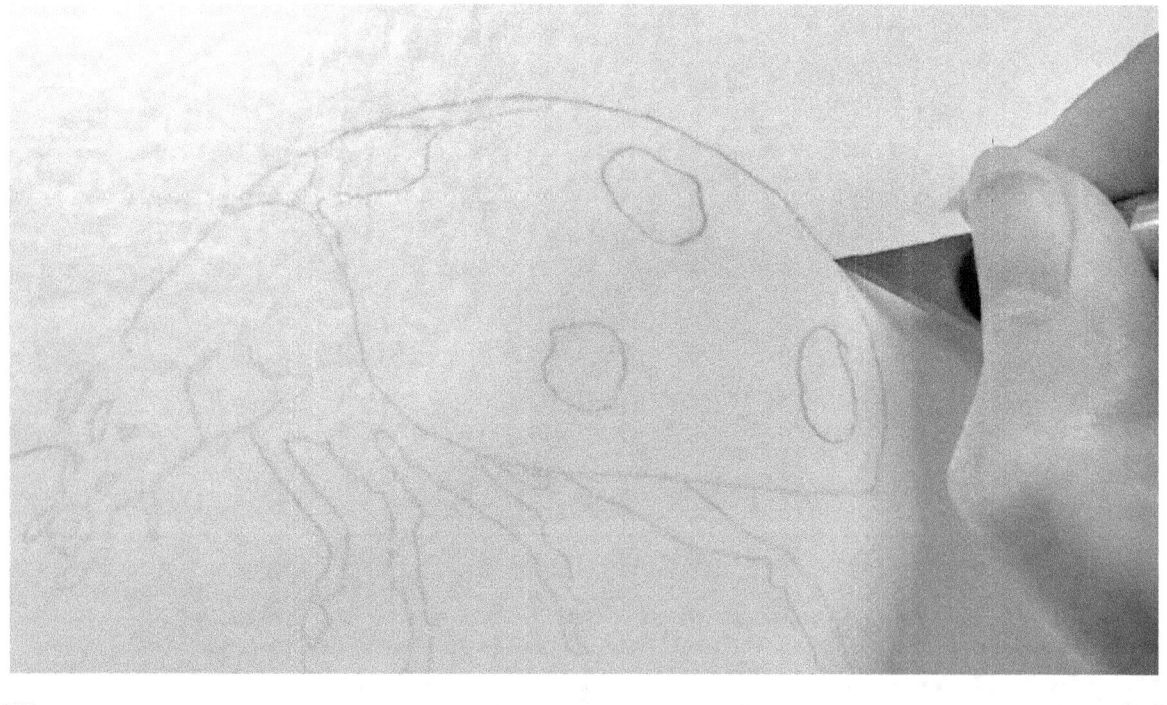

Shading the Ladybug's Shell

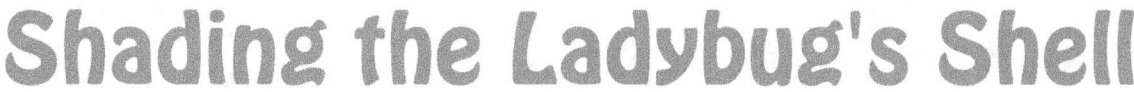

Now that we have the area of the shell exposed, let's proceed with shading. Before applying the graphite powder to your drawing, test it on a separate piece of paper to see the grade it will produce. Also, be cautious not to touch your paper with your fingers, as it could leave unwanted marks once the graphite powder is applied. To avoid this, I always rest my hand on a separate piece of paper while working on my drawing. This ensures that my hand doesn't come into contact with the artwork, keeping it clean and free from smudges.

Dip your finger, wrapped with a tissue, in graphite powder. Carefully apply this graphite over the area, starting with the shadowed part on the right side and pressing with decreasing pressure as you shade towards the left side. This technique will create a gradient transition between the dark and light shades. Remember to always start on the right side after dipping your tissue in graphite powder, applying it for the shadowed area. The remaining graphite on the tissue will be sufficient for the lighter area on the left. Applying circular movements will help you achieve a smooth transition between the shades.

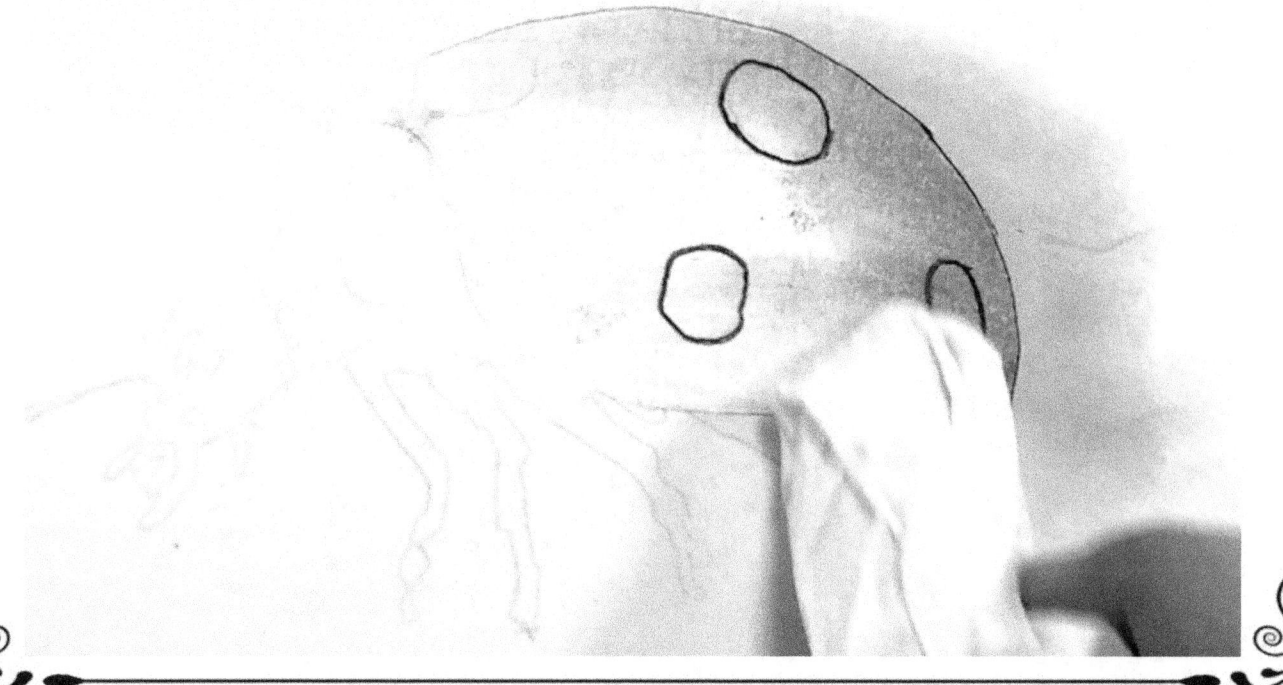

Layering and Unmasking

Proceed layer by layer, carefully building up the shades until you achieve your desired result. The choice of graphite powder shade is important; in my case, I use a B shade. If you have a darker shade, you may want to remove some graphite from your tissue before applying it to your drawing to prevent it from becoming too dark and difficult to erase. On the other hand, if you have HB or lighter graphite powder, it may not be dark enough for the shadowed area.

After removing the Frisket Masking Film, you should observe that your shaded area resembles the one in my next image. However, if you find that your result is not satisfactory, I recommend starting anew on a fresh sketch. Since you are only at the initial stages of the drawing and haven't invested much effort yet, repeating this step until you are content with the outcome is a wise approach. I hope you'll find this shading technique engaging, especially considering that it is both faster and results in a smoother appearance compared to using graphite pencils and blending. Take your time to master this method before moving on to the next step, and feel free to explore and experiment with the process until you achieve the desired effect.

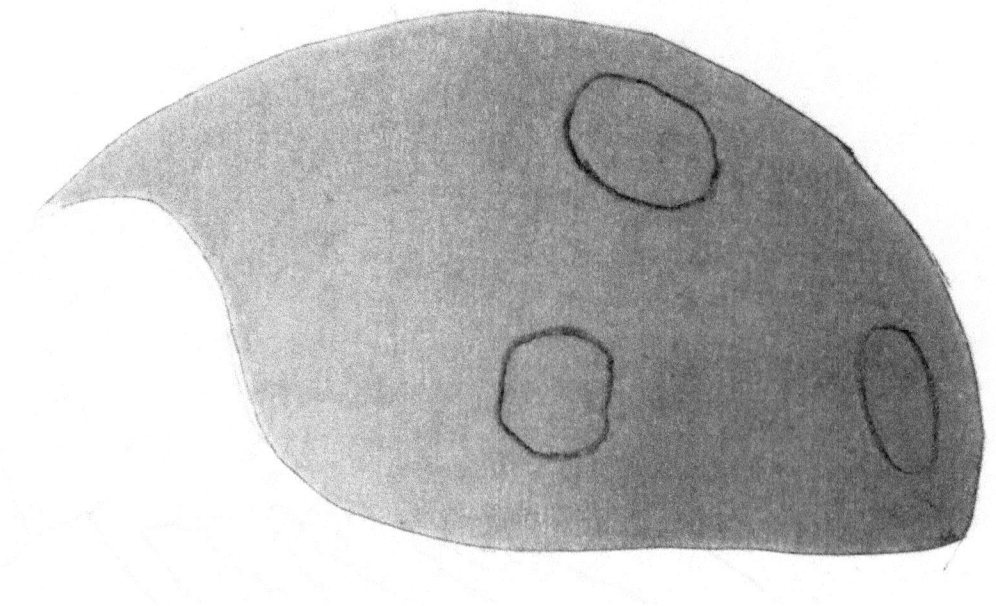

Drawing the Black Spots

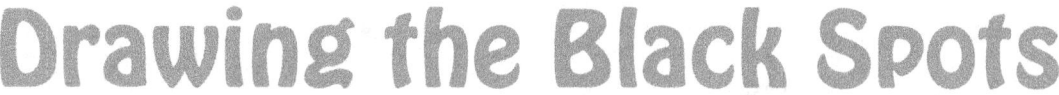

In the next step, we will focus on adding the distinctive black spots to the ladybug's shell. To achieve this, take your 14B pencil and apply firm pressure while drawing these spots. The goal is to create a deep and contrasting shade that stands out against the surrounding graphite shading.

As previously mentioned, don't feel restricted by the reference photo when drawing the spots on the ladybug's shell. You have the creative freedom to interpret and position them as you see fit. In my case, I accidentally lost the initial sketch for the spot on the top of the shell, but I have now added it back by approximating its position.

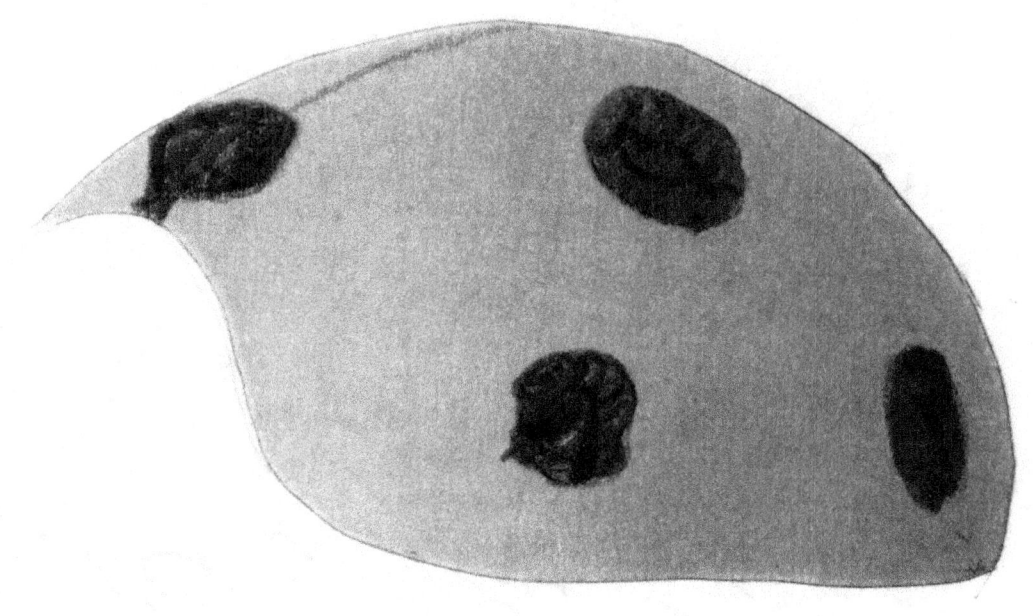

Creating Highlights

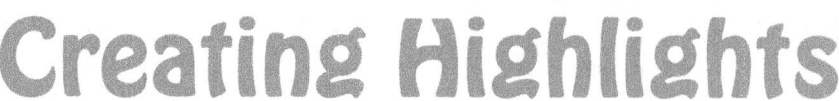

Next, we'll enhance the ladybug's shell with some highlights. To achieve this effect, I gently lift off a bit of graphite using a kneaded eraser, as demonstrated in the next image. For a more pronounced highlight, I employ my electric eraser to brighten the center of this area. This added brightness gives the shell a beautifully rounded appearance.

Additionally, I meticulously erase the two white spots near the head to preserve their whiteness, enhancing the contrast and making them stand out elegantly

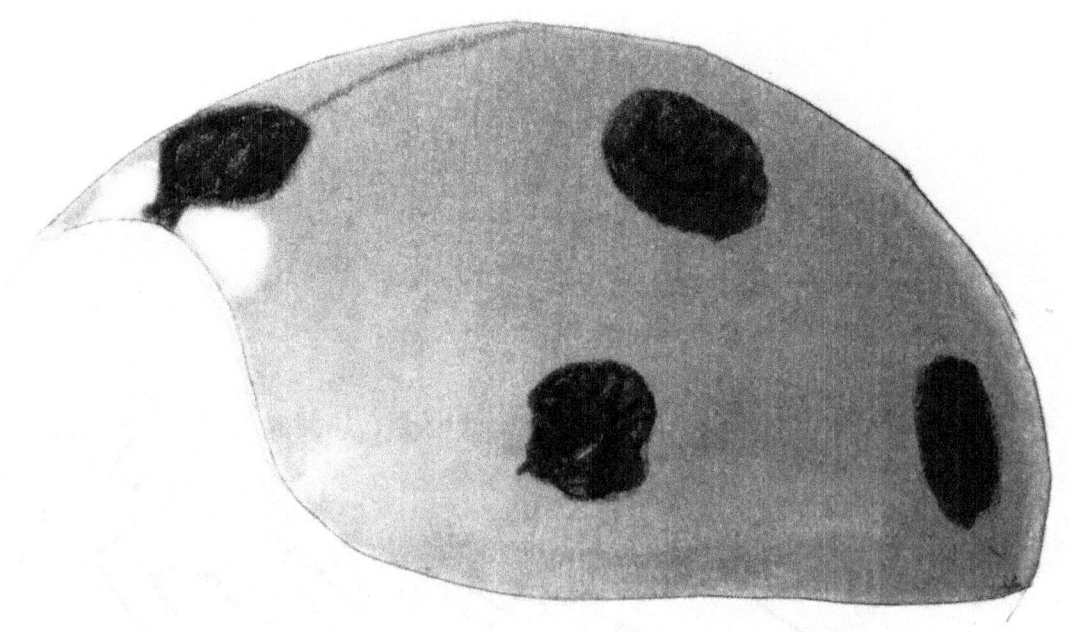

Drawing the Darkest Areas

Let's proceed by shading all the darkest areas using the deepest shade, such as **14B**. Refer to the image below to observe precisely which areas I have shaded, while leaving certain tiny sections white. Take time to study both the reference photo and my step-by-step process to grasp the necessary actions for your drawing.

It's important to note that I have intentionally left the black highlighted part over the pronotum (the black area between the head and the shell) untouched. This area will be shaded with a lighter grade to indicate the shine it possesses.

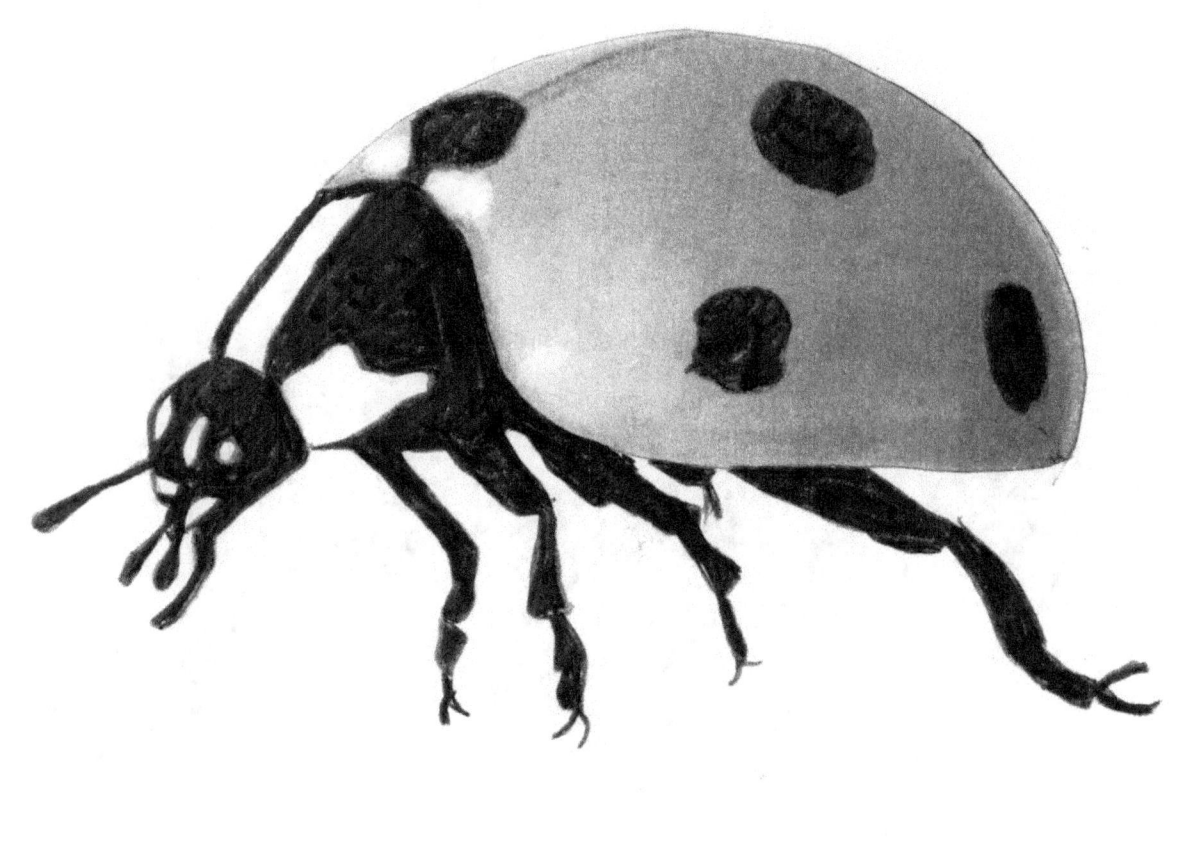

Blurring and Shading the Details

Next, we will shade the previously untouched area over the pronotum. Begin by using an HB pencil at the top of this area, gradually transitioning into the **14B**-shaded region. Afterward, blend the edge between these shades with a 6B pencil to achieve a smooth gradient.

Additionally, take a blending stump and carefully blend the edges of the legs in the background to give them a slightly blurry appearance. This effect will create the impression that these legs are positioned behind the legs that are closer to the viewer's eyes. Also, blend the edge of the shell next to the pronotum to ensure a seamless transition between the two sections.

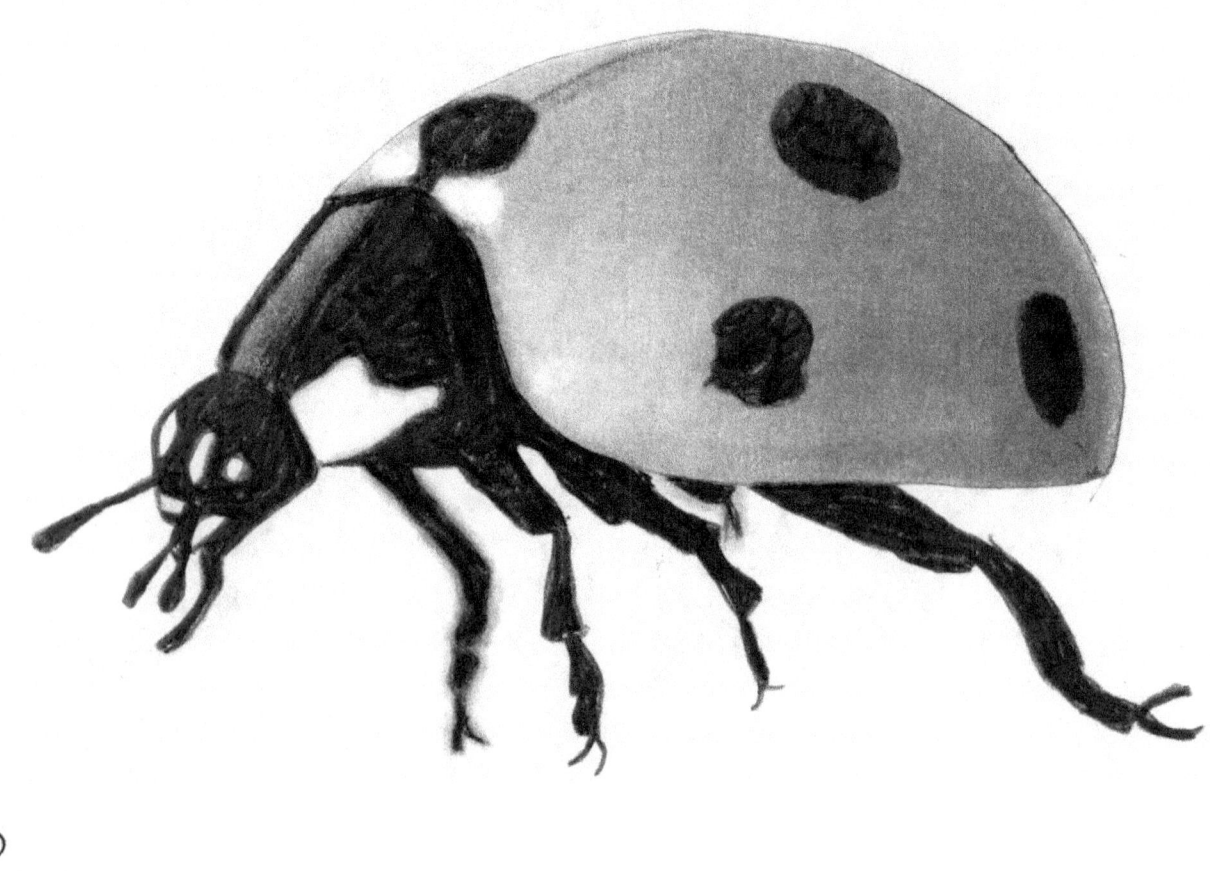

Hairing the Legs

As evident from the reference photo, the legs possess a hairy texture. To achieve this effect, we'll utilize a wax colorless blender. By gently placing its tip along the edge of the leg and drawing it outward in the required direction, we can create the appearance of tiny hairs, as demonstrated in my drawing. This technique enhances the fluffiness, imparting a realistic and lifelike quality to the legs in the artwork.

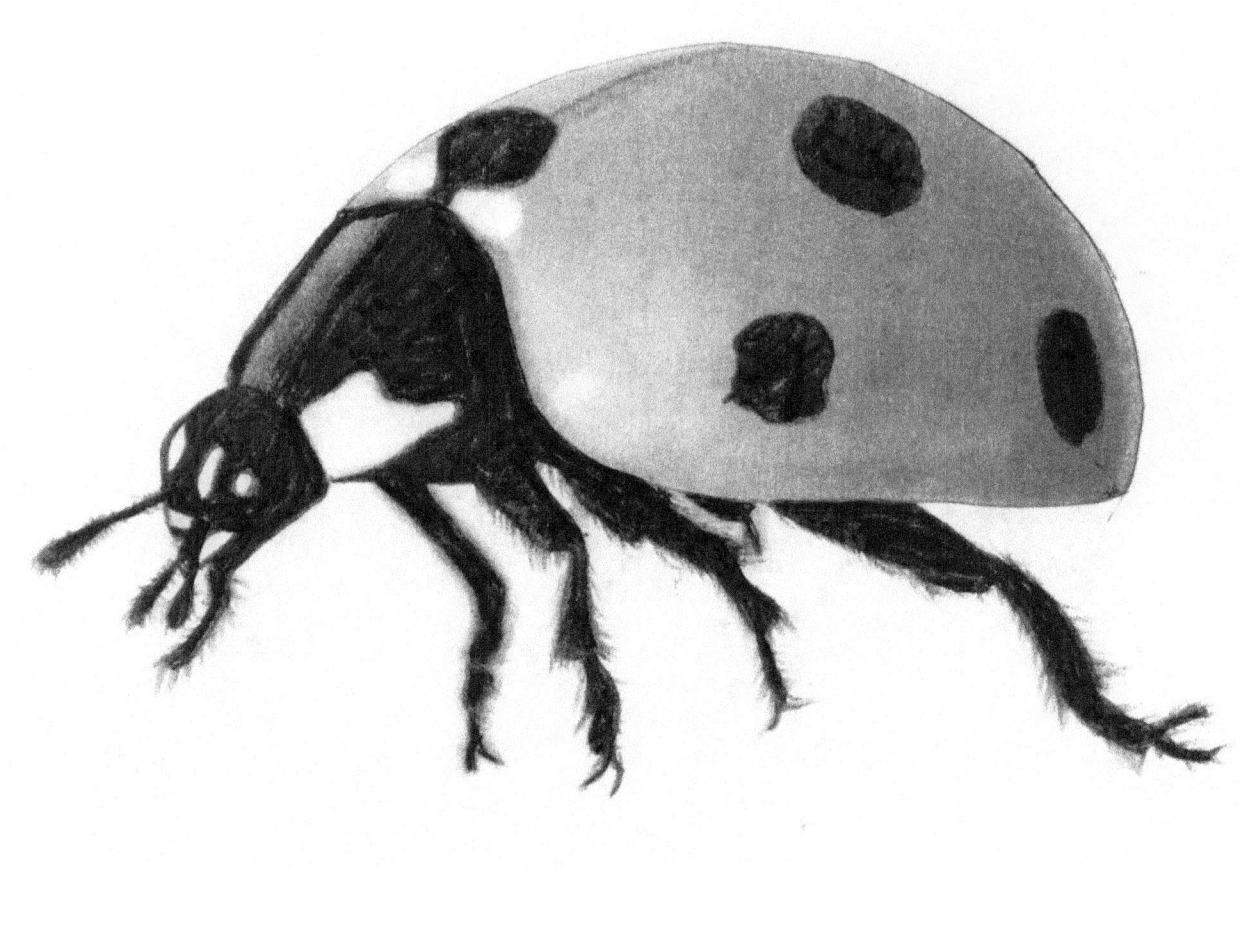

Enhancing with Tiny Highlights

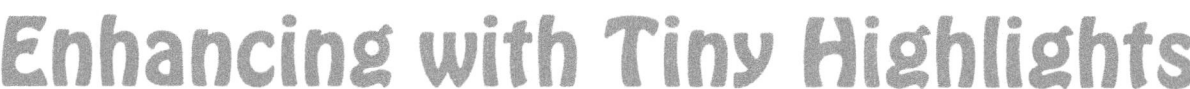

Now, it's time to add the finishing touches by incorporating tiny highlighted spots where appropriate. To achieve this effect, I used the sharp tip of my electric eraser, carefully eliminating graphite and creating bright highlights. For areas that required a pure white value, I applied a white ink gel pen.

In the accompanying image, you can observe numerous small white dots that I meticulously placed all over the ladybug, even on its legs.

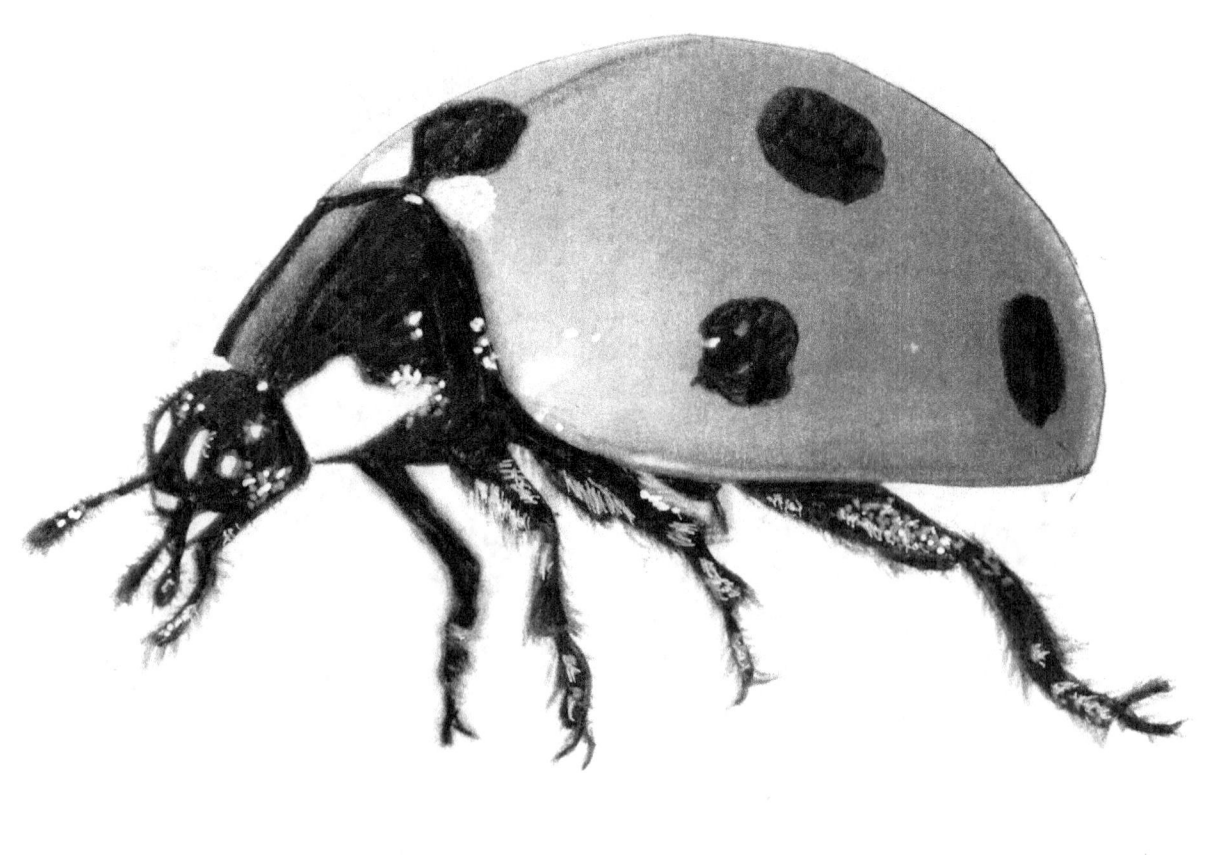

Mastering Cast Shadows for Realism

Once you are content with the overall appearance of your drawing, it's time to enhance its three-dimensional and lifelike feel by creating a cast shadow under the ladybug. To achieve this, I used graphite powder and a painting brush, employing back and forth movements to apply the shadow.

The shadow should appear darker next to the ladybug's legs and gradually fade into the background. When applying graphite powder with a brush, start by focusing on areas that require a darker shade. As you shade outwards, you will have less and less graphite powder on the brush to use, creating a smooth gradient transition between the cast shadow and the background. This technique results in a realistic and dimensional effect for the drawing.

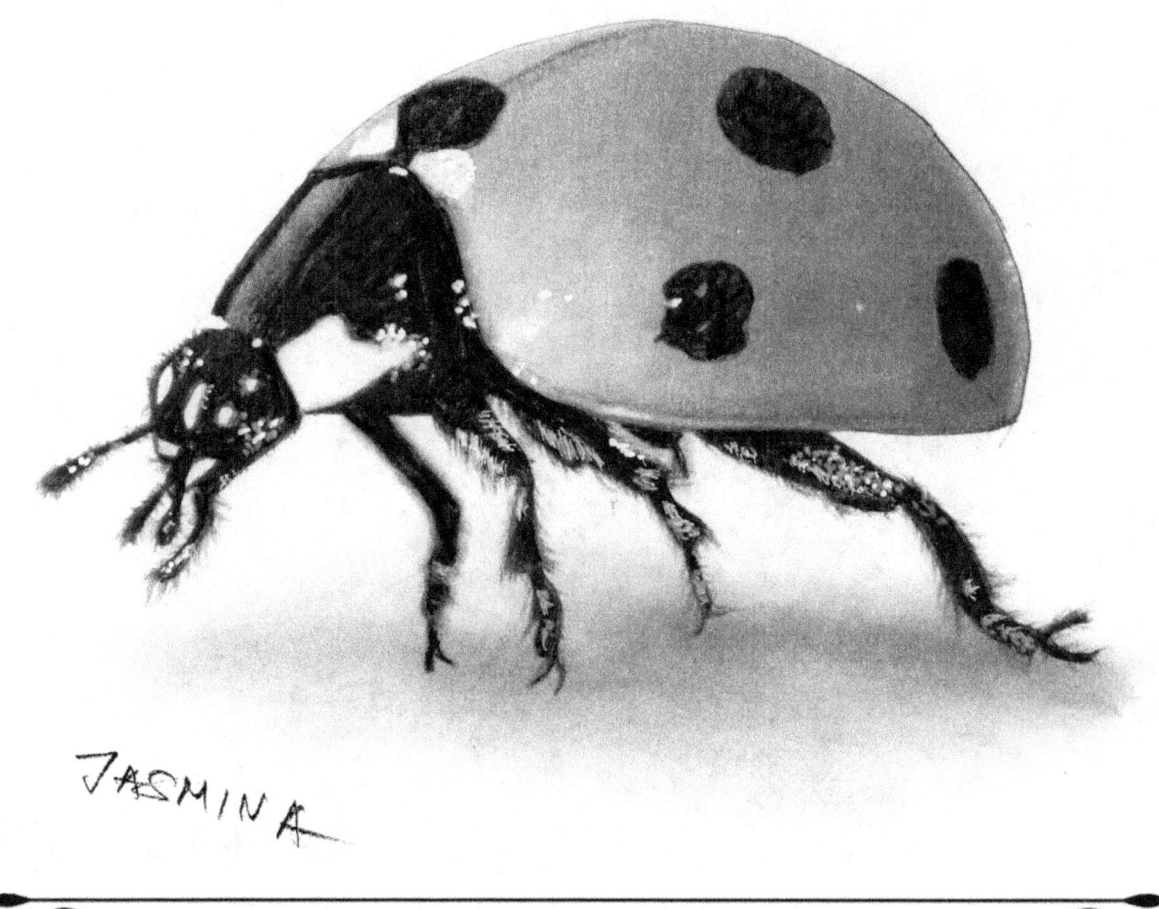

JASMINA

How to Draw a Bumblebee

With their fluffy bodies and distinctive black and yellow coloration, bumblebees are fascinating subjects for artistic exploration. Bumblebees are known for their gentle and docile nature, making them a beloved presence in gardens and natural habitats. As an artist and nature enthusiast, I have personally planted clover in my expansive garden specifically to attract and provide food for honey bees and bumblebees. Observing them buzzing happily among the vibrant flowers is a true joy and inspires me to capture their charm on paper. By creating artwork that showcases their beauty, we can raise awareness about the importance of protecting these valuable and endangered species.

The Reference Photo

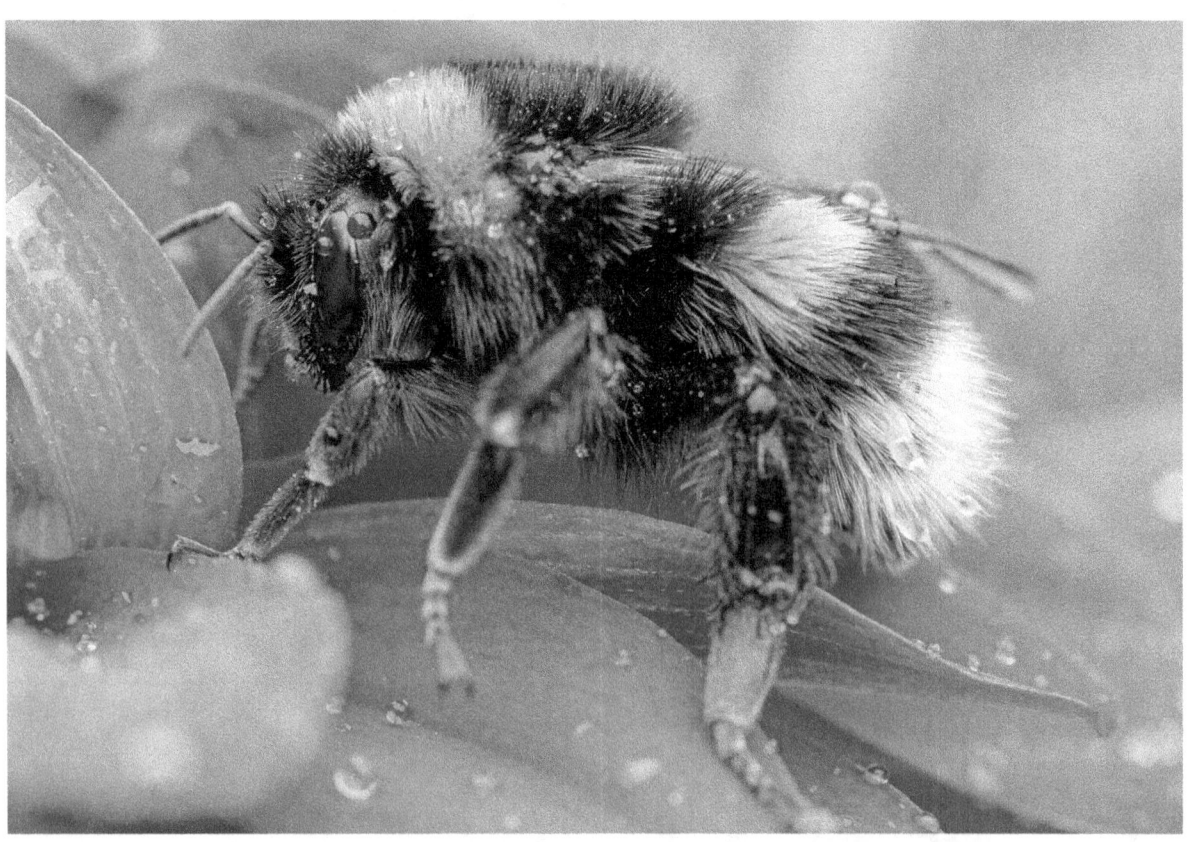

Sketching and Basic Shapes

In my approach, I've emphasized the significance of outlining the main body and legs, as well as delineating the border between the striking black and yellow segments with zigzag lines. Remember, not every detail in your sketch needs to perfectly match the reference photo. Feel free to experiment and explore, even deviating from the exact wing positions if you're inspired to do so.

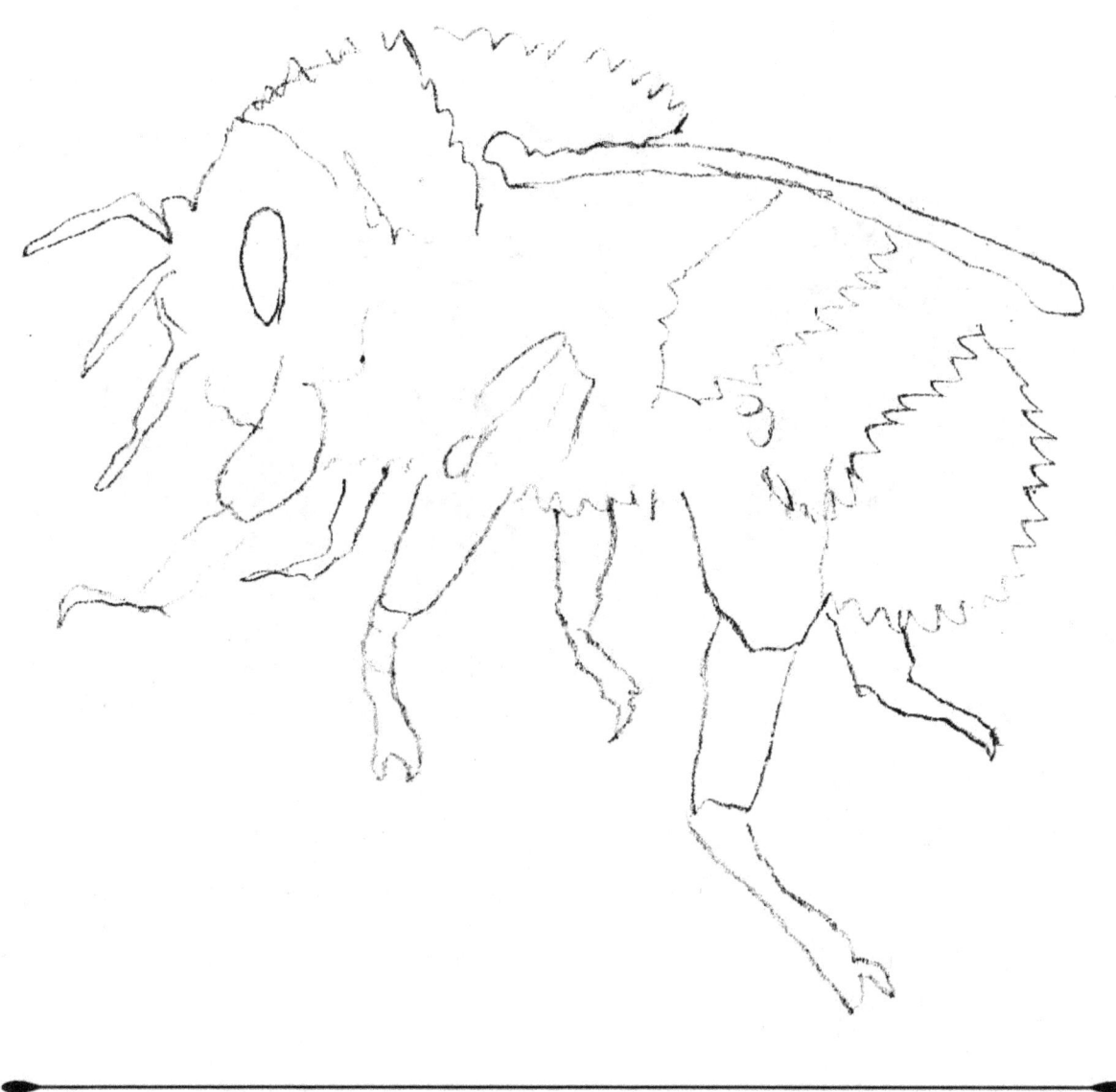

Drawing the Darkest Areas

With a 14B pencil, begin by sketching the regions that should be entirely black. Recognizing these areas within the reference photo might be somewhat challenging, so please refer to my step to observe where I have applied the deepest shade.

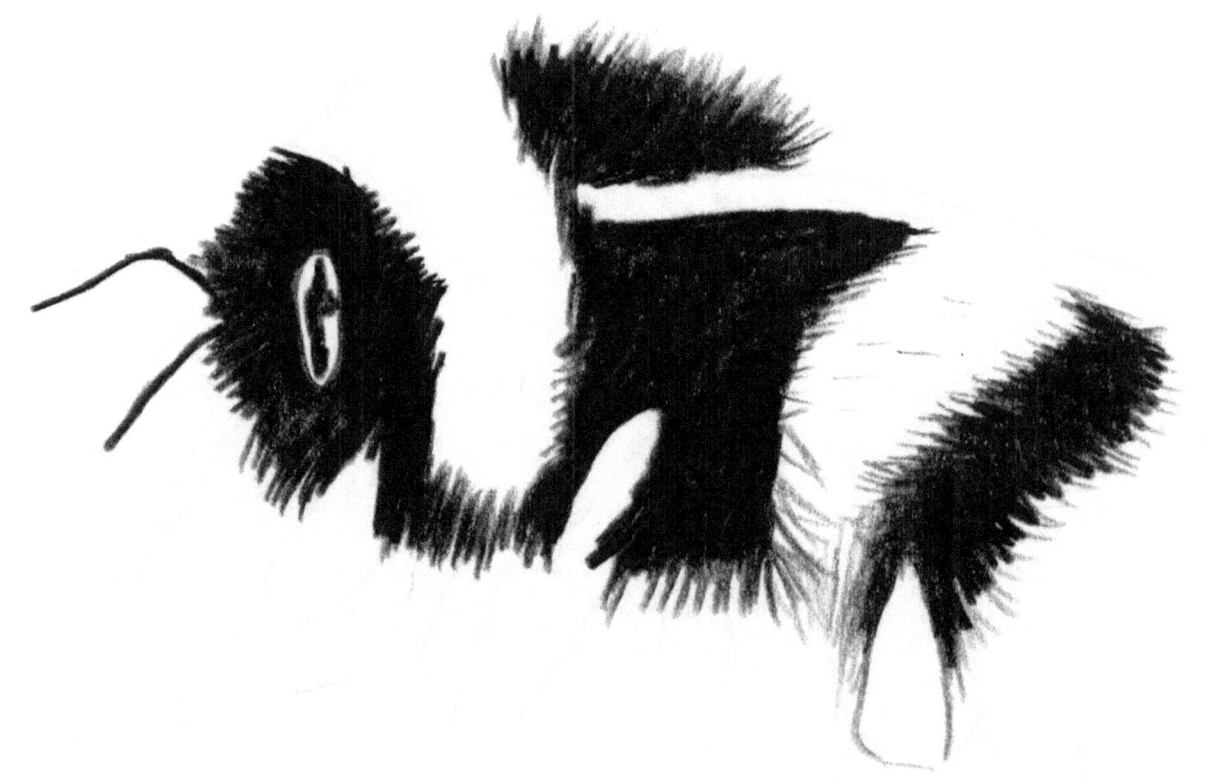

Drawing Lighter Hairs

Bumblebees are recognized for their distinctive black and yellow stripes, often culminating in a white-tipped section, akin to a tail. Now, using an HB pencil, focus on sketching the delicate hairs over the two yellow segments. Gradually reduce the density of these strokes for the white-haired section.

As with previous steps, ensure you're aligning your pencil strokes with the natural growth and flow of the hairs.

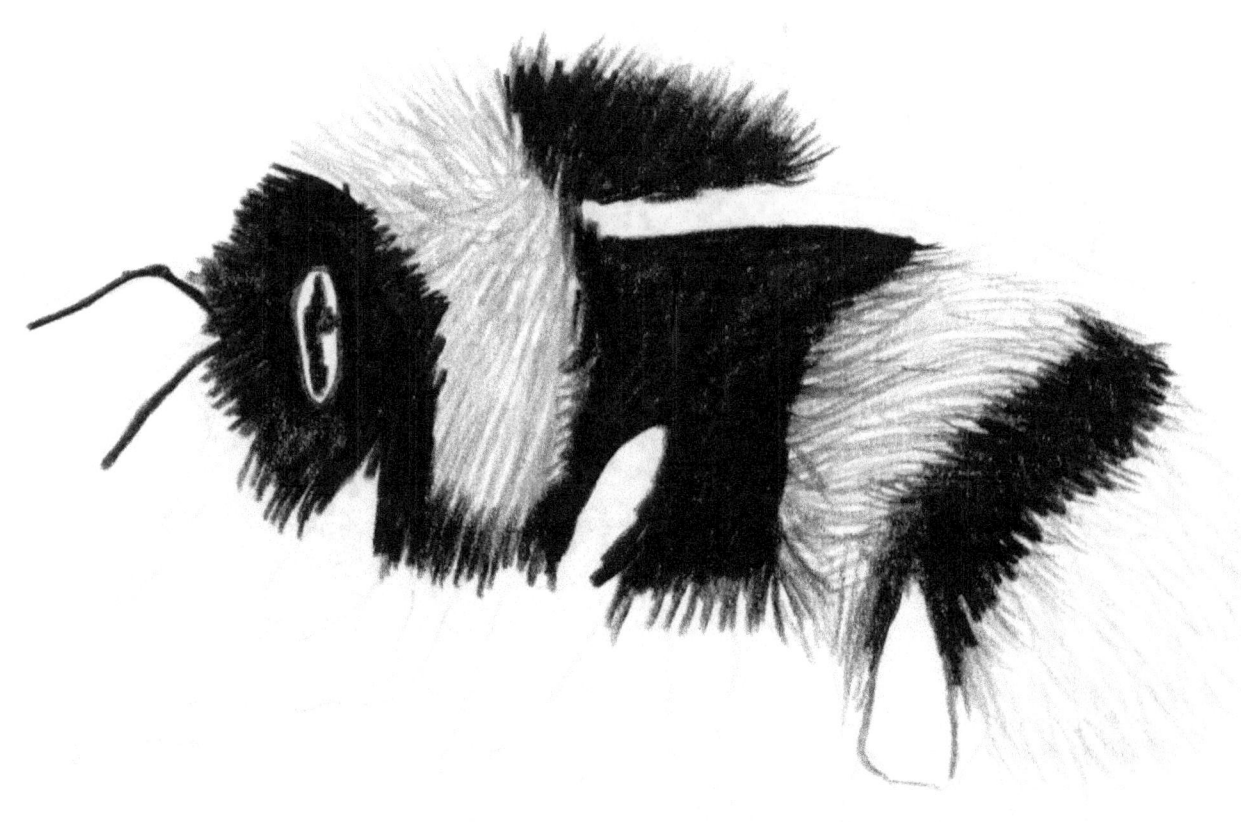

Blending the Lighter Hairs

To achieve a softer and more natural look, employ a blending stump or a Q-tip to meticulously blend the hairs you've sketched. This blending process will prevent the hairs from appearing sharp and distinct, contributing to a more realistic and gentle texture.

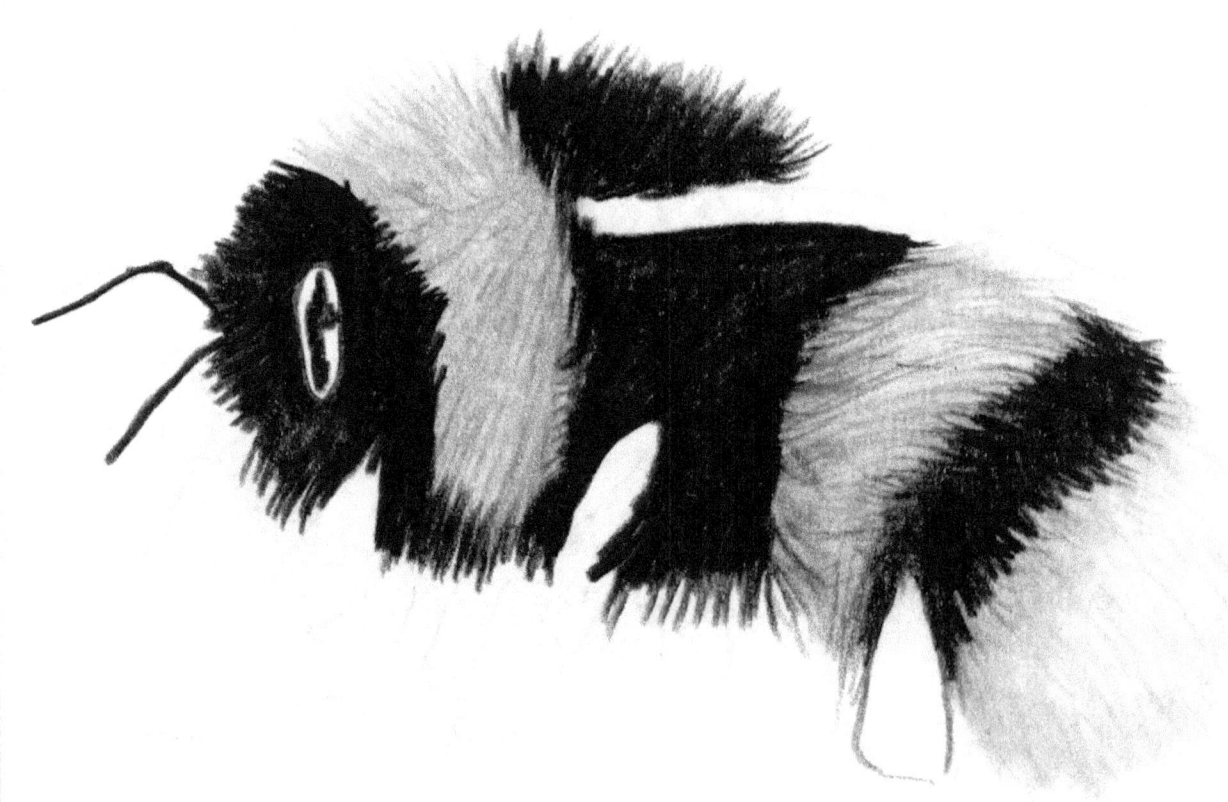

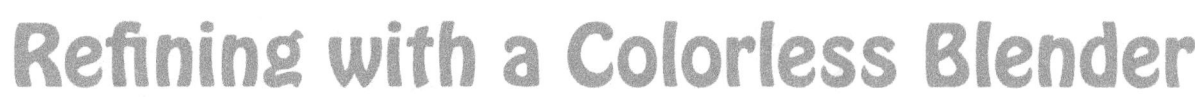

Refining with a Colorless Blender

For this stage, I employed a colorless blender from Prismacolor Premier to meld the ends of the black hairs I sketched using a 14B pencil. This blending is applied to the black hairs that extend over the yellow and white parts of the bumblebee, as well as those along the outer edge against the background. To execute this, position the tip of the blender on the black area and swiftly stroke in the required direction. While a 2B pencil can also be used for this task, I noticed that the blending effect is more delicate and textured when utilizing this specific blender.

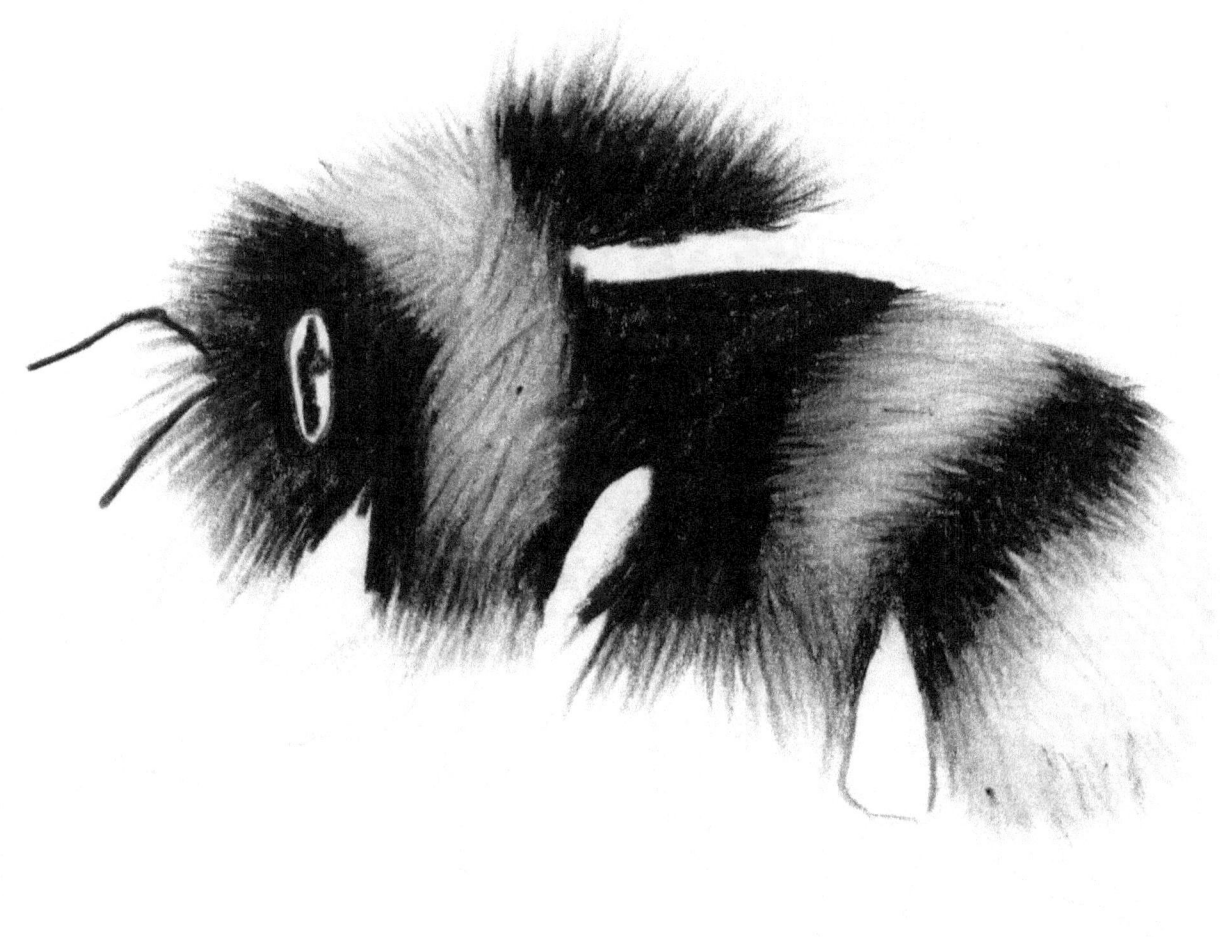

Adding Highlighted Hairs

Moving forward, we'll introduce some delicate highlighted hairs at the juncture of the black sections, where they meet the yellow and white regions. You have the option to craft these fine, bright hairs using either an electric eraser or a white ink gel pen. Should the highlights appear overly luminous after using the gel pen, a simple solution is to gently stroke them with a blending stump once the ink has dried, achieving a slightly darker tone.

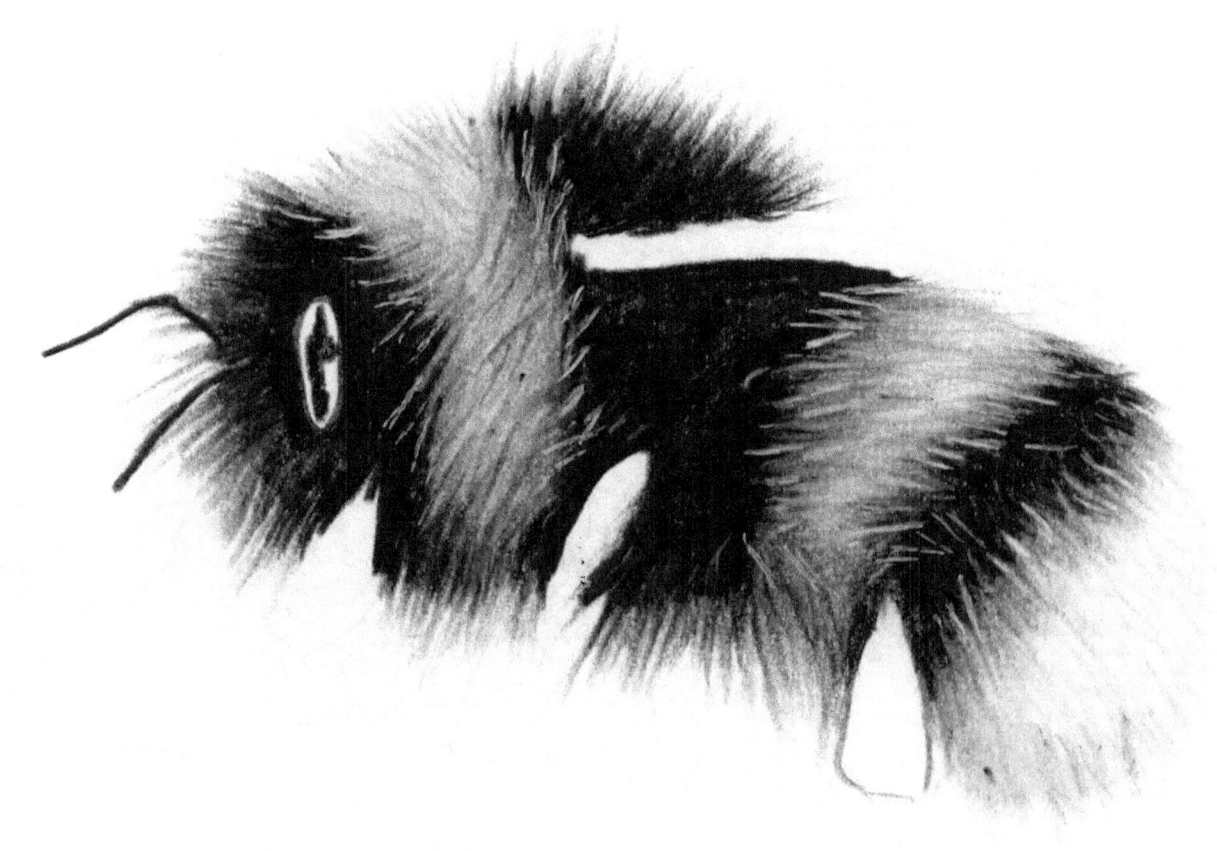

Shading Antennae, Eye, and Wing

In this phase, we will proceed to shade the upper sections of the antennae with an HB pencil. Utilizing the same pencil, shade the eye and the wing as well. While shading the wing, make sure to adjust the pressure you apply to create a textured effect that is less uniform and more three-dimensional.

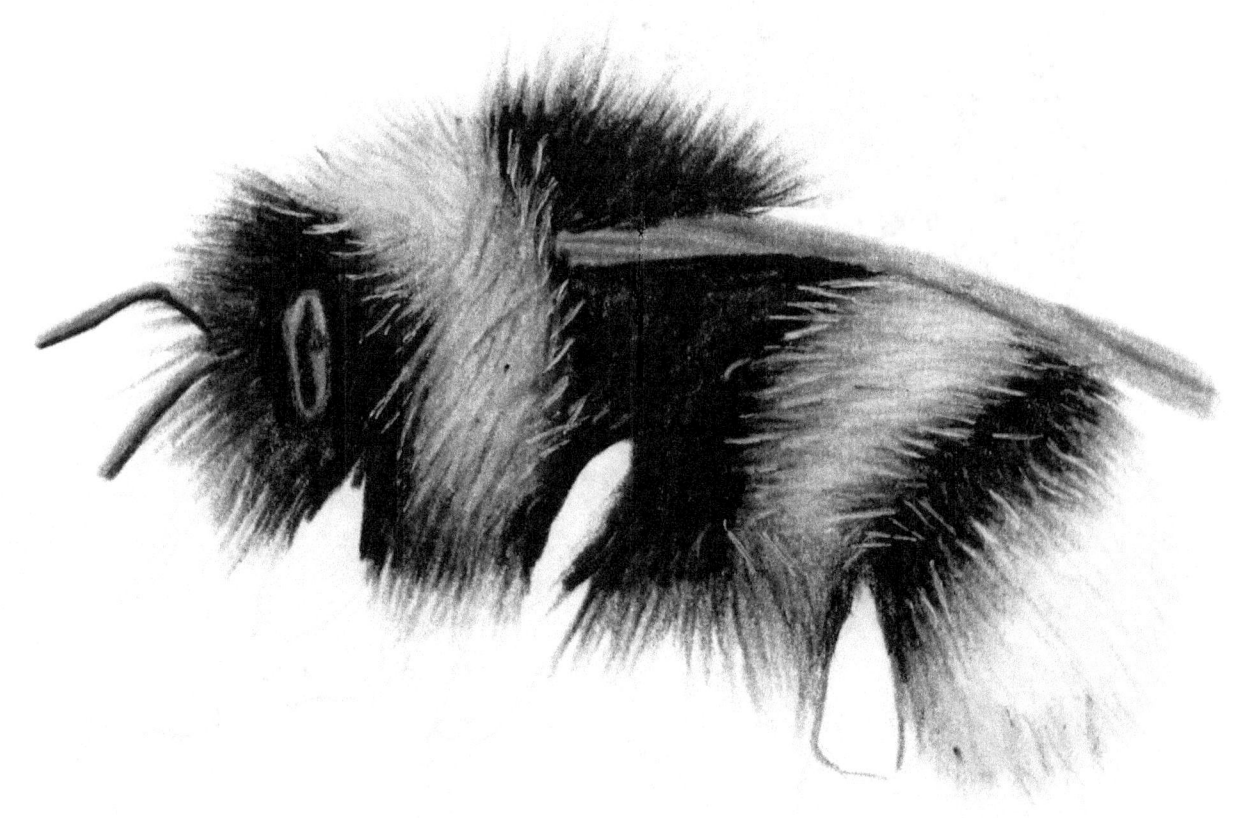

Commencing Leg Drawing

When you're prepared, we can embark on sketching the legs.
To achieve a sense of all-around illumination and roundness,
I employed a 2B pencil to shade the outer sections of the legs.
Observe the accompanying image to identify the specific
regions I've shaded in this instance.

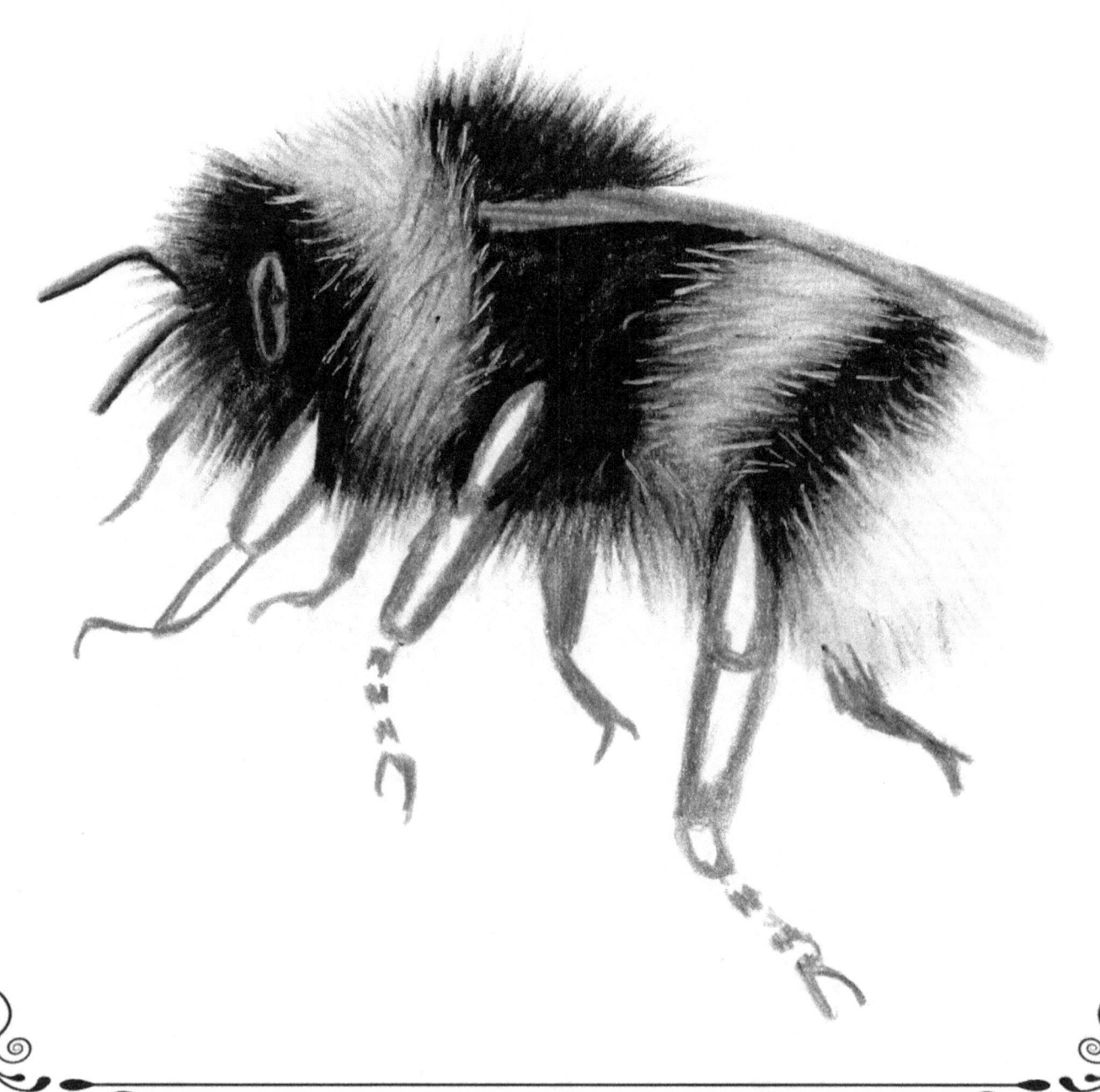

Continuing Leg Shading

Proceed to shade the areas that were left untouched in the previous step, focusing on the middle sections of the leg parts. Utilize a 10B pencil for this shading. Afterward, use a 6B pencil to blend the transitions between the two shades, ensuring a gradual and seamless flow between them. This blending technique will produce a rounded effect for the legs.

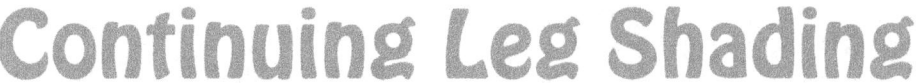

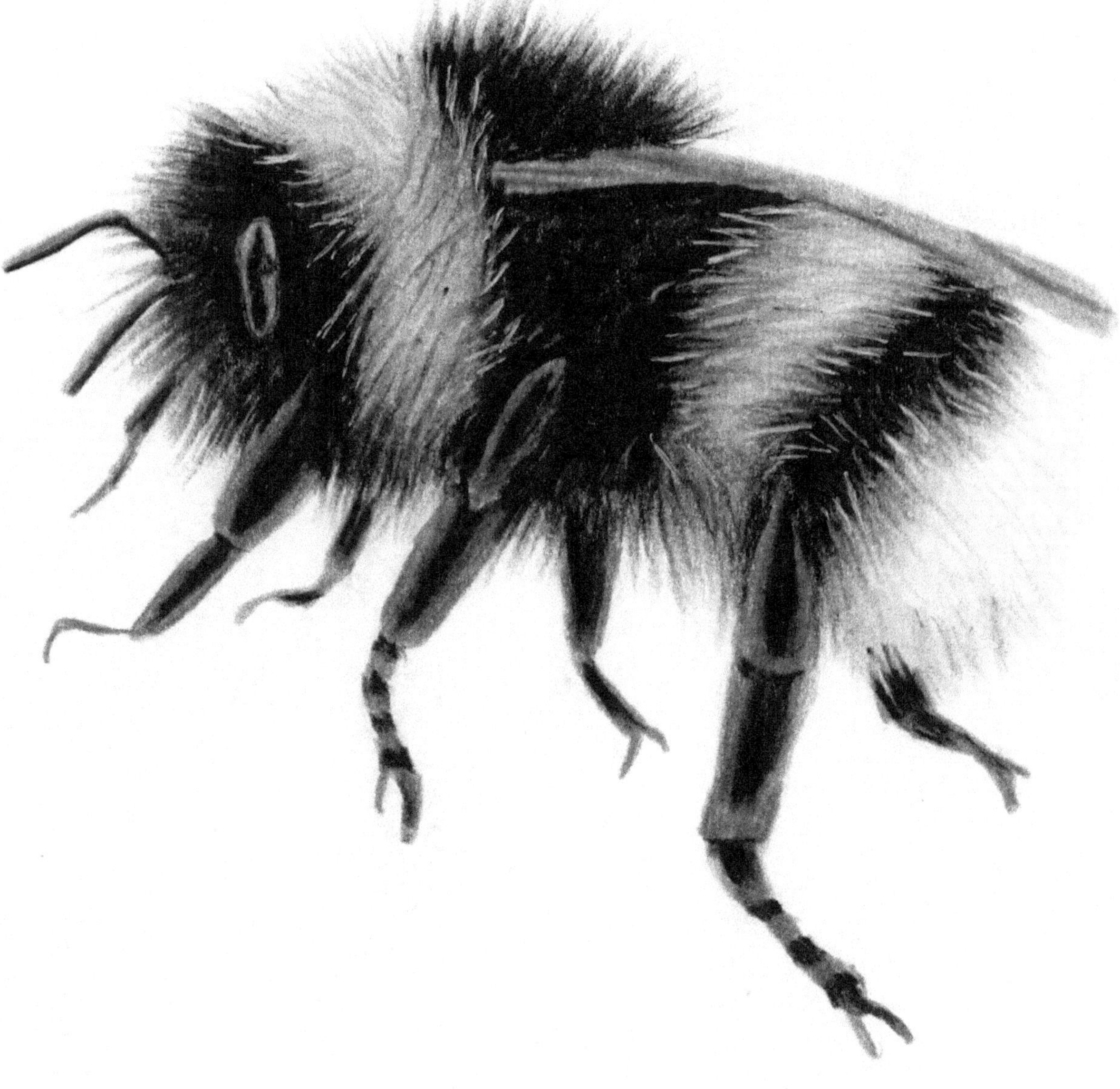

Refining Leg Details

Moving forward, employ a 2B pencil to carefully draw the small hairs that adorn the entire surface of the legs, following the visual guidance provided in my accompanying image.
Once you're satisfied with the result, proceed to blend these drawn hairs using either a colorless blender or a lighter shade, such as HB. This blending will create a harmonious and textured appearance for the leg hairs.

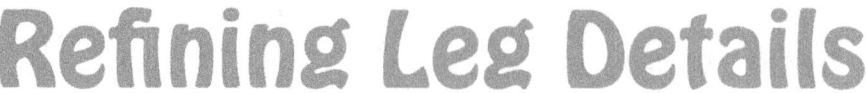

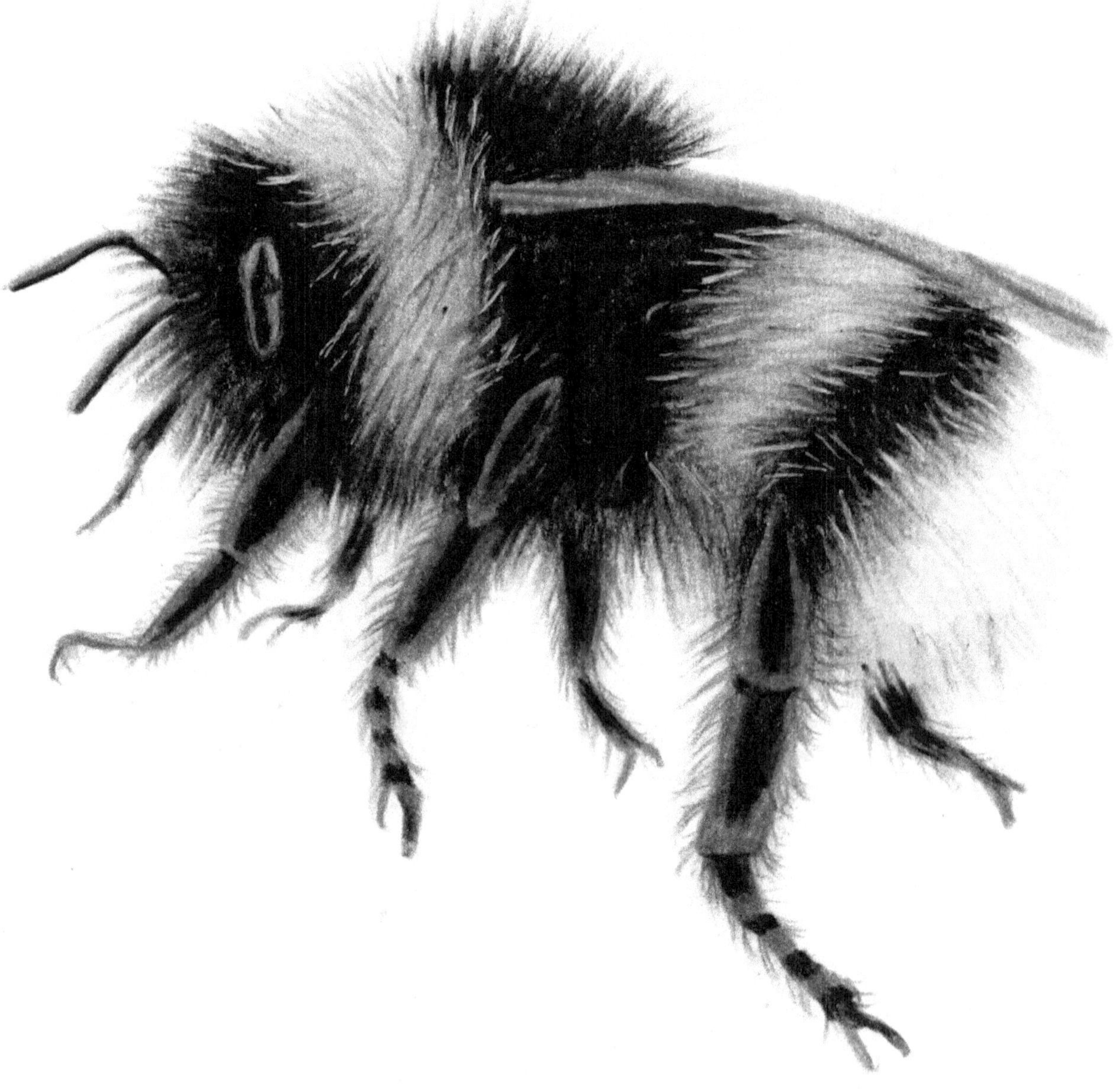

Enhancing Leg Details and Adding Pollen

Continuing onward, utilize a white ink gel pen to delicately craft the minuscule hairs that grace the legs. These hairs often gleam in the light or bear traces of pollen, warranting their depiction with the precision of a white ink gel pen or an electric eraser. Additionally, sprinkle some diminutive dots strategically across the bumblebee's form, conveying the idea of pollen and its diligent foraging. This will infuse your artwork with a touch of life and vibrancy.

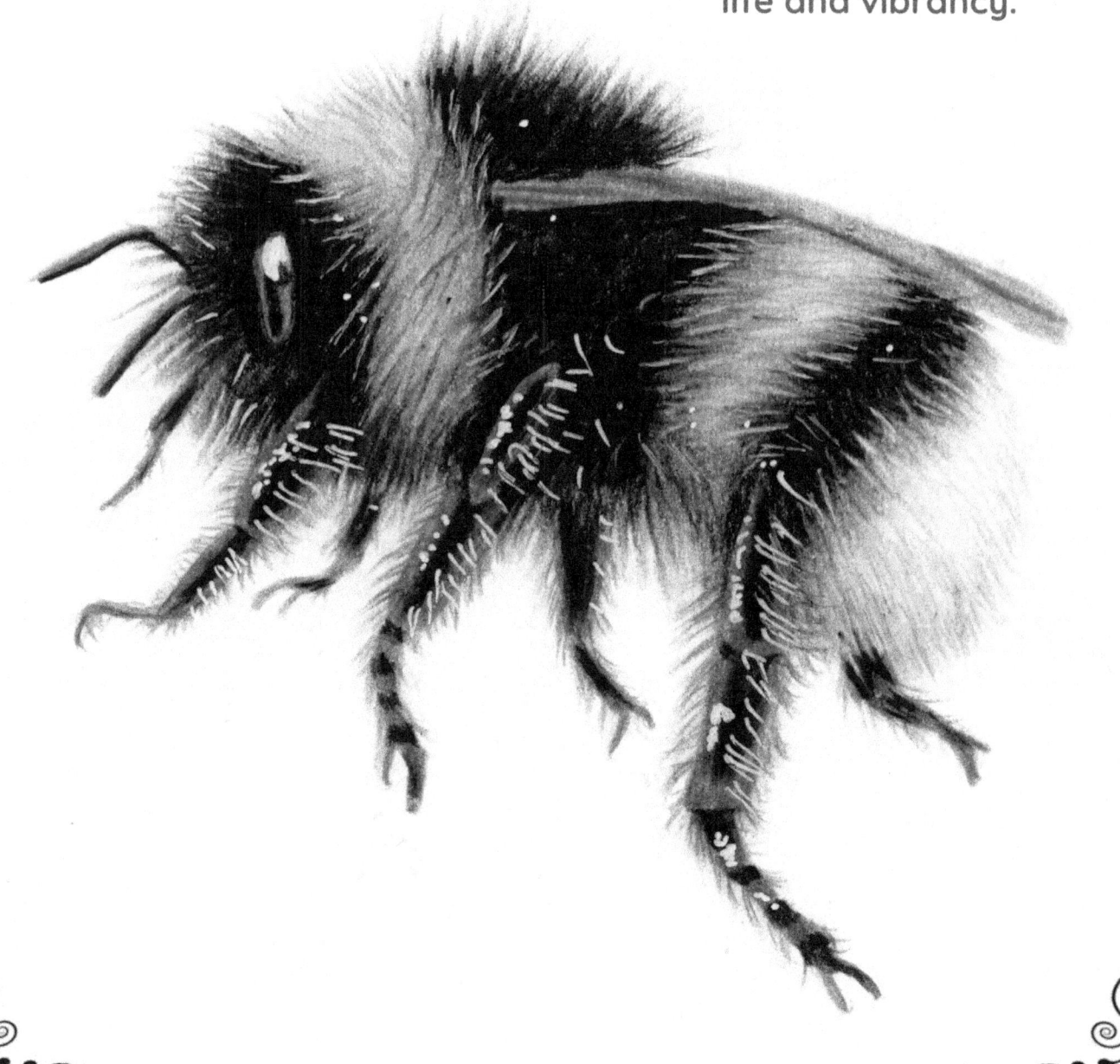

Concluding the Bumblebee Artwork

Should you find yourself content with your rendition of the bumblebee, you may consider extending your composition by illustrating a flower beneath it, as if it were perched upon it. To add an extra touch of realism, I opted to portray the shadow cast by the bee upon the imagined surface. This was achieved by gently applying graphite powder with a brush, thus lending a subtle and atmospheric dimension to the scene.

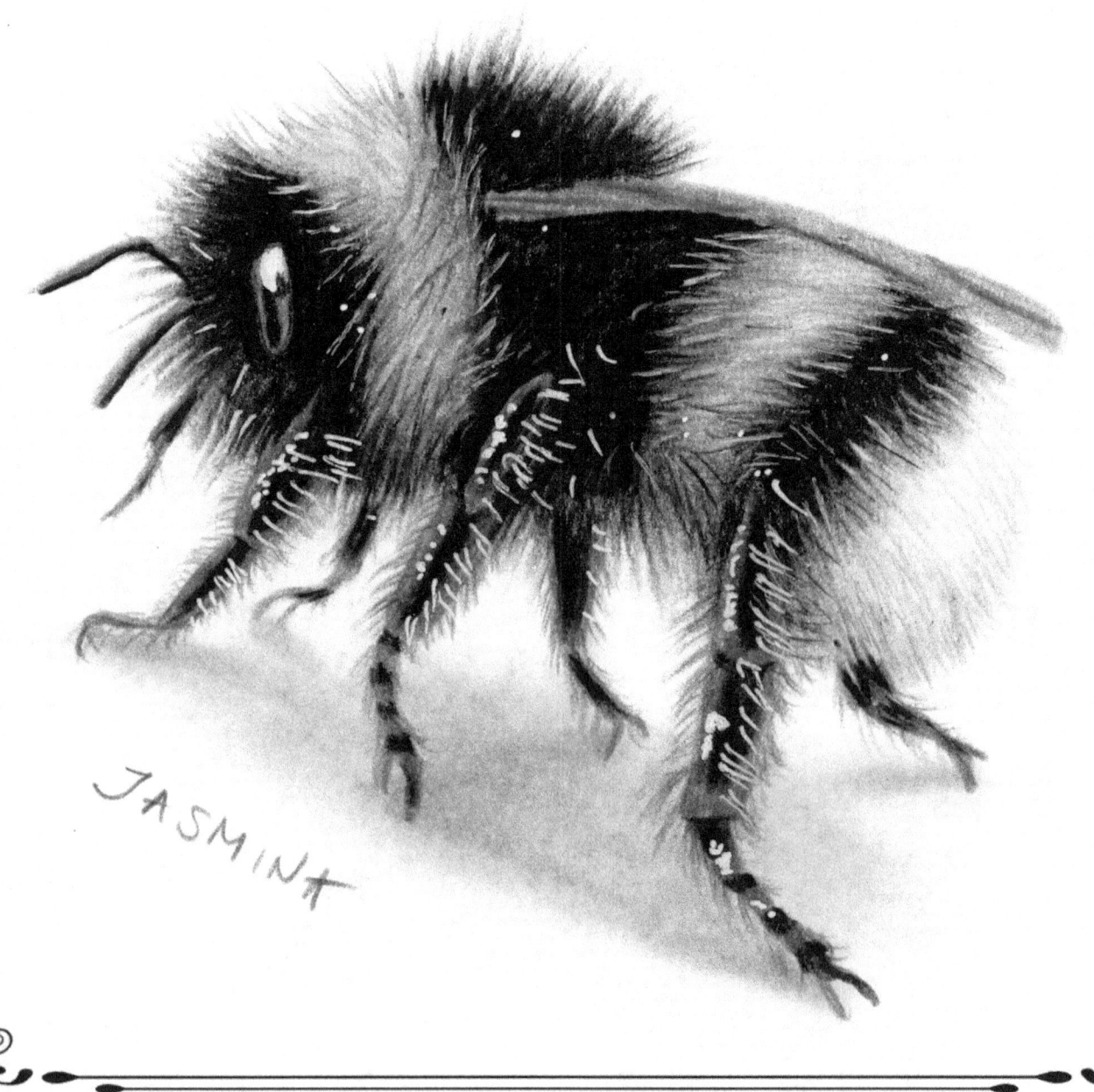

Drawing Interludes

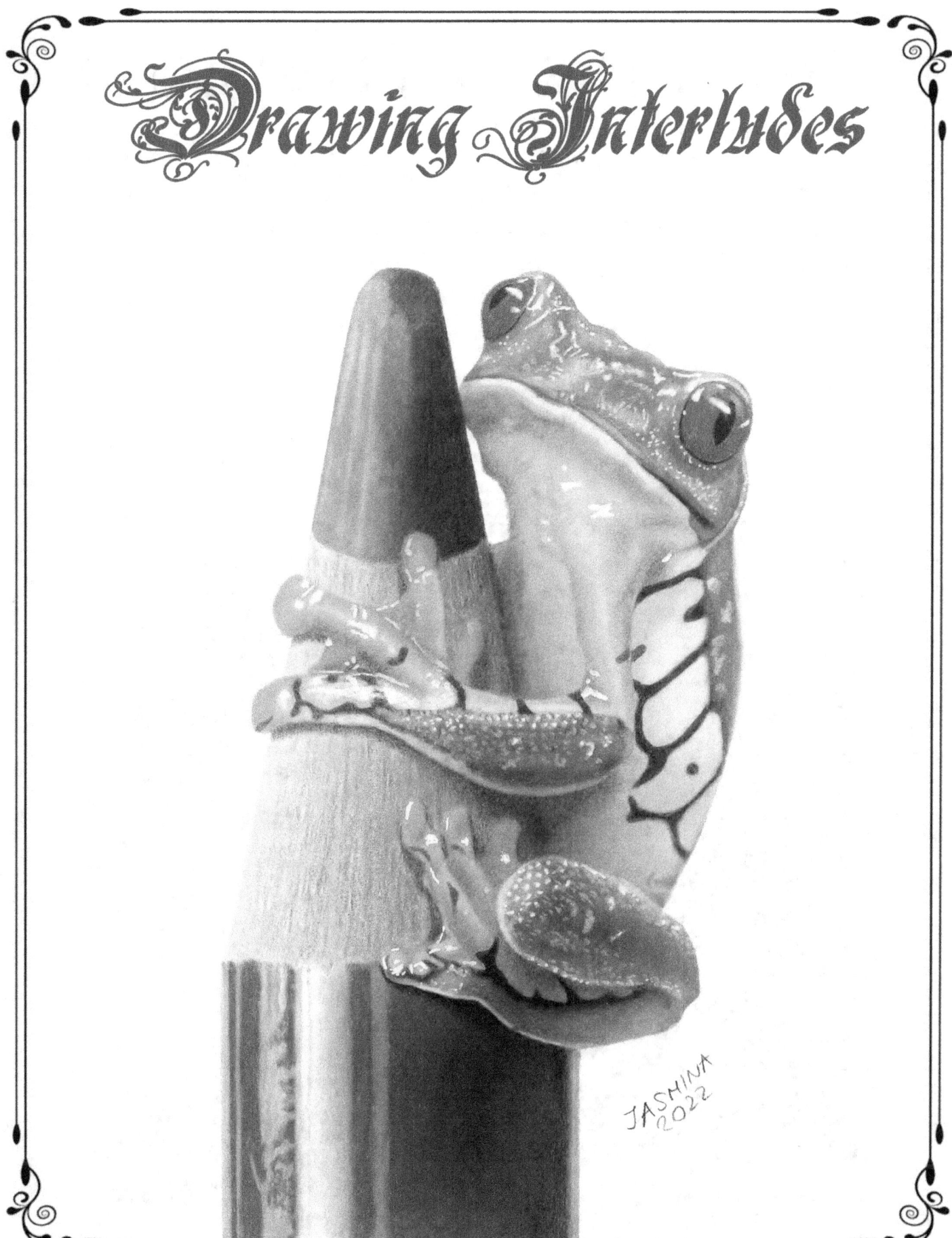

JASMINA
2022

How to Draw a Black Swan

Drawing the black swan offers a chance to practice textures, shades, and intricate details, while exploring how light plays on dark feathers, enhancing your artwork's realism and appeal. Appreciate nature's elegance and develop your artistic skills by capturing the beauty of the black swan. Let's bring it to life in our drawing.

The Reference Photo

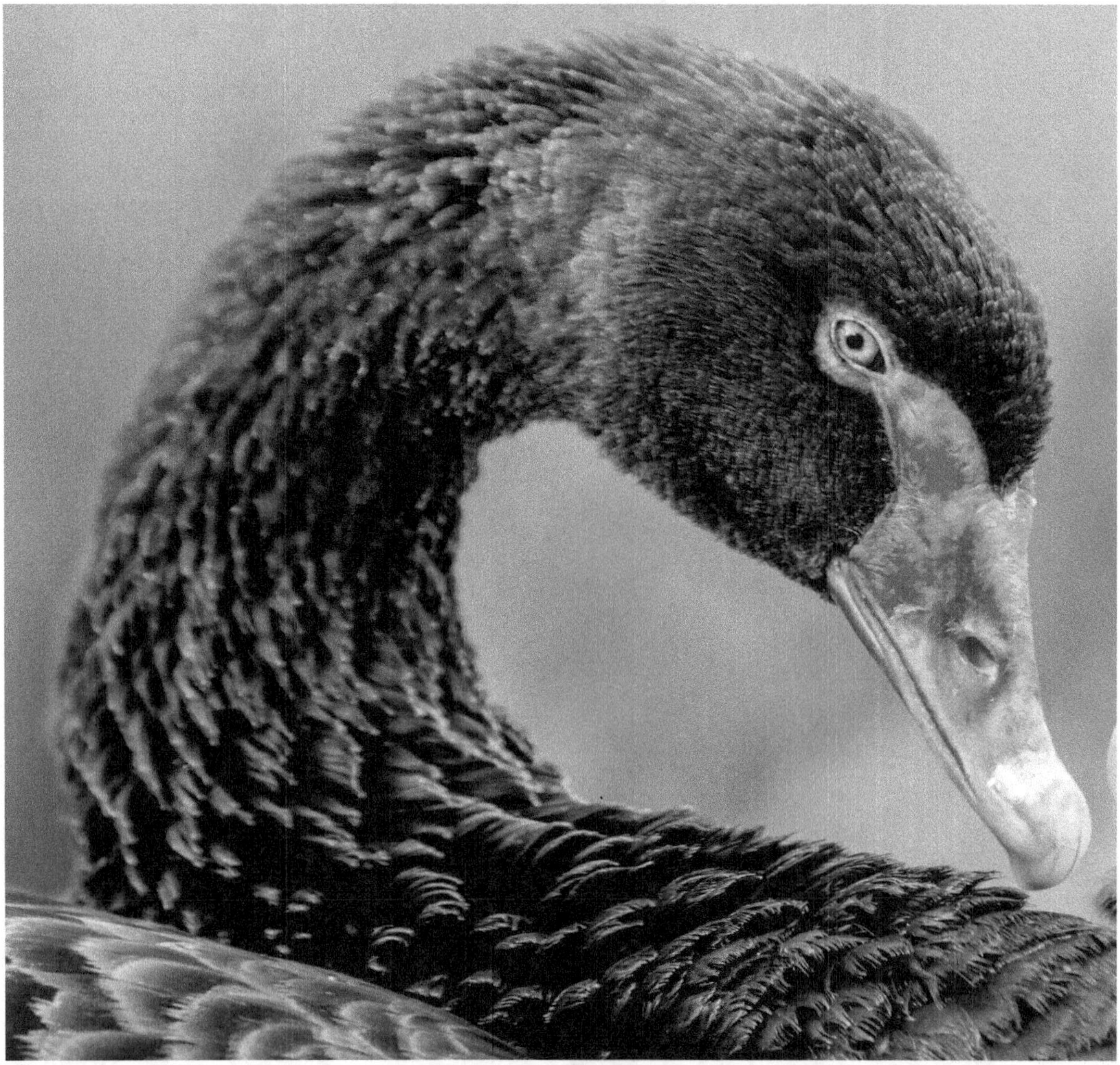

84

Sketching and Basic Shapes

In the next image, you will find my pencil sketch that I have scanned. Take a moment to study and analyze the lines that I have found important and significant in my drawing. These lines have been carefully chosen to capture the essence and character of the subject. Observe the details, the curves, and the precision in each stroke, as they contribute to the overall composition.

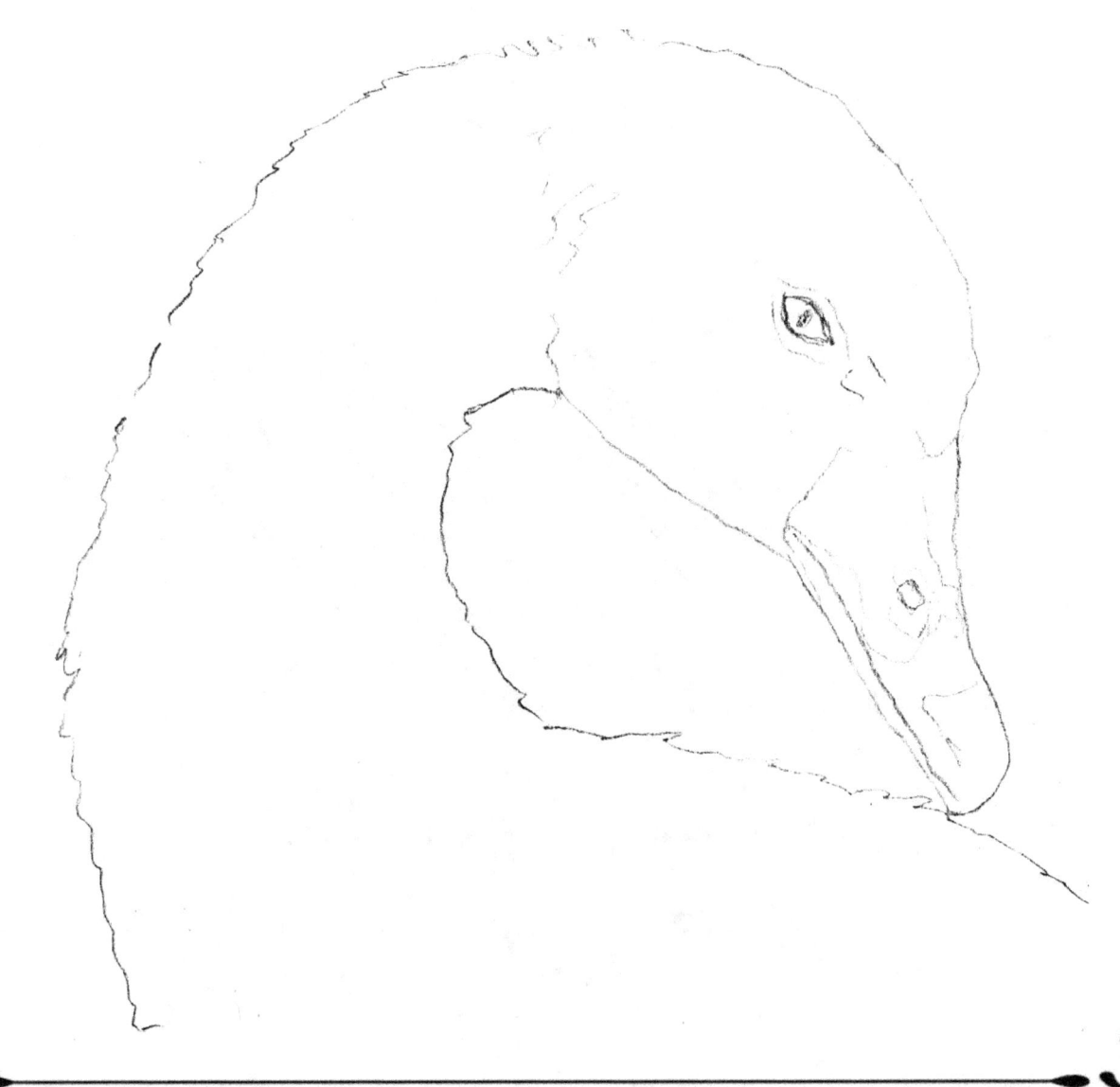

Analyzing the Black Swan's Values

Let's begin by analyzing the photograph of the beautiful black swan and breaking it down into different value levels.

To do this, you can use any image editing app that offers a Posterize effect. I have created a free tool for this called Posterize Image Online Free Tool, which is available on the Pencil Drawing Tutor website www.pencildrawingtutor.com

Upload image

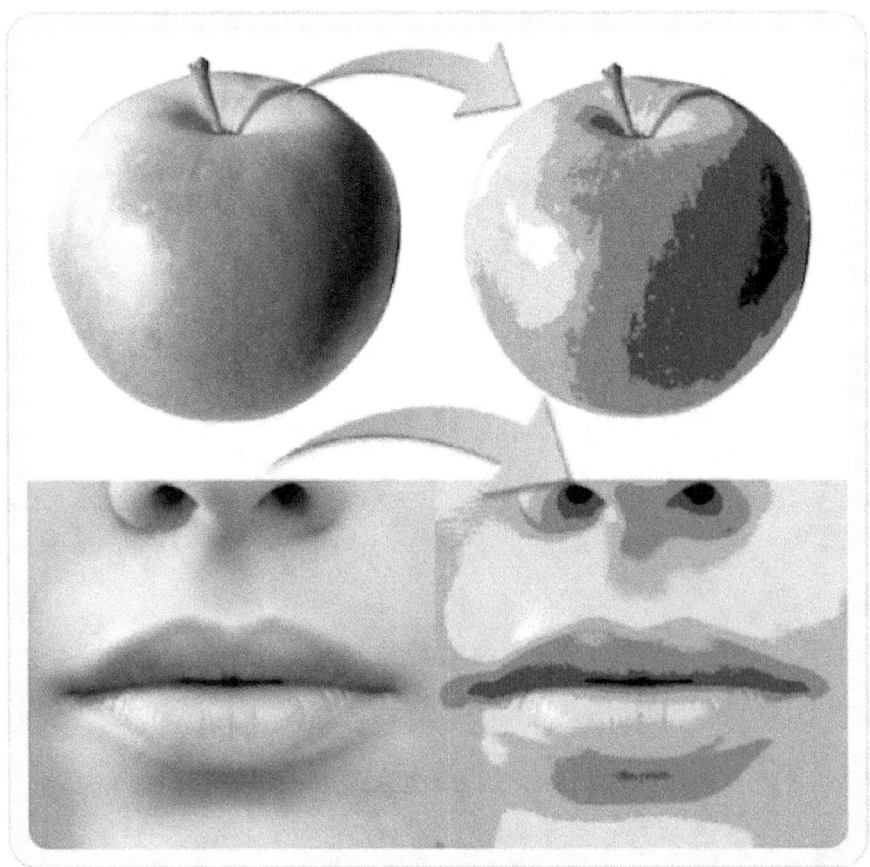

When you upload your photo to the Posterize Image Online Free Tool, move the scale below the image to select the desired number of value levels. For example, if you choose 2 levels, the image will display only black and white. With 3 levels, one gray value is added between black and white.

In the screenshot shown, I selected 4 levels, which results in black, white, and both lighter and darker shades of gray. These four values are sufficient for breaking the photo down into clear areas for shading. While you can experiment with five or more levels, I find that starting with these four values provides a solid foundation, considering the amount of detail we will add later.

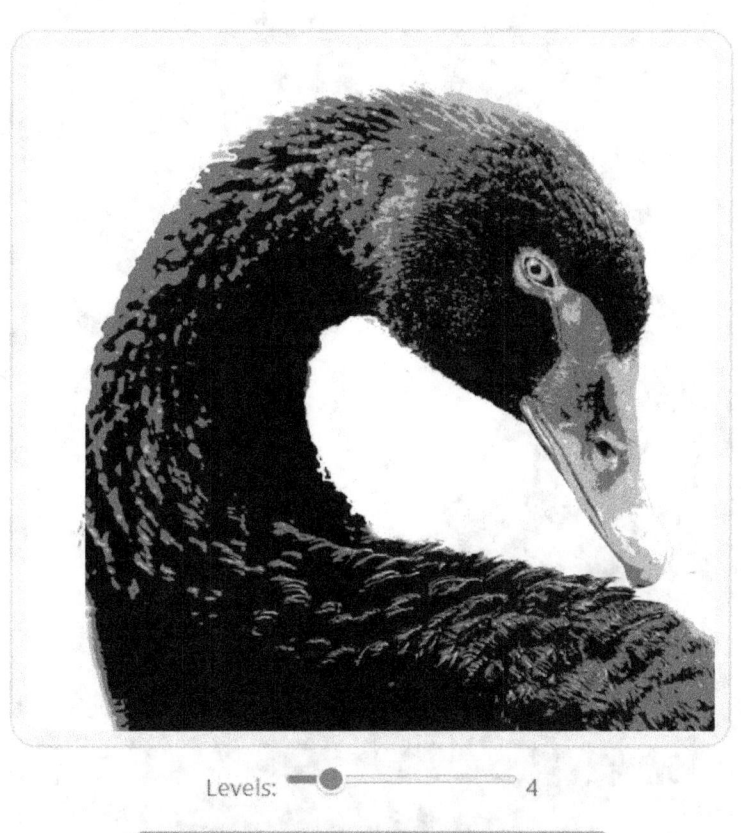

Levels: ━●━━━━━ 4

Download posterized image

Finding the Correct Shades

In the next image, you will find the "posterized" image that I have created. It shows the black and two shades of grey that I have selected. I have connected each shade with a line to the corresponding swatch. This approach helps us identify the values clearly, free from any distractions caused by surrounding grades or intricate details.

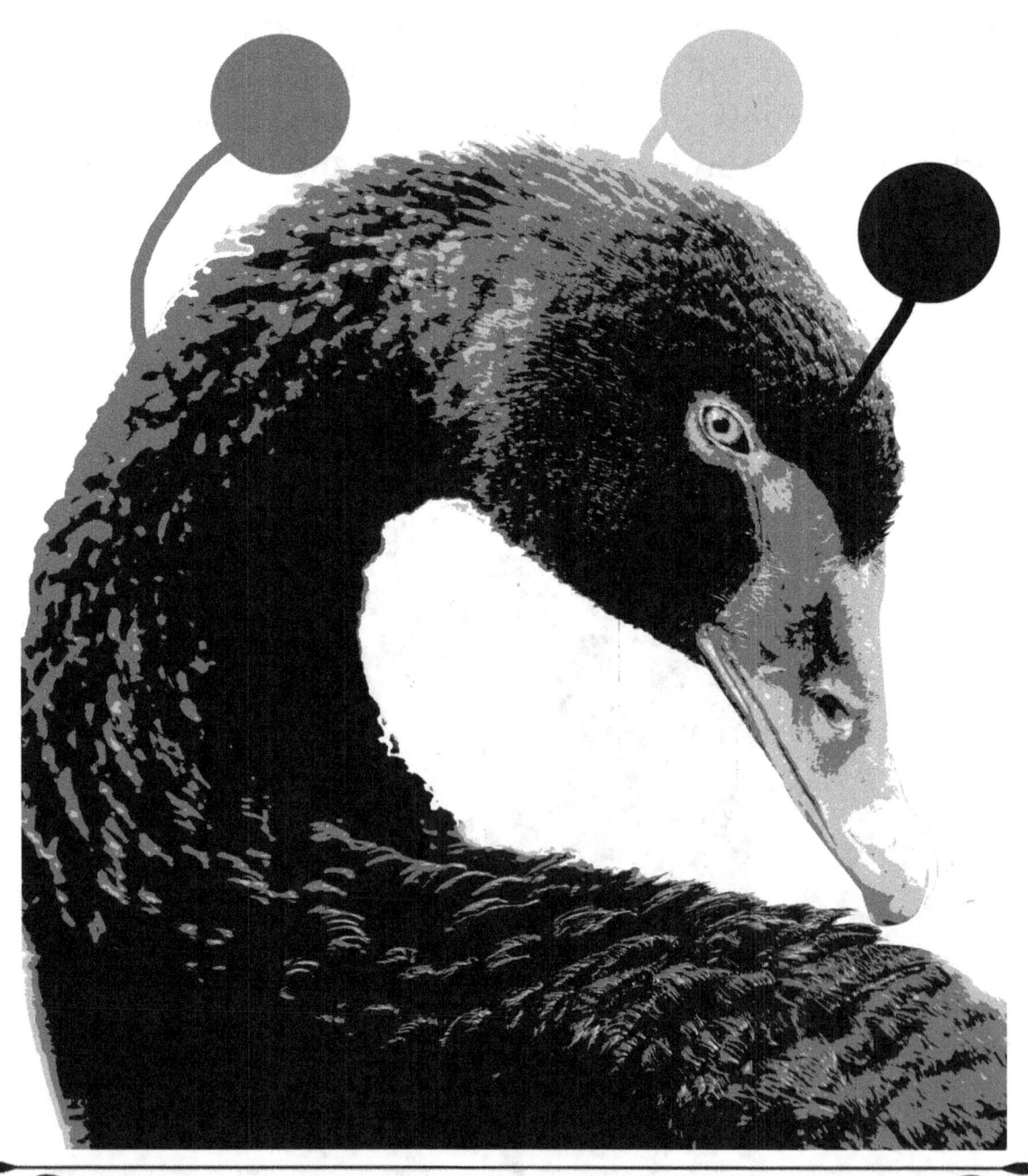

Selecting the Right Pencils

By simplifying the image in this manner, we can readily identify the ideal pencils for our drawing. In my judgment, these three pencils are a perfect match for the various swatches. However, adjustments can always be made during the shading process. At this stage, having the right grades of pencils is crucial to lay the foundation for our artwork.

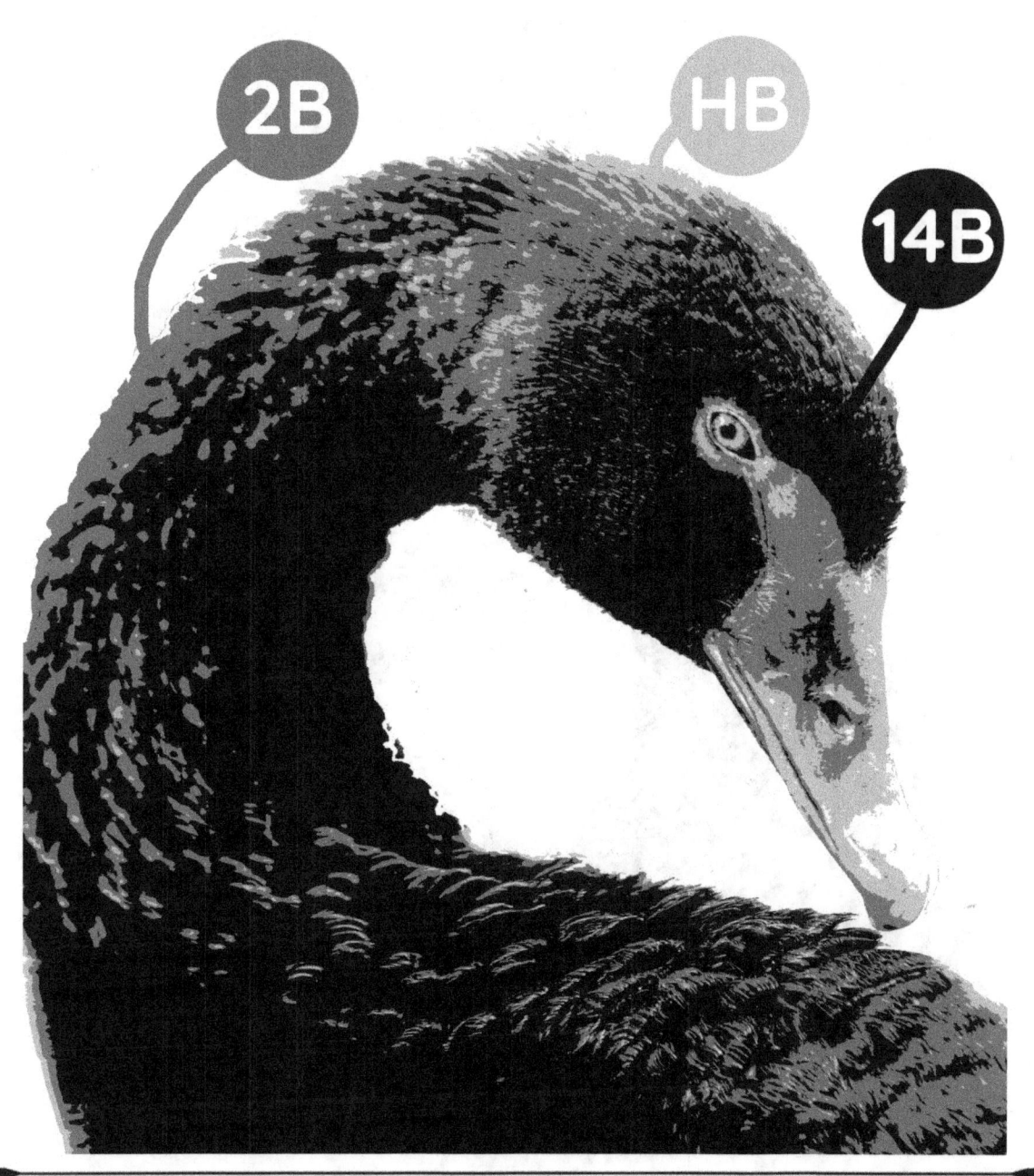

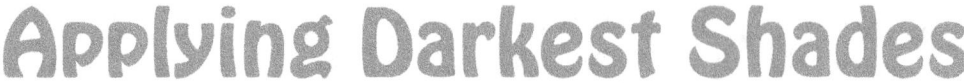

Applying Darkest Shades

To simplify the process, we will focus on the eye and beak later. For now, let's shade the black feathers.

Let's begin by using a **14B** pencil to shade the areas visible in the accompanying image. Apply firm pressure while shading to achieve a rich and deepest shade. Remember, we don't need to draw each feather individually, as seen in the reference photos. Instead, focus on approximating the shading to capture the deepest shades found between overlapping illuminated black feathers.

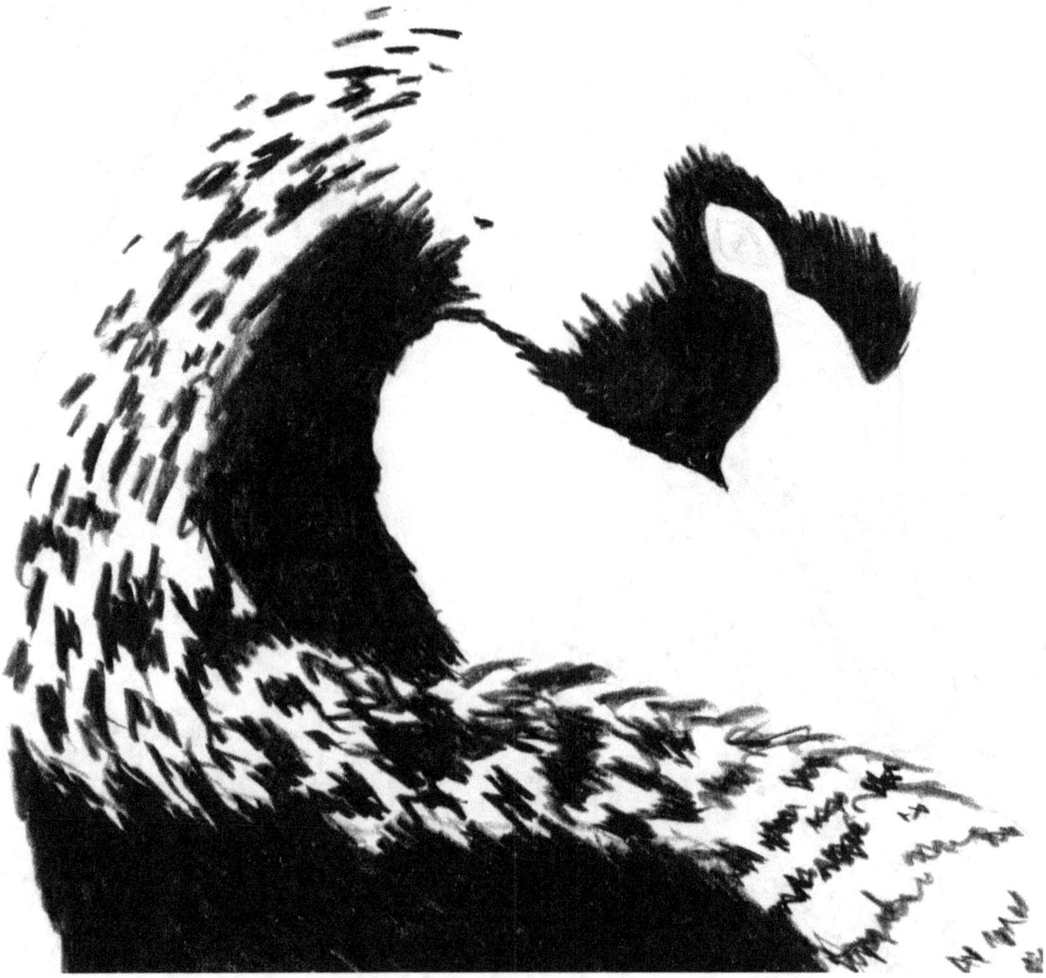

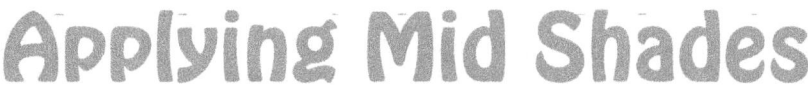

Applying Mid Shades

Following the values shown in the image in the "Selecting the Right Pencils" step, let's proceed with a 2B pencil to shade all the designated areas, ensuring a consistent and even application. Reserve the sections intended for the brightest tone, which we will shade using an HB pencil.

Always draw strokes in the direction of the feather's flow and growth. Additionally, draw around the outer edges, follow just next to the 14B edges to create reflected light, as the black edge is often slightly illuminated.

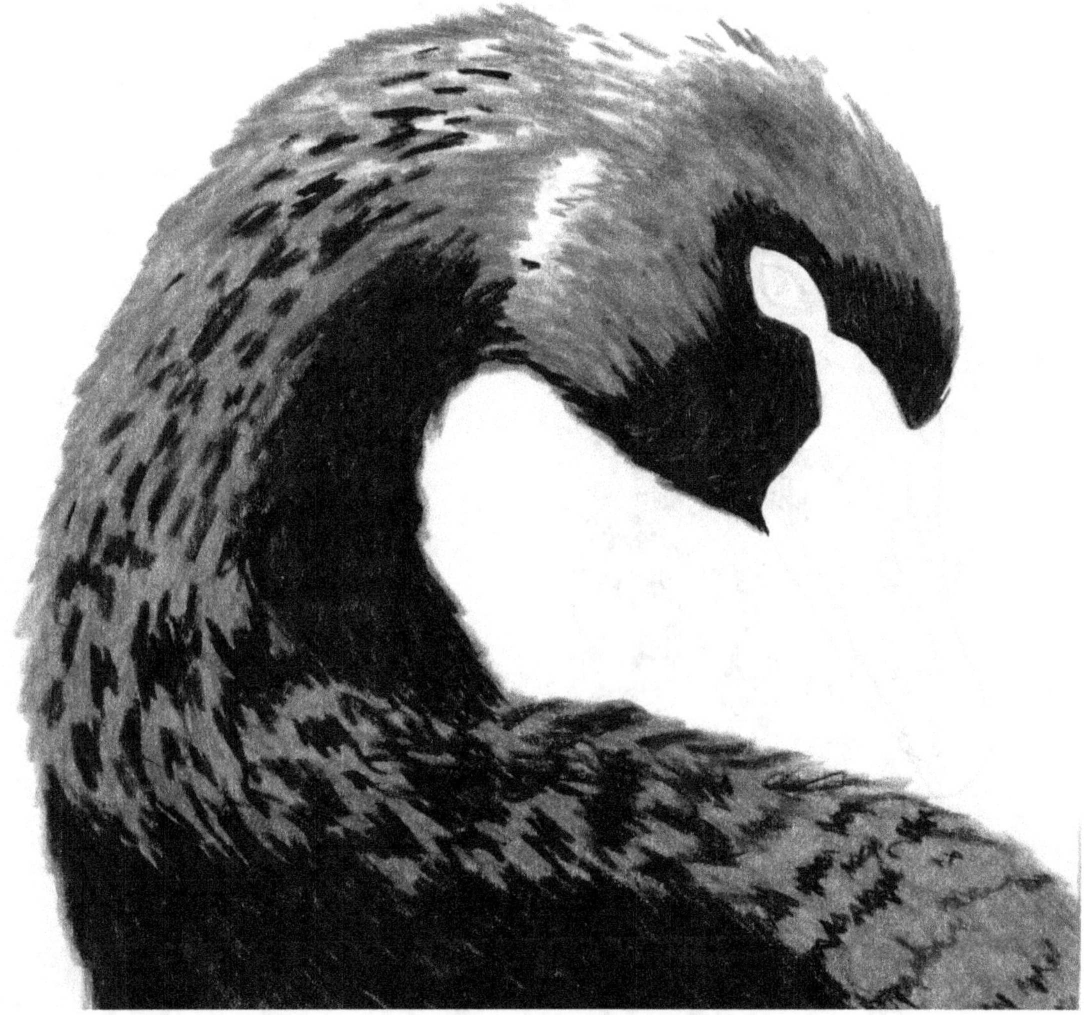

Applying Lightest Shades

In this step, let's use the HB pencil to delicately cover the remaining smaller areas. Focus on creating the lightest shades that add depth and dimension to the black swan's feathers. After applying the highlights, blend these areas carefully using a blending stump.

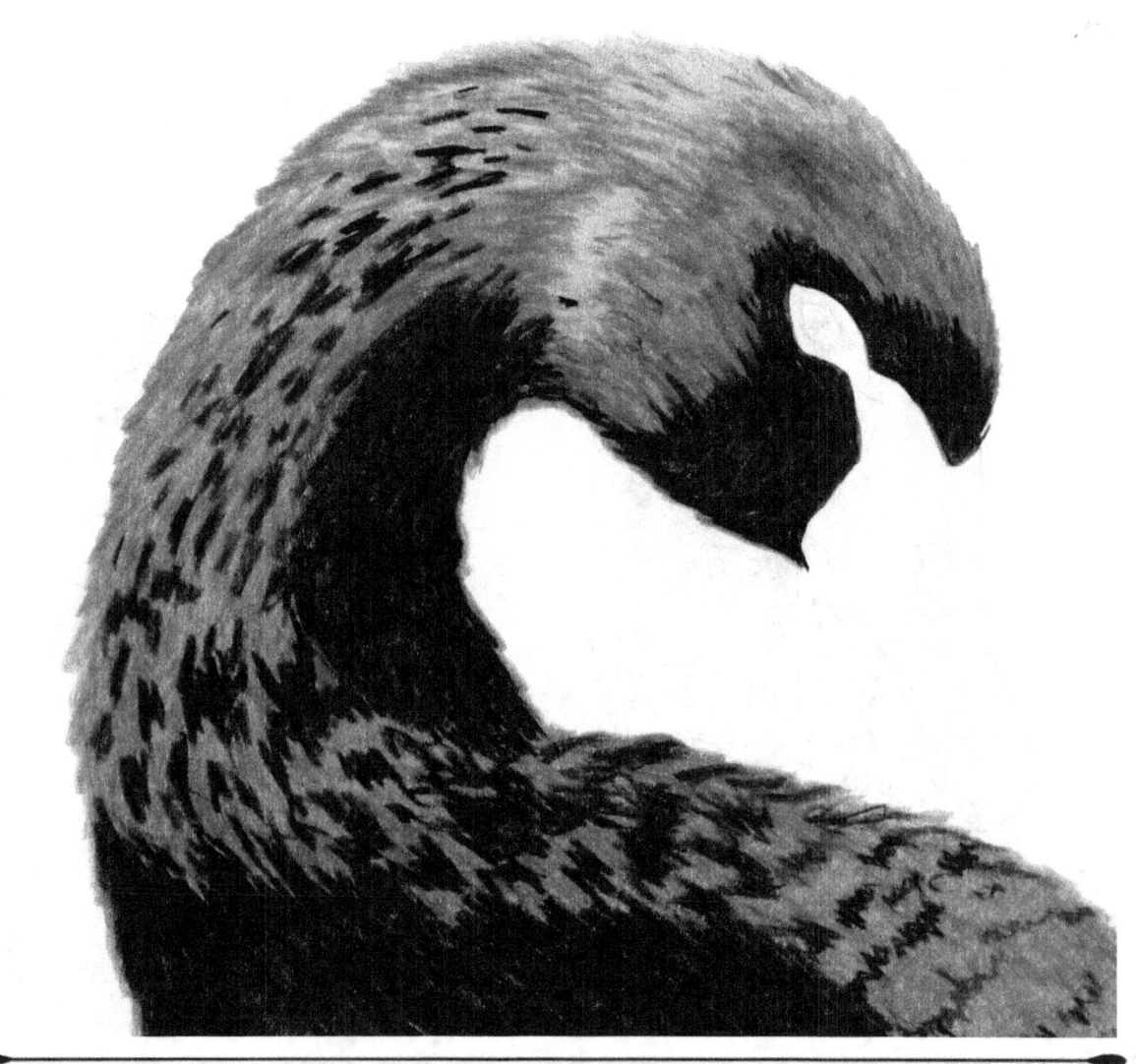

Smoothing Shades Transitions

Next, blend the 14B and 2B shades seamlessly using a 6B pencil, which sits between them. Adjust your pressure to create a smooth transition: lighten pressure away from the 14B areas into the 2B areas, and vice versa. This technique eliminates visible edges and make these shades flow into each other without any edges visible. Since we started with only 3 values, we can now create additional shades by skillfully shading in between these values.

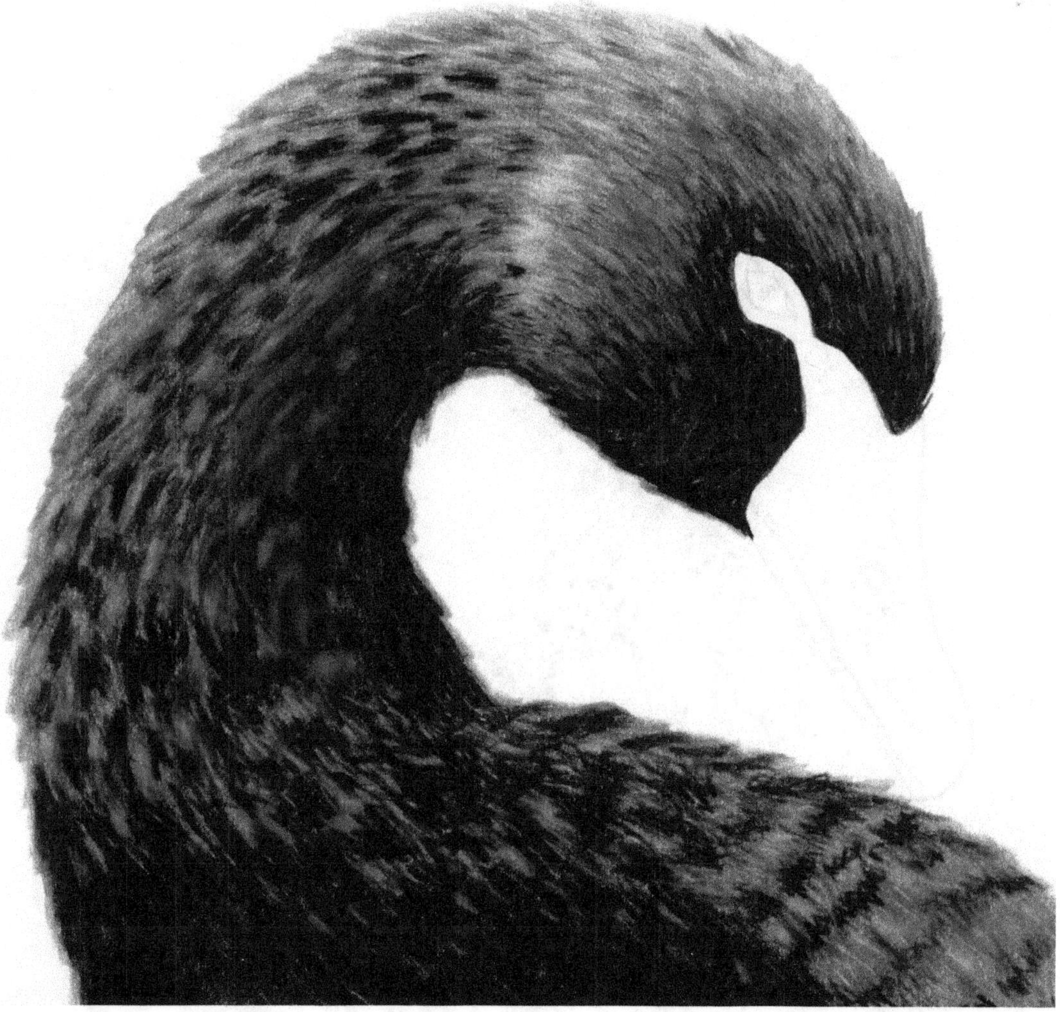

Creating Highlights

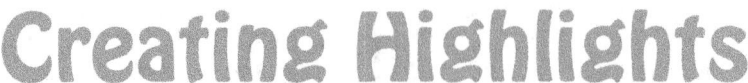

Now, let's enhance our drawing by adding highlights to the 2B areas using an eraser. Remember, increasing the range of values will make your drawing more lifelike. Take a moment to compare your current image to the previous one to observe the impact of these highlights. If the kneaded eraser isn't sufficient for removing enough graphite, consider using a plastic or gum eraser for better results.

To achieve a flawless flow between the highlights and the 2B shade, make their edges slightly darker by erasing less on the edges of the highlights, or shade these edges with any pencil.

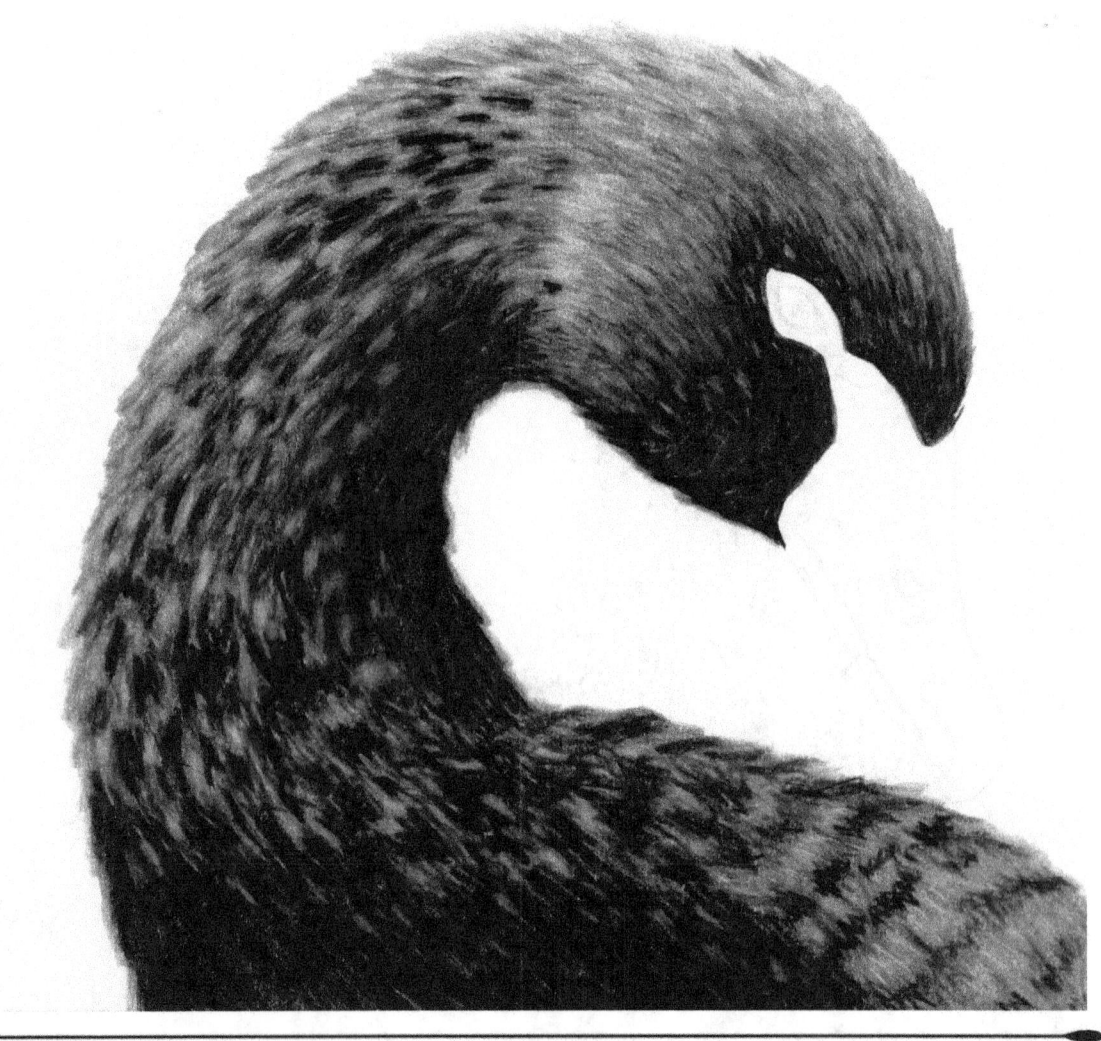

Drawing the Darkest Beak's Areas

If you are satisfied with the feather, the next focus is on the beak. To begin, use a **14B** pencil to create the darkest parts, such as the pupil, the outline of the eye, the nostril, and the line between the upper and lower beak, as depicted in the image below.

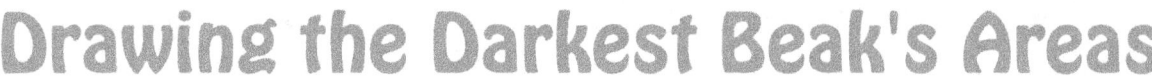

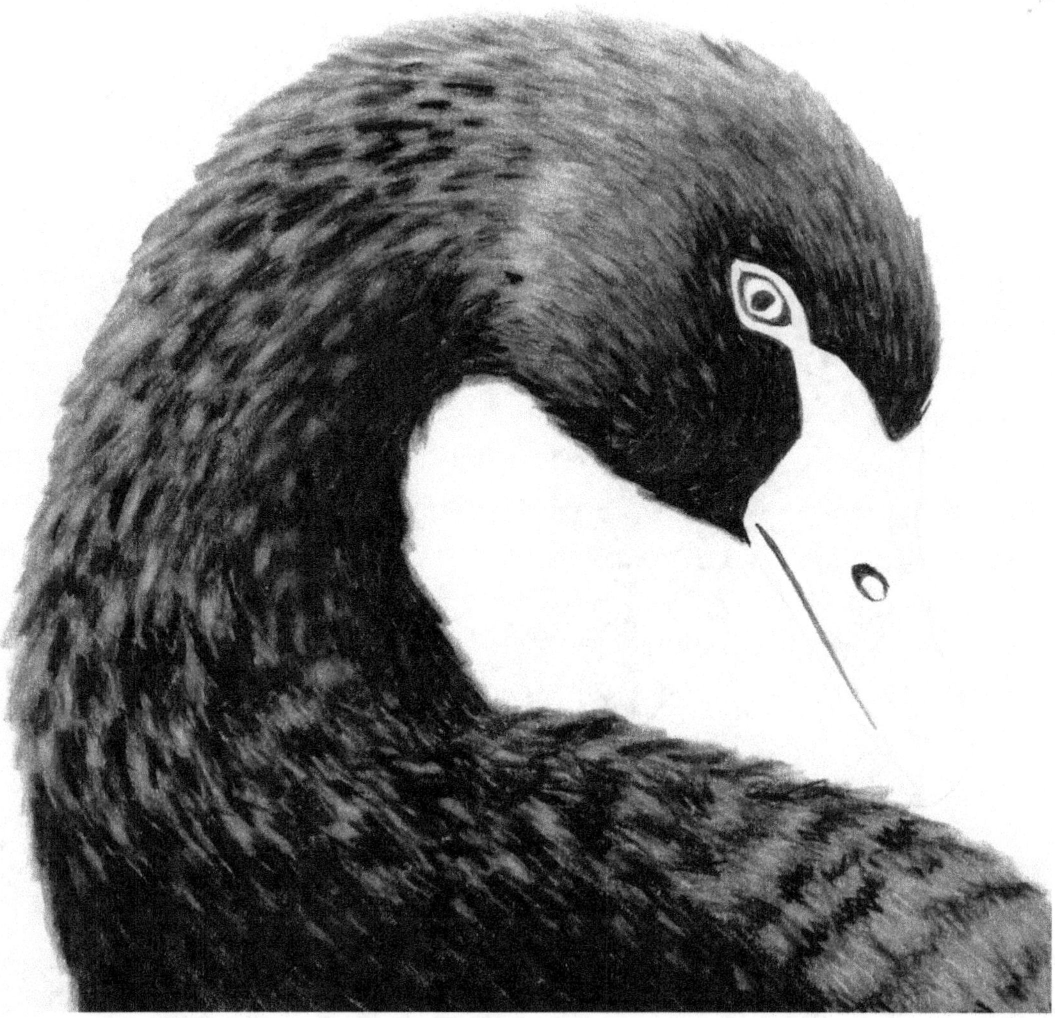

Drawing Beak's Midtones

Begin by gently layering the 2B pencil strokes, gradually building up the midtones to achieve a smooth transition from the darkest areas. Be mindful of the beak's unique structure, capturing its graceful curves and subtle texture with each stroke. As you progress, continually refer to the reference image for guidance, analyzing the interplay of light and shadow on the beak's surface. Remember to use varying pressure to control the pencil's darkness, adding a touch of depth and realism to your drawing. Practice blending techniques to seamlessly merge the mid tones, resulting in a cohesive and harmonious appearance.

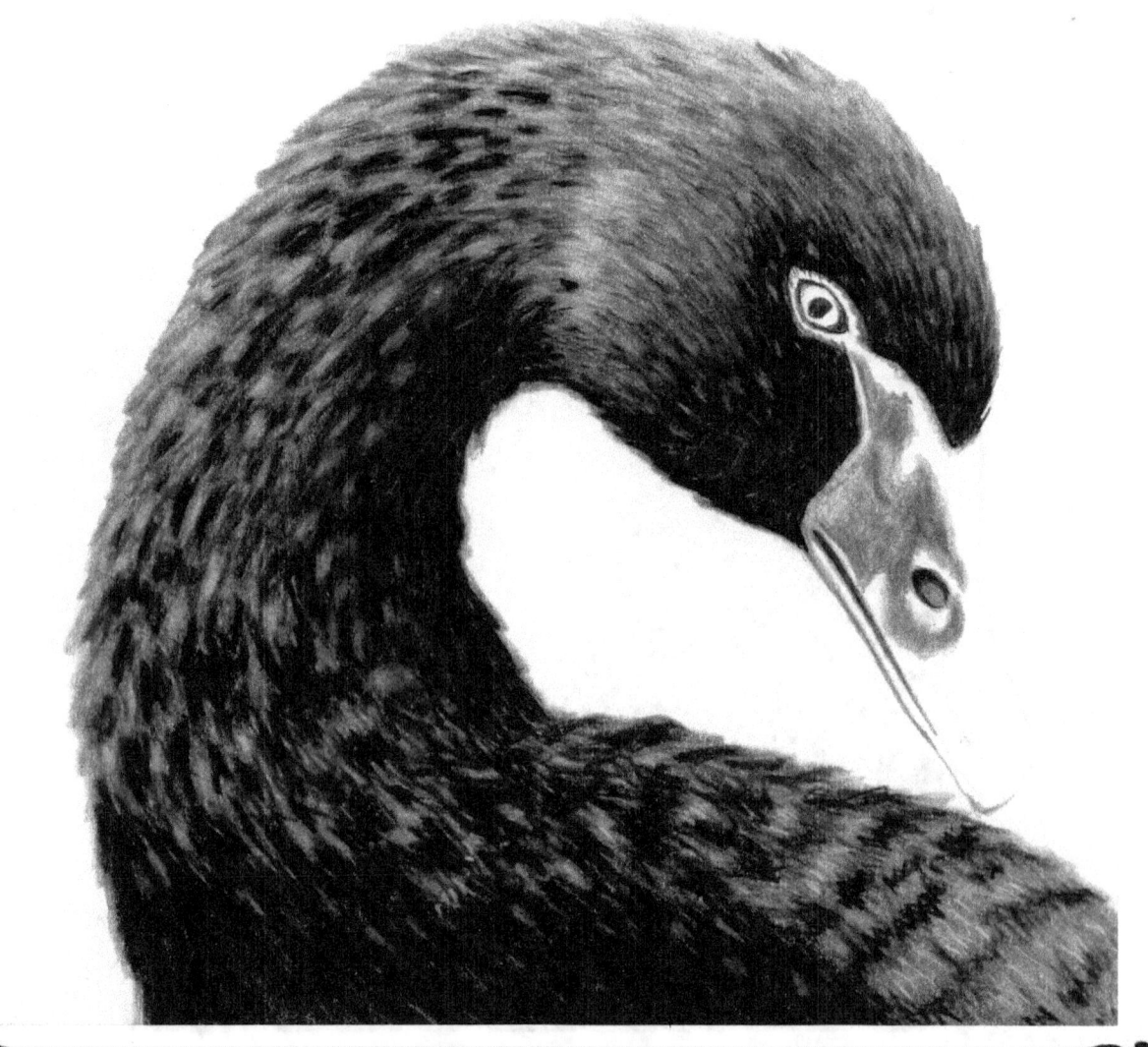

Drawing Beak's Highlights

To complete this drawing, we'll use an HB pencil to add highlights to the brightest parts of the beak. Apply varying pressure,
as even among the highlighted areas, there are different
shades to capture. For a seamless look, use a blending stump
to carefully blend these areas, ensuring no lines are visible.
If needed, use a kneaded eraser to gently erase the brightest
highlights. If the highlights appear too intense, you can easily
adjust them by shading over them with a pencil and then
blending everything together.

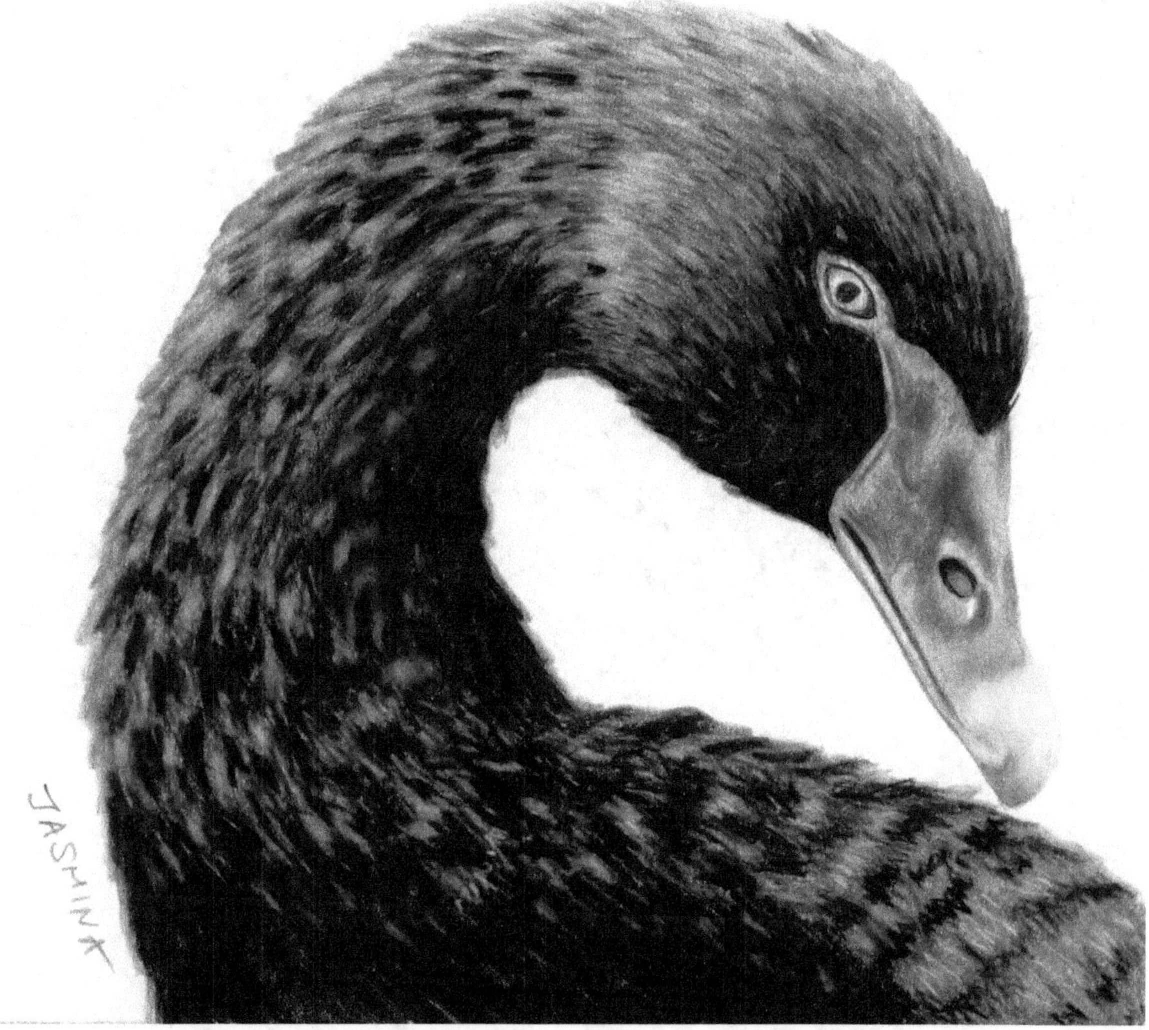

How to Draw a Ragdoll Cat

Drawing a ragdoll cat with its long, fluffy fur and beautiful mesmerizing eyes can be a captivating and rewarding artistic endeavor, offering an excellent opportunity to showcase texture, depth, and personality in your artwork.

The Reference Photo

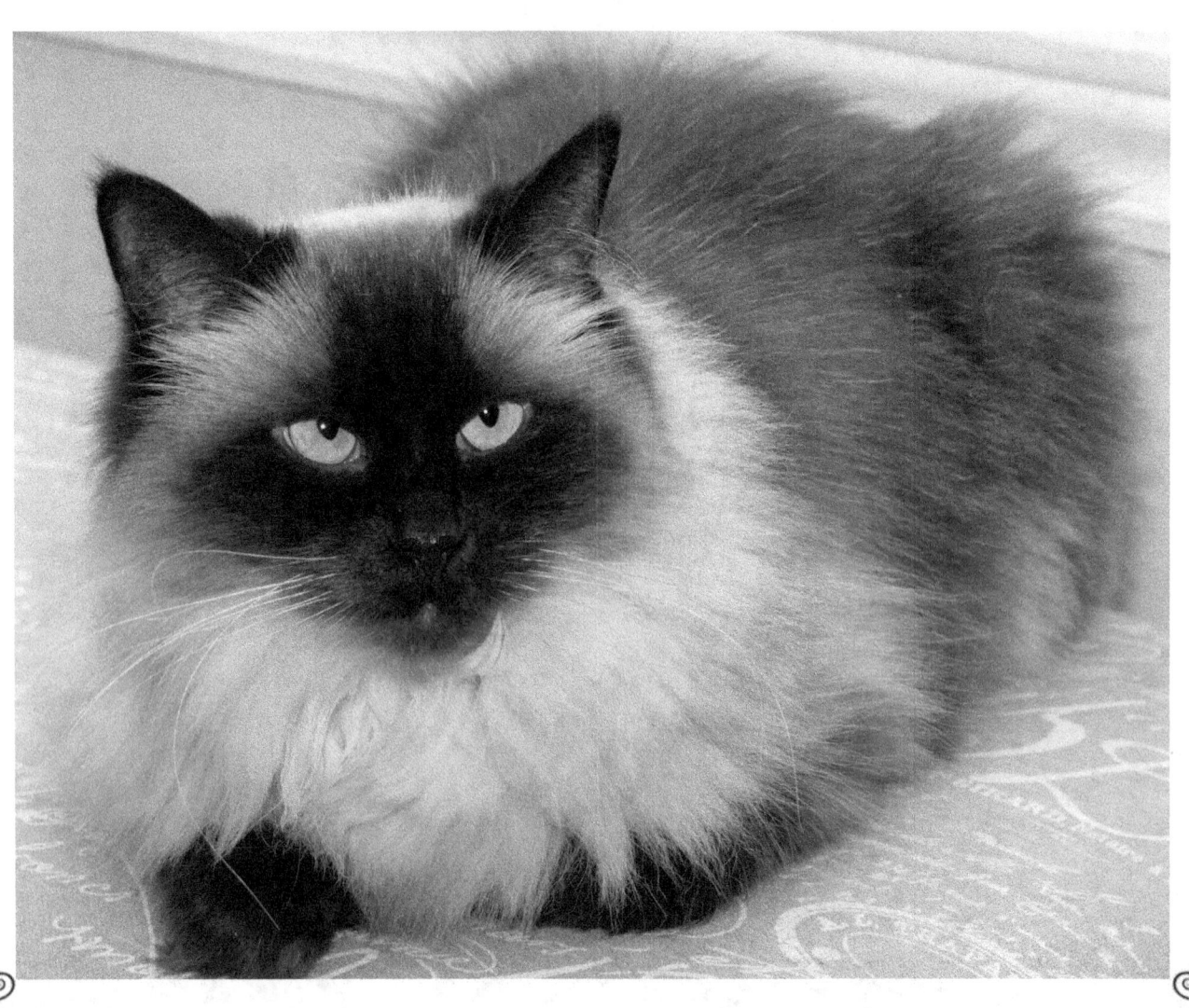

While working with this reference photo of a ragdoll cat, I noticed that the eyes in the image were crossed, which didn't align with the desired expression I wanted to portray. I also wanted to emphasize larger and more expressive eyes to truly capture the charm of this breed. As such, I decided to select and incorporate eyes from a different reference photo that better reflected the look of the eyes I envisioned.

However, I decided not to use the entire photo as the reference because the cat was depicted in an unnatural position within a cartoon box and the

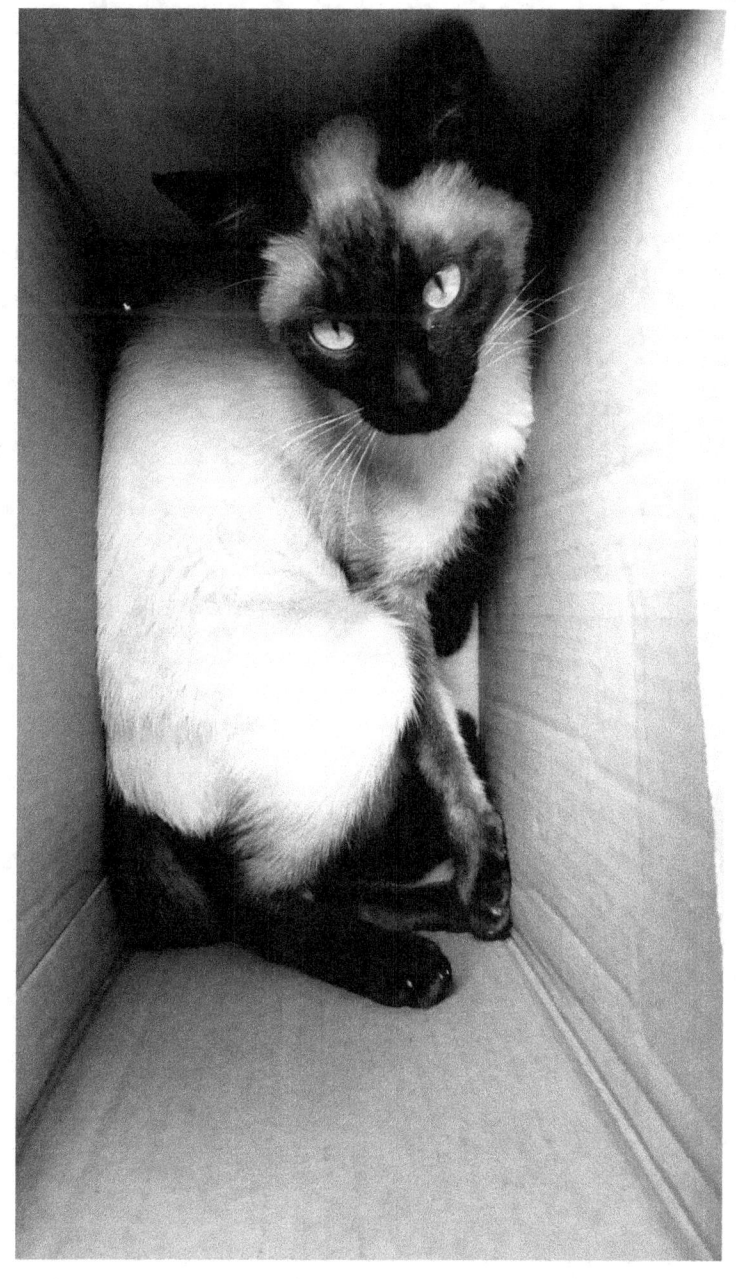

lighting on the fur didn't align with my vision for the drawing. So, I used only the eyes from this photo. The rest of the drawing was based on the first photo that showcases the cat in a more natural position and provided the desired lighting and fur details. I encourage everyone to use reference photos as a foundation but feel free to modify or combine elements from various sources as they see fit. This approach allows for a more personalized representation of the subject.

Sketching and Basic Shapes

In the sketch displayed below, pay close attention to the essential lines I've emphasized. The precise positions of the cat's eyes, head, and ears are crucial focal points. Instead of a straight line, I've used zig-zag sketch lines to mark the edge between the brighter and darker fur, but these were not drawn in their precise position, as their placement can vary from cat to cat, giving us a little freedom to relax and make desired variations as we please. Additionally, the exact placement of the whiskers is also not crucial and can be approximated at the end of the drawing.

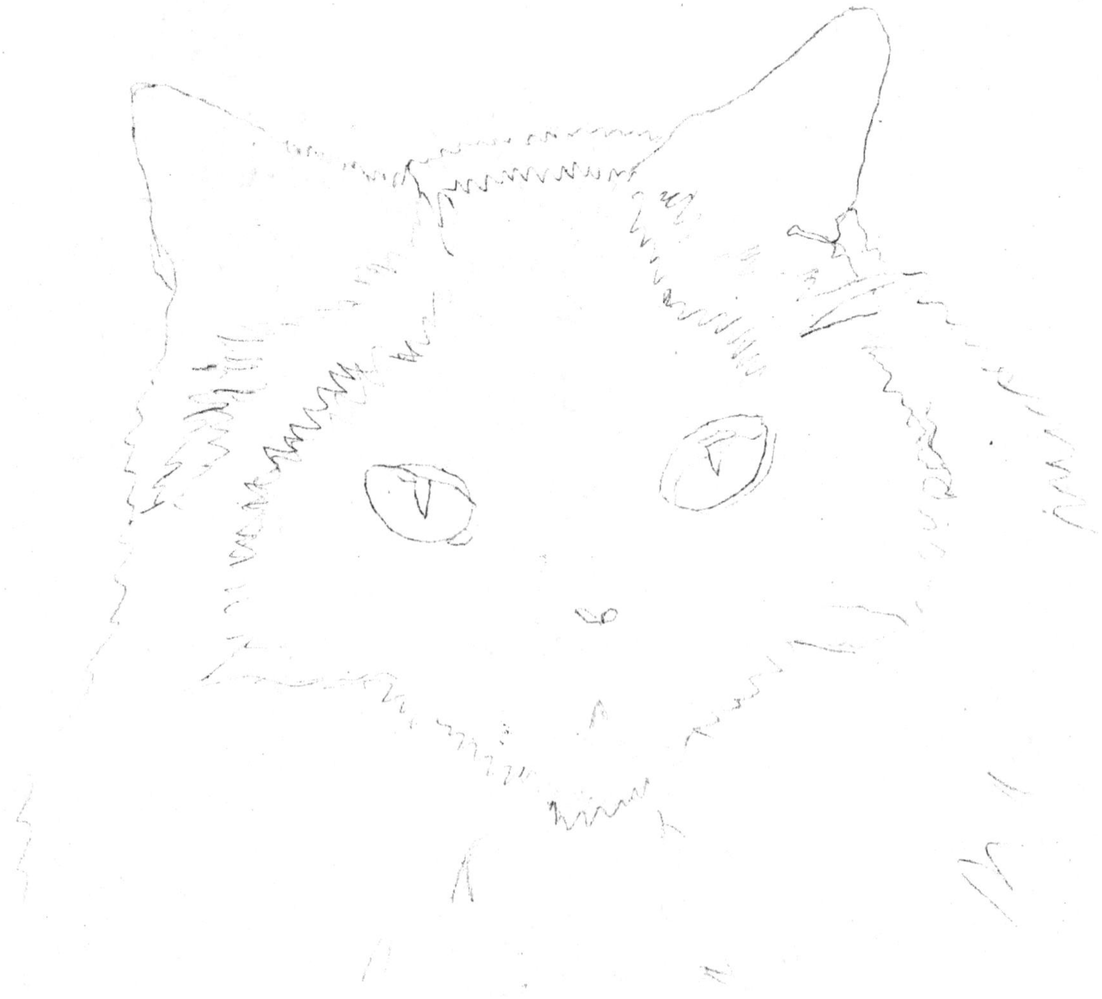

Creating the base for the eyes

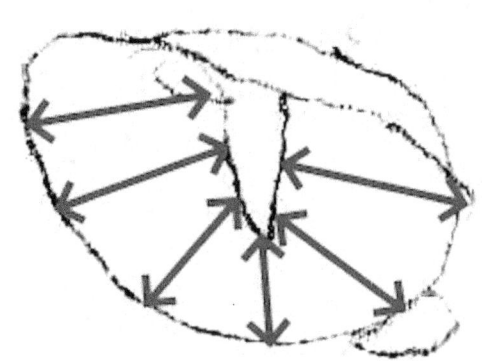

Let's begin with the eyes, a crucial aspect that I prioritize not only in drawing animals but also in my human portraits. Achieving satisfying results with the eyes sets the tone for the entire artwork, allowing me to proceed confidently with the rest, where absolute precision is not always necessary.

Now, let's begin by shading the irises. The key is to draw spokes originating from the iris boundary and extending towards the center of the pupil, as depicted in this image with digitally placed arrows over my sketch. Each spoke should radiate from the exact center of the eye, creating a realistic effect.

To shade the irises, I recommend using an HB pencil. For the shadow cast by the upper eyelid over the iris, use a darker pencil like 2B. There are two approaches you can take: you can either skip the areas for the highlights and draw around them, or shade the entire iris and later create the highlights using an eraser or a white ink gel pen once the eyes are fully shaded.

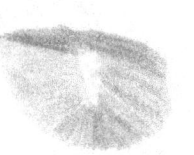

Blending and Detailing the Irises

Next, blend the previously shaded areas with a blending stump to impress the graphite into the paper. As a result, you will notice that the areas may become slightly darker, but there's no need to worry, as we can easily create the highlights over these parts.

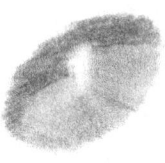

But, let's draw the darker patterns over the irises first. I used a 2B pencil for this, placing them approximately in the same areas as in the reference photo. Without these patterns, the eyes can look flat. Adding these tiny details and "imperfections" can make the drawing look more lifelike, creating a natural texture that distinguishes it from digital art.

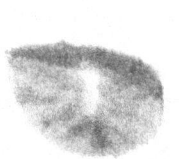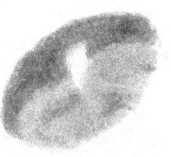

Next, use an eraser to create the highlights. Analyze the reference photo to identify the brightest areas on the irises and carefully erase to mimic those highlights on your drawing. This attention to detail will bring life to your artwork and enhance the realistic appearance of the eyes.

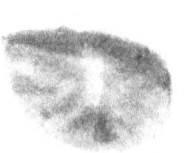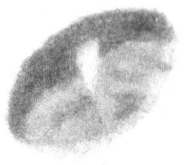

Introducing Darkest Shade

Let's take a bold step by adding the deepest grade, 14B, all around the irises to observe how the values of the eyes interact with the dark surroundings. This will help us determine whether the irises need adjustments in darkness or lightness.

Additionally, shade the pupils with the darkest pencil you have, applying firm pressure to achieve a rich black color that represents the deepest shade in the drawing.

Carefully blend the edges between the newly created black areas and the irises using a 2B pencil, softly eliminating any sharpness that may have occurred. The tip of the blending stump might be too thick for this task, so we need the precision of the pencil to achieve the desired dark blending effect.

If you have nothing to change on the irises, you can start drawing the fur.

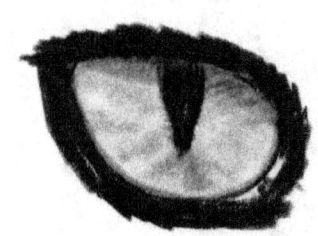 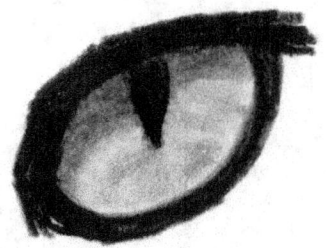

Analyzing Fur Growth and Flow

Observe a cat closely or study images of cats, and you'll notice a fascinating pattern: all the hairs, whether long or short, seem to radiate from the center of their faces, right between their eyes.

In the following image, you'll notice a dot placed over the crucial point I mentioned, accompanied by arrows indicating the direction of the hairs' growth and flow.
This guide will be invaluable throughout the entire process of drawing the fur, helping you confidently direct your pencil strokes and achieve a realistic and lifelike texture in your artwork.

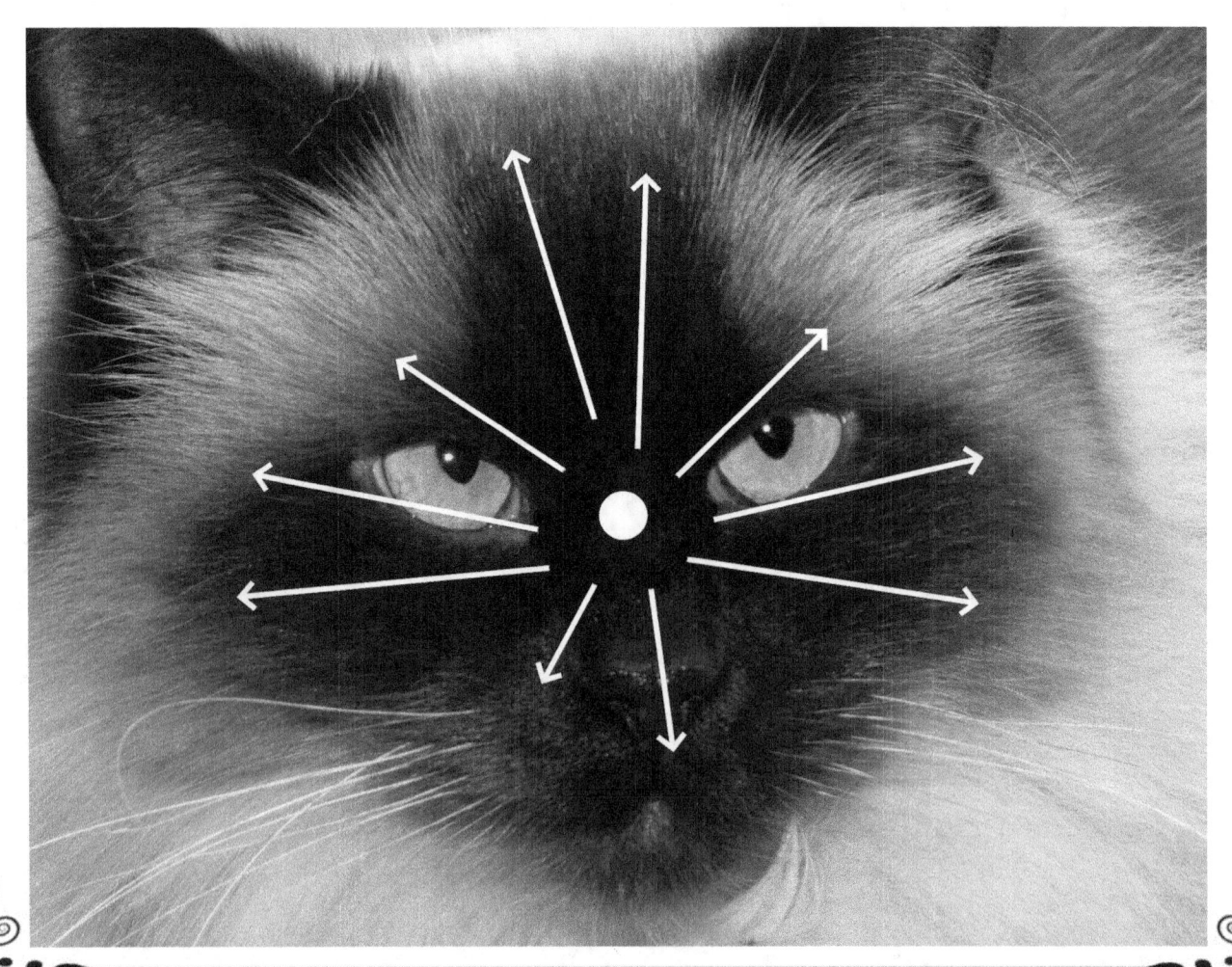

Drawing Black Fur on the Face

Following these directions, confidently draw the lines with a 14B pencil, pressing firmly and placing them closely next to each other to achieve complete coverage of the paper and create the black areas, as demonstrated in the next image.

Take note of the hairlike strokes along the edge of the drawn area to replicate the lifelike texture. Additionally, omit the highlight over the nose and the highlighted area on the right side, as these subtle details enhance the overall realism of the artwork.

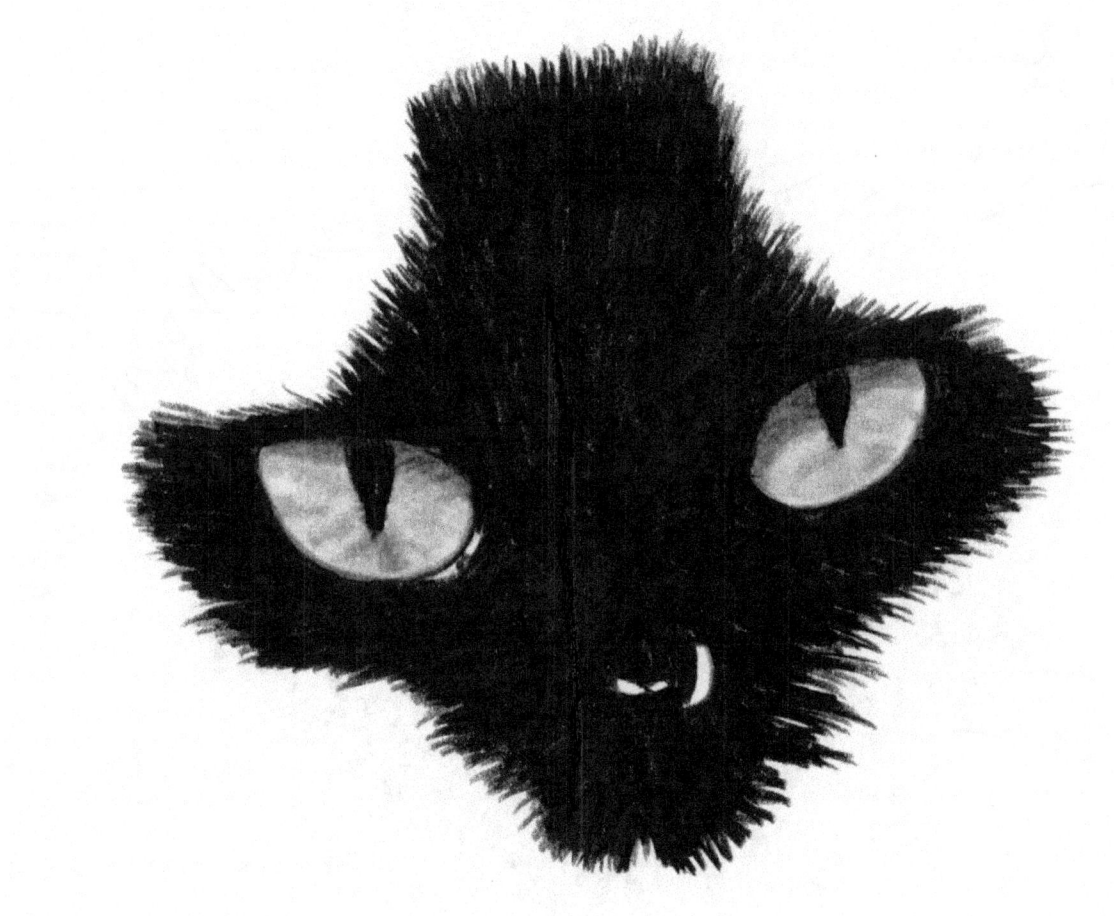

Blending for Fluffy Hair Effect

Maintaining the direction of all pencil strokes originating from the center of the face, proceed to blend the edges using a colorless blender by Prismacolor. Position the tool's tip deeper into the area, slightly away from the edge, allowing it to pick up a generous amount of graphite for creating long and smooth lines as you blend outward.

As you follow these instructions, you'll experience the overwhelming satisfaction of creating the fur's fluffiness, making the process incredibly gratifying. Mastering this technique will elevate your drawings, bringing your artwork to life with remarkable realism and attention to detail.

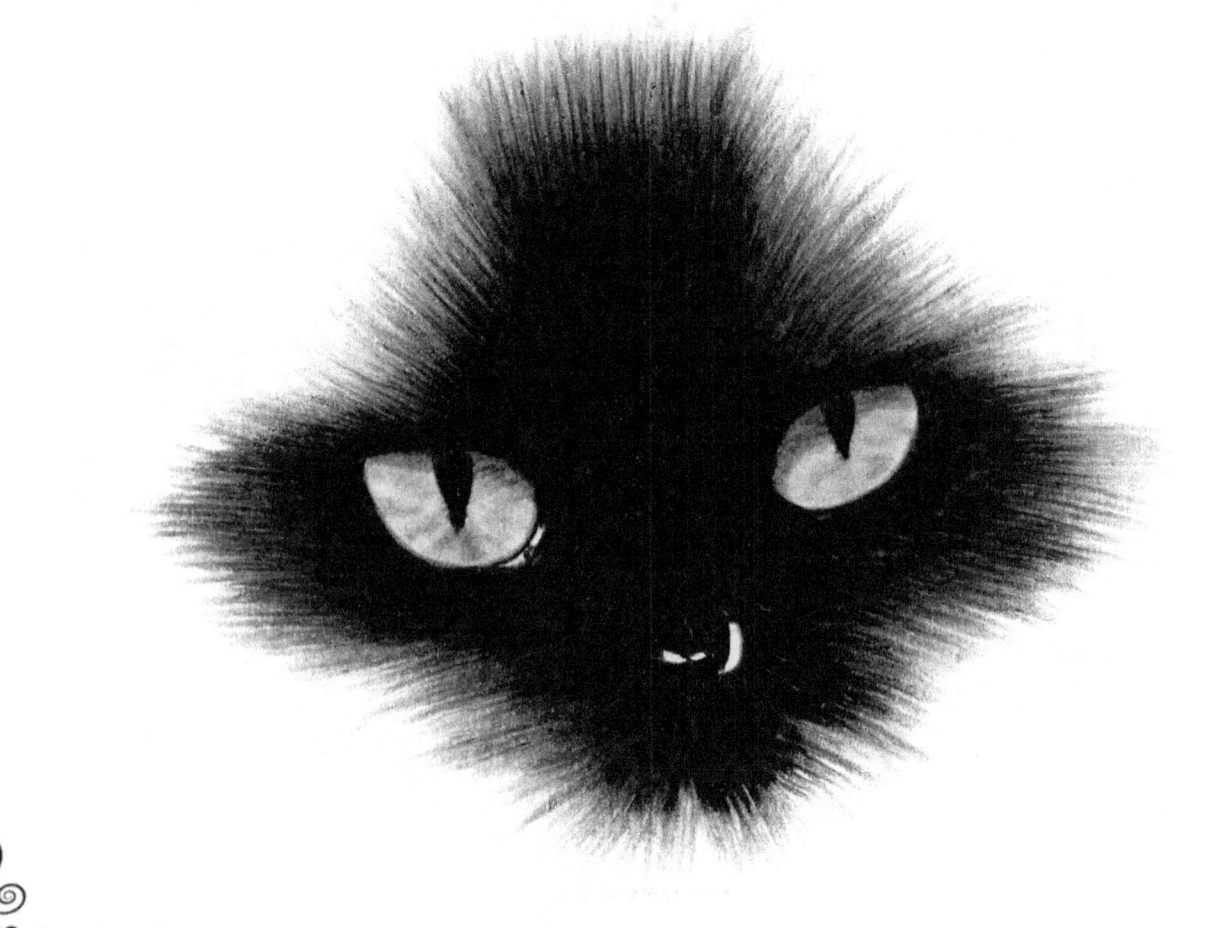

Highlighting the Face and Eyes

Next, delicately erase a bit of graphite to create the highlights around the nose, aiming for a dark grey shade to maintain depth. Similarly, highlight the lower eyelids, achieving a slightly lighter tone than black as showcased in the accompanying image. Additionally, erase the reflected lights above the irises and over the pupils, then consider adding a dot with a white ink gel pen to enhance their radiance. Observe how the cat's eyes and face come to life with these reflected lights, infusing your drawing with an extra layer of photorealism and captivating detail.

Even if these reflected lights are not present in the reference photo, you have the artistic freedom to infuse your drawing with a vibrant sense of life and soul by skillfully incorporating them.

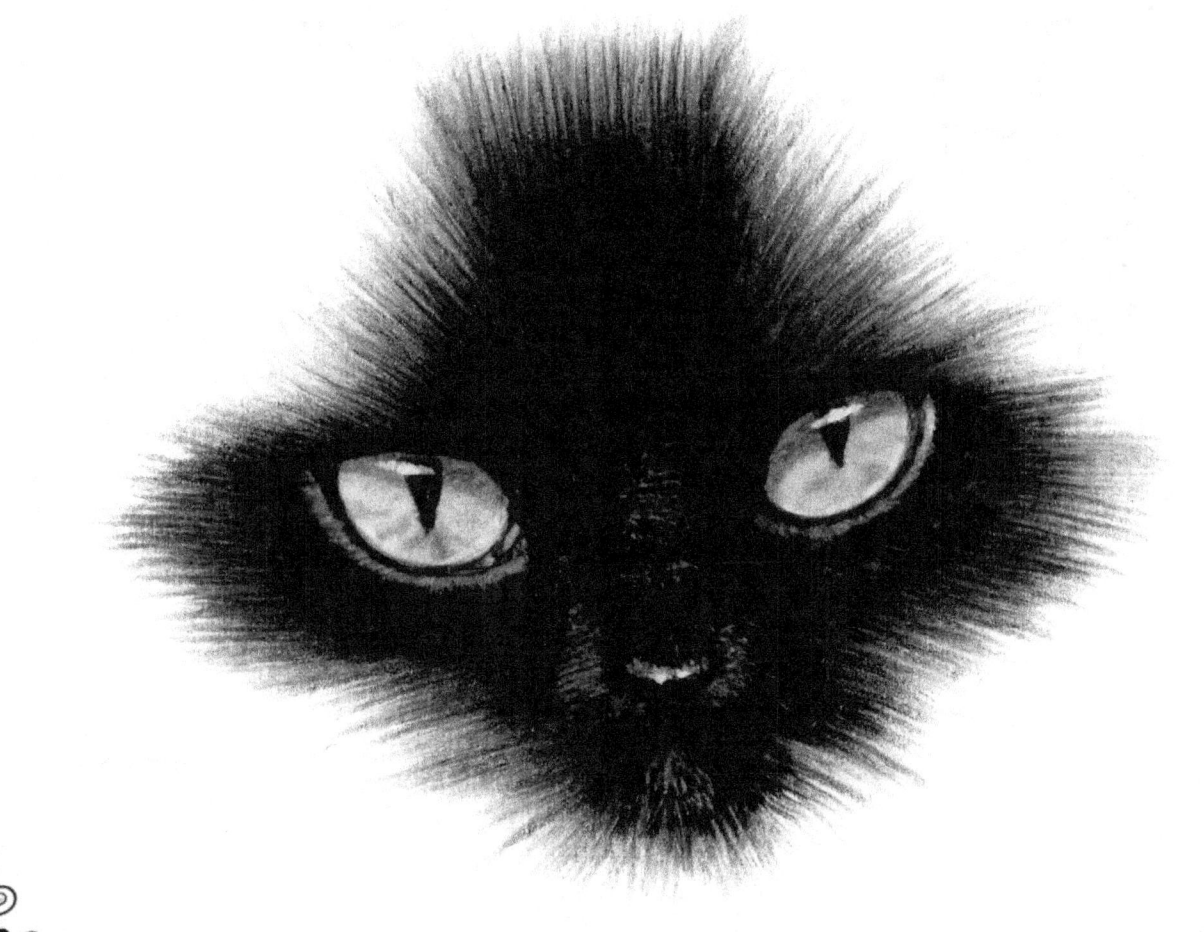

Creating Darkest Areas on the Ears

In this step, we'll work on the ears to finalize the upper part of the head by skillfully connecting the long hairs between the center of the face and the ears. Using a 14B pencil, carefully replicate the darkest parts of the ears while paying close attention to the reference photo to understand the direction of the hair's flow. To achieve a realistic and textured look, make sure the edges of these areas are drawn with hair-like strokes, creating a seamless transition between the darker and lighter hairs. By skillfully using the dark pencil, we'll be drawing the space between the bright hairs, as shown in the next image.

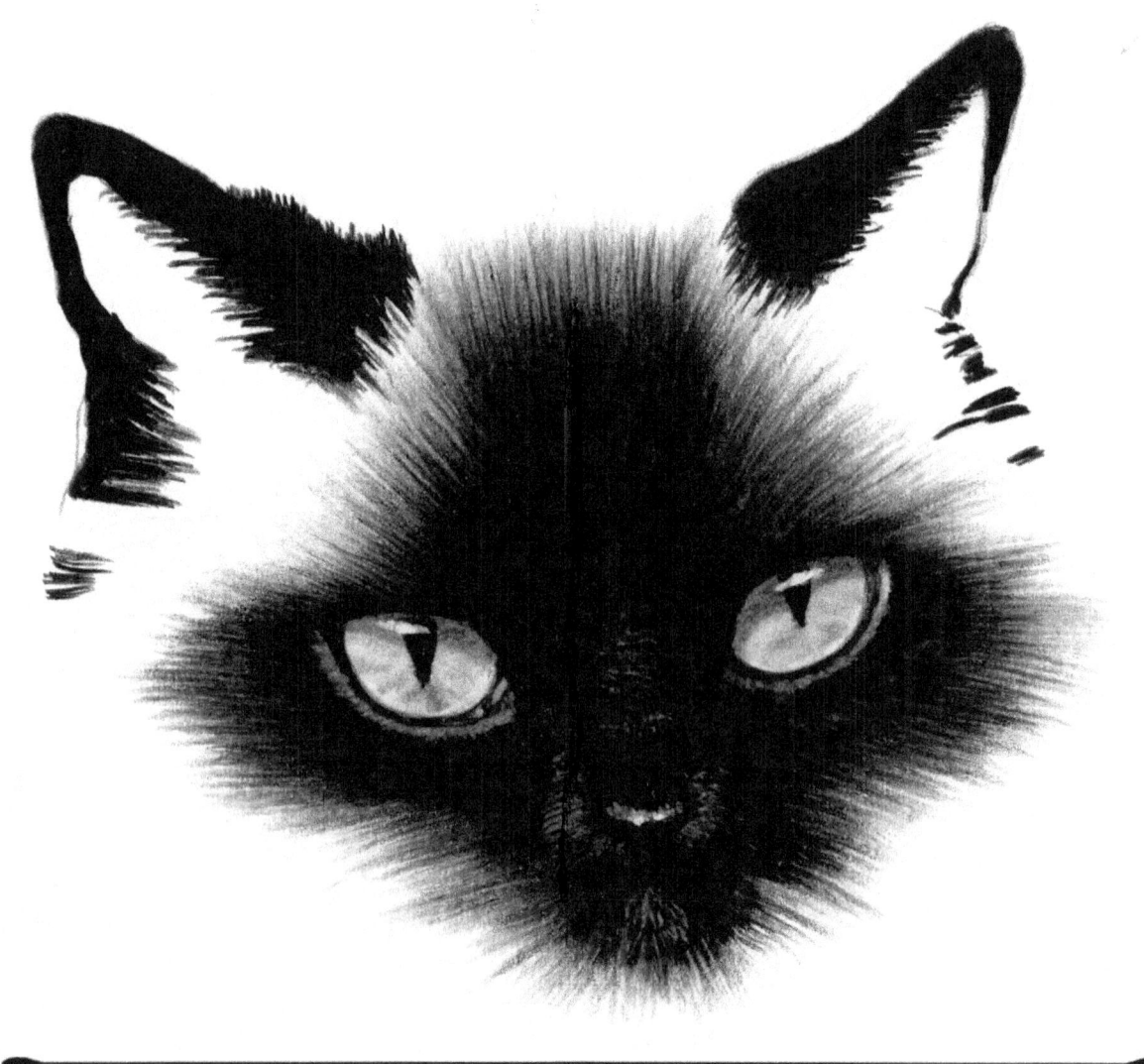

Adding Mid Tone

In this step, we'll focus on shading the inner parts of the ears using an HB pencil, carefully capturing the subtle details that add depth and dimension to our drawing. Additionally, we'll add intricate, tiny dark hairs downward on both sides of the face, infusing the artwork with a lifelike appearance. For better guidance, compare this image with the previous one to precisely follow the areas where these pencil strokes have been placed. Finally, use a blending stump or a Q-tip to artfully blend the inner parts of the ears, creating a smooth transition of tones.

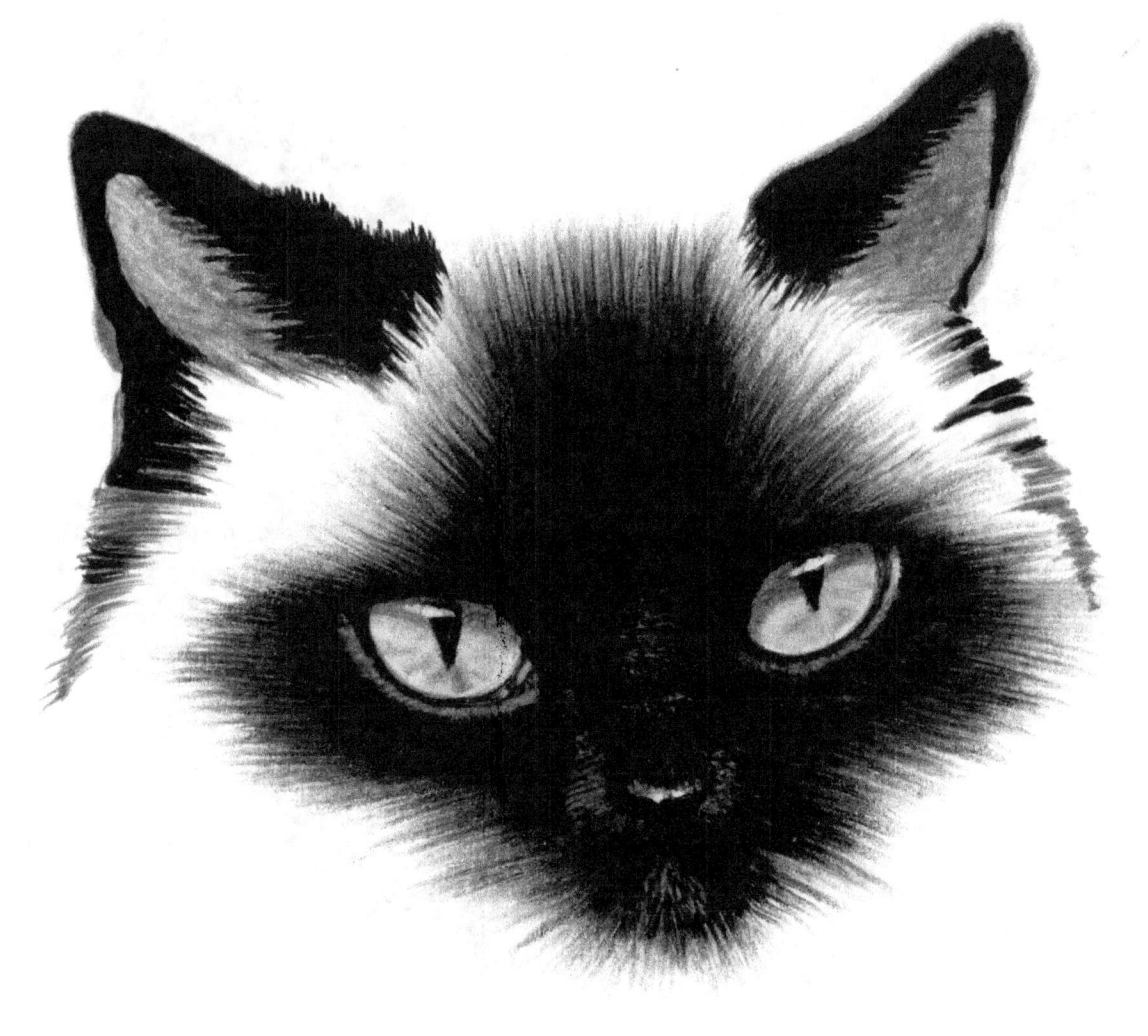

Mastering Intricate Ear Hair Detailing

Let's carefully replicate the intricate hairs from the reference photo using a 14B pencil, starting over the black areas and the previously drawn HB inner parts of the ears. Take note of how these artfully rendered hairs subtly soften the prominence of the inner areas while maintaining their visibility against the bright background.

Blend these hairs using a blending stump or a colorless blender for a seamless and realistic appearance.

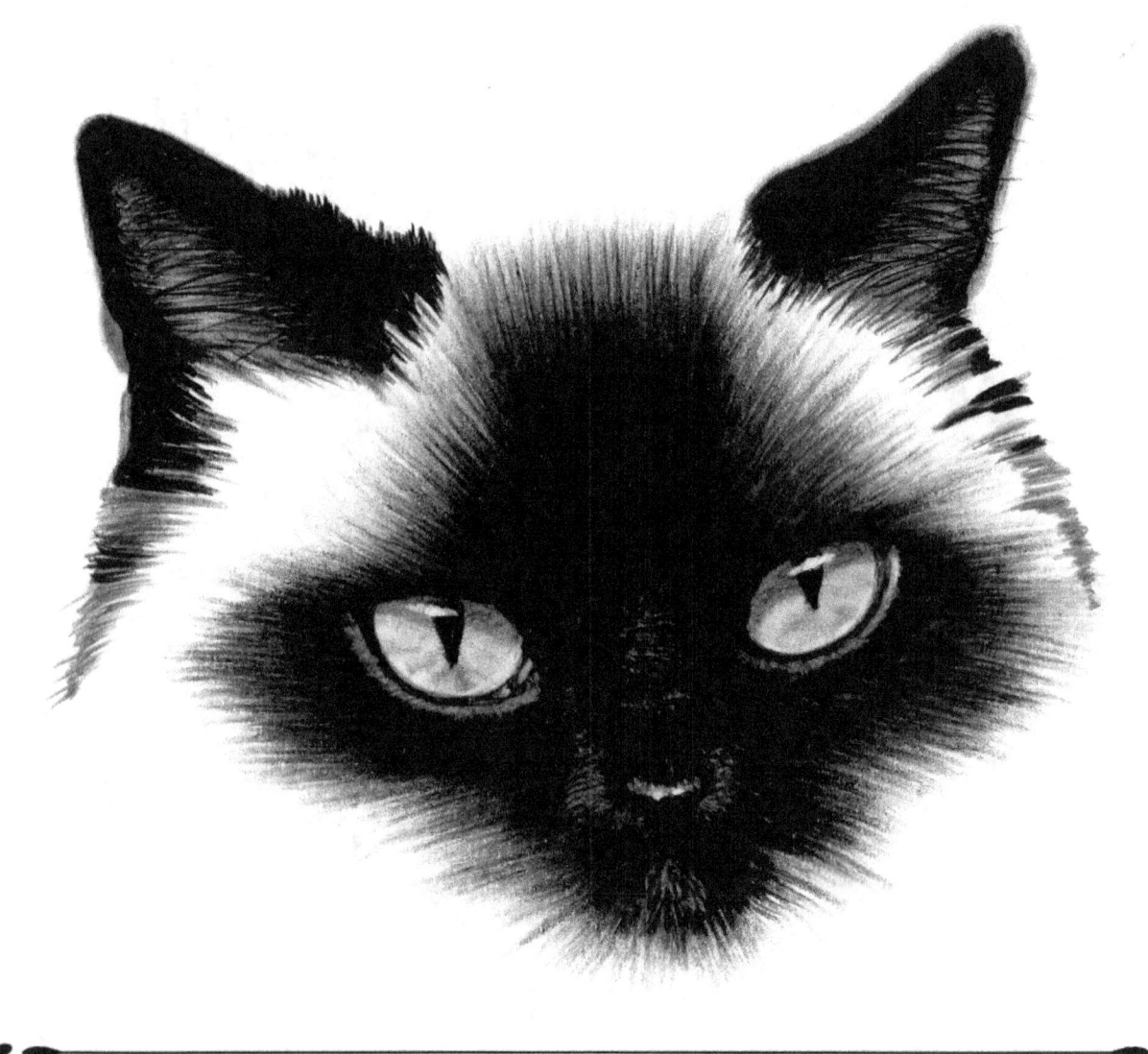

Fluffing the Ears

In this step, utilize a colorless blender to achieve a fluffy texture on the outer edges of the ears. Place the tip of the blender over the 14B pencil lines and move it outwards, creating short strokes for a realistic effect. Take note of the reference photo for the direction of these hairs, and make the lines on the top of the ears slightly longer for accuracy, as shown in the next image.

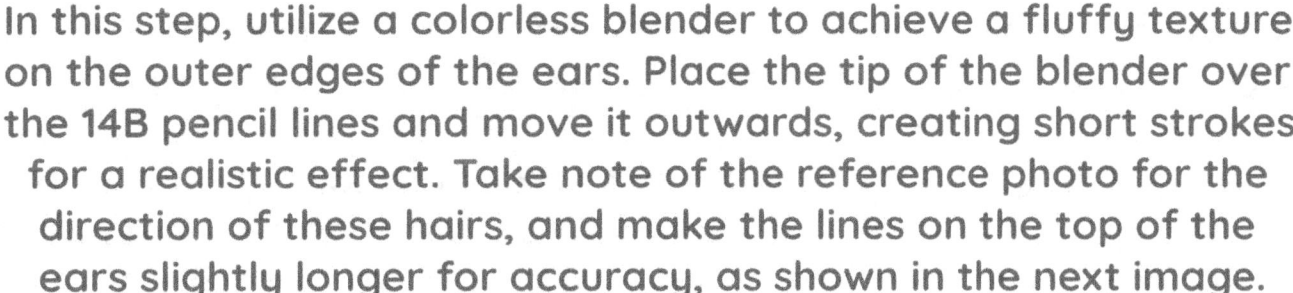

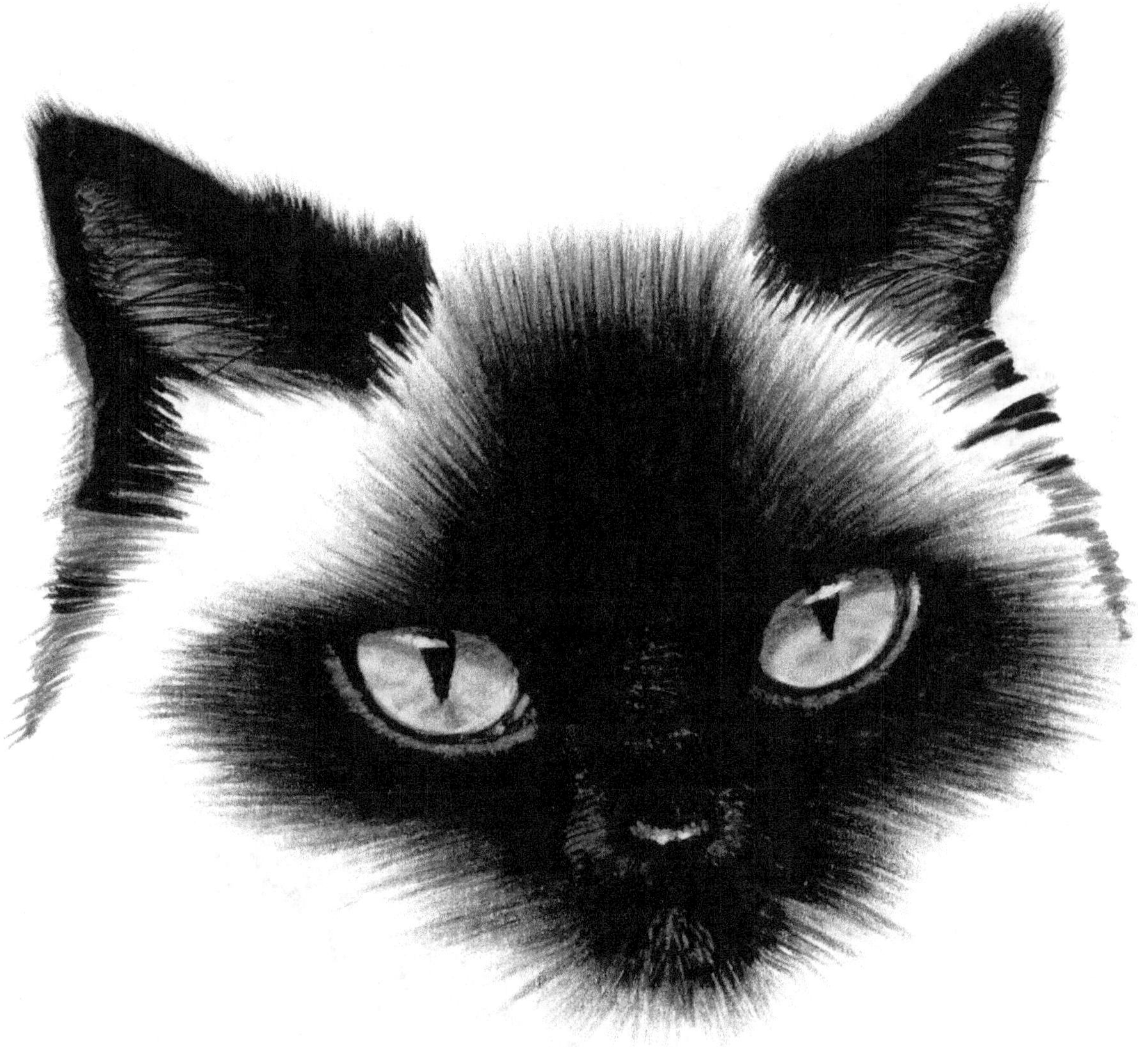

Understanding Fur Direction

Now, it's time to blend all the bright fur in the upper part of the head, now that we have completed the surrounding areas. For this blending process, I'll be using a colorless blender by Prismacolor.

Before we proceed with blending, it's crucial to take a moment to study the image of the fur direction. To aid in this process, I have provided digitally placed arrowed lines over the previous step, showing the precise direction in which the strokes were drawn. Carefully examining this guide will allow us to understand the flow and movement of the fur, which is pivotal in achieving a realistic and fluffy texture. Once we have thoroughly studied and grasped the fur's natural direction, we can confidently move on to the blending stage.

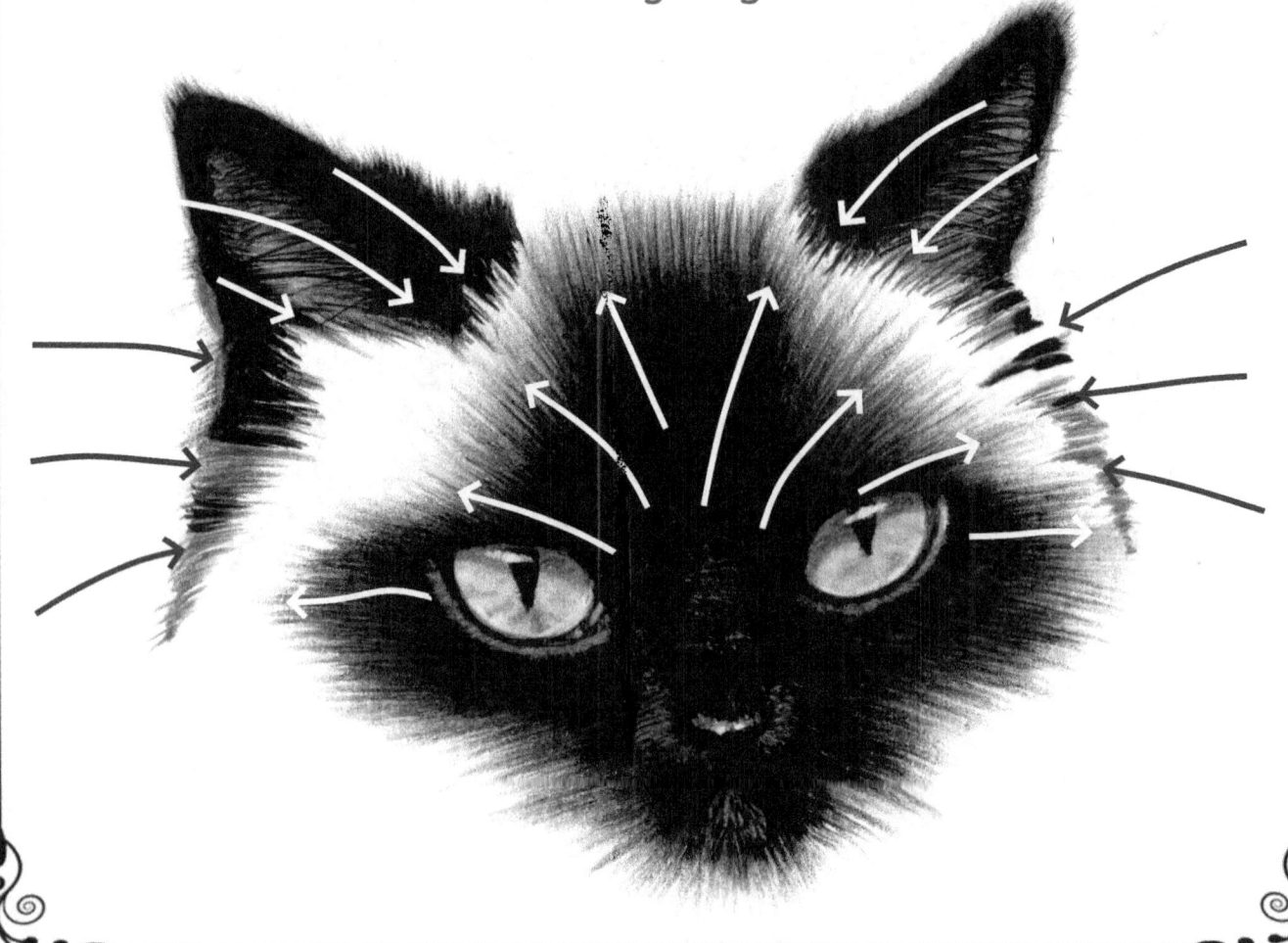

Creating Fluffy Bright Fur

To create the fluffy appearance of the bright fur, blend the lines by skillfully picking up the graphite from the dark areas on both sides – starting from the center of the face and extending outwards towards the ears, and from the ears inwards on the bright fur, following the direction indicated by the arrows in the previous image. For ease and precision, feel free to rotate the paper to make it more comfortable for your hand to apply the strokes in the required direction. Keep in mind that every part of the bright fur should receive some graphite, as you'll observe when studying the reference photo. There are no completely white areas in the fur, so it's essential to cover these regions completely, varying the darkness and brightness to match the natural texture and depth of the fur in the reference image.

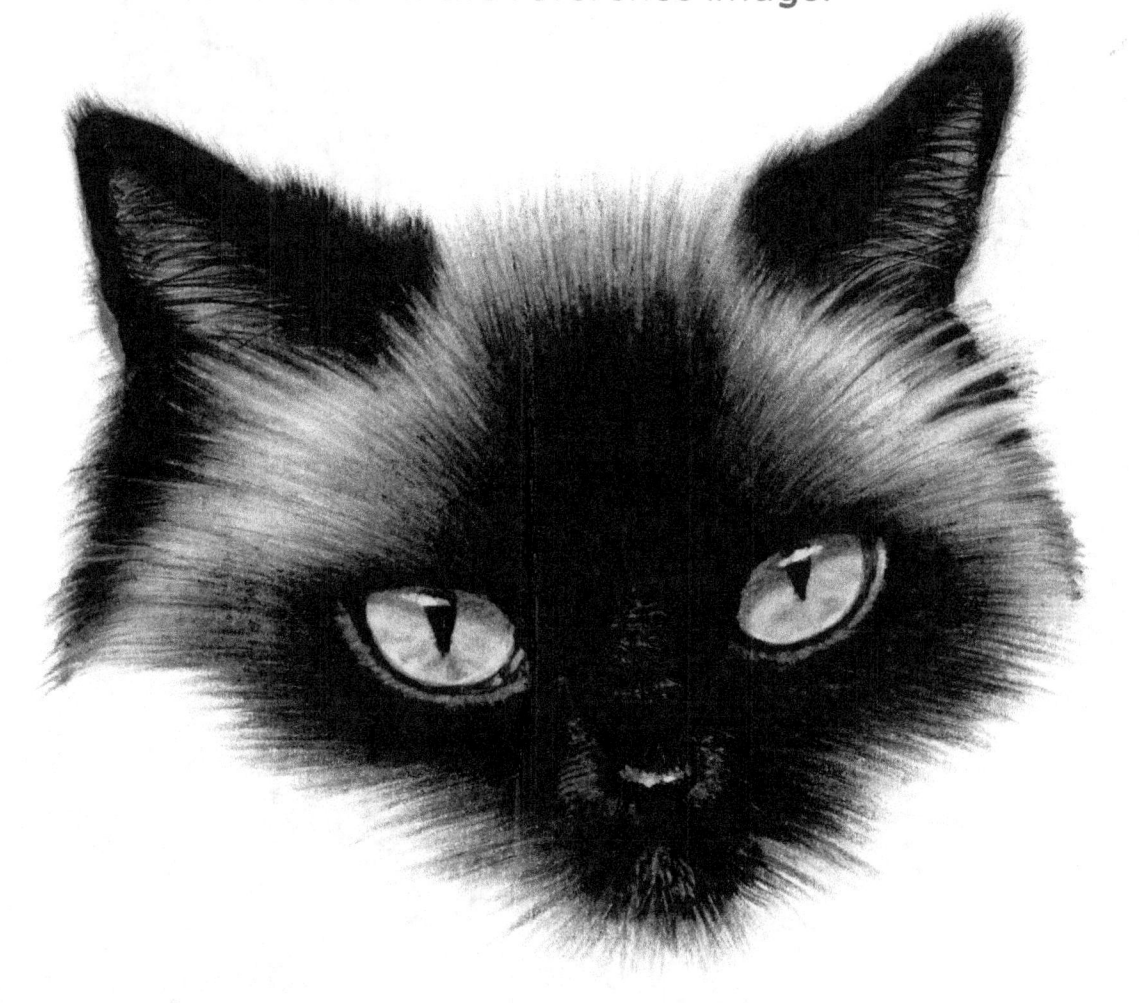

Refining with Delicate Details

To complete the upper part of the head, I'll draw some "fresh" lines over the bright, fluffy fur using a well-sharpened 14B pencil, following the same directions as before. Additionally, I'll create a few brighter lines using a white ink gel pen, which I found to be most helpful for this purpose. In the next image, you can see where I've added these hairs. If the lines appear too white to you, simply wait for the ink to dry and then gently go over them with a blending stump. This will make the lines slightly darker while still ensuring they stand out on the dark areas.

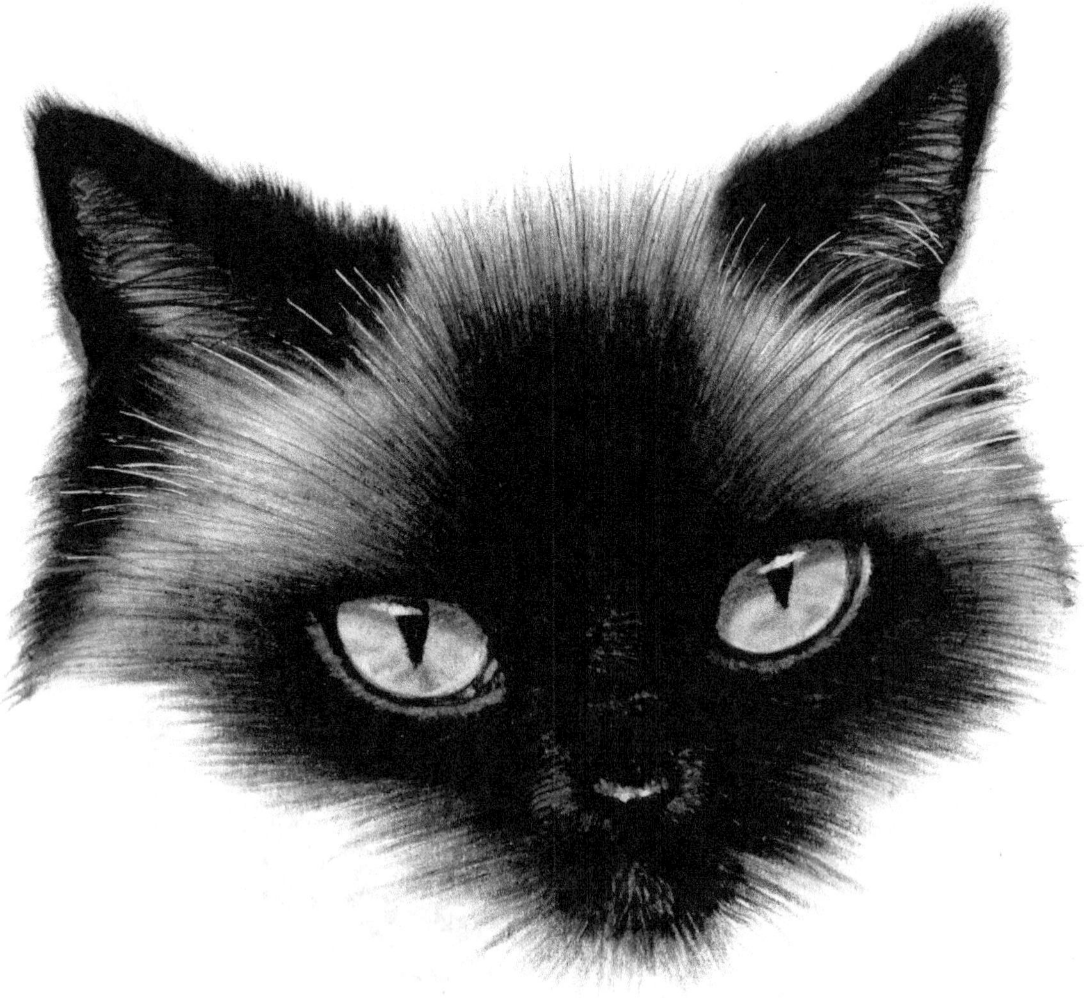

Creating a Soft Base for the Torso

Next, let's shift our focus to the lower part of the picture, specifically the cat's torso. The hairs in this area have a softer and more delicate appearance, creating a unique texture that doesn't require individual hair-by-hair drawing. Despite lacking white fur, this region maintains a brightness that can be achieved by gently shading graphite powder with a tissue wrapped around our finger, following the natural flow of the hair.

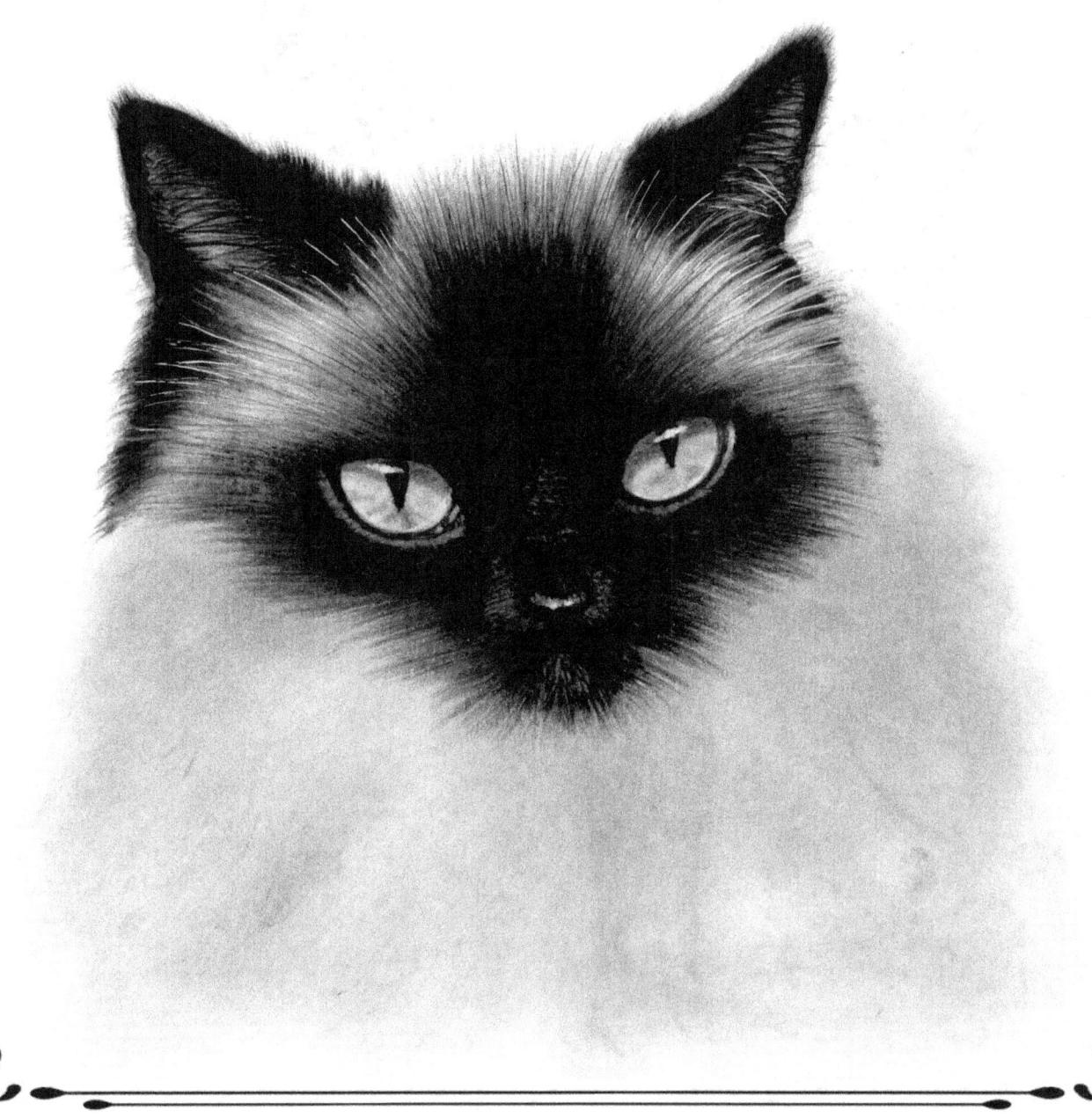

Adding Darker Shades

As we progress, it's time to add depth and dimension to our drawing by focusing on darker shades in specific areas. To achieve this, take your blending stump and gently dip its tip into the graphite powder. Apply the powder carefully to the targeted regions, creating rich shadows and emphasizing the contours, as demonstrated in the following image.

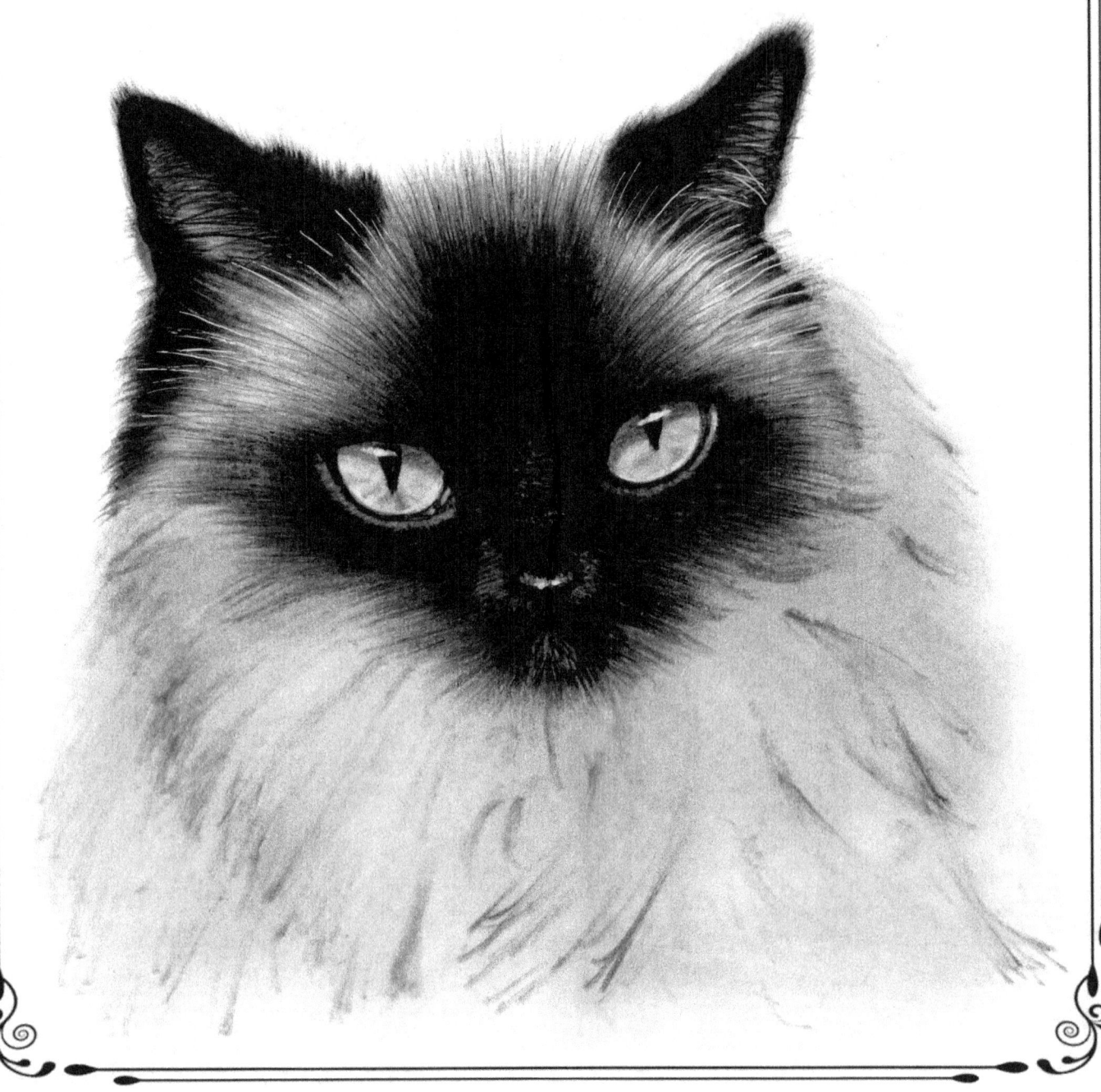

Highlighting the Torso Fur

Now that we've added darker shades to enhance the depth, it's time to bring out the highlights. For this delicate task, I highly recommend using a kneaded eraser, as it allows for precise control and ensures that the texture remains fluffy and natural. Carefully work with the kneaded eraser, removing graphite little by little until you achieve the desired values, effectively creating those bright and captivating highlights.

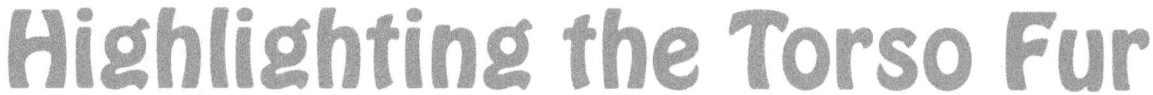

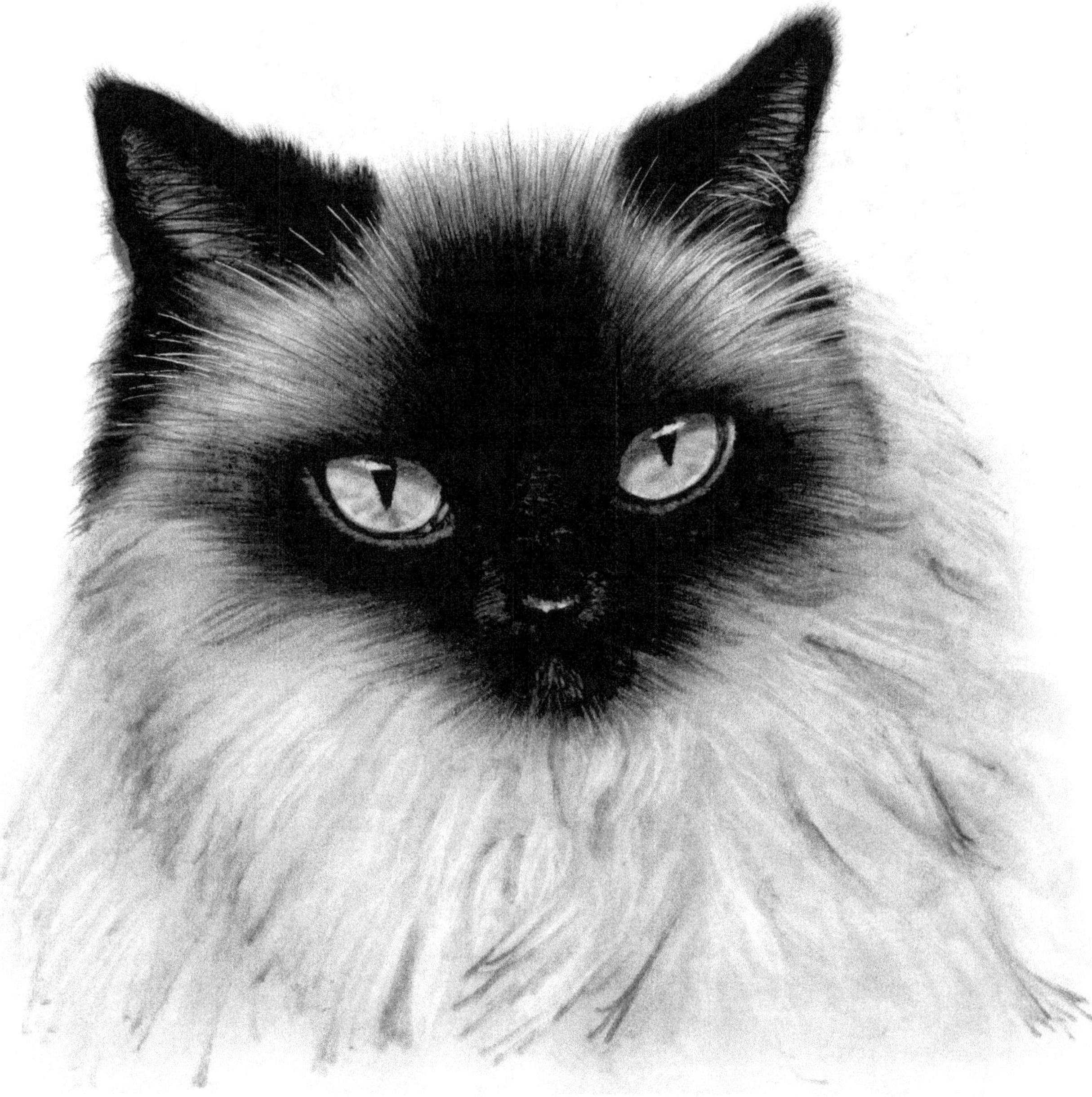

Seamlessly Blending the Head and Torso

By carefully picking up the graphite with the tip of the colorless blender by Prismacolor, I blend the previously drawn dark hairs from the lower part of the face towards and over the torso, extending them seamlessly into the fluffy texture of the torso's fur. This technique ensures that the dark areas blend in naturally.

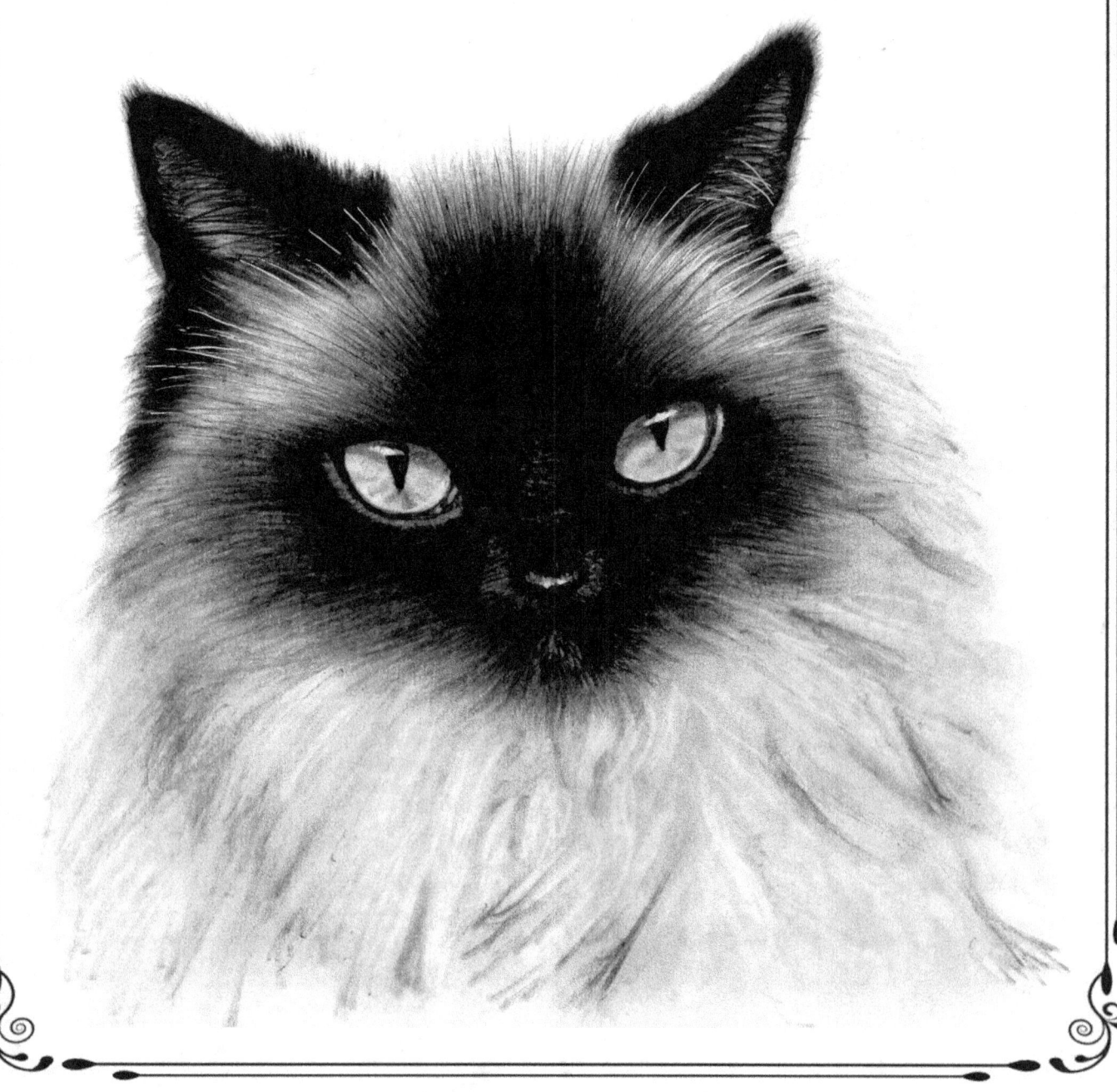

Adding Individual Hairs

To further enrich the texture of the torso, we'll carefully draw long individual hairs across the surface, following the natural flow as we've done before. Utilizing a well-sharpened HB pencil, employ quick, confident strokes in a random pattern. Some of these strokes can originate from the dark fur of the lower part of the cat's face, creating a seamless transition between the two areas.

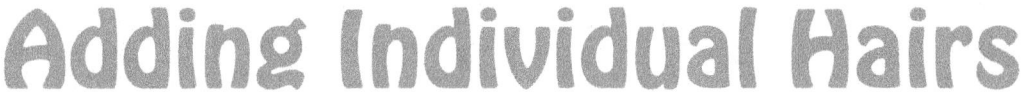

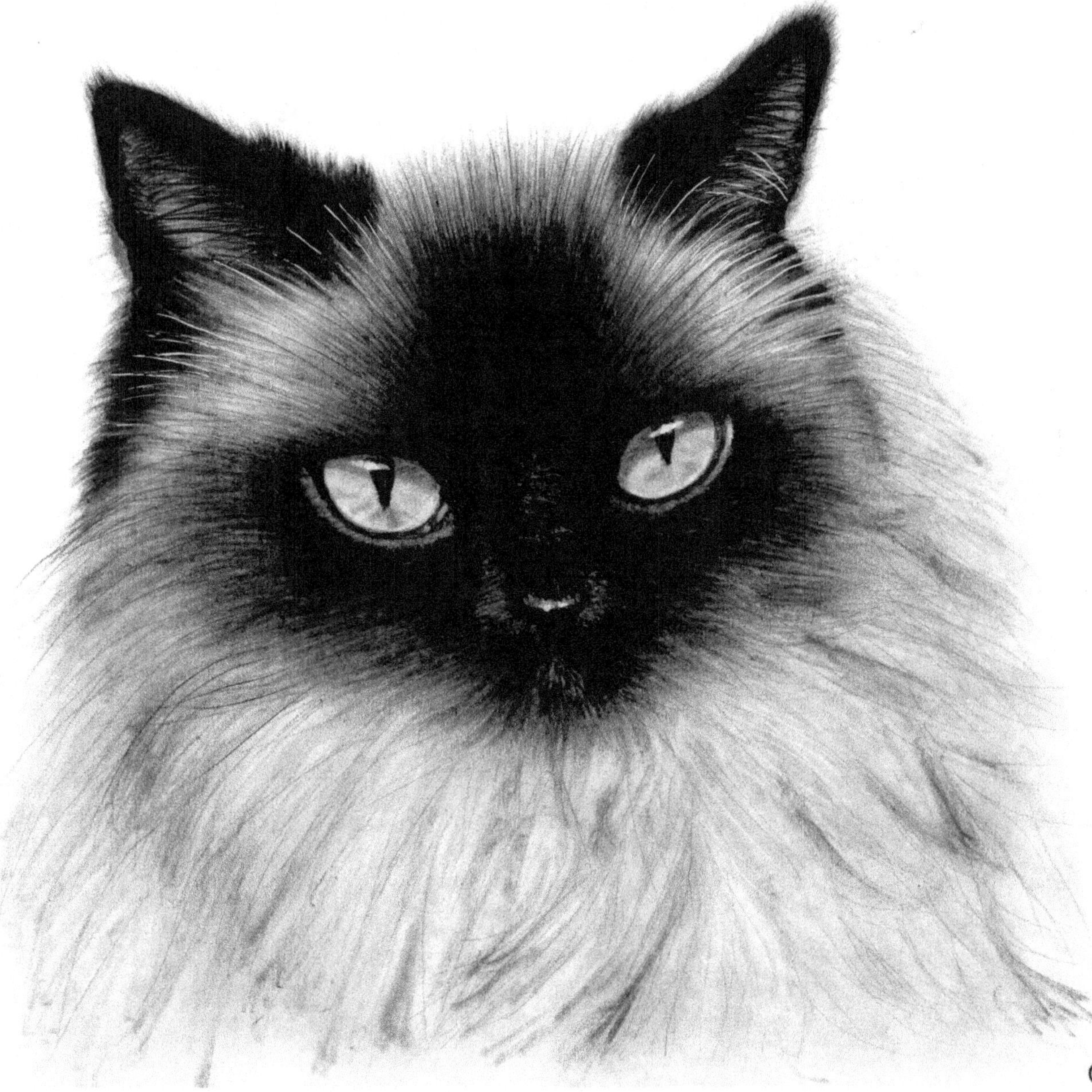

Drawing Whiskers

The famous quote by Leonardo da Vinci, "Art is never finished, only abandoned," holds true, but I have reached a point where I feel content with the drawing, and there's nothing more I'd like to change or add. However, feel free to explore further and make any adjustments you see fit in your own artwork.

So, if everything looks good, we can conclude the drawing by adding whiskers with a white ink gel pen.

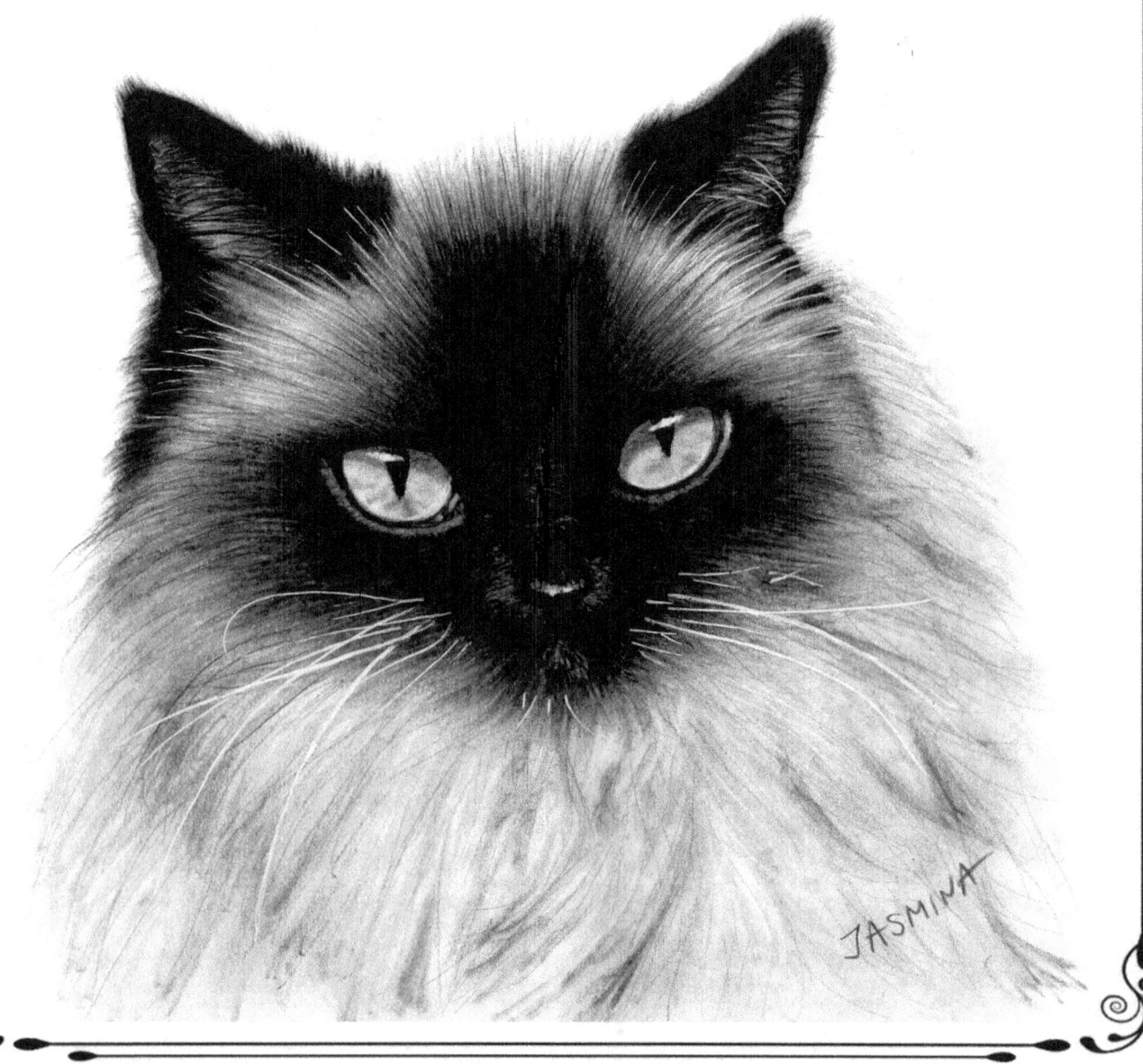

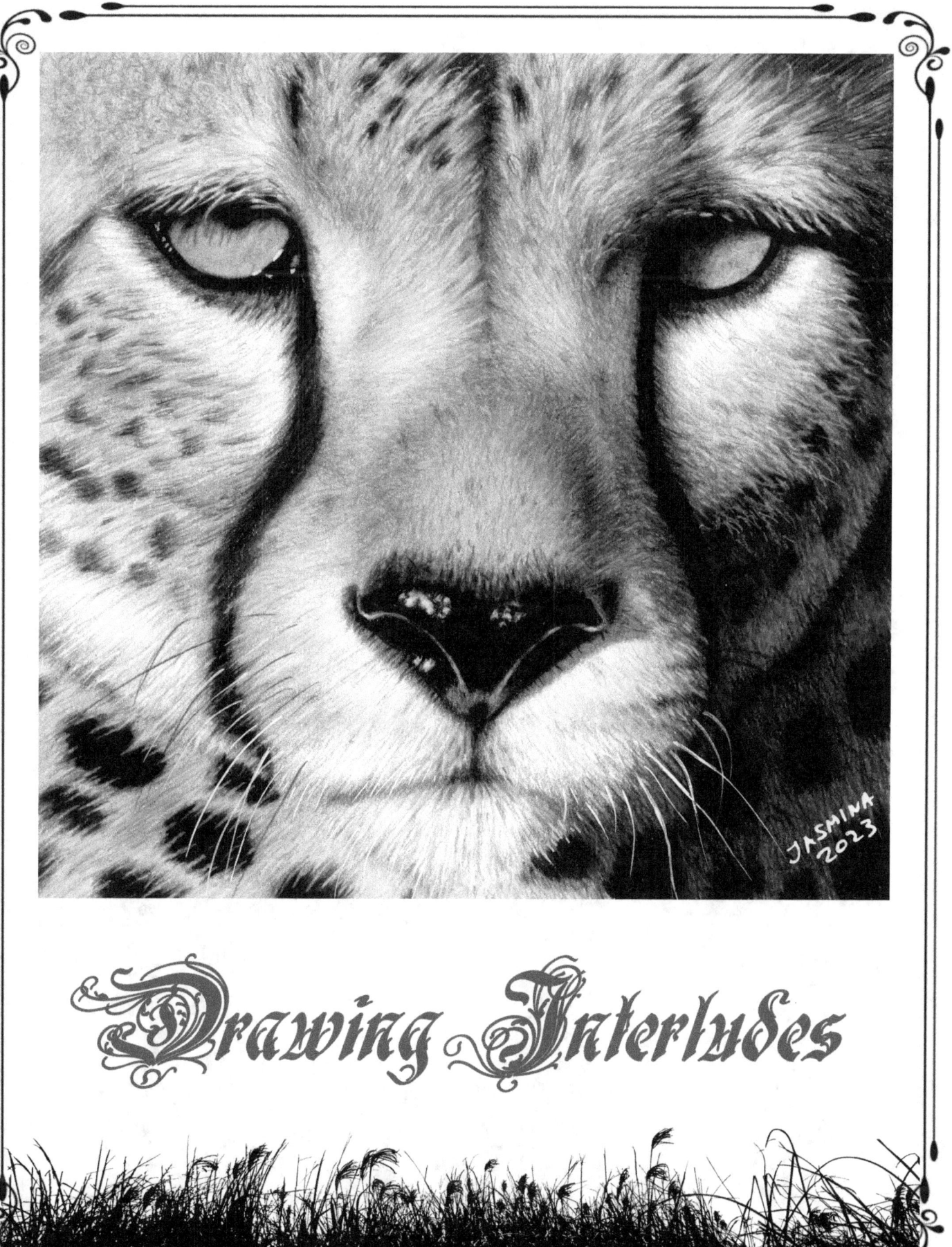

Drawing Interludes

How to Draw a Zebra

Drawing a zebra provides a wonderful opportunity to delve into the world of patterns, contrast, and unique textures. The zebra's distinctive black and white stripes offer a visually striking subject that challenges our observation and drawing skills. By studying and drawing a zebra, we can enhance our understanding of light and shadow, develop our attention to detail, and explore the fascinating interplay between positive and negative spaces. Let's appreciate the beauty and diversity of the animal kingdom and capture the mesmerizing beauty of the zebra on paper.

The Reference Photo

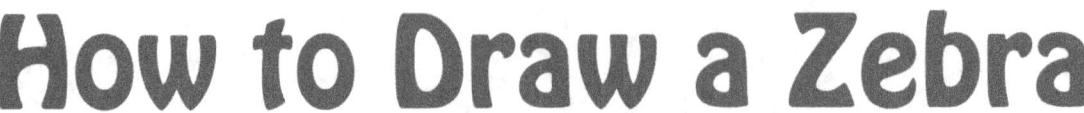

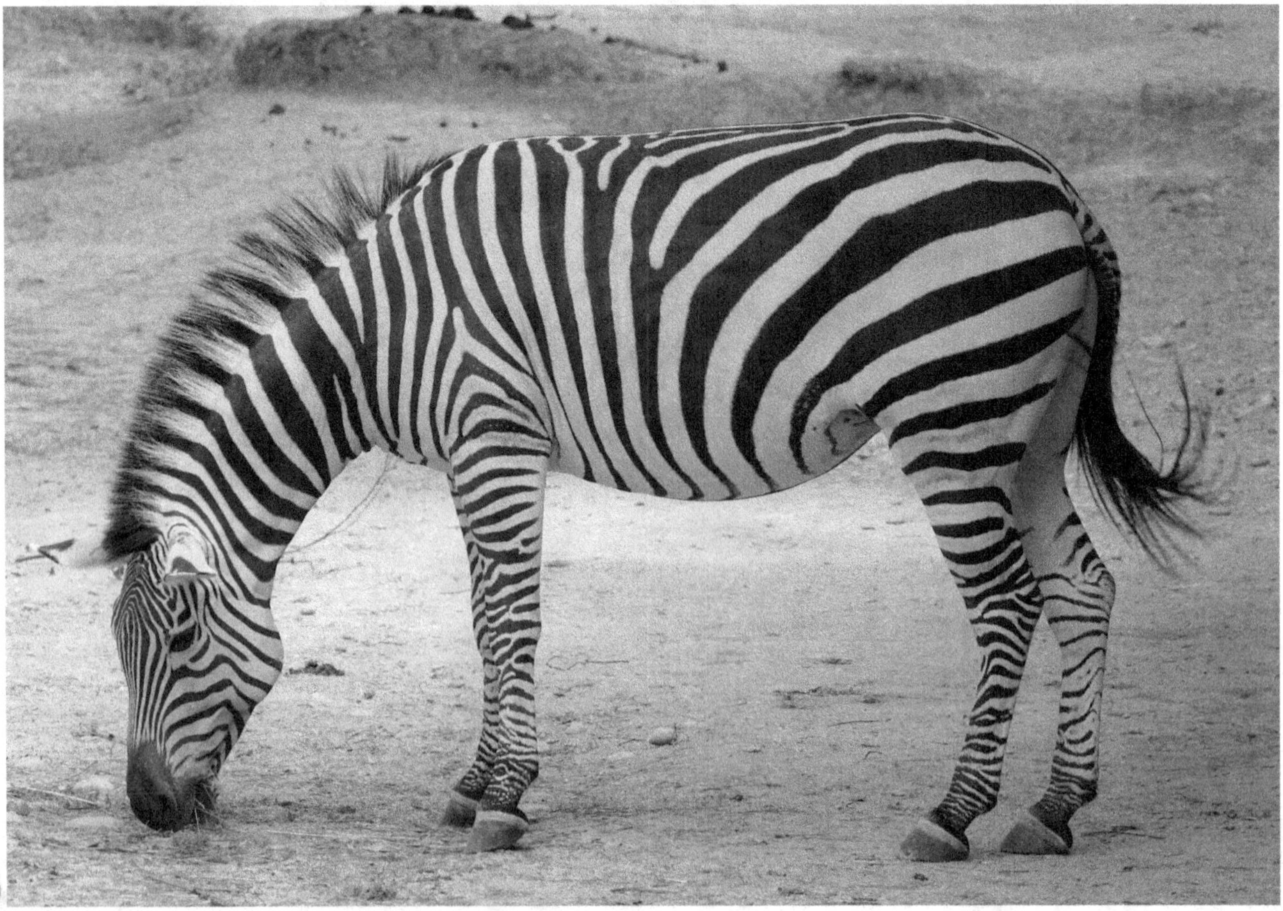

122

Sketching and Basic Shapes

In the next image, I have highlighted the lines that I consider important. Using the grid method, you can create the main outline of the zebra. While sketching the zebra, it is not necessary to strictly adhere to the grid method for the black and white stripes. They can be created randomly. However, in this case, I have chosen to sketch every single detail as depicted in the reference photo to provide a clear comparison between my drawing and the original image. In my sketch image, I have marked the black stripes with small "x" marks to distinguish them from the white stripes. This helps me avoid confusion and ensures that I accurately shade the areas that should be black.

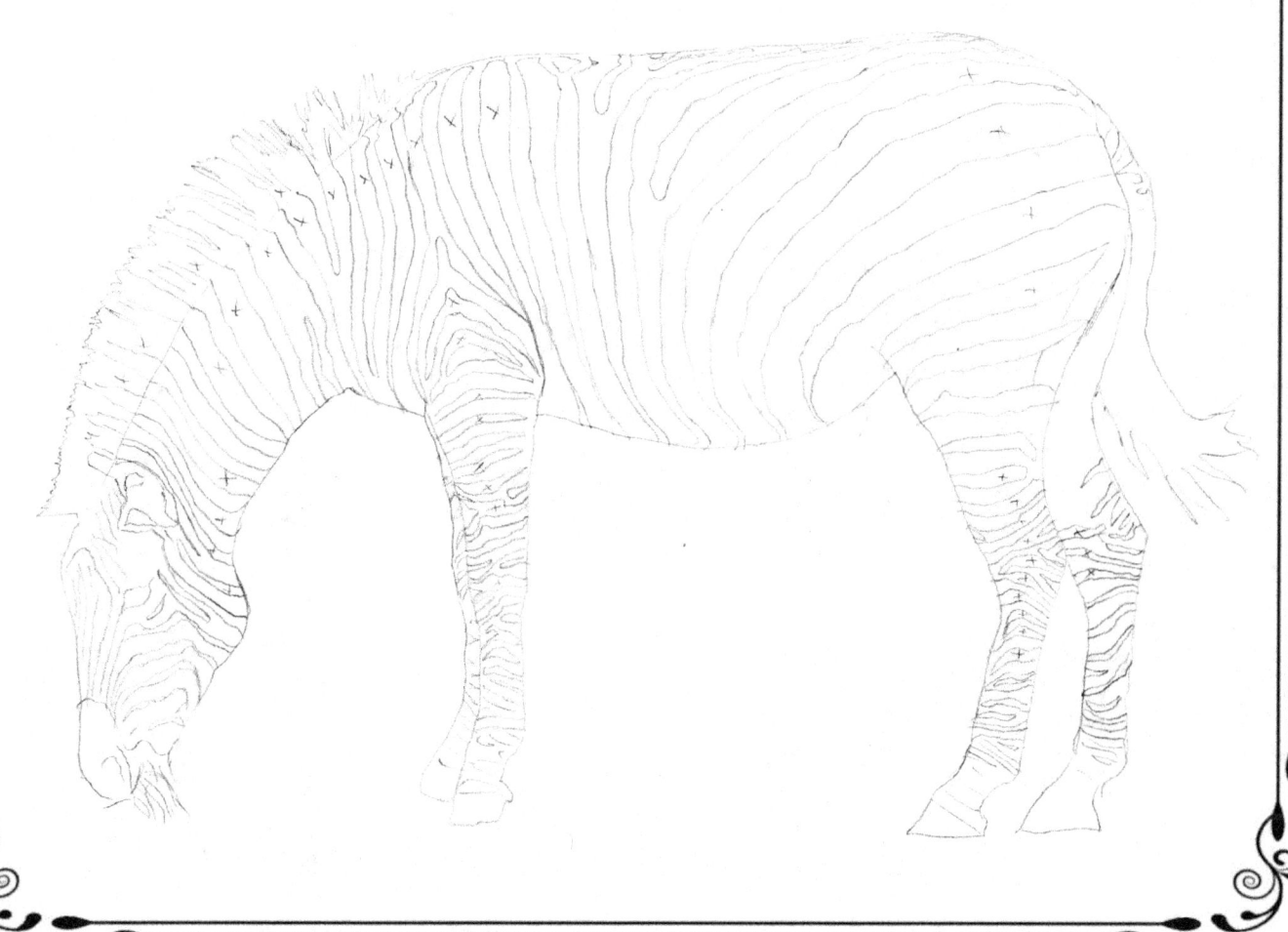

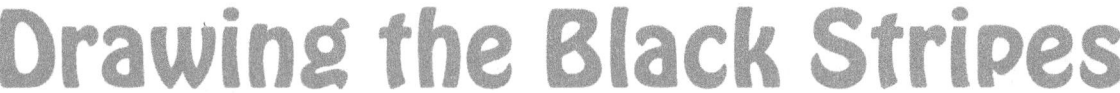

Drawing the Black Stripes

Start by using a **14B** pencil to cover the areas that are absolutely black in the reference photo. In this step, we will intentionally leave the upper areas of the black stripes untouched for now, as they will require a lighter value to represent the illuminated areas. While these parts may not be visible in the reference photo, we want to focus on creating contrast and depth in our drawing.

Apply the pencil with firm and even pressure to create a rich, dark tone. If you feel unsure or want to make adjustments, you can use an HB pencil with a lighter touch to fill in these areas before committing to the darker value. Once you are confident with the placement and look of the black areas, you can go over them with a very dark pencil, such as an 8B or darker, to further enhance the depth and richness of the black tones.

This step is crucial and requires careful attention. Completing this step alone required a substantial amount of time, approximately 2.5 hours in my case. So, take your time, especially when working on the intricate details such as the thin stripes over the legs and the head.

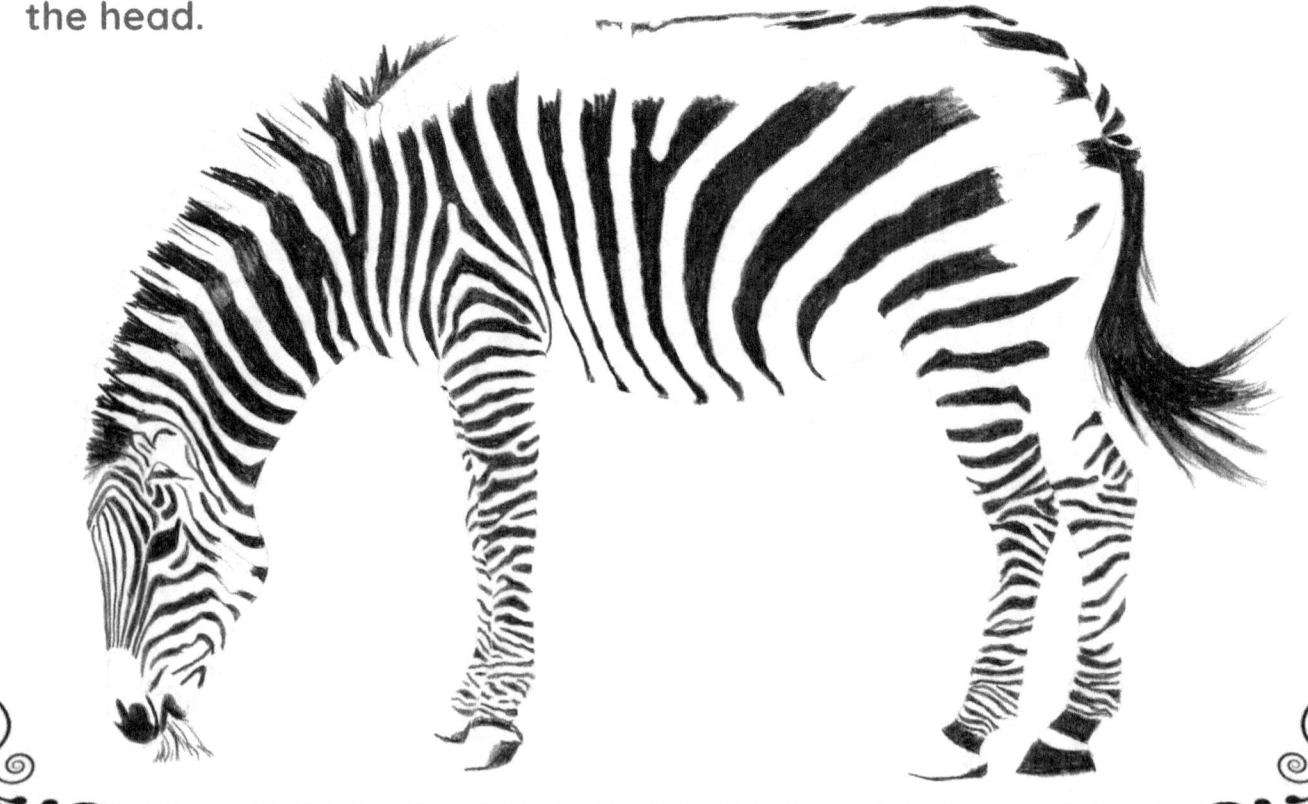

124

Highlighting the Black Stripes

In the next step, shade the highlighted black stripes that were previously left untouched in the image. Use an HB pencil for this part of the process. Moreover, lighten the upper portions of the black stripes over the neck, specifically under the roots of the mane hairs, as these areas possess a slight highlight. You can achieve this effect by carefully using an eraser.

It's important not to rush and to draw with precision to achieve the desired effect. Each person has their own pace, and dedicating sufficient time to each step ensures accuracy and attention to detail.

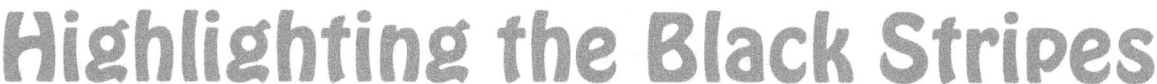

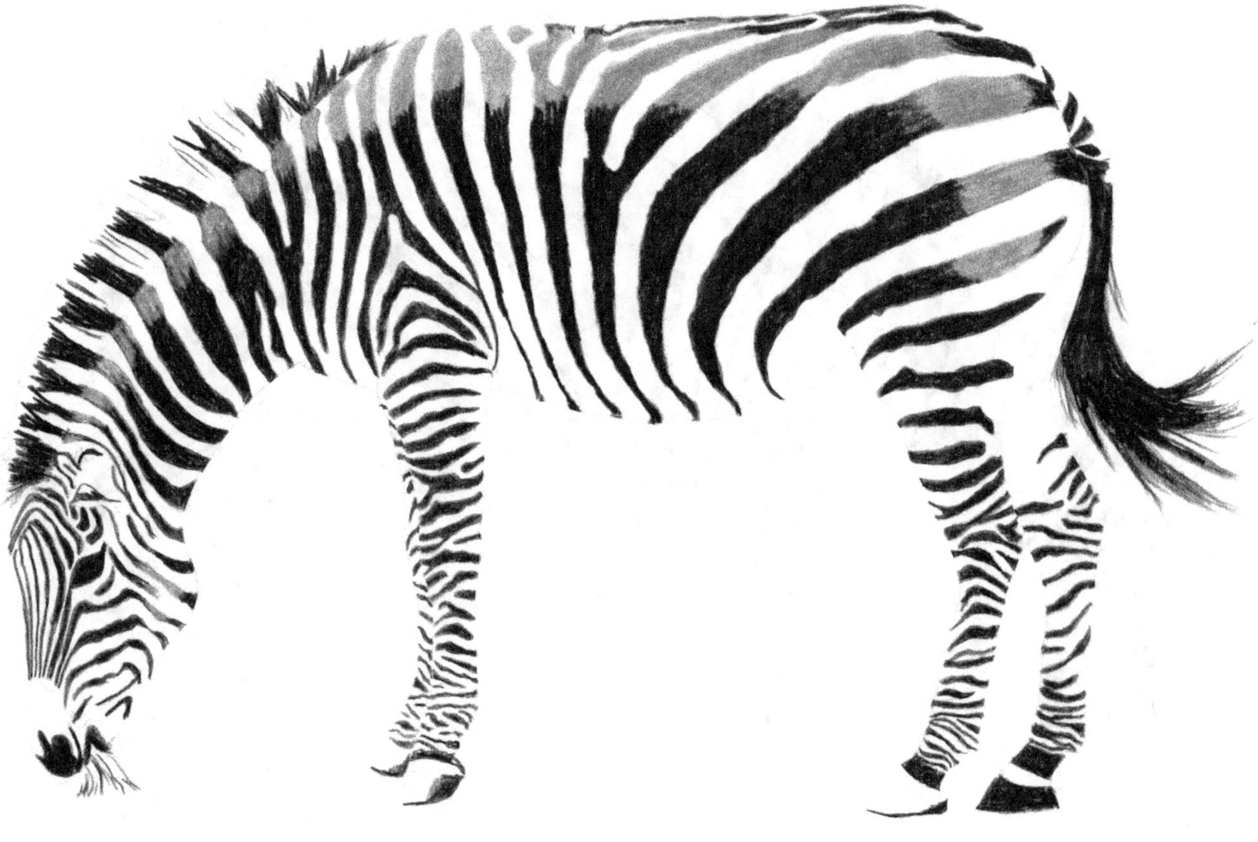

Smoothing Tone Transitions

In the next step, we want to focus on blending the edges between the two shades we previously applied. The goal is to create a smooth transition where the shades seamlessly flow into each other. If you have practiced the technique discussed in the "Smooth Gradient" chapter, this is the perfect opportunity to utilize it.

To begin, I recommend using a 4B pencil for blending. As you blend, you can gradually increase the pressure on the pencil, particularly in the areas where you shaded the darkest parts of the stripes using the 14B pencil. You can use gentle, circular motions or back-and-forth strokes to smooth out the transition and create a seamless flow between the shades. This blending technique will help give the zebra a more three-dimensional appearance, adding depth compared to the previous flat look.

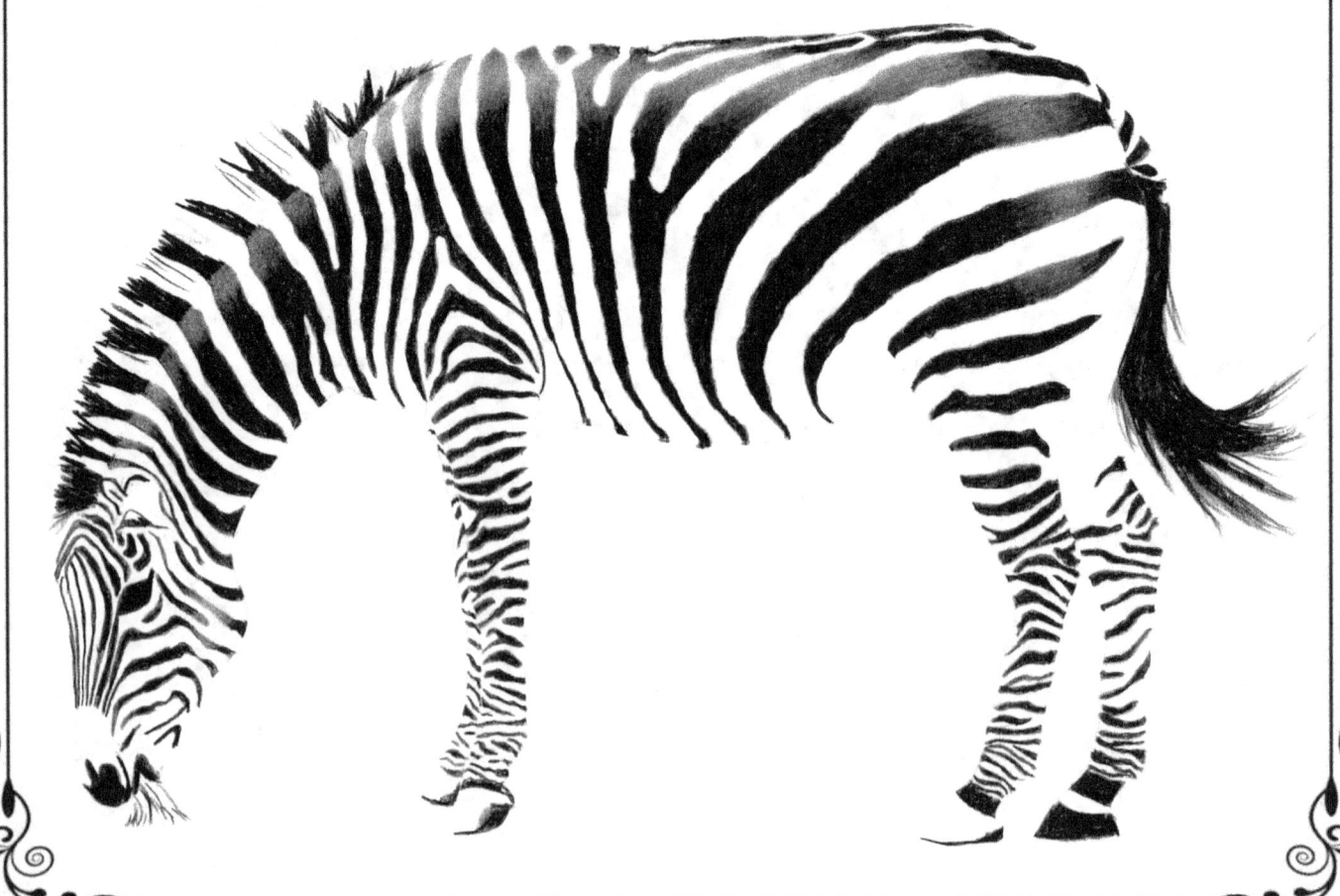

Shading the Hooves and Muzzle

In the next step, we'll focus on shading the hooves and muzzle of the zebra using an HB pencil. Refer to the accompanying picture to identify the specific areas that require shading. Take note of the shadows, highlights, and texture in the reference image to guide your shading technique.

If necessary, you can use a blending stump to gently blend and soften the shaded areas.

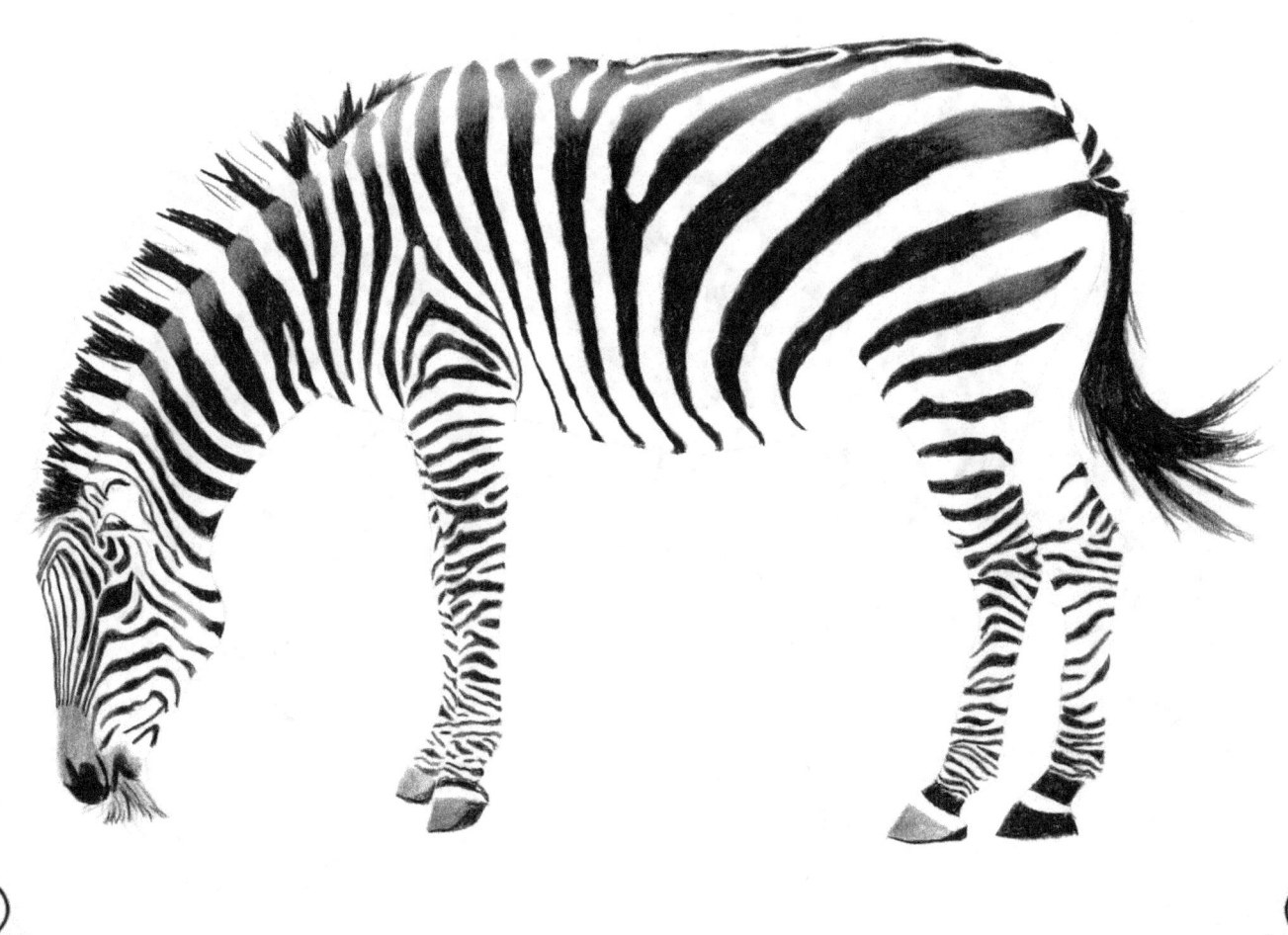

Blending Tone Transitions

In this step, we will create a seamless gradient transition between the previously shaded hooves and muzzle and the sections drawn with **14B**. To accomplish this, we will use an **8B** pencil and gradually lessen the pressure as we shade from the shadows to the highlighted parts. If an area appears too light or lacks sufficient shading, simply add more layers of shading to build up the desired tone. Use your pencil to carefully apply additional shading, gradually building it up until the desired consistency is achieved.

On the other hand, if certain areas appear too dark or require lightening, you can lightly use an eraser to lift some graphite from those specific areas. Be gentle and cautious when using the eraser, as you don't want to remove too much or damage the paper. After lightening the darker areas, you can then smooth out the transitions and blend them with the surrounding tones.

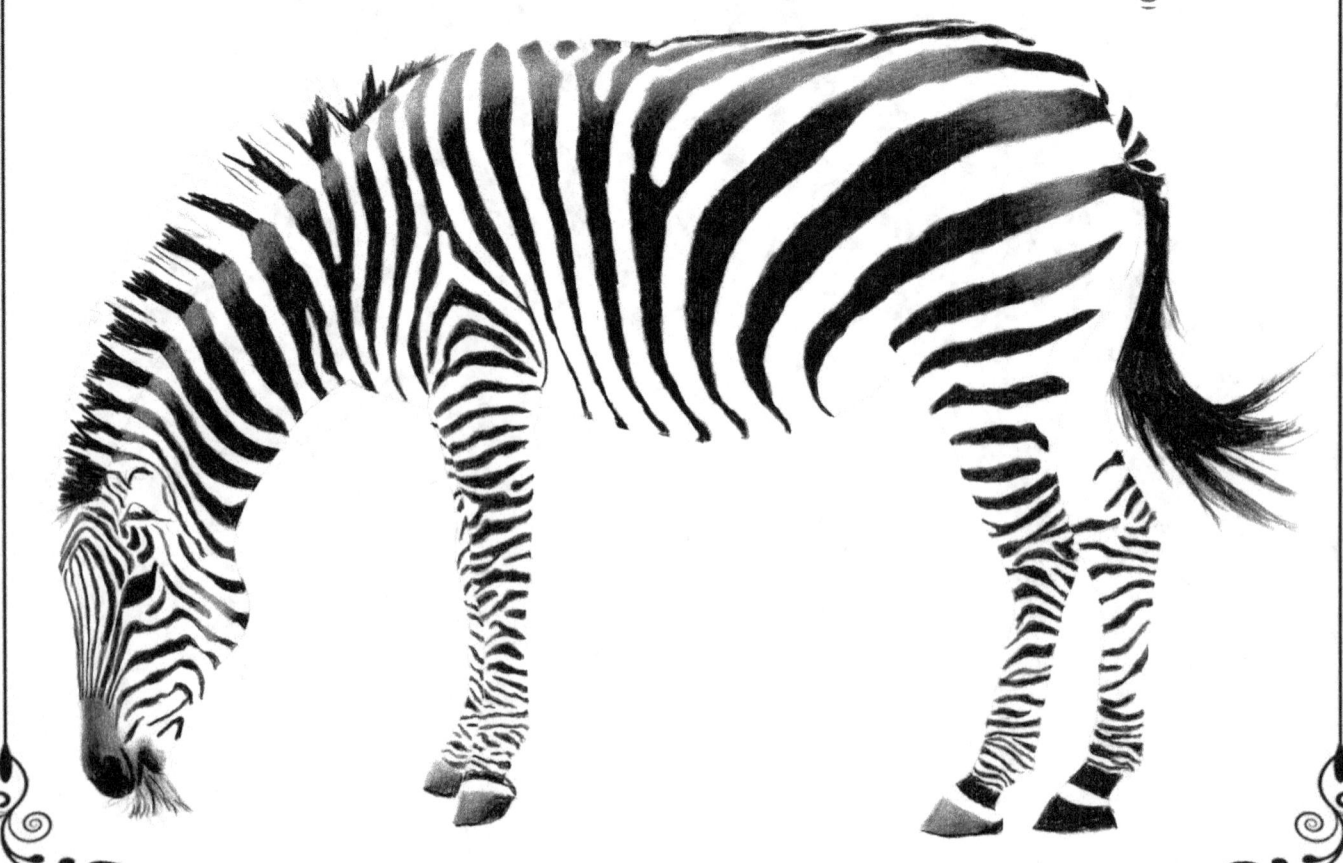

Shading the White Areas

Now, let's focus on shading the white coat. Although it may initially seem counterintuitive to shade white coat, we can achieve the desired effect by using a light touch and building up additional layers. In the next image, observe the areas shaded with an HB pencil as a reference for your own shading. Note that I pressed firmly near the edges and gradually lightened my touch as I approached the highlights. You can use either an HB pencil with lighter pressure or switch to a harder pencil like 2H for lighter shading This gradual transition allows the lightest shade to blend seamlessly into the brightness of the highlights.

Don't forget to create reflected lights in areas like the hindquarters next to the tail. By lightly pressing the pencil and applying slightly darker pressure further from the edge, you can add a three-dimensional effect. Even if not visible in the reference photo, these reflected lights enhance the roundness of the subject.

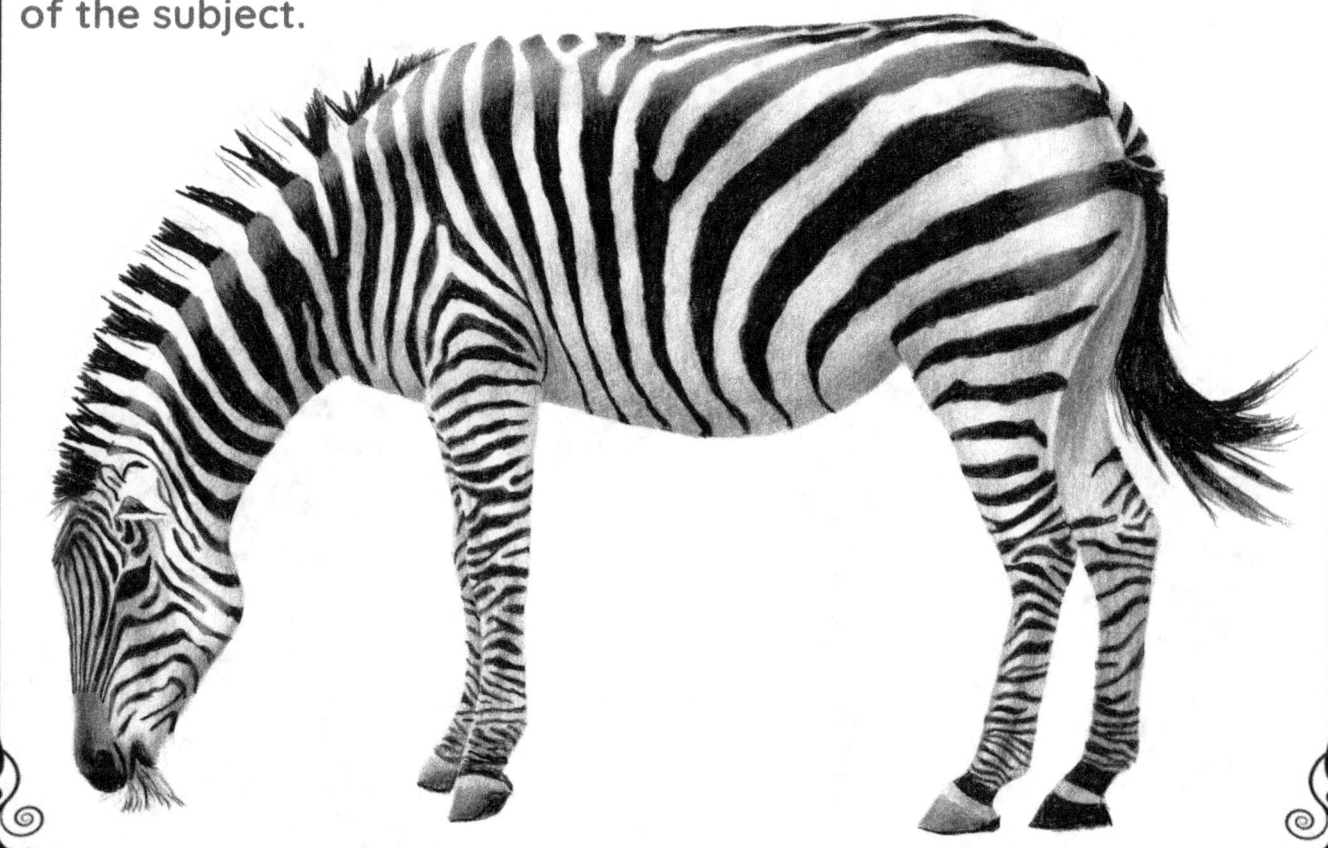

Intensifying the Shades

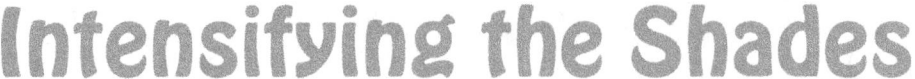

Let's assess whether further shading is needed. Upon observation, I've noticed that the self-shadow on the zebra's belly appears too light. To address this, I recommend switching to a 4B pencil and applying firm pressure along the edges, gradually lightening the pressure as you move away. Additionally, the shadowed upper part of the neck and under the eyes require additional shading. In addition, it is important to note that the hinder part of the zebra's body, shadowed by the tail, needs to be significantly darker. When comparing this image to the previous one, you can clearly observe the difference in values. To achieve the desired effect, use a darker pencil, such as a 4B or 6B, and apply ample pressure while shading. This will create a stronger contrast and enhance the shadowed area, adding depth and dimension to the drawing.It's crucial to shade every part, except for the highlights. You'll notice that by shading the shoulder with lighter pressure compared to the surrounding shadows, it will appear brighter and stand out more prominently on the paper.

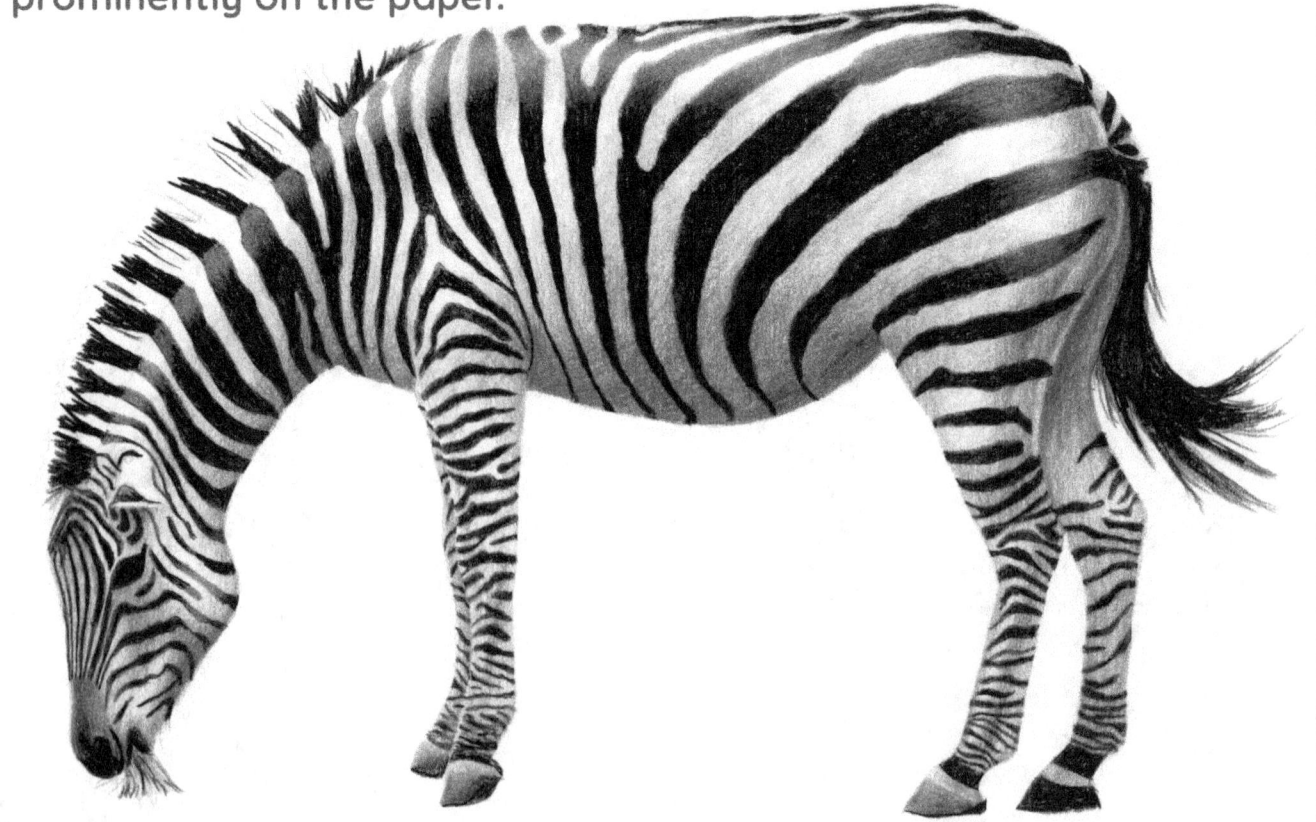

Blending and Refining

Now, it's time to carefully blend all these areas using a blending stump or a Q-tip. Start by using a clean tip of the blending tool next to the highlights, and gradually work towards the darker areas. If the tip becomes saturated with graphite, it's advisable to switch to a clean Q-tip or blending stump to avoid unintended smudging in the highlight areas. Remember, the goal is not to blend everything to achieve absolute smoothness Preserving some "imperfections" like individual hairs, scars, spots, or traces of dirt on the coat will enhance the realism of the animal. If the white coat is perfectly smooth, it may appear more like a digital drawing or a vector illustration, which can come across as artificial or "fake". Adding tiny, random details will contribute to a more lifelike representation. By embracing these slight deviations and incorporating subtle, unexpected elements, you will create a more authentic and natural rendering of the animal.

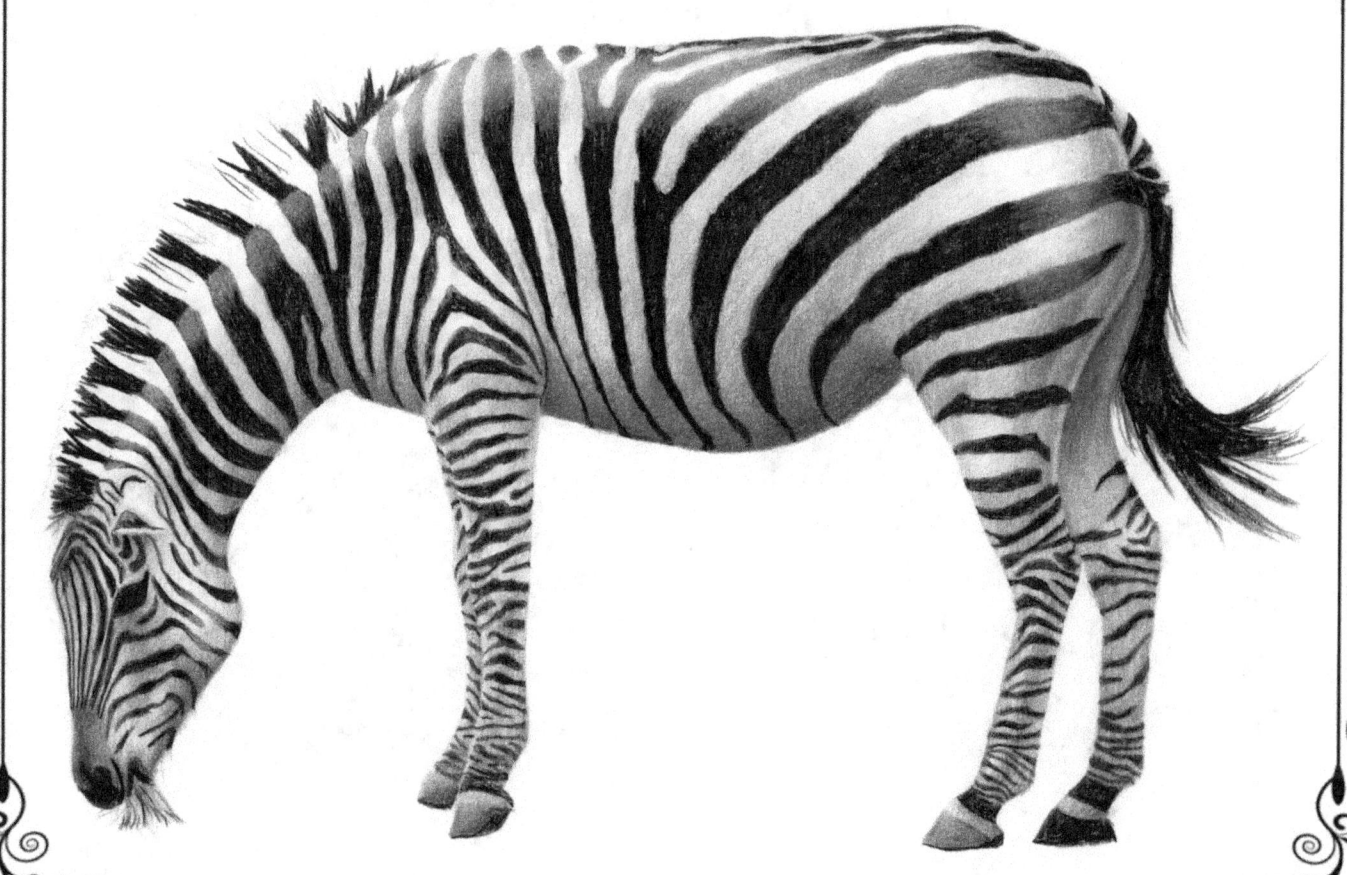

Delving into Intricate Details

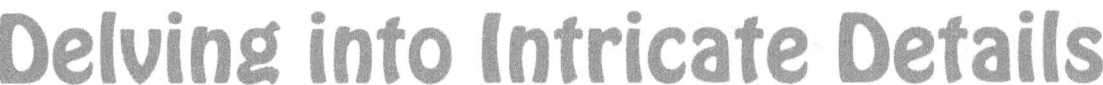

Now it's time to incorporate some intricate details that may not be immediately visible but contribute to the realism of the drawing. For this, I utilize a colorless blender by Prismacolor to create tiny, delicate hairs along the edges where the black and white stripes meet. These hairs mimic the fine texture found in the zebra's coat and add an extra level of hyper-realism to the artwork.To blend these edges, I position the tip of the colorless blender over the edge of the black stripes and gently glide it outward, across the white stripes. The blender's tip selectively picks up the necessary amount of graphite, resulting in the creation of these fine hairs with fluffy ends.

It's important to note that this step requires meticulous attention to detail and can be time-consuming. While it may not be readily noticeable in a thumbnail view, I recommend taking every opportunity to practice patience and indulge in this process. However, if time constraints are a concern, you can choose to skip this step without compromising the overall impact of the drawing.

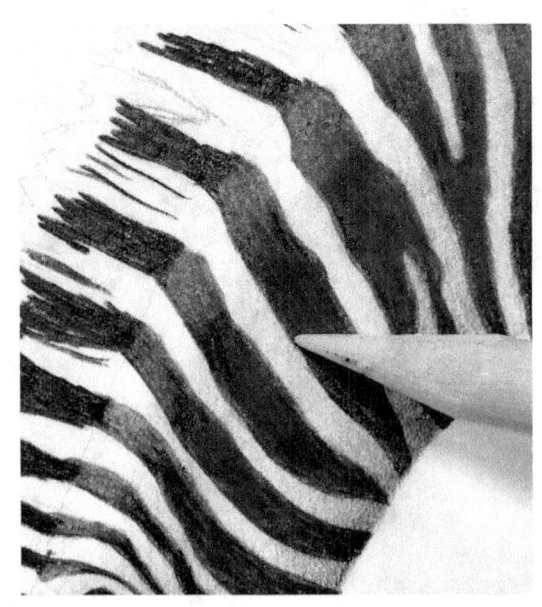
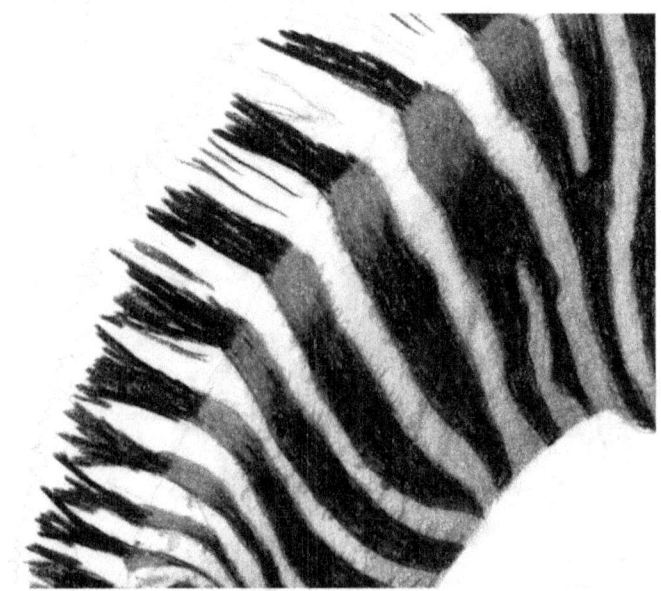

Adding Subtle Elements for Realism

To further enhance the details, let's incorporate some elements that are visible in the reference photo. Specifically, there are darker stripes between the two black stripes over the white ones. To achieve this effect, use a 2B pencil and lightly layer it, gradually building up the value until the desired darkness is achieved. Take your time with this process, ensuring that the layers are applied evenly and smoothly.

For a clear comparison, I recommend examining the previous image alongside the current one to identify the specific areas where these stripes have been added. Take note of the subtle details and study the reference photo as well.

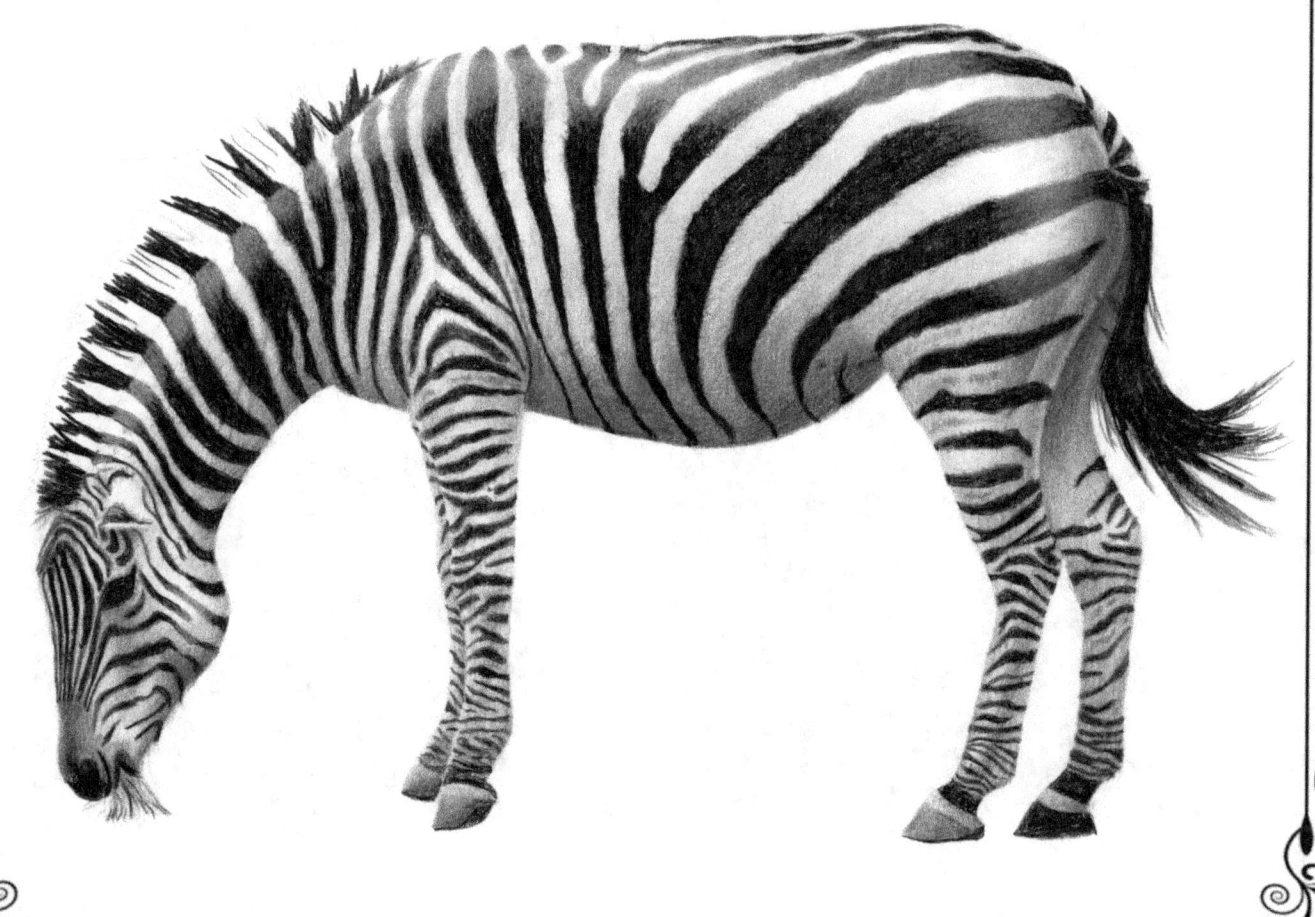

Softening Long Hairs

To create a soft and fluffy texture for the ends of the tail and the mane, blending is key. I recommend using a wax-based colorless blender by Prismacolor in conjunction with a blending stump. The blender's tip will pick up the right amount of graphite to smoothly finish the line, allowing it to gradually disappear into the background. Meanwhile, the blending stump will create a slightly blurred effect along the edges.

To achieve this, position the tip of your blender on the desired area and use quick, confident strokes to spread the graphite outwards. As you approach the background, slightly lift the tip of your pencil to create a fading effect. The difference in texture and blending can be seen in the before-and-after image below, showcasing the significant impact of this blending technique.

Before   After

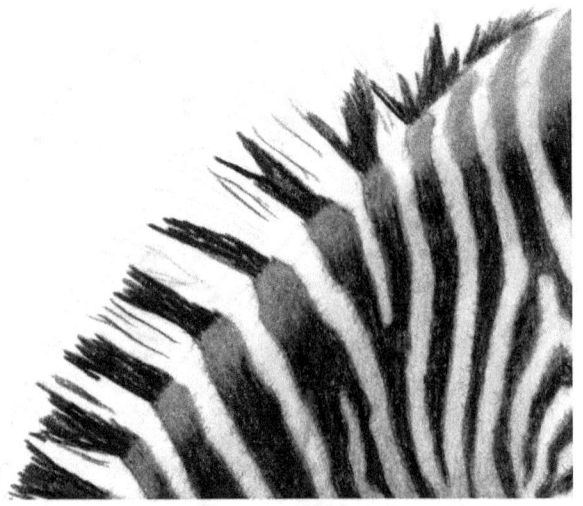 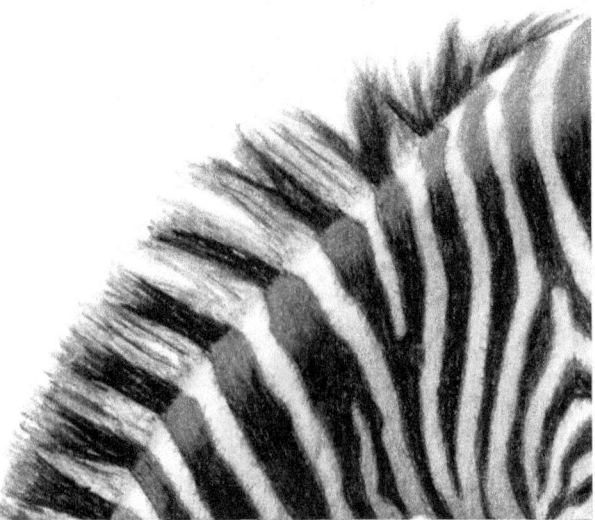

In addition, while blending the ends of the mane, it's important to create lines following the direction of the hair flow on the white parts of the mane. This technique adds a realistic touch to the drawing, mimicking the natural flow of the mane's individual hairs.

I must say, this step was truly captivating and engaging.
It held my interest throughout the process, and I found great satisfaction in creating intricate details and textures.

I'm curious to know if you had a favorite part of the drawing process I would be delighted if you could share your thoughts and experiences with me.

Once you have completed the blending process, you can further enhance the effect by drawing some individual hairs with an 8B pencil or a darker shade.

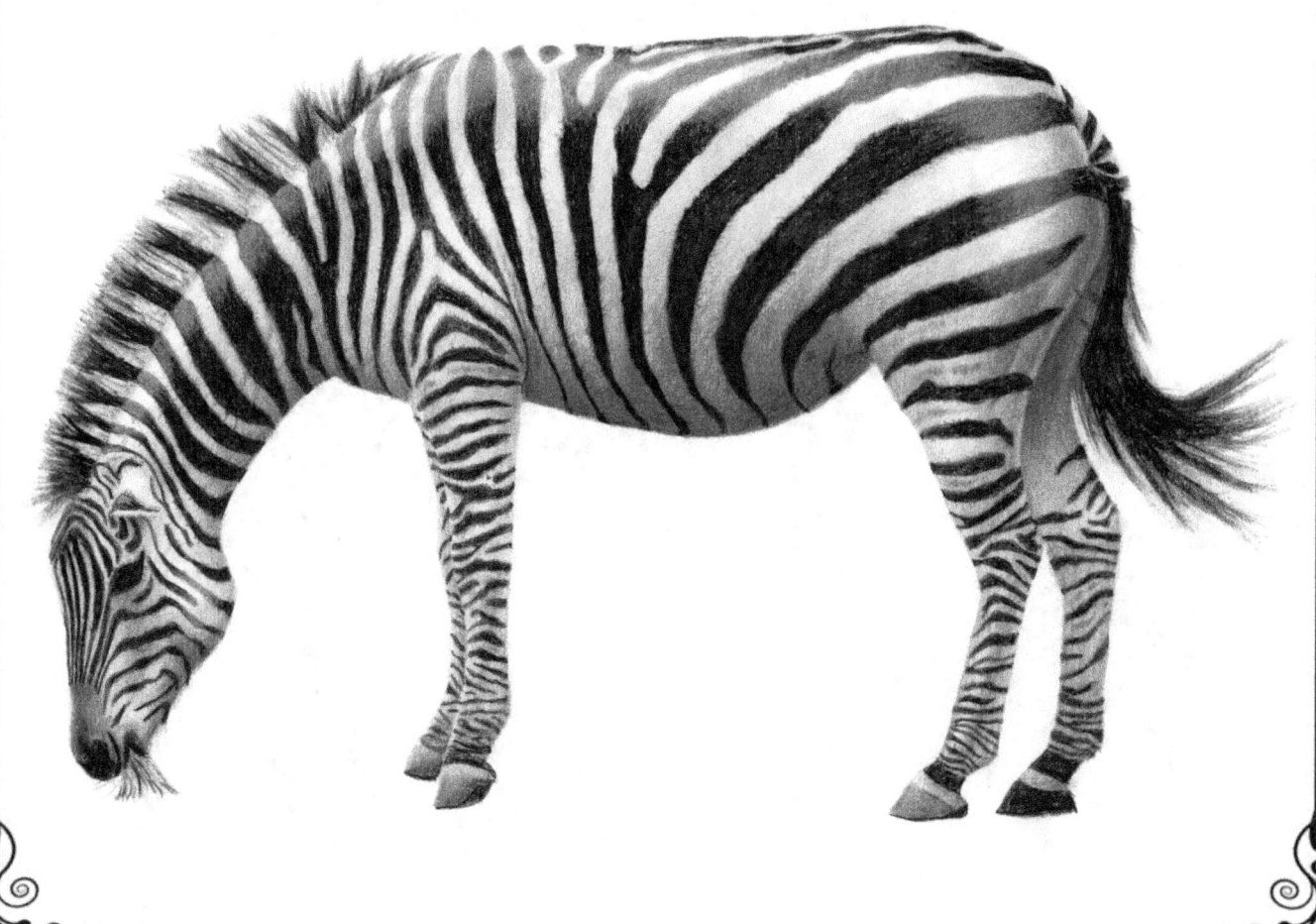

Creating the Zebra's Cast Shadow

To complete this drawing, if you are satisfied with the overall result and feel that no further additions are necessary, you can now consider adding the shadow cast by the zebra. In the reference photo, you will notice that the shadow cast by the zebra's head and legs appears darker adjacent to those body parts, gradually fading into the surrounding area. Additionally, create a larger cast shadow in the middle, aligning horizontally with the hooves to indicate the shadow cast by the zebra's body. You can achieve this effect by using graphite powder applied with a simple painting brush or by gently spreading it with a tissue using back and forth motions. This will help enhance the overall depth and realism of the drawing. When aiming to portray the zebra standing in direct sunlight, it's essential to have sharp edges for the cast shadow to achieve a realistic effect. In contrast, if the lighting conditions suggest a softer illumination, the shadow over the animal should appear blurry.

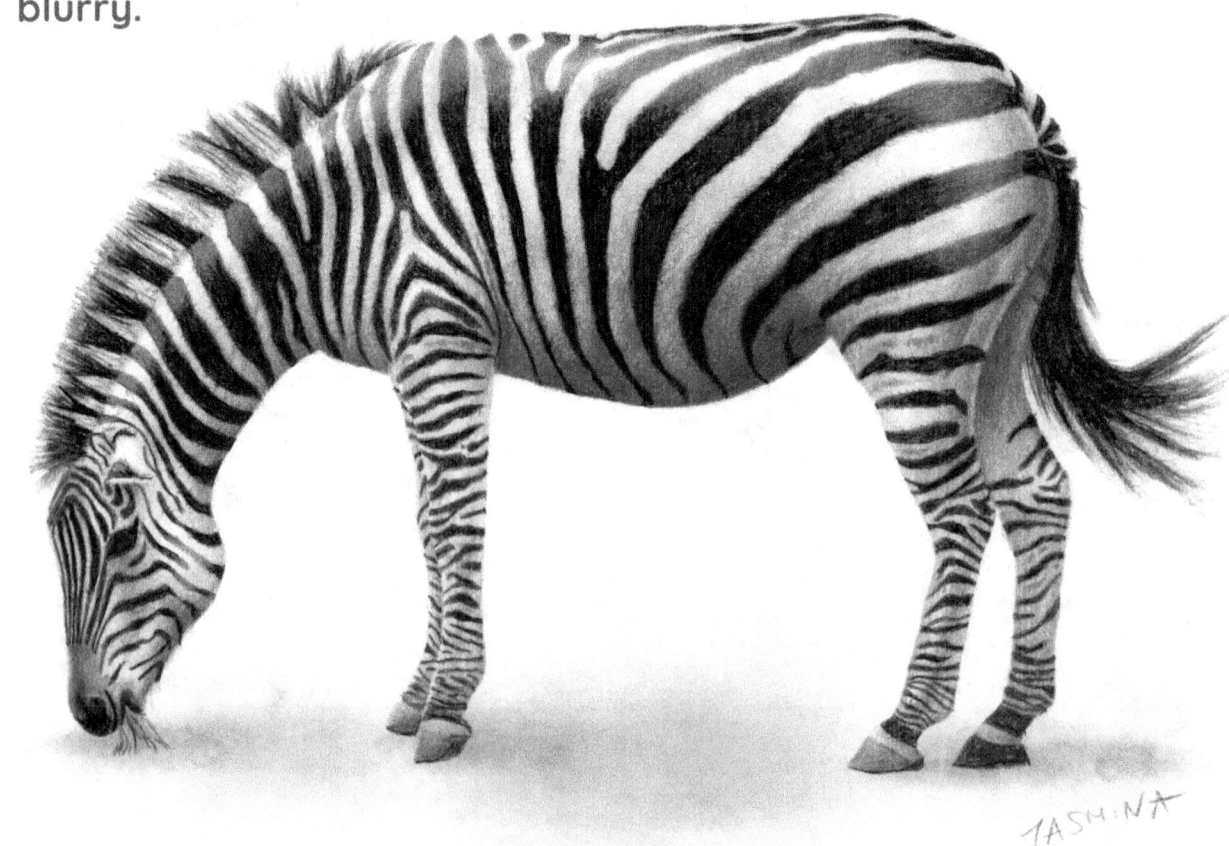

JASMINA

Drawing Interludes

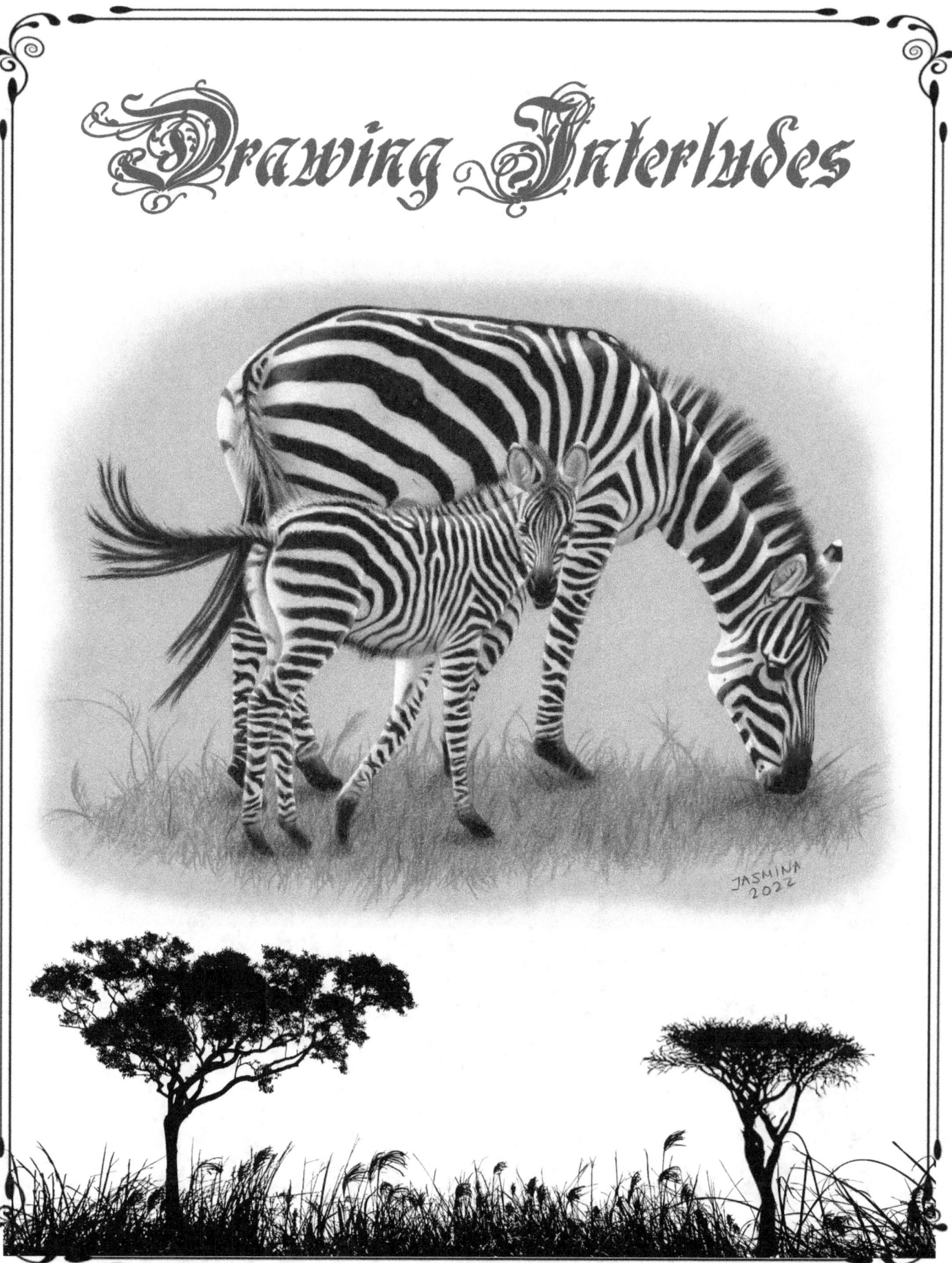

How to Draw an Elephant

Embarking on an elephant drawing presents an exciting avenue to delve into the art of crafting intricate textures beyond fur. The elephant's unique skin, with its wrinkles, folds, and tactile characteristics, allows artists to master the art of detailing and realism. Exploring the challenges of replicating this remarkable texture enhances your drawing skills and opens doors to a world of artistic possibilities, making it a fascinating and rewarding subject for any artist.

The Reference Photo

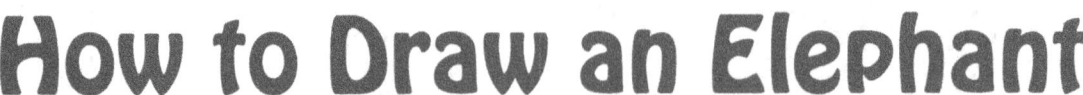

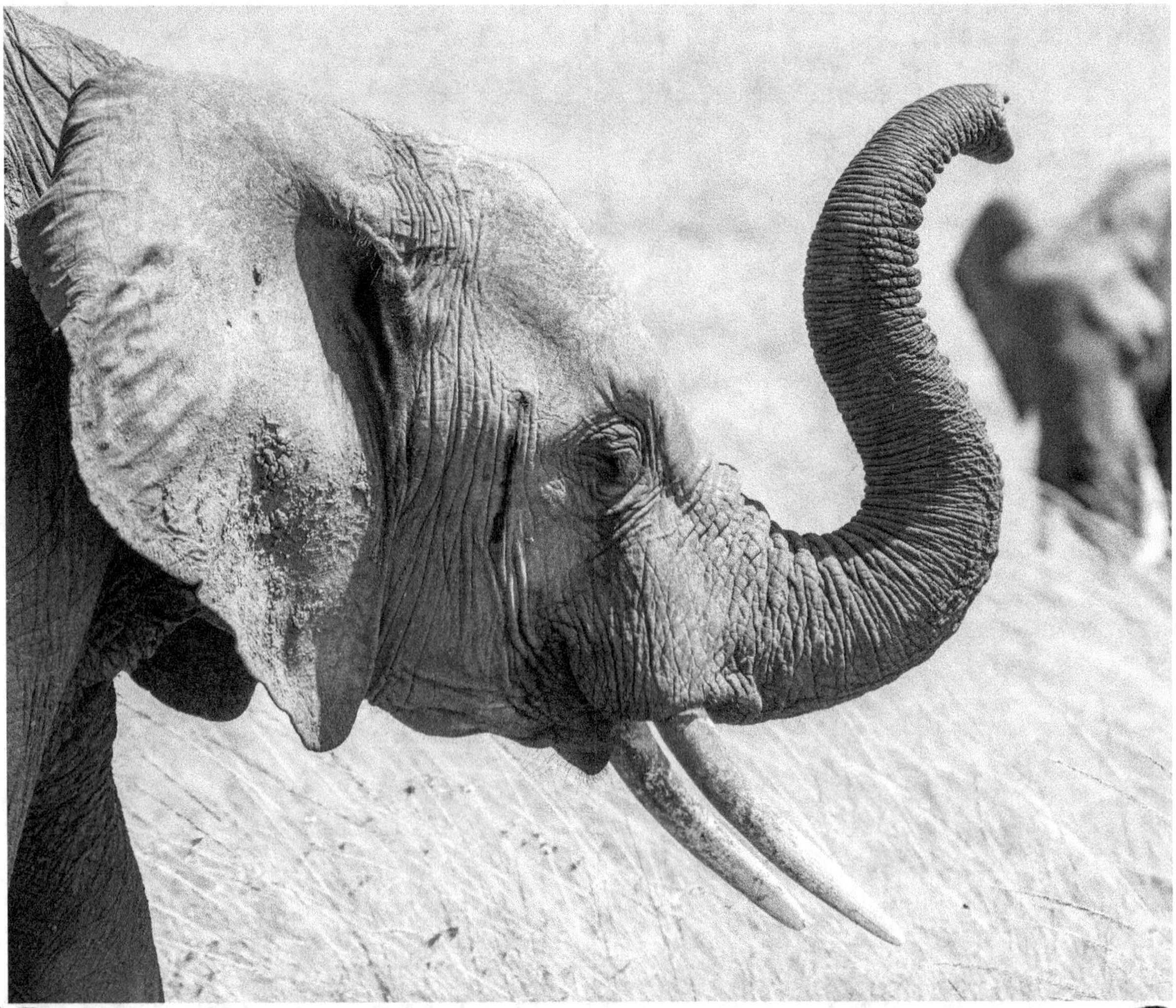

Sketching and Basic Shapes

For achieving lifelike depictions of elephants, selecting the right reference photo is crucial. Look for images of elephants bathed in direct sunlight, as this lighting creates strong cast shadows and self-shadows. As a result, the uniformity of the elephant's skin texture is broken, and a variety of tonal values emerge, adding depth and dimension to the artwork. By capturing the captivating contrast between light and dark, your drawings will become truly eye-catching, showcasing the majestic beauty of these magnificent creatures. In the image below, you'll notice that I've marked the outline of the elephant's body and highlighted the edges between the contrasting dark and bright areas. Additionally, I've added some finer details, like the eye and subtle wrinkles.

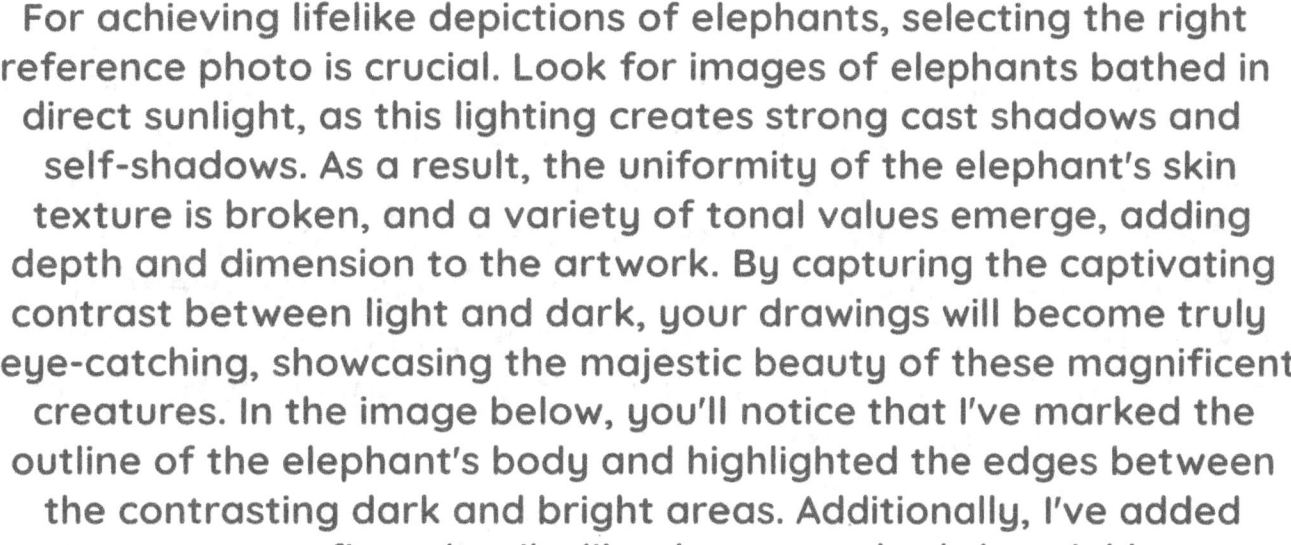

Analyzing Skin Values

Next, it's important to identify the brightest areas on the elephant, even though there may not be any completely pure white values. To do this, I use the Highlight & Shadow Isolator Online Free Tool that I created on the Pencil Drawing Tutor website www.pencildrawingtutor.com, which you can use for free to see both the darkest areas and the brightest highlights in your reference photo. I moved the scale toward Highlights to reveal the brightest parts on the elephant.

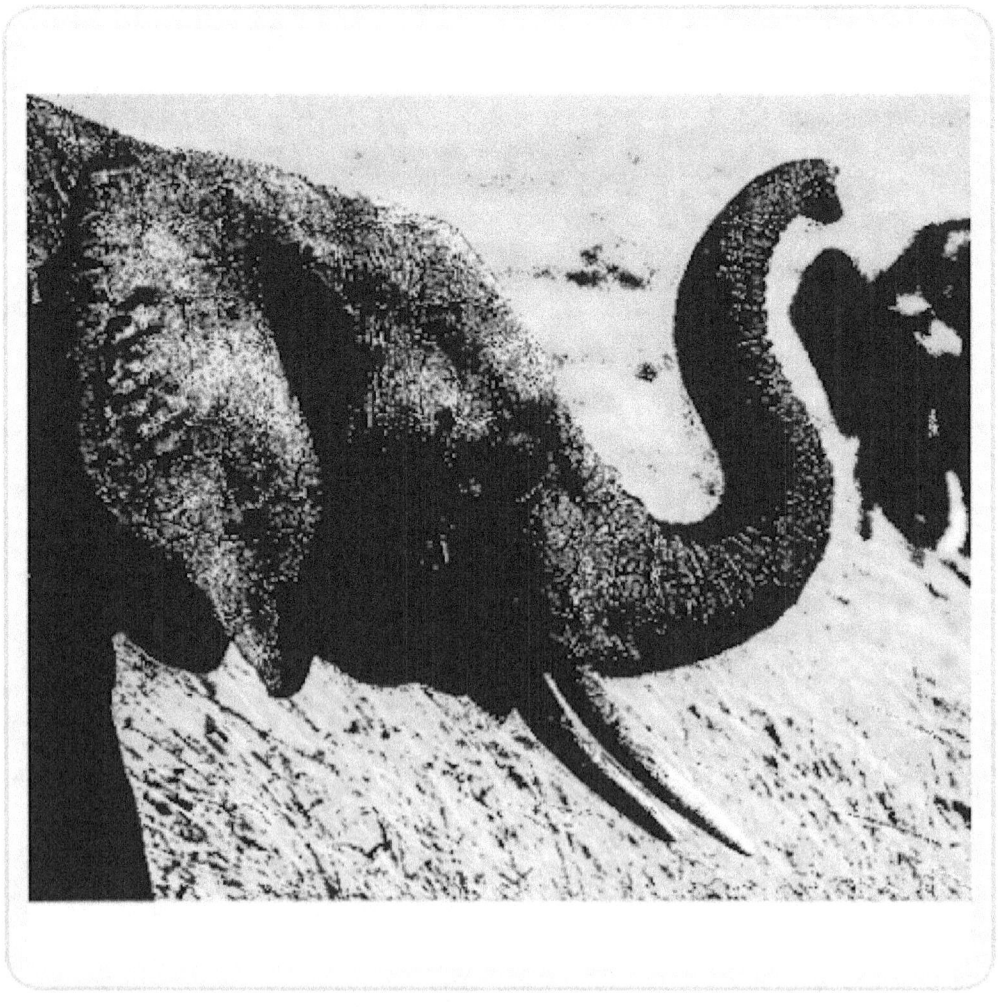

Shadows ◄ 0 ► Highlights

Next, to find the darkest areas of the reference photo, move the scale toward Shadows. The further you move it to the left, the purer the black areas become, as you can see in the screenshot I've provided. This technique helps you clearly identify the darkest values, which are essential for creating depth and contrast in your artwork.

I highly recommend incorporating this editing step into your drawing routine, whether you are sketching furry animals, human portraits, or any other subject. It will help you develop a deeper understanding of tonal values and add a new level of realism to your drawings.

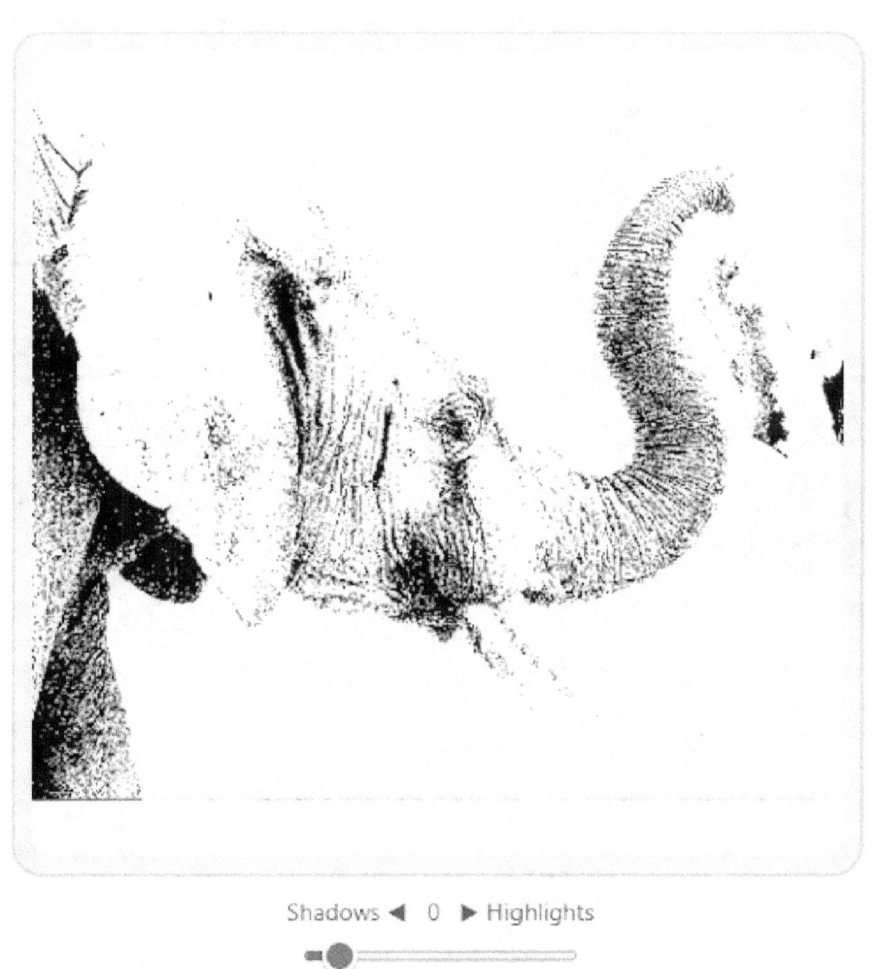

Shadows ◀ 0 ▶ Highlights

Drawing the Deepest Shadows

So, following the previous guidelines, focus on drawing the darkest parts of the picture. For this, use a 12B pencil to shade the areas as shown in the image below. Apply firm pressure to create rich, deep tones. Remember, these darker areas will add depth and dimension to your drawing.

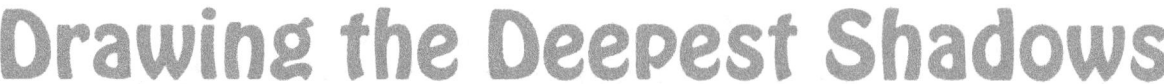

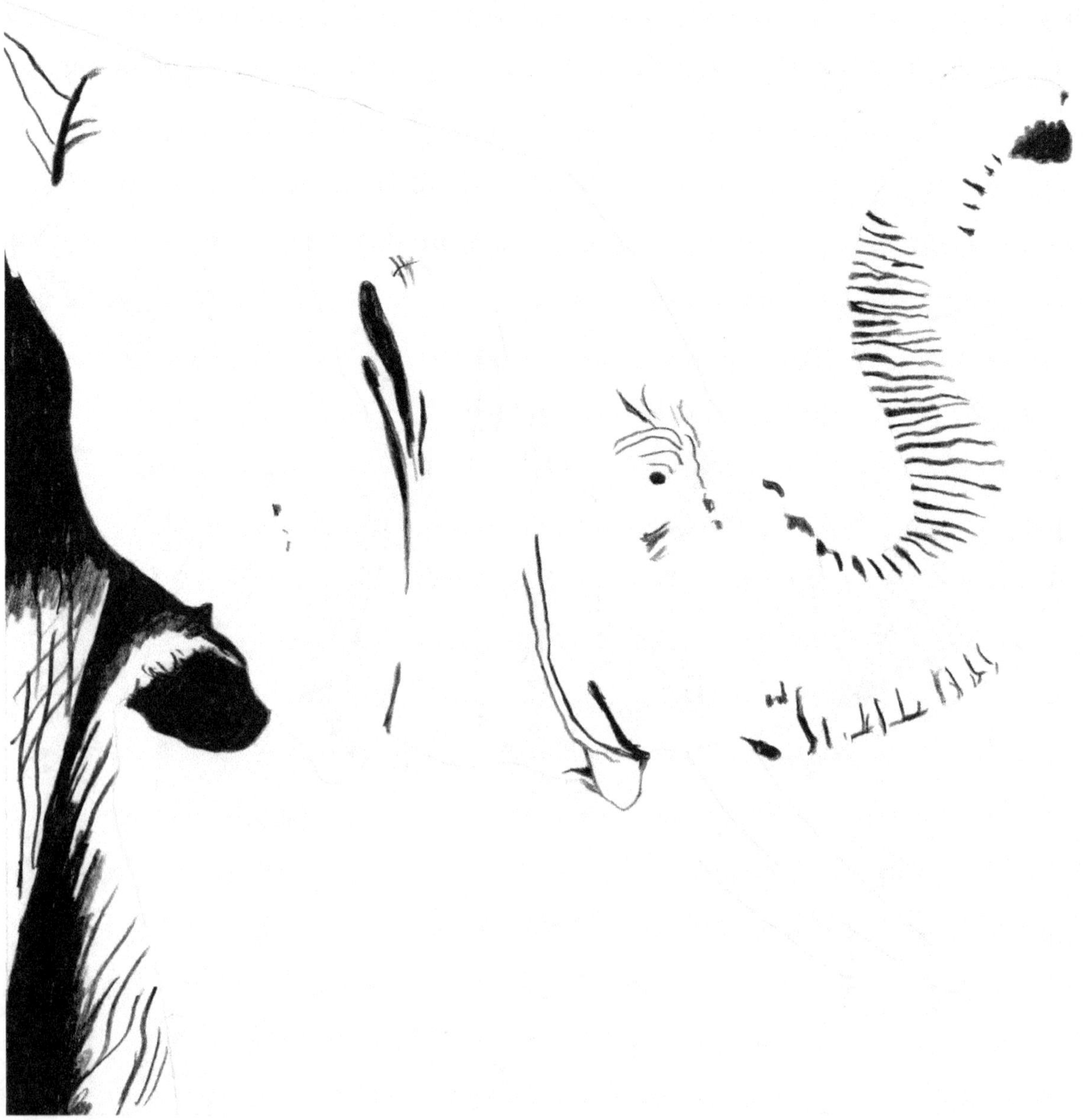

Creating Softer Shadowing

Next, we'll employ a 2B pencil to shade the regions adjacent to the ones we previously drew. This pencil is excellent for creating dark areas, though not as intense as the 12B pencil. It serves as a lighter dark value, allowing us to smoothly transition to mid-tones. Be sure to carefully mark all the wrinkles over the trunk, head, and ear with this pencil.

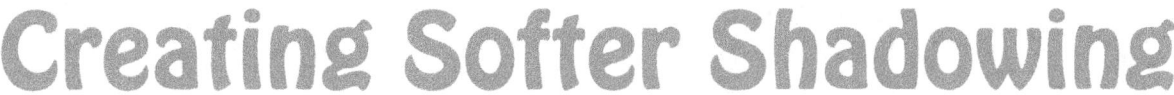

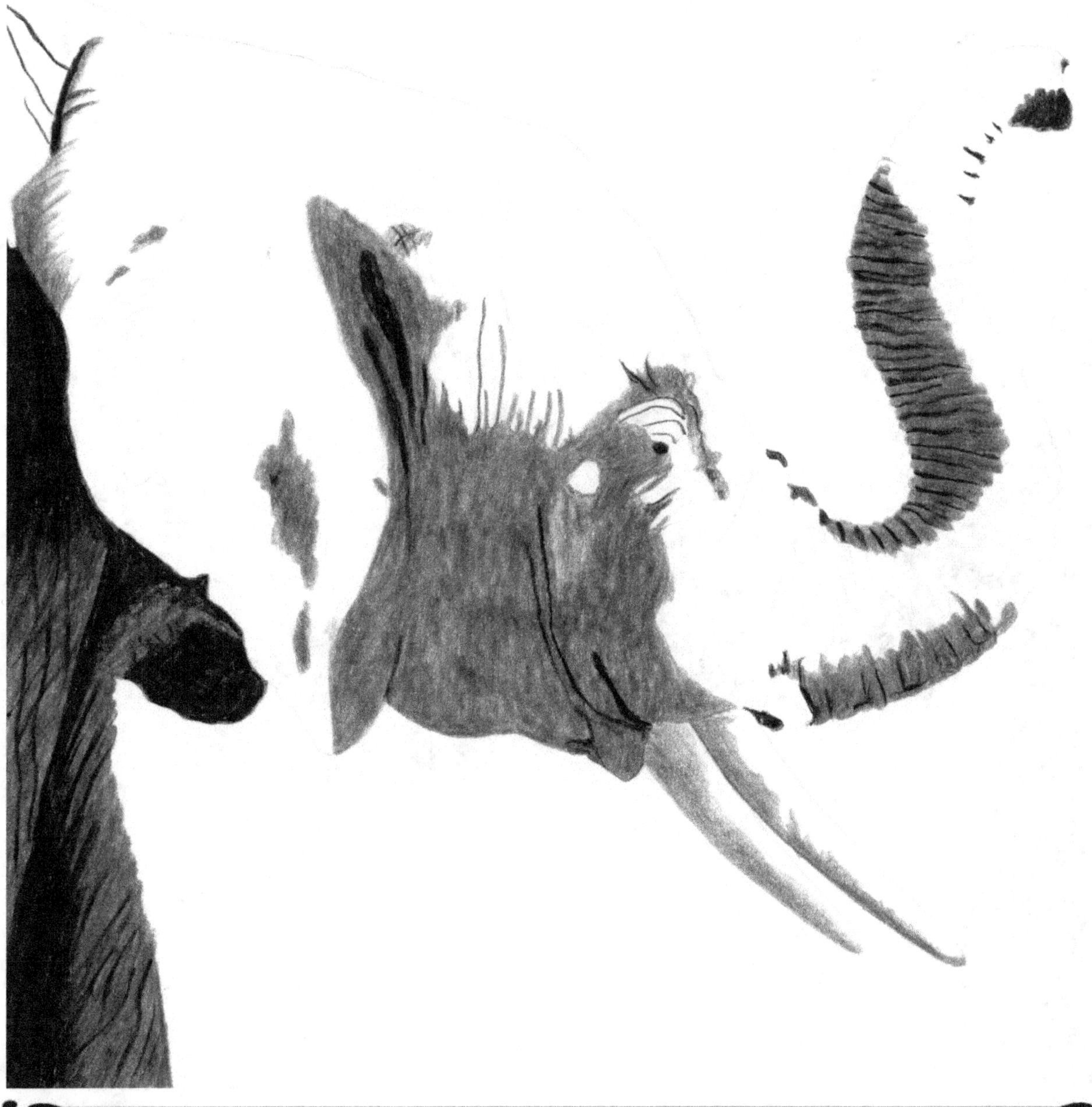

Applying Mid Tones

Moving on, use an HB pencil to shade the entire remaining area, following the direction of the wrinkles and textures. Be gentle with your strokes over the highlighted areas, applying lighter pressure. For areas that require a slightly darker touch, like wrinkles and certain sunken areas that were not meant to be shaded with a 2B pencil, apply a bit more pressure to the pencil.

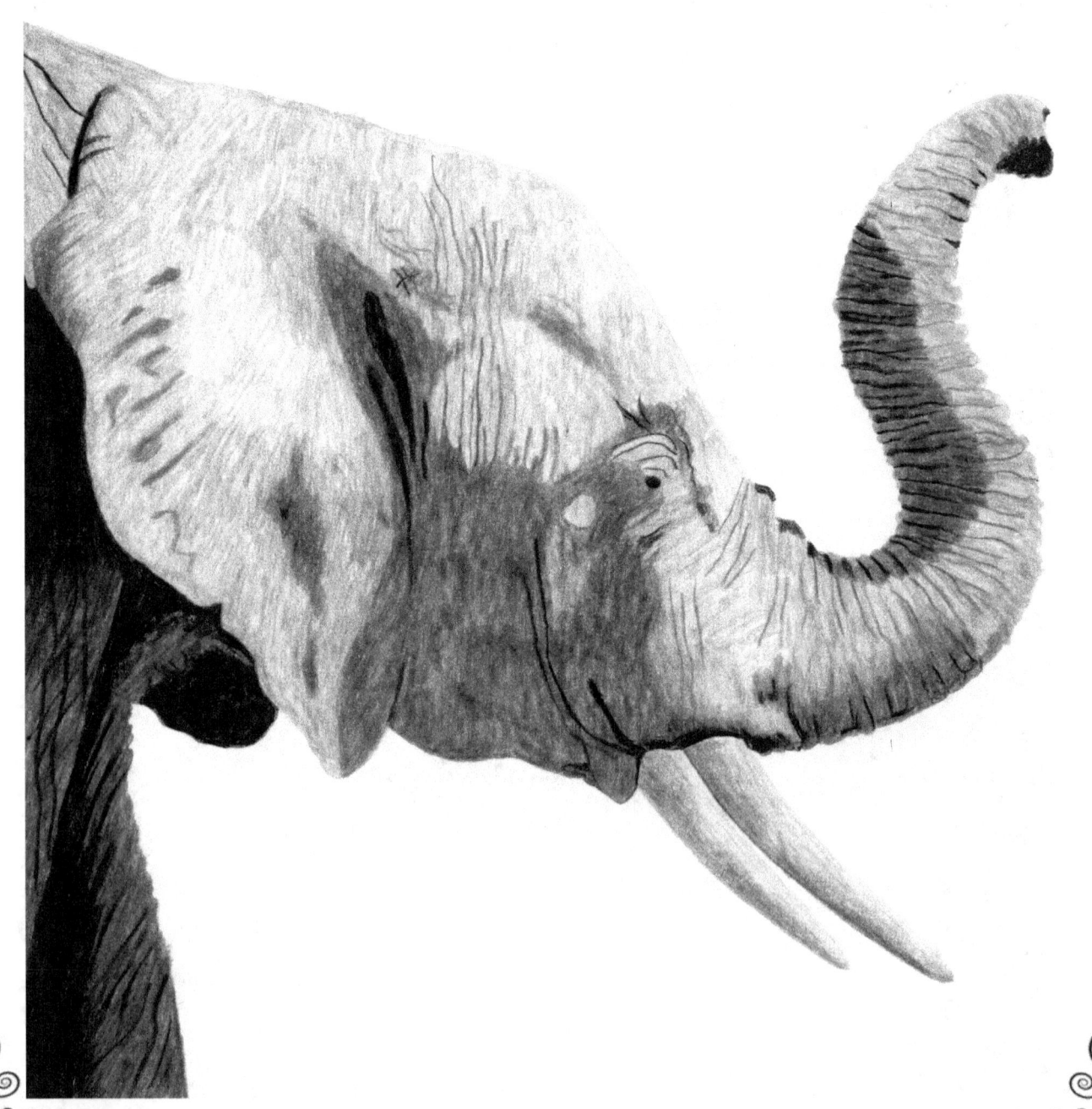

Blending the Mid Tones

In this step, take a tissue wrapped around your finger or a cotton pad and blend the entire area shaded with an HB pencil by applying firm pressure. This blending technique will impress the graphite into the fibers of the paper, resulting in a slightly darker and smoother appearance. For areas near the edges of the drawing, use a blending stump. If you accidentally applied graphite beyond the outline of the elephant and onto the background, use an eraser to carefully remove those unwanted marks.

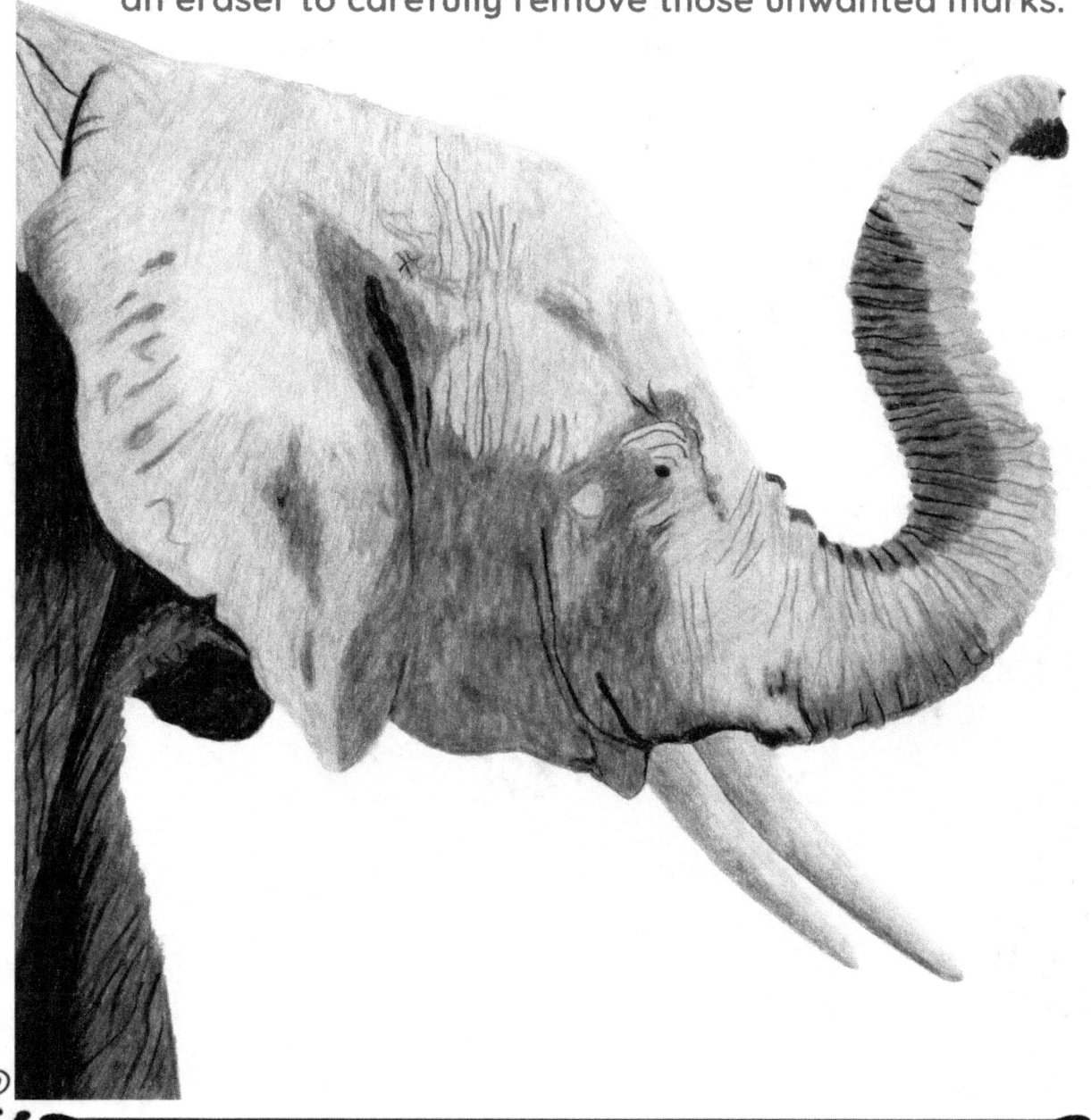

Detailing Shadowed Areas

Now, let's go back to the areas shaded with a 2B and create intricate wrinkles using a darker pencil such as 8B, 10B, or even 12B. When drawing wrinkles, apply firm pressure with the dark pencil to emphasize the deepest parts of the wrinkles. Gradually lessen the pressure as you shade away from the deepest point, allowing for a smooth transition between the darkest areas of the wrinkle and the basic shade of the surrounding area. This technique will create multiple shades inside the shadowed regions, which are essential for achieving a photorealistic effect.

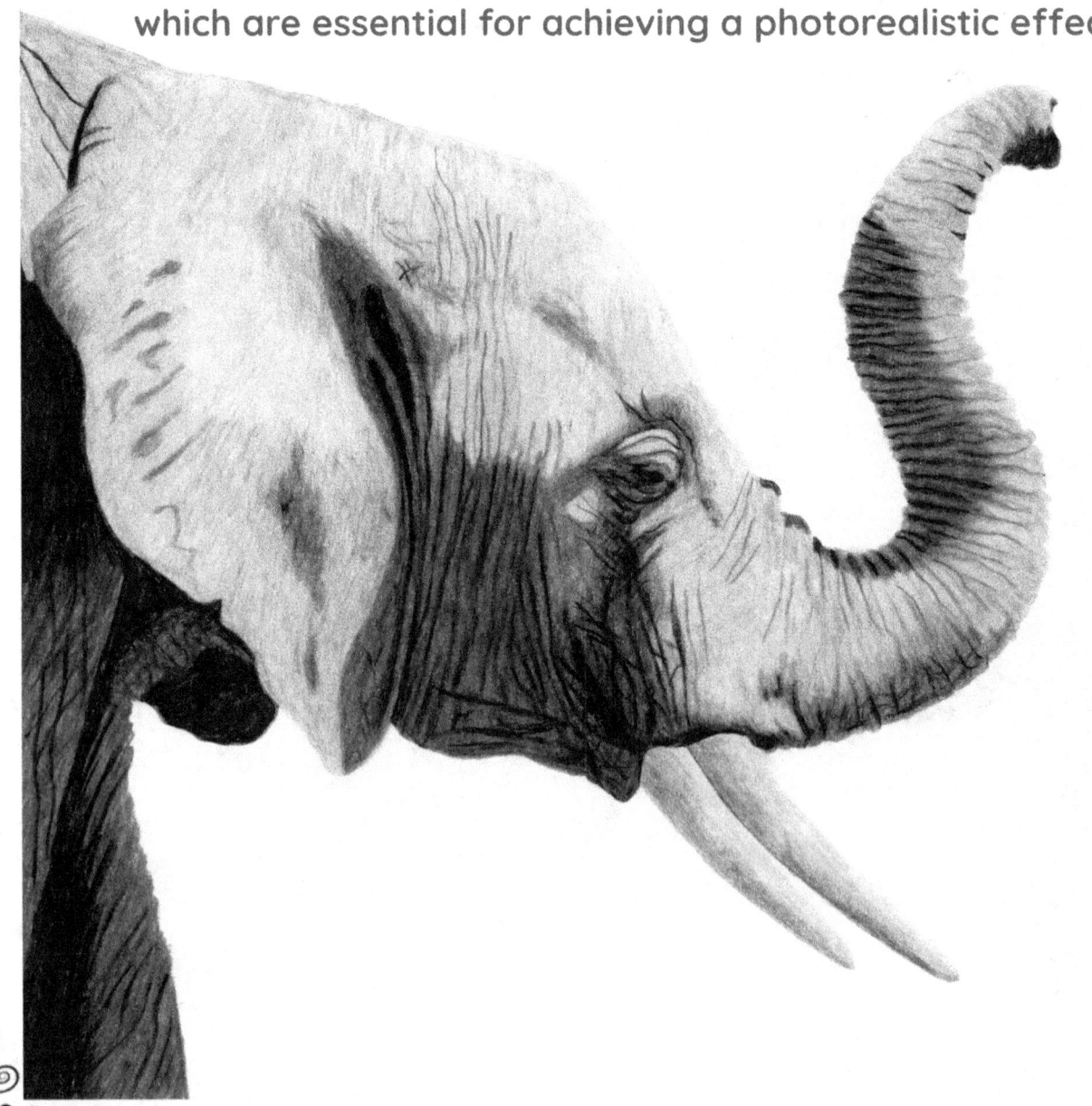

Creating Mid Tone Values

Using an HB pencil, intensify the areas over the mid tones that you've previously shaded with an HB and blended. Ensure that only the brightest highlights remain untouched. If you want them to be more prominent without making them lighter, just add shade around them. Vary your pencil pressure to generate a range of values, facilitating a seamless tonal progression between mid tones and highlights. Observe the specific sections of the ear where I've applied more shading and those I've intentionally left unshaded.

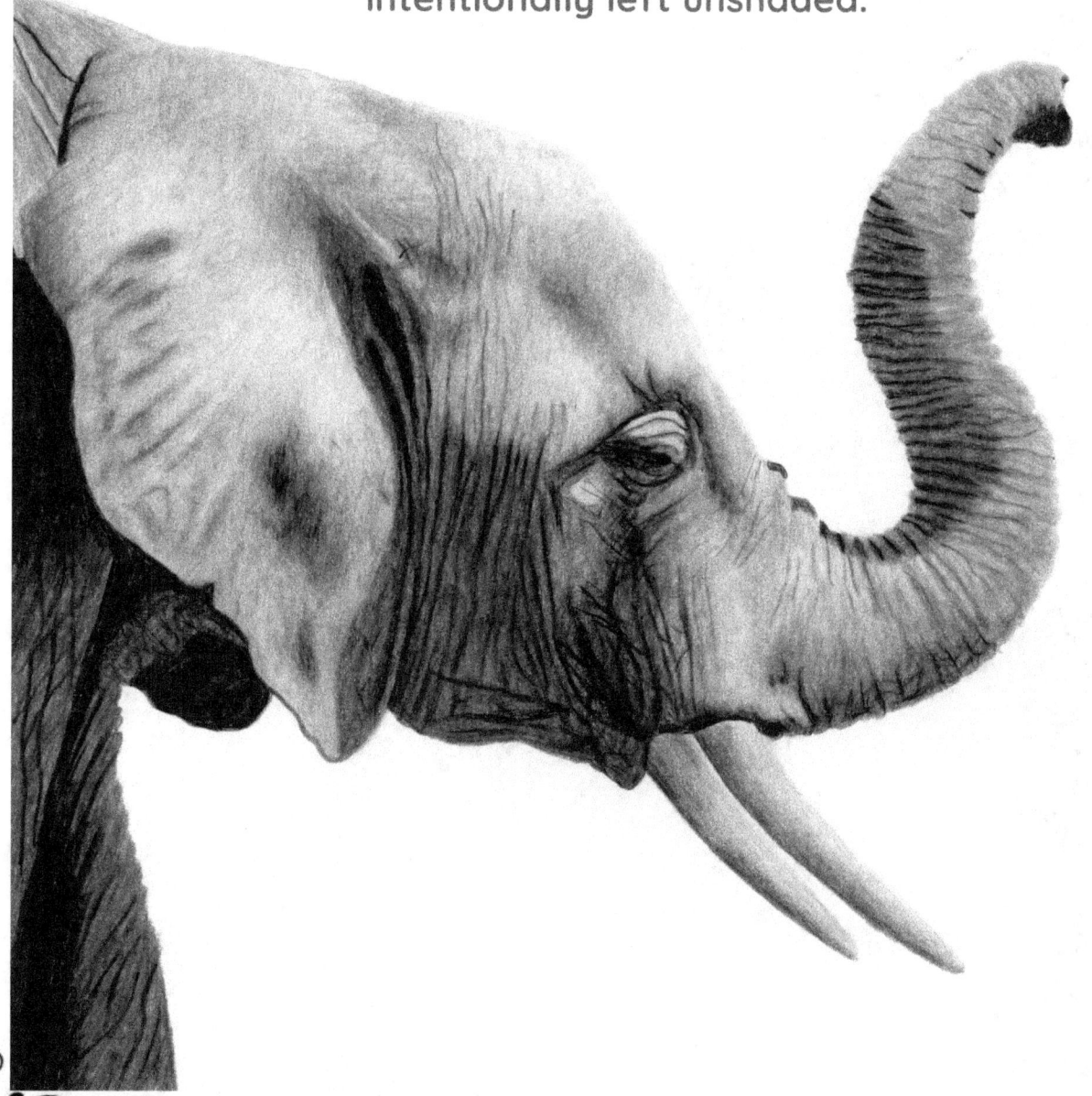

Adding the Wrinkles

With a 4B pencil, sketch the wrinkles across the HB-shaded region, including those above and under the eye, as well as along the entire trunk. While the wrinkles need not replicate the reference photo exactly, ensure that they follow the trunk's direction, contributing to its form.

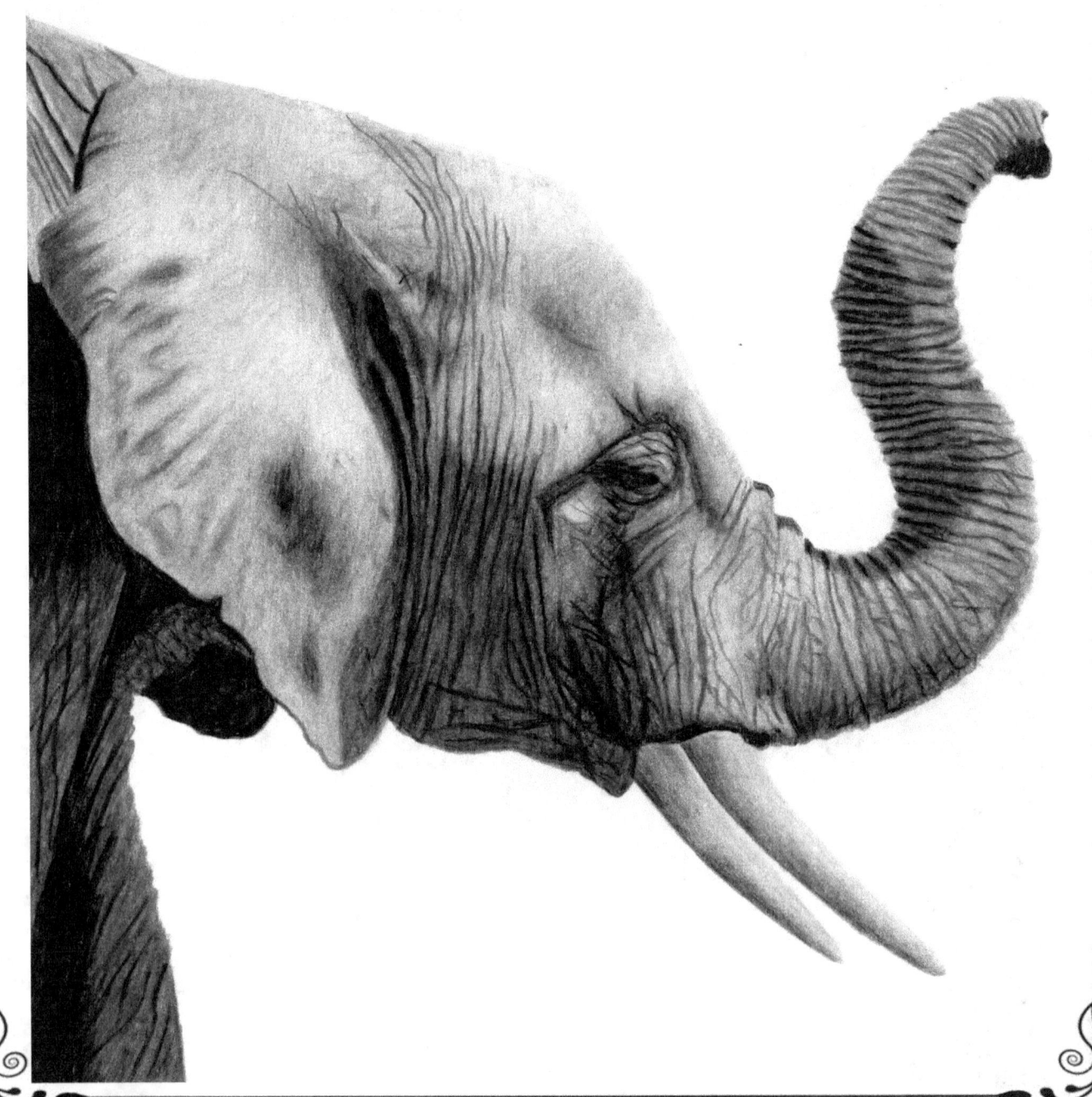

Softening the Wrinkles

Given that the wrinkles currently appear quite sharp and pronounced, it's necessary to soften them using a lighter pencil like HB. While a blending stump might not achieve the required darkness around the wrinkles, it remains crucial for blending these transitions smoothly.

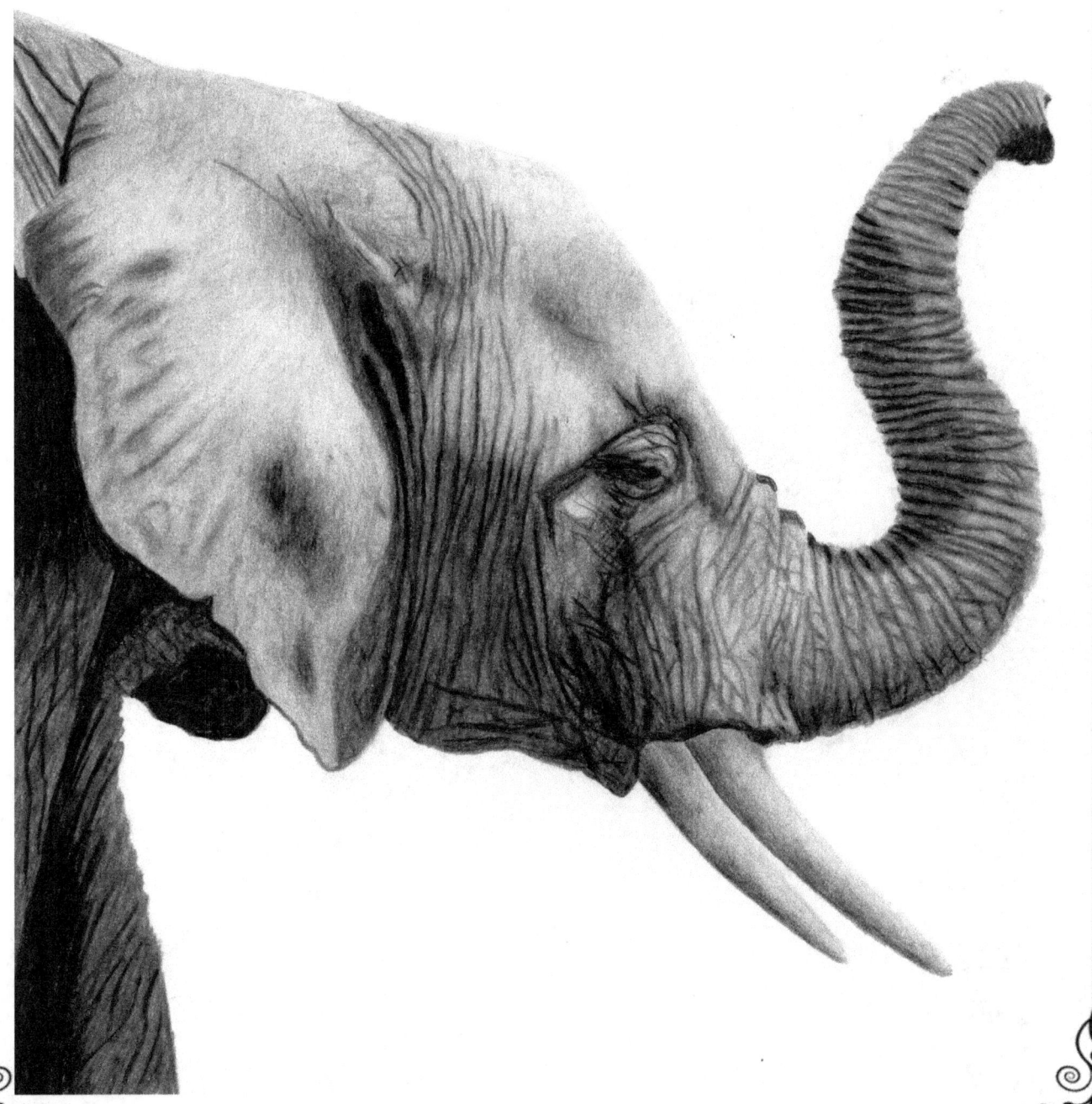

Details and Highlights

Conclude by incorporating any desired intricate details, like subtle imperfections and dirt akin to those evident in the reference photo or other areas of your choosing. Employ an eraser to craft highlights atop the protruding sections, thus completing the process.

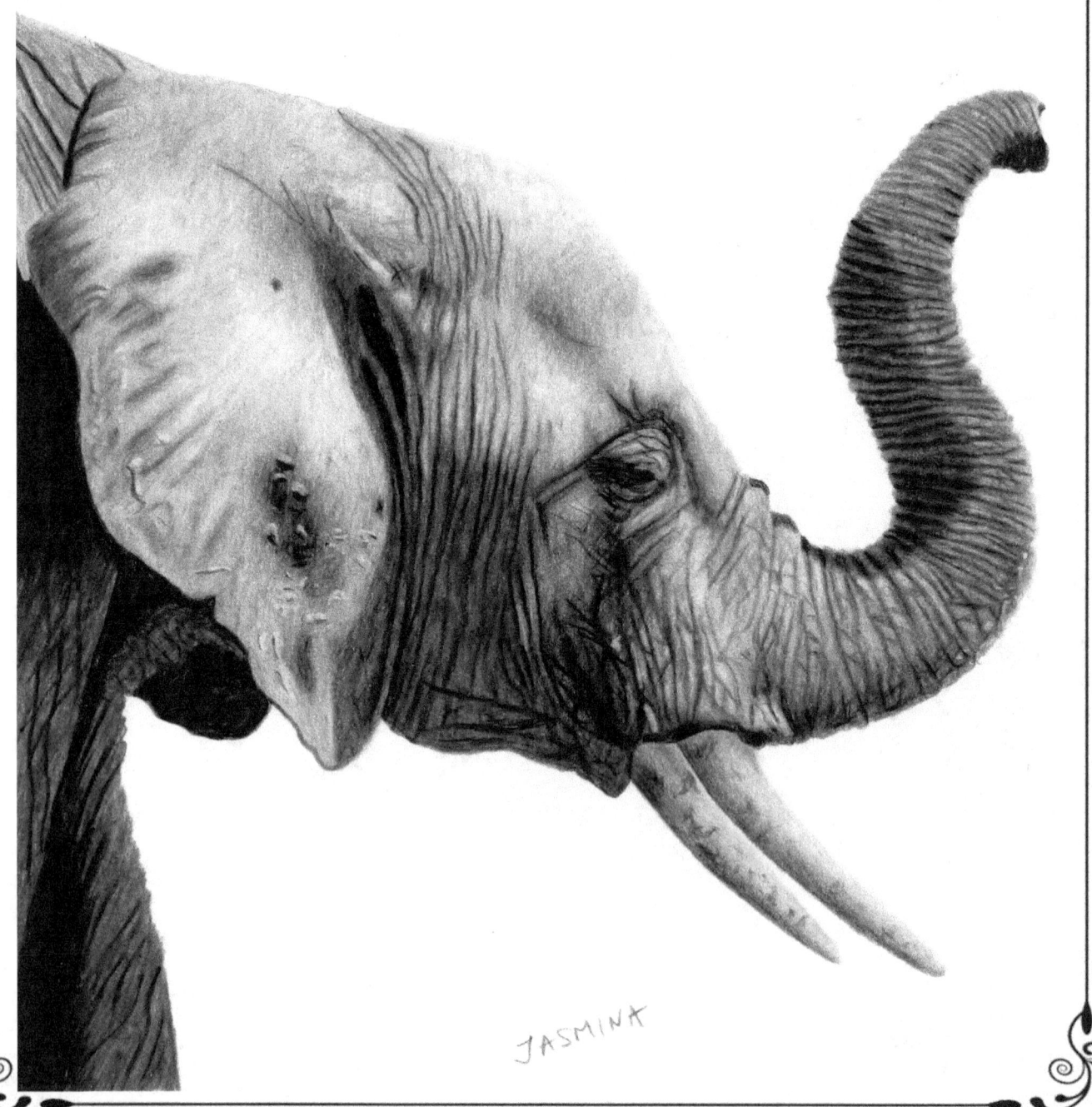

JASMINA

Drawing Interludes

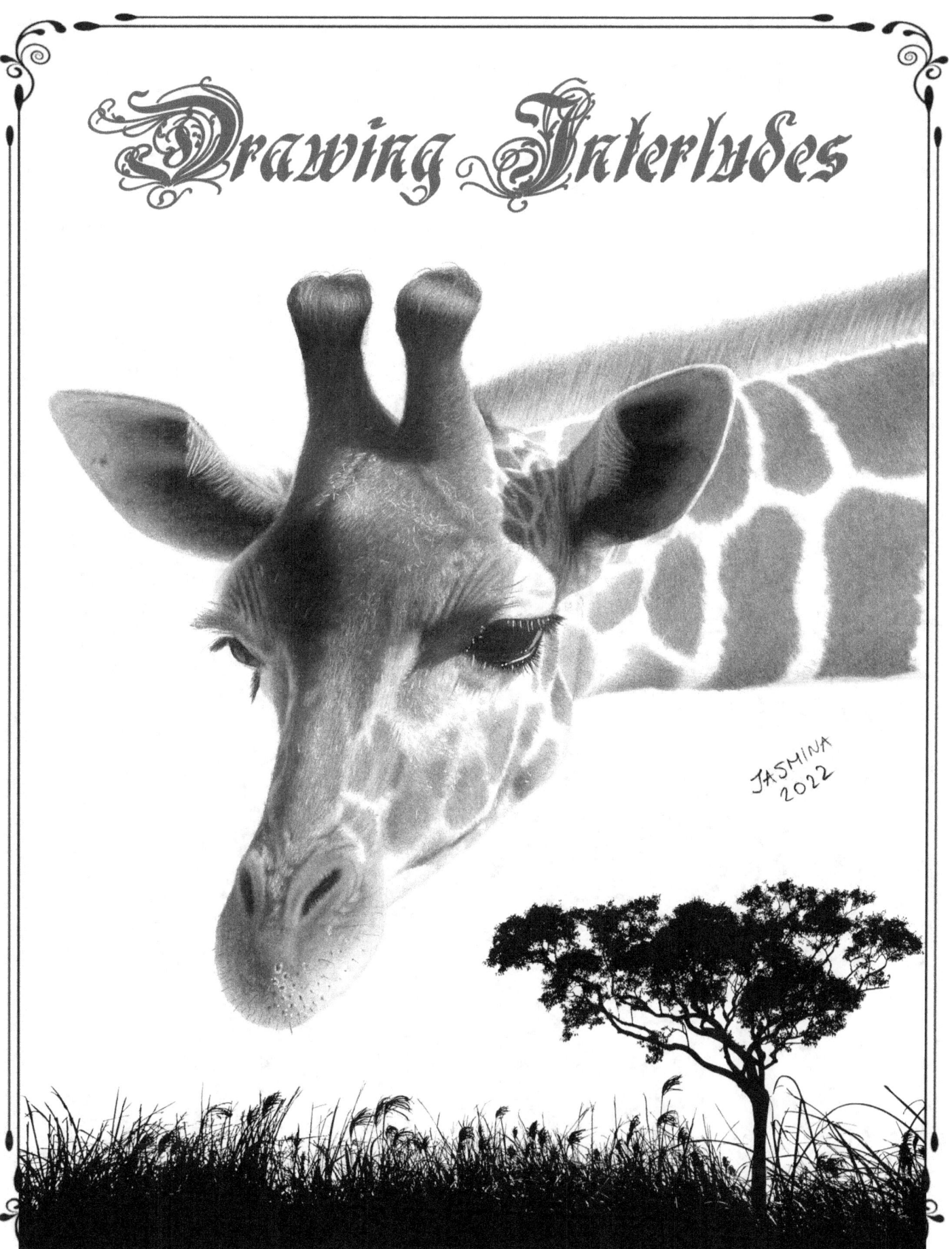

JASMINA
2022

How to Draw a Horse

Horses possess a grace and beauty that make them captivating subjects for artists. Their muscular forms, flowing manes, and expressive eyes provide a wealth of details to capture on paper.

The intricate textures of their coats, the play of light and shadow on their bodies, and the intricacies of their features provide valuable opportunities to practice shading, rendering, and capturing depth.

The Reference Photo

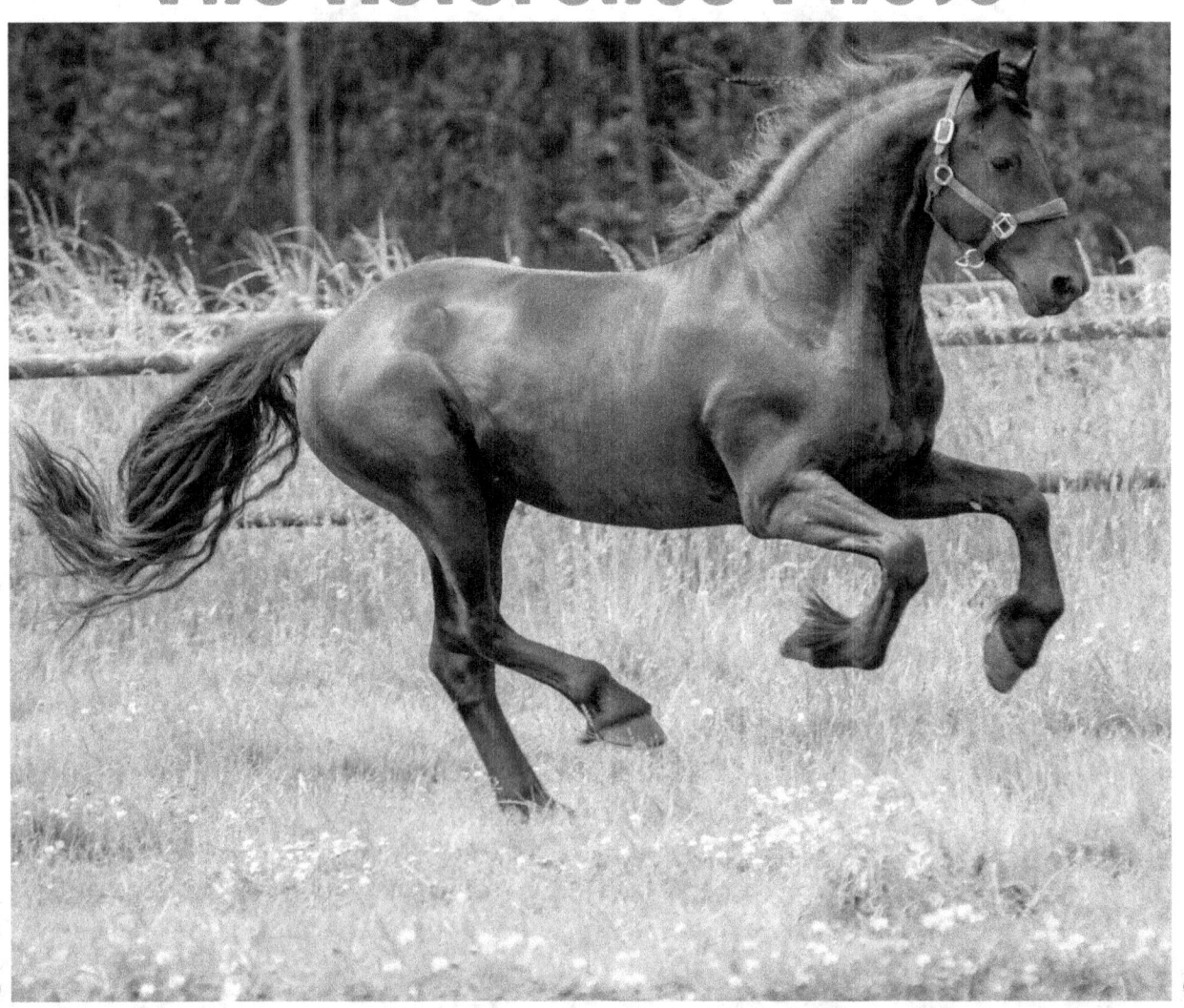

Sketching and Basic Shapes

In the initial stages, it's pivotal to set the groundwork for your drawing. I've strategically marked significant sketch lines that play a vital role: outlining the core body structure, earmarks, expressive eyes, flowing mane, and the subtle boundary separating shaded and illuminated sections. It's worth noting that these regions can be refined during shading and they don't need to align precisely with the reference photo. For instance, the Friesian horse breed's characteristic wavy tail and mane can be portrayed uniquely, allowing you to infuse your artistic vision into the representation.

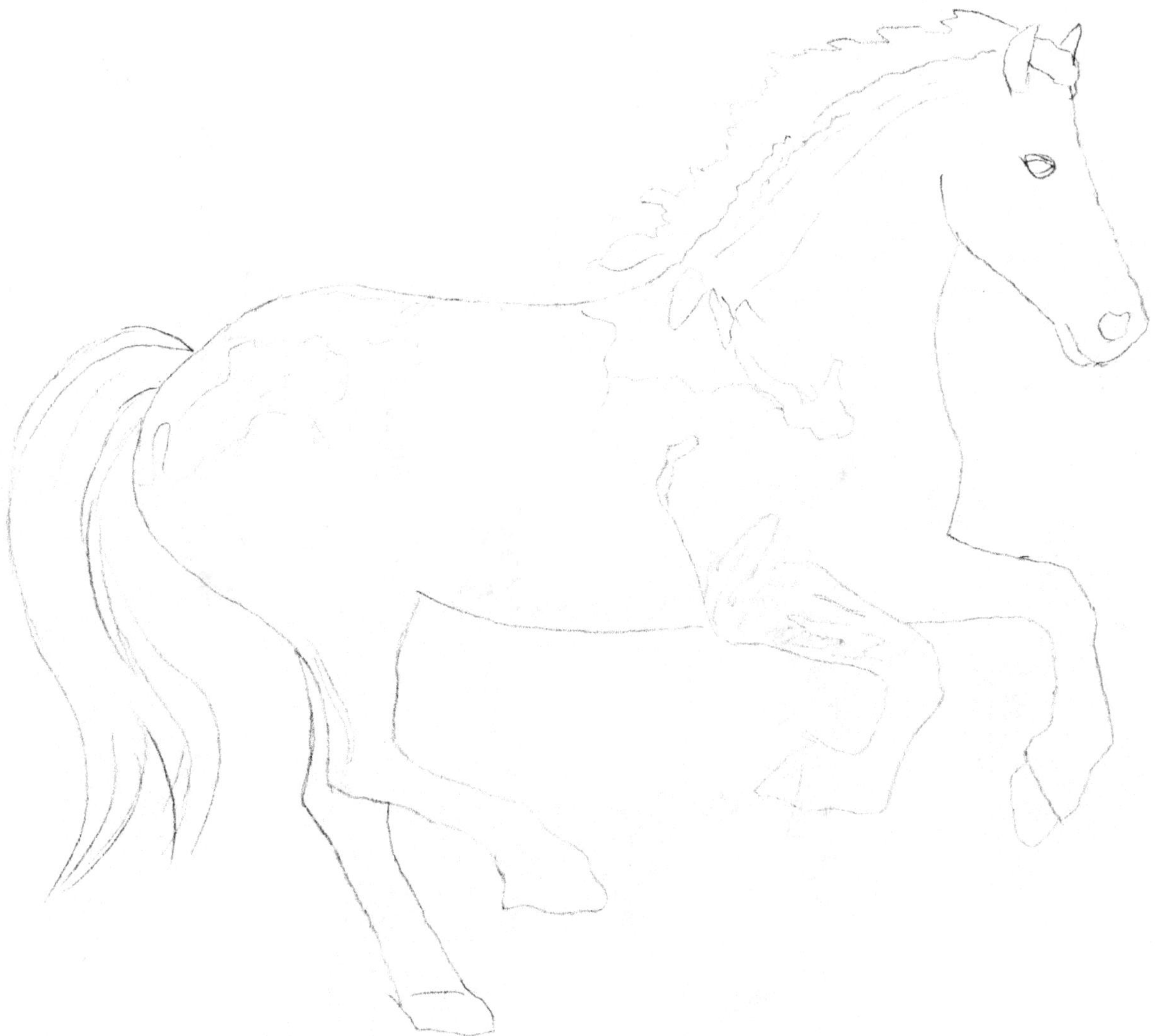

Defining the Deepest Shadows

Employing a 14B pencil, I've meticulously outlined the regions that remain shrouded in complete darkness – these encompass the shadowy expanses beneath the belly, neck, hip, eyes, and ears, among others. As you follow the visual cue provided in my subsequent step, remember to exert firm pressure with the pencil to capture the essence of a profound, velvety shade.

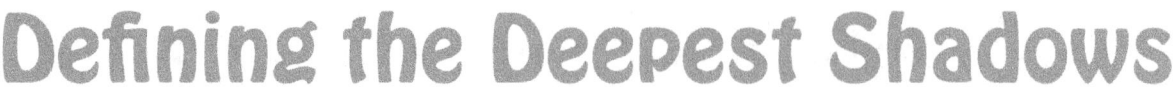

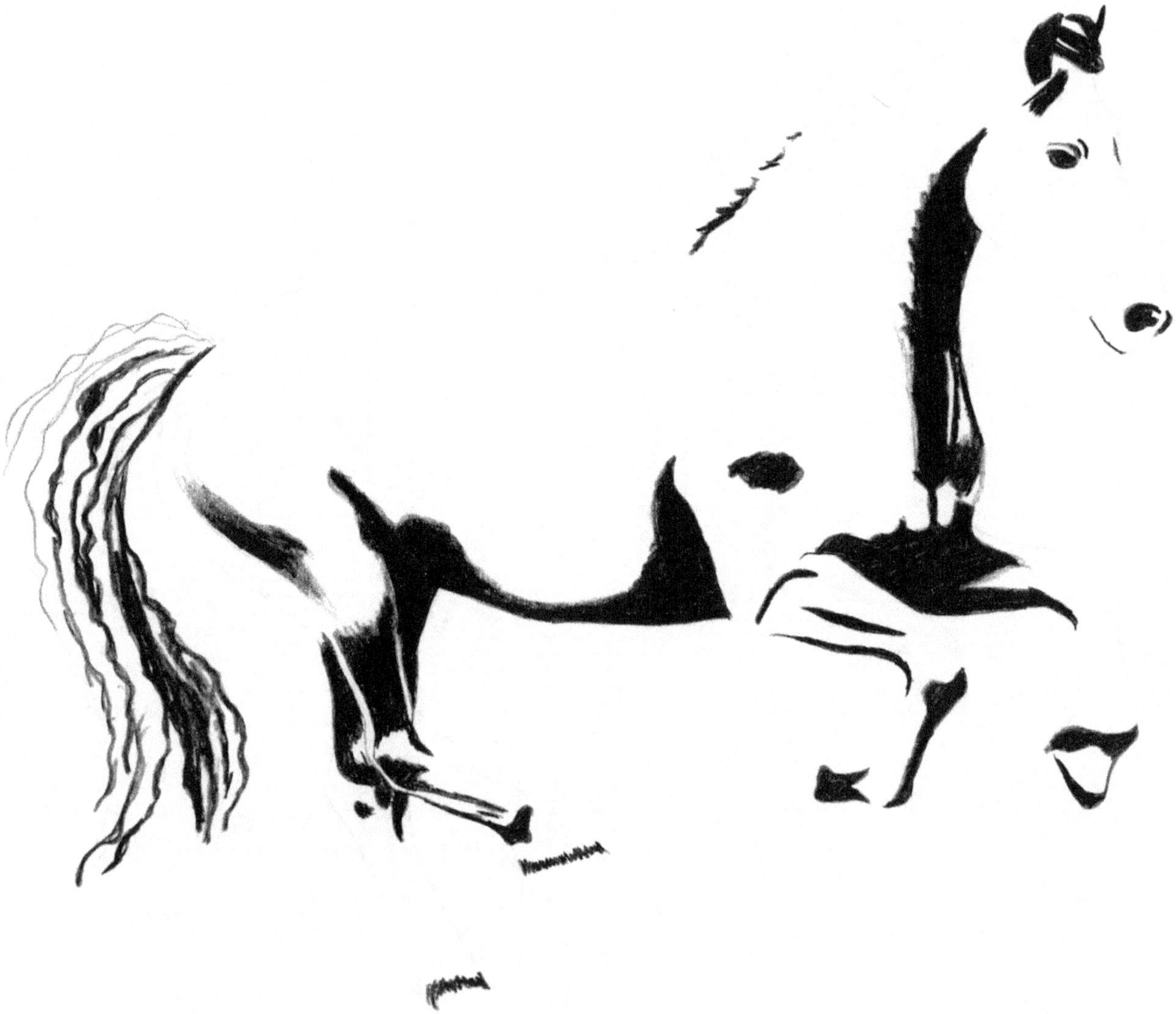

Isolating the Background

When pursuing the goal of reproducing the glossy and silky look of this particular horse breed, I recommend avoiding traditional pencil strokes. Instead, consider employing graphite powder to attain a refined and velvety texture. To do this, I've opted to use self-adhesive Frisket Masking Film, adhering it to my drawing paper. Following this, I meticulously used a precision knife to trace the outer contour of the horse. Subsequently, I peeled away the film portion covering the horse, allowing me to exclusively shade the body, head, and legs while leaving the background untouched.

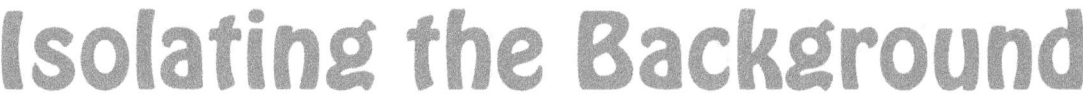

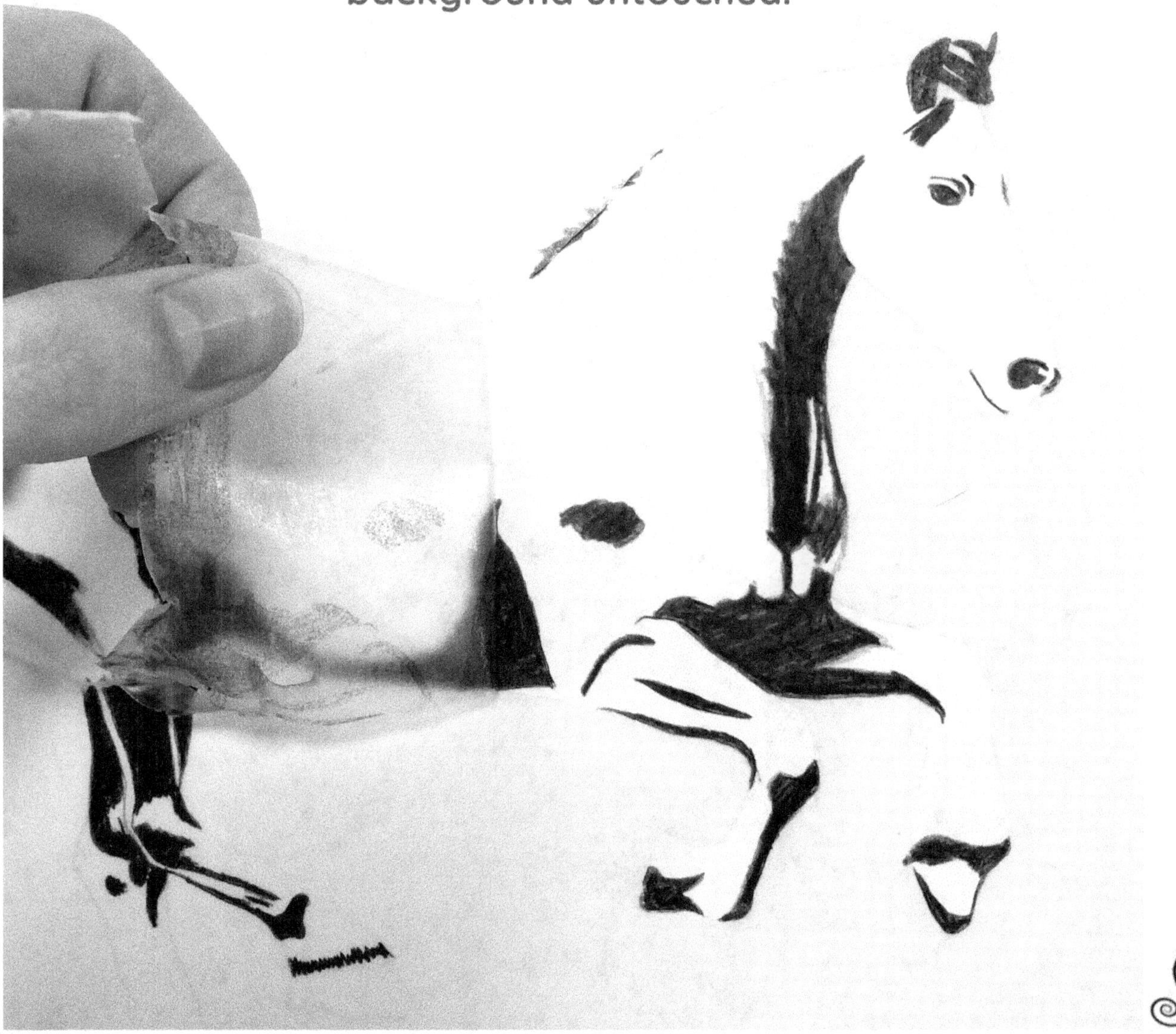

Introducing Graphite Powder

Let's delve into the application of graphite powder to shade the entire uncovered area. I opted for a B-grade graphite powder, generously applying more over the shadowed sections adjacent to the darkest parts rendered with a **14B** pencil. I find that using small circular motions with a tissue wrapped around my finger offers greater control. After loading your tissue with graphite powder, begin by targeting the darkest areas. Gradually shift your focus to mid-tones and highlights as the powder on your tissue diminishes.Keep in mind that the cotton pad/tissue might become quite dark and potentially smudge darker tones onto lighter areas. To prevent this, consider switching to a fresh cotton pad/tissue periodically. Referencing the provided image, you can observe the initial stages of applying graphite powder.

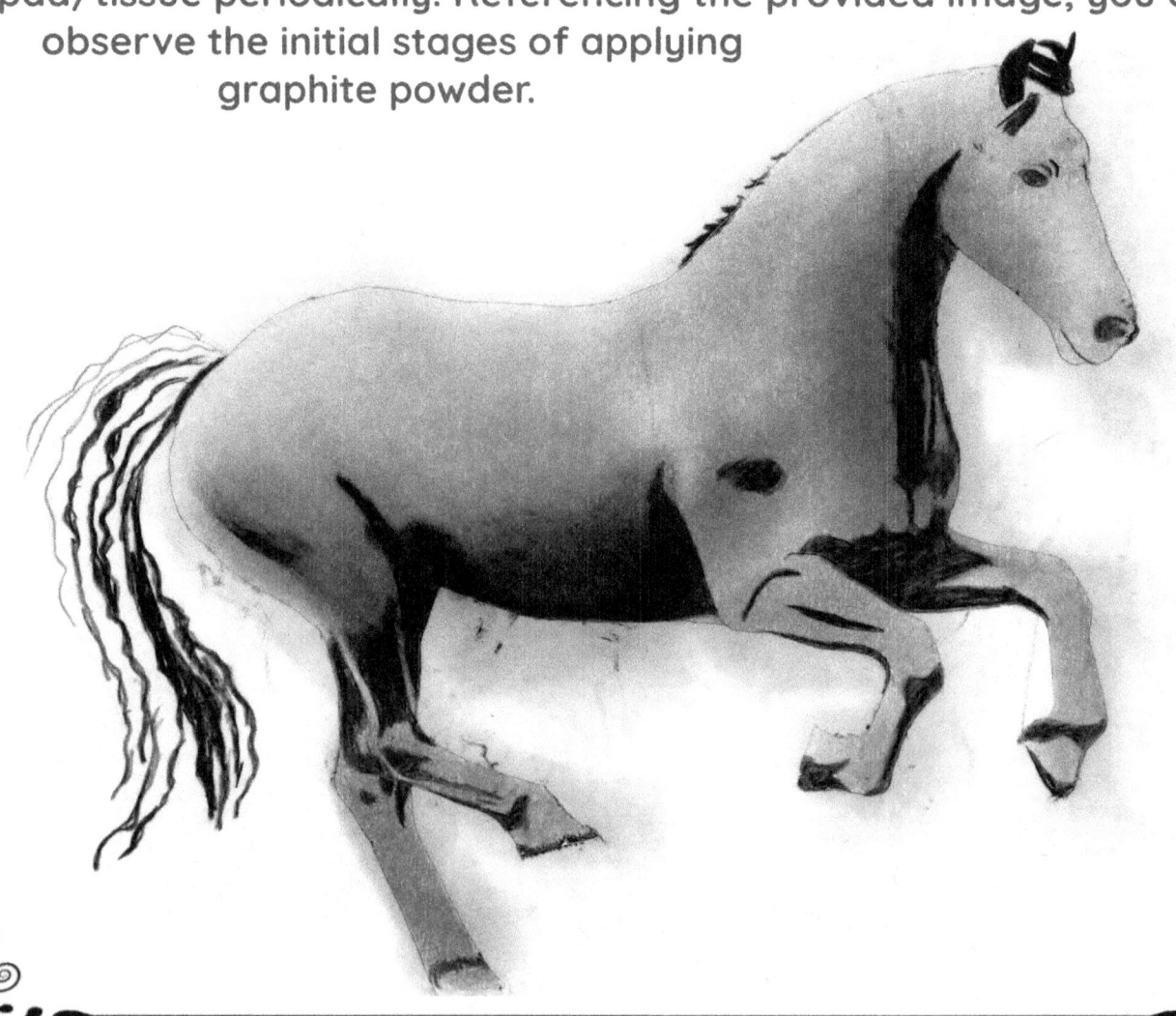

Switching to Darker Graphite

Next, let's use the graphite powder made out of darker shades such as 6B or darker. I created my graphite powder out of 14B Pitt Graphite Matt pencil because I didn't seem to find such graphite powder to purchase anywhere. So, the point was to use this graphite matt that doesn't reflect and shine as a common graphite. So, I rubbed this pencil onto the sandpaper to get that powder and applied it with a tissue over the areas that have to be very dark as seen in my image. Compare my previous image to this one to note the areas that are darker now. So, under the belly, the neck, and 3 legs that are in shadow etc.

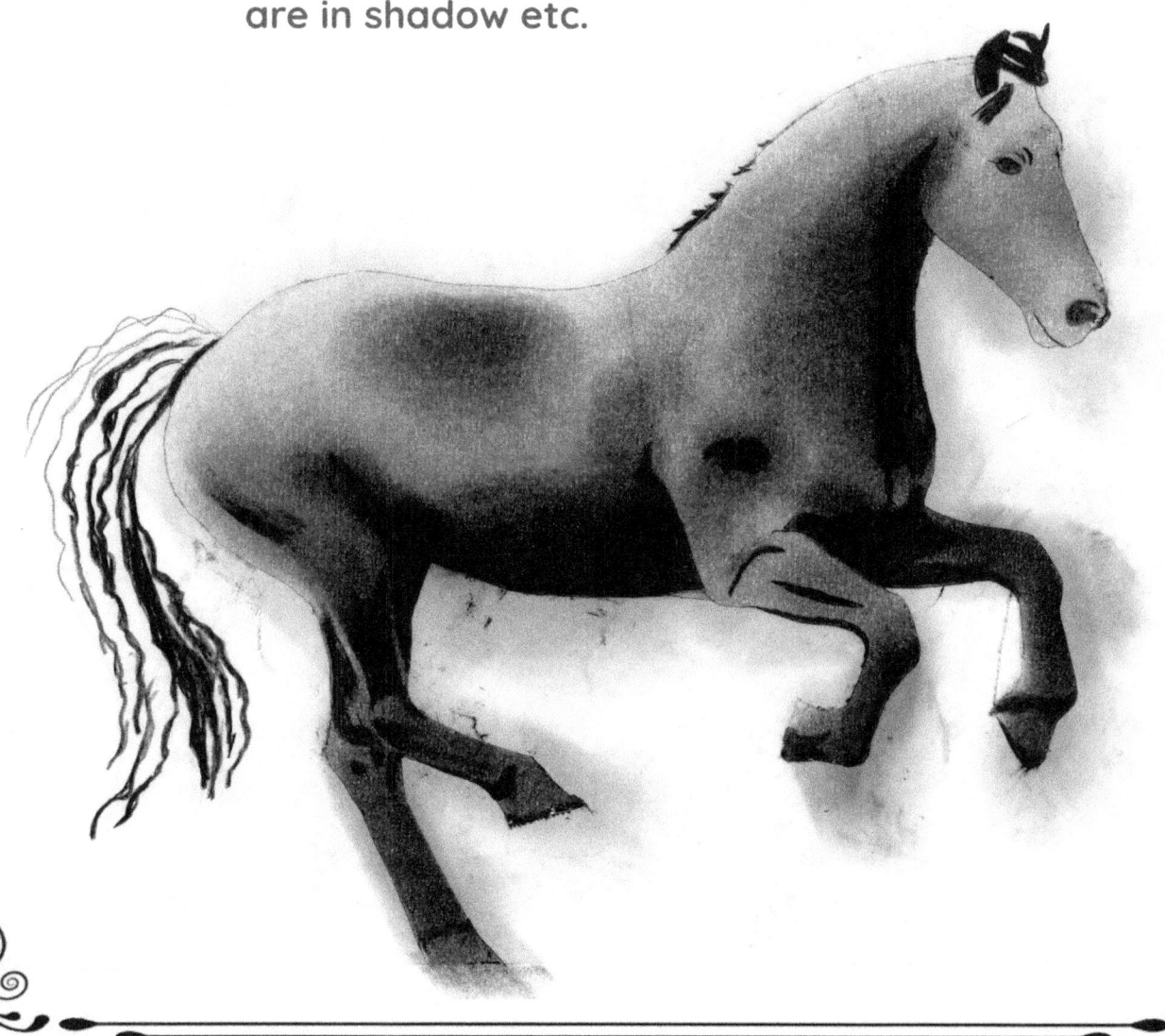

Refining with Graphite Powder

Moving forward, as I've realized that using a tissue is a bit unwieldy for the finer details I intend to shade with darker graphite, I've turned to a Q-tip and a blending stump for this purpose. I dip the tips of these tools into the graphite powder created from the 14B pencil residue on my sandpaper, resulting from rubbing the pencil onto it. This powdered graphite is then carefully applied to introduce subtle shadows within the intricate details. This approach is essential to ensure these details remain smooth, as they wouldn't appear as refined if drawn with a pencil. In this stage, I've extended the shading to encompass portions of the head and the area just beneath the highlight next to the mane. As you can observe, I've taken meticulous care to achieve even smoother shadowing all over the body. To enhance the effect, I've added additional layers of shading and meticulously smoothed them out, resulting in the seamless gradient of shading evident in this image.

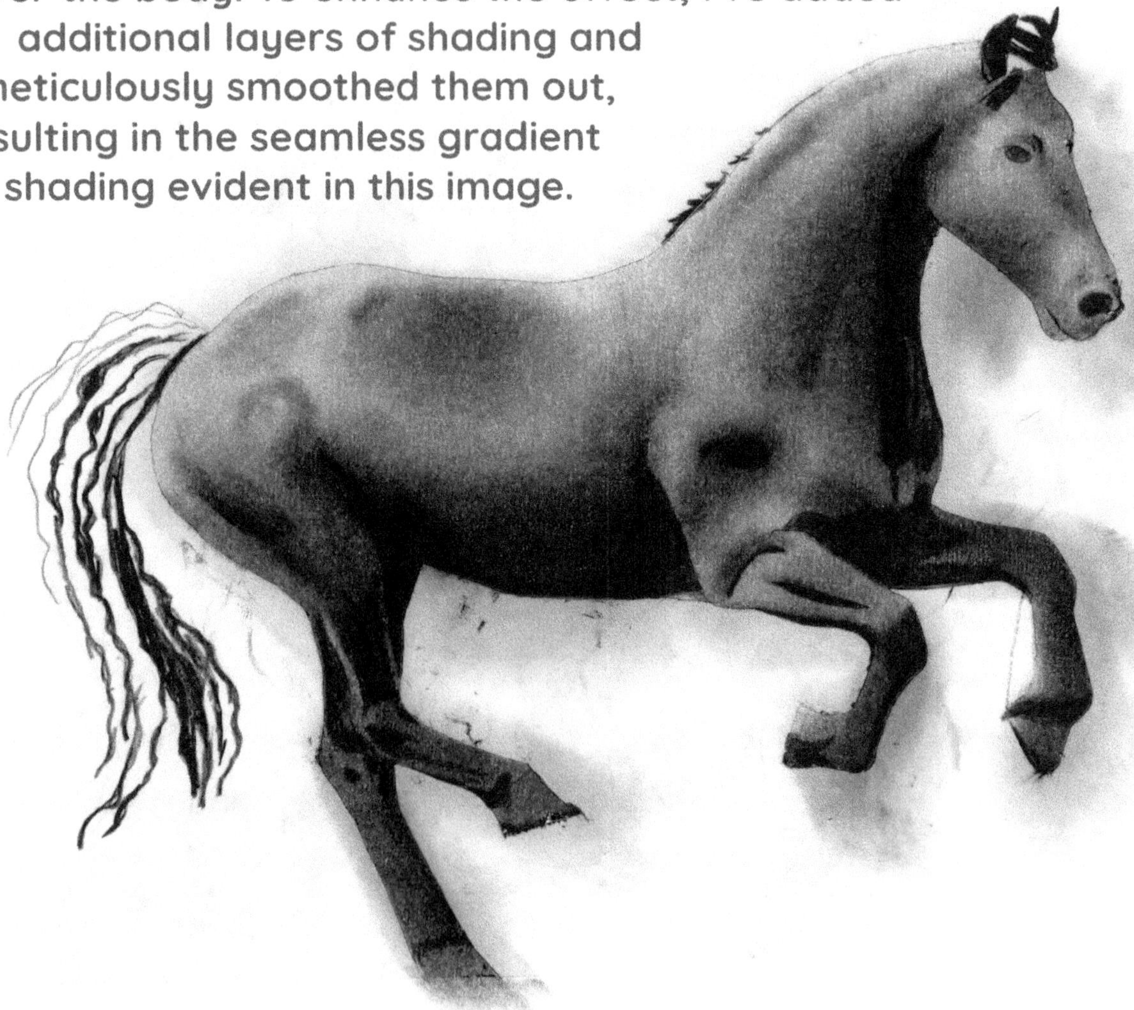

Developing Highlights

Domesticated horses boast a somewhat glossy coat, resulting in distinct highlights adorning their bodies. In this drawing, these highlights primarily grace the shoulders, hips, beneath the mane atop the neck, and one of the unshadowed legs. Let's employ an eraser to craft the necessary highlights. While a kneaded eraser might prove too soft, repeatedly lifting off graphite with it can achieve the desired effect. An electric eraser could risk over-erasing, though you can always reintroduce graphite to darken it. In my case, I opted for a mechanical eraser, providing finer control over the highlighting process. Feel free to experiment with various tools to determine your preference. Observe my image to witness how these highlighted areas imbue the horse with a radiant and sleek appearance.

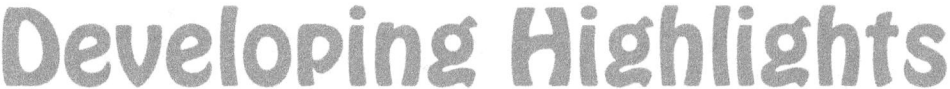

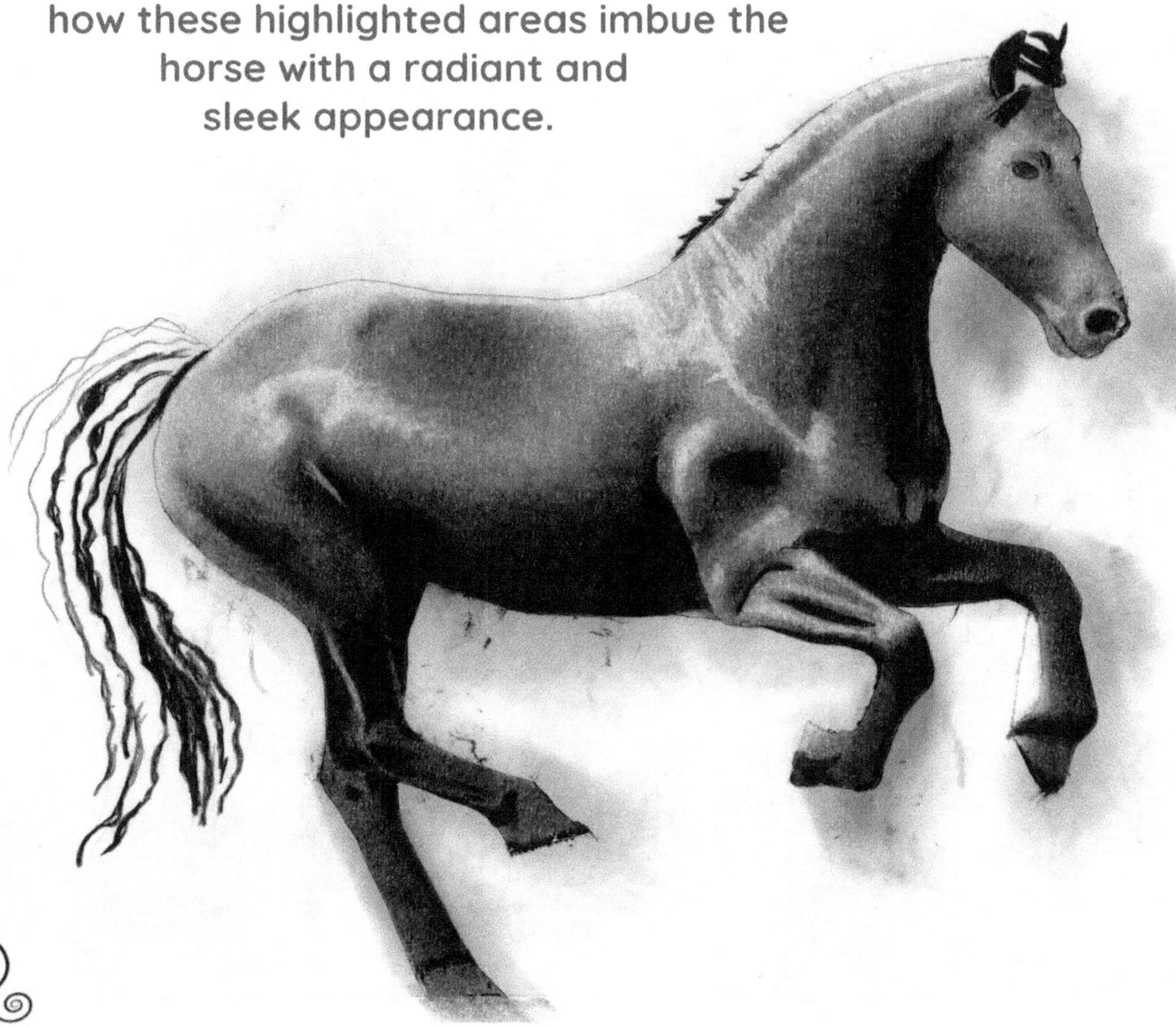

Refining with Subtle Shading

Continuing our progress, let's deepen the mid tones around these highlights to introduce more intricate details. I employed a blending stump, which I dipped into my B-grade graphite powder for this purpose. Notice that I also shaded the head, achieving a much darker appearance. In the reference photo, the face remains unilluminated, rendering the eye positions challenging to discern due to the overall darkness. Only the edge of the nostril should retain a hint of illumination.

During this step, I even utilized a pencil as soft as 12B to infuse additional detailing, subsequently smoothing them using a blending stump. You'll also observe delicate lines between the highlights; these depict the textured, wrinkled skin or coat. Don't overlook these nuanced details while applying them.

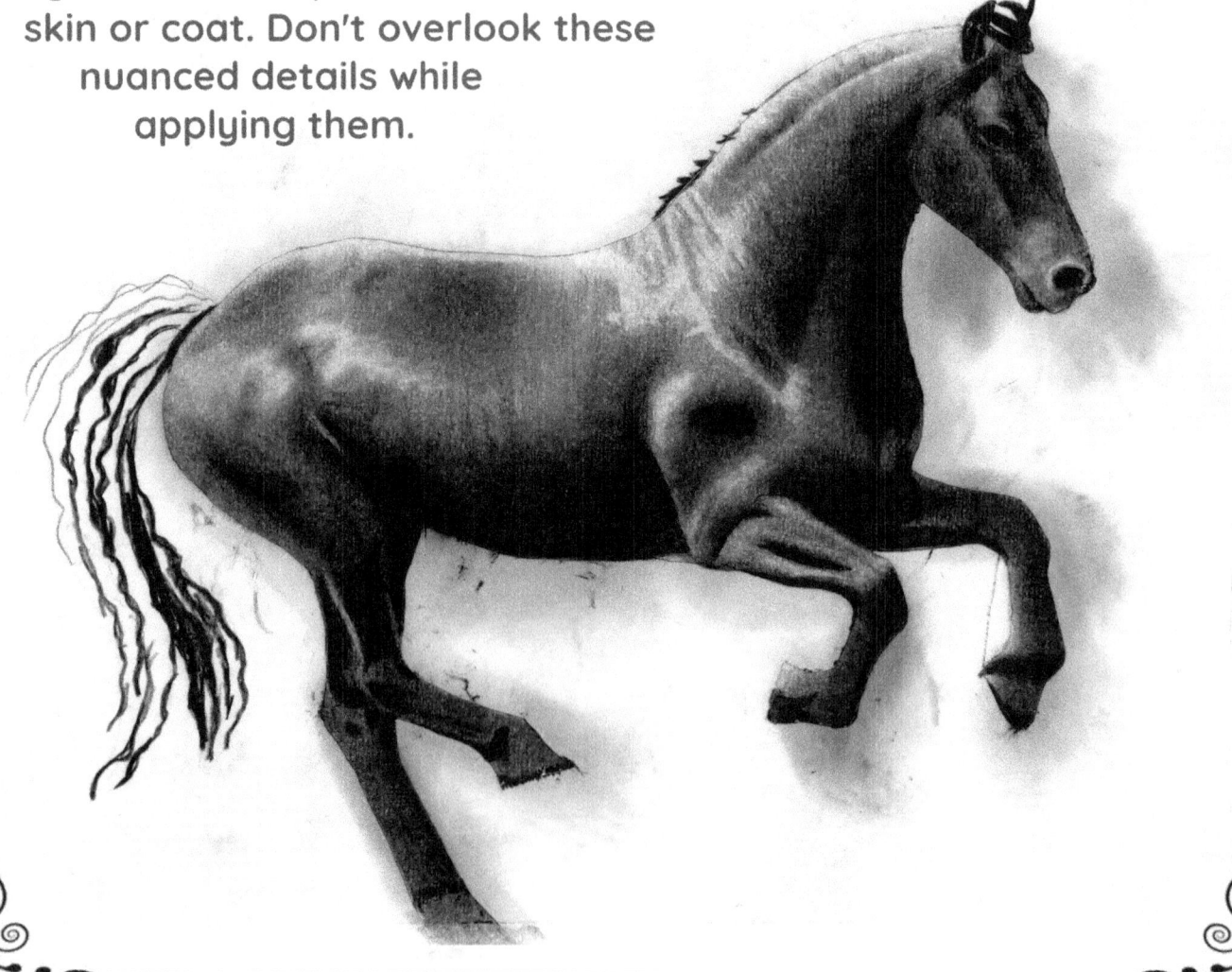

Removing the Masking Tape

Once you've completed the graphite powder application, it's time to carefully remove the Frisket Masking Film that was covering the background. While this doesn't signify the end of shading, the bulk of it is complete, and the protective covering can be safely removed. Be aware that areas like the mane and tail were intentionally left covered, as we'll now shift our focus to detailing them.

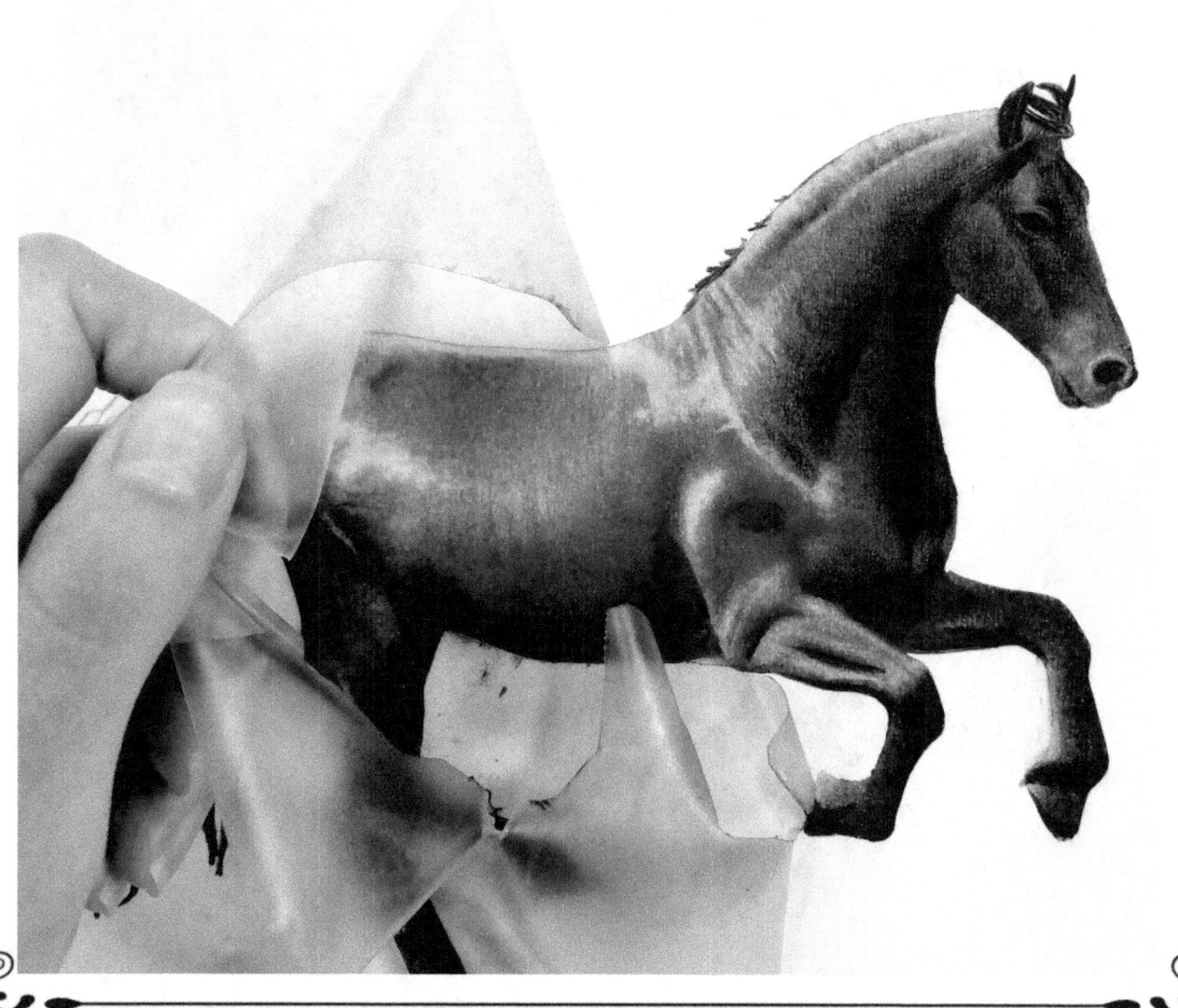

Revealing the Unmasked Horse

In this step, I present my scanned work without the masking film that previously covered the drawing paper. This reveals the strikingly sharp edges of the horse's outline that I managed to achieve. While this tape technique may not be necessary when focusing on background shading or creating a landscape, it allowed me to concentrate exclusively on the horse. This contrast highlights the depth of the shades I've established when compared to the blank background.

Furthermore, I encourage you to consider this concept. Once you complete this horse, you can experiment by placing it within an environment, such as a grassy field with a horizon line in the center. You can gently shade the sky using graphite powder as well.

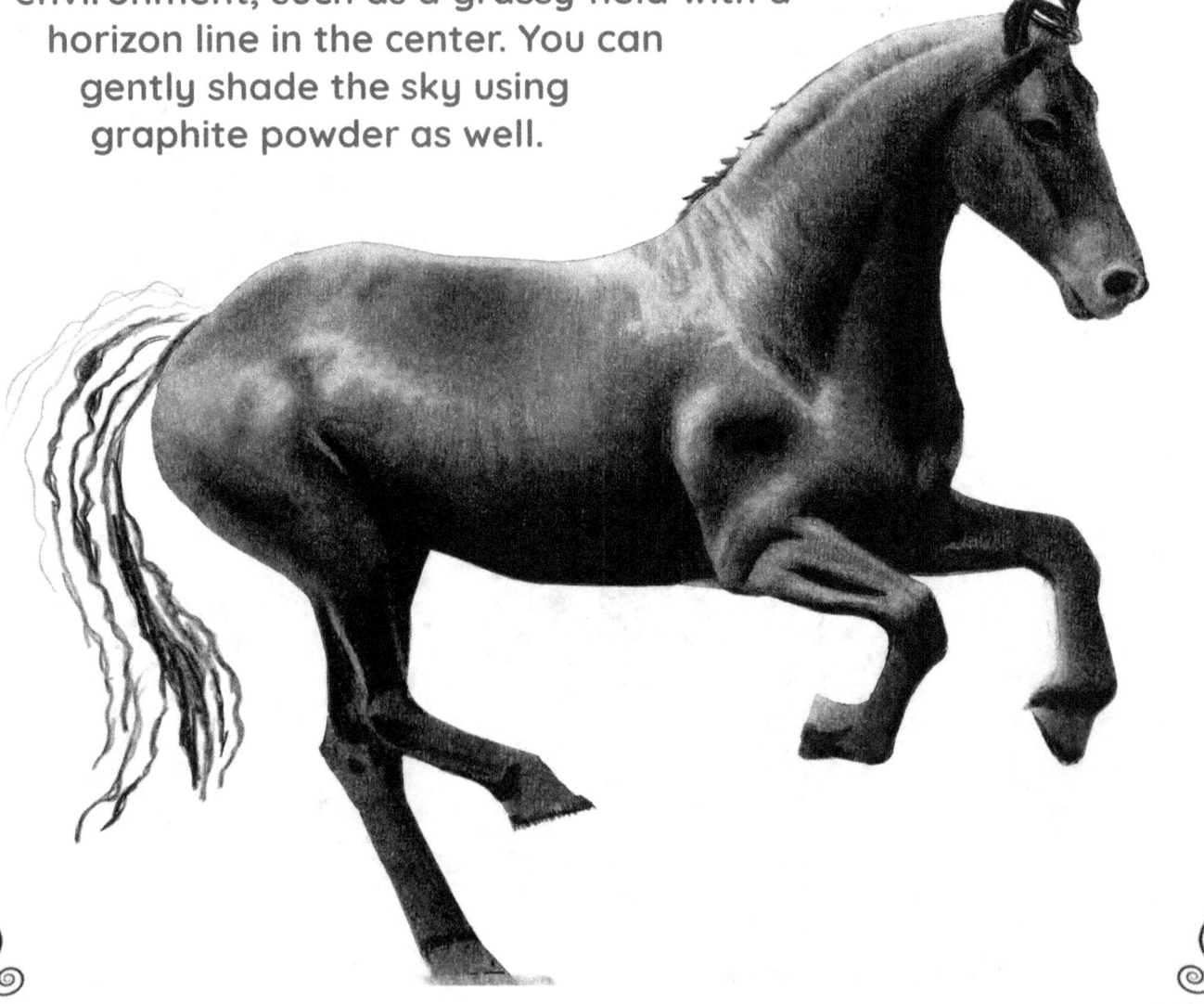

Crafting the Mane and Tail

Using a 6B pencil, I carefully drew the darker strands of hair along the horse's neck. As I completed each stroke, I gradually lifted the pencil to create a soft transition into highlights. On the opposite side of these highlights, I added more hairlines with a touch of randomness for a natural look.

For the tail's shading, I aimed to capture its flowing texture by carefully shaping the hairs with varying degrees of darkness and softness. I also added a sense of spontaneity by creating waves and curls in some of the strands.

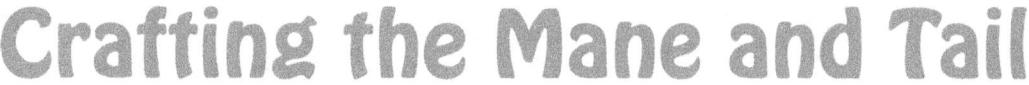

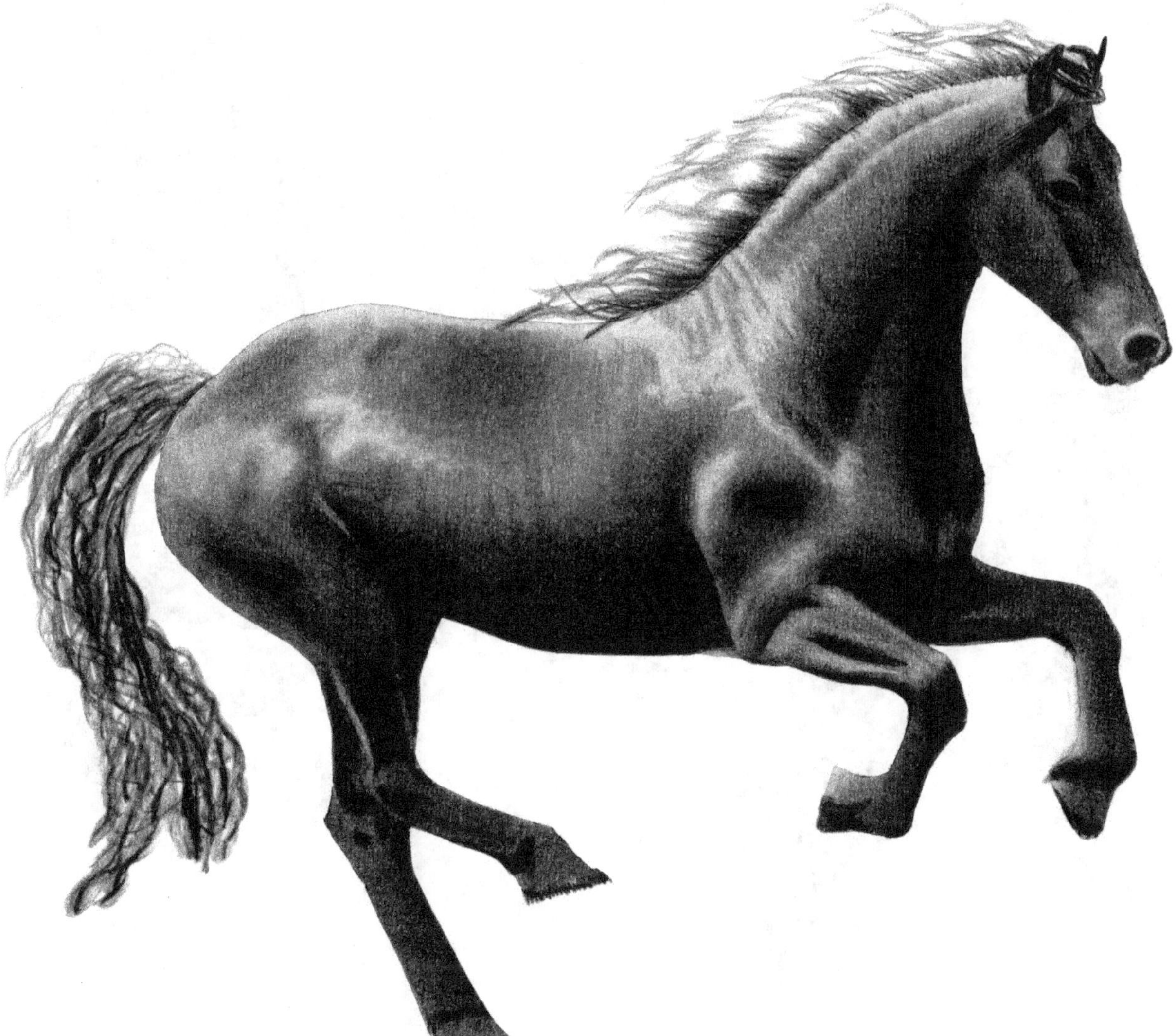

Refining Highlights and Blending

Continuing with the mane, delicately sketch over the highlighted areas using an HB pencil, carefully following the natural flow of the hair. Transitioning to the rest of the tail, apply shading using the same HB pencil. To achieve a seamless blend between these tones, gently use a Q-tip or blending stump to soften and merge the graphite on the paper. This process will give the mane and tail a more unified and polished appearance.

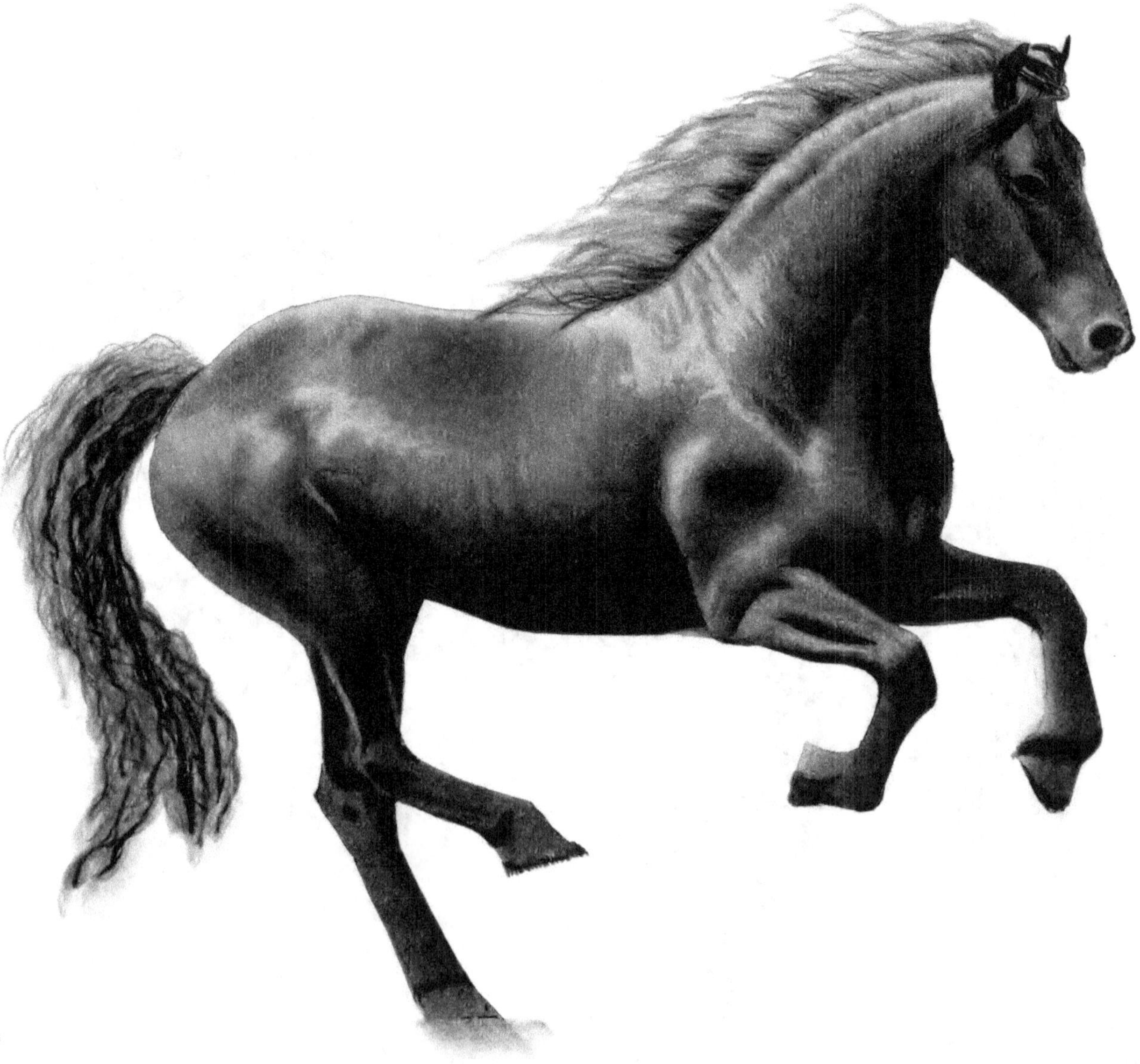

Adding Flyaways

With a finely sharpened 10B pencil, introduce random and confident strokes to both the tail and mane, lending them a more natural appearance. Feel free to vary the strokes, introducing occasional waves, and afterward, lightly blend them using a blending stump.

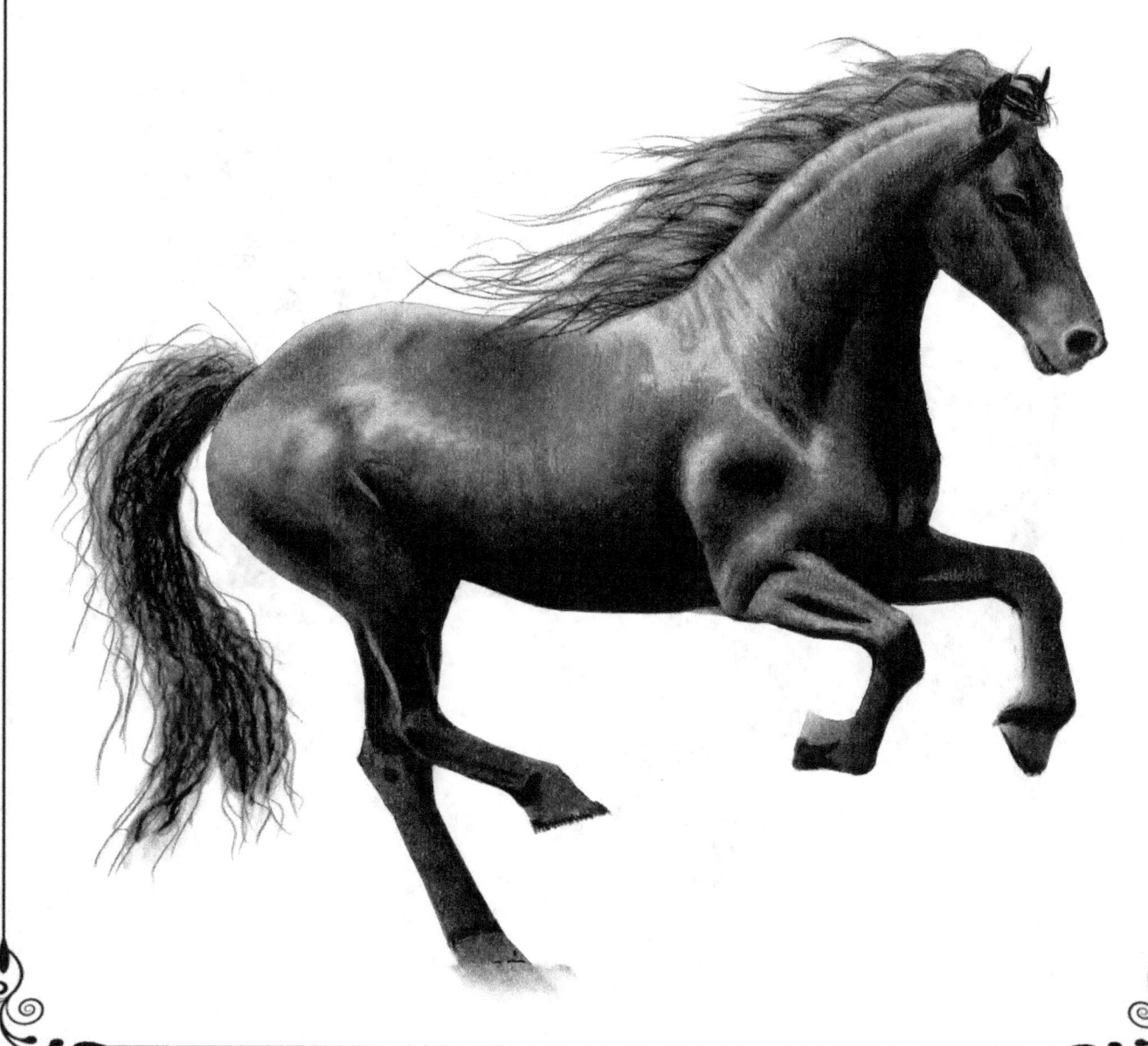

Drawing the Hooves

With an 8B pencil, apply shading to the hooves, and utilize a 2B pencil in the center to give them a rounded appearance. Study the provided step for a clear understanding of the technique. Afterward, use a blending stump to achieve a seamless blend of these shaded areas.

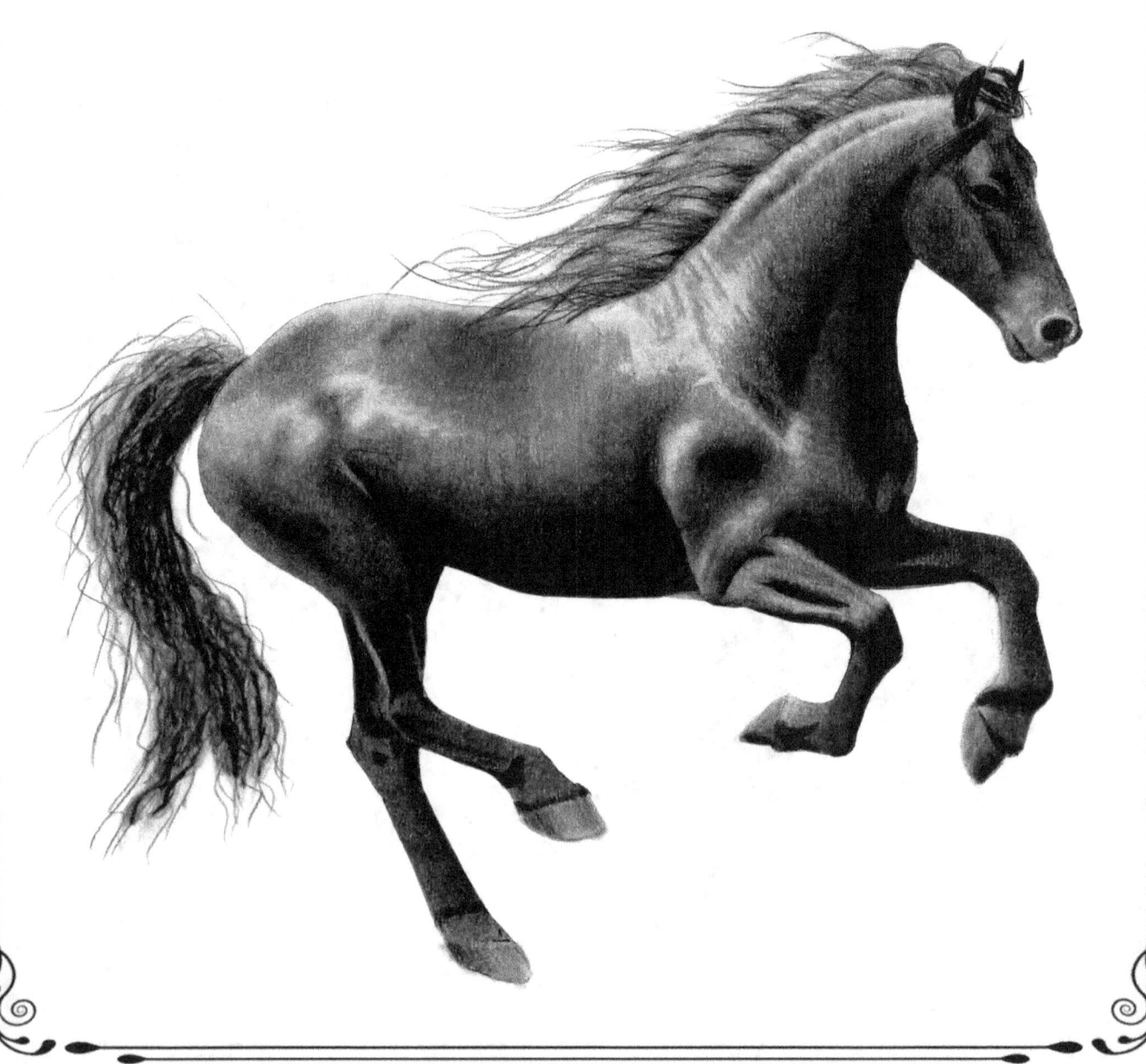

Enhancing Feather Texture

The next step involves using a 12B pencil to draw short, quick strokes that follow the flow of the feathers, as depicted in the reference photo. Once these strokes are in place, blend them with a colorless blender like the Prismacolor Premier. To achieve a fluffier appearance, position the tip of the blender over the ends of the strokes and move it outwards in a continuous manner. If you don't have a colorless blender, you can use an HB pencil, as its lighter shade can create a similar effect.

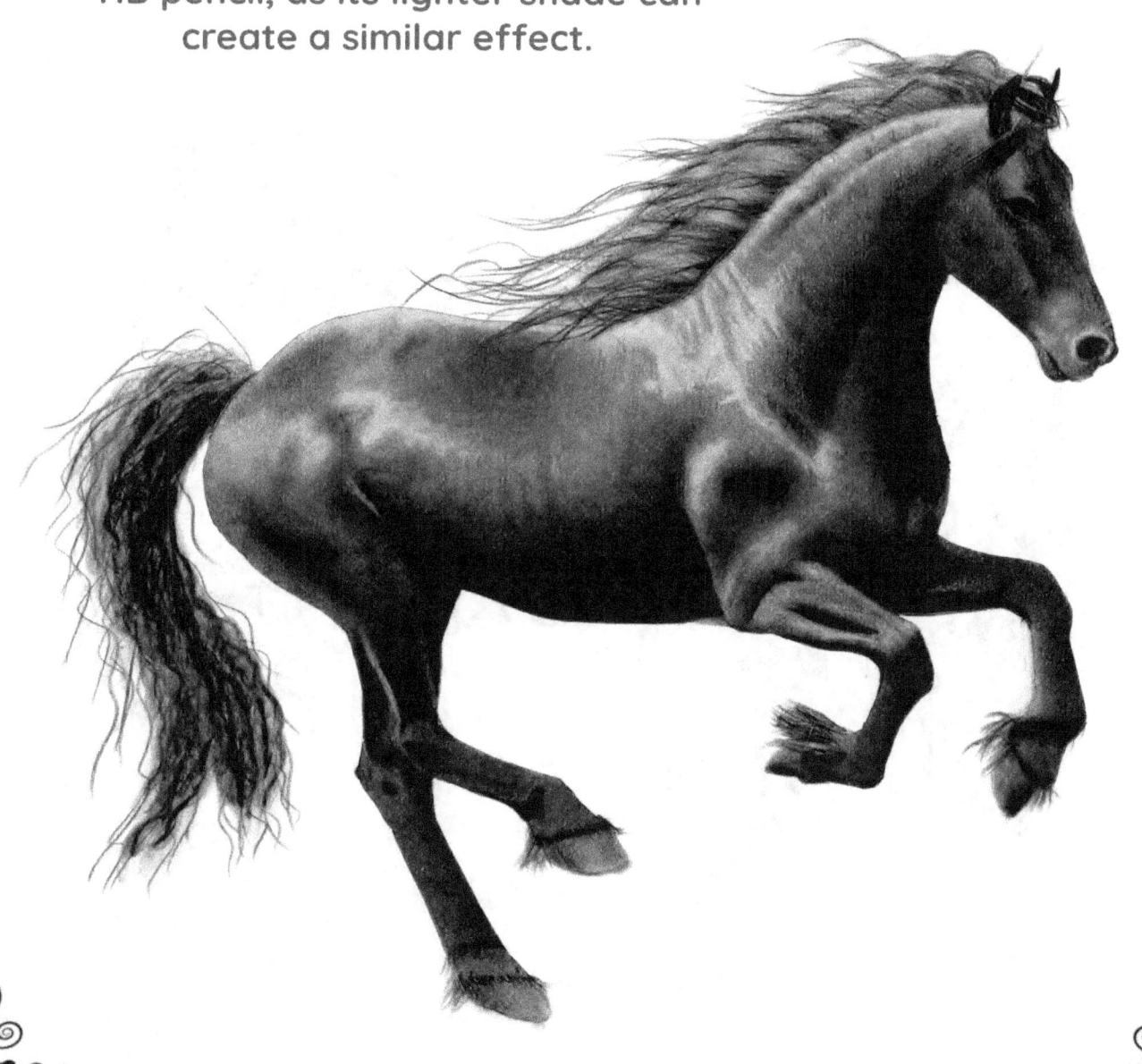

Creating Horse's Shadow

Once you're content with your horse's depiction, consider introducing its shadow onto the surface below. To achieve this effect, I utilized graphite powder applied with the motion of a paintbrush in back-and-forth strokes. I concentrated a heavier application of graphite adjacent to the leg that rests on the ground, allowing the shadow to naturally transition into the background as it diminishes. Please note that my horse turned out darker than the one in our reference photo, and that's perfectly acceptable.

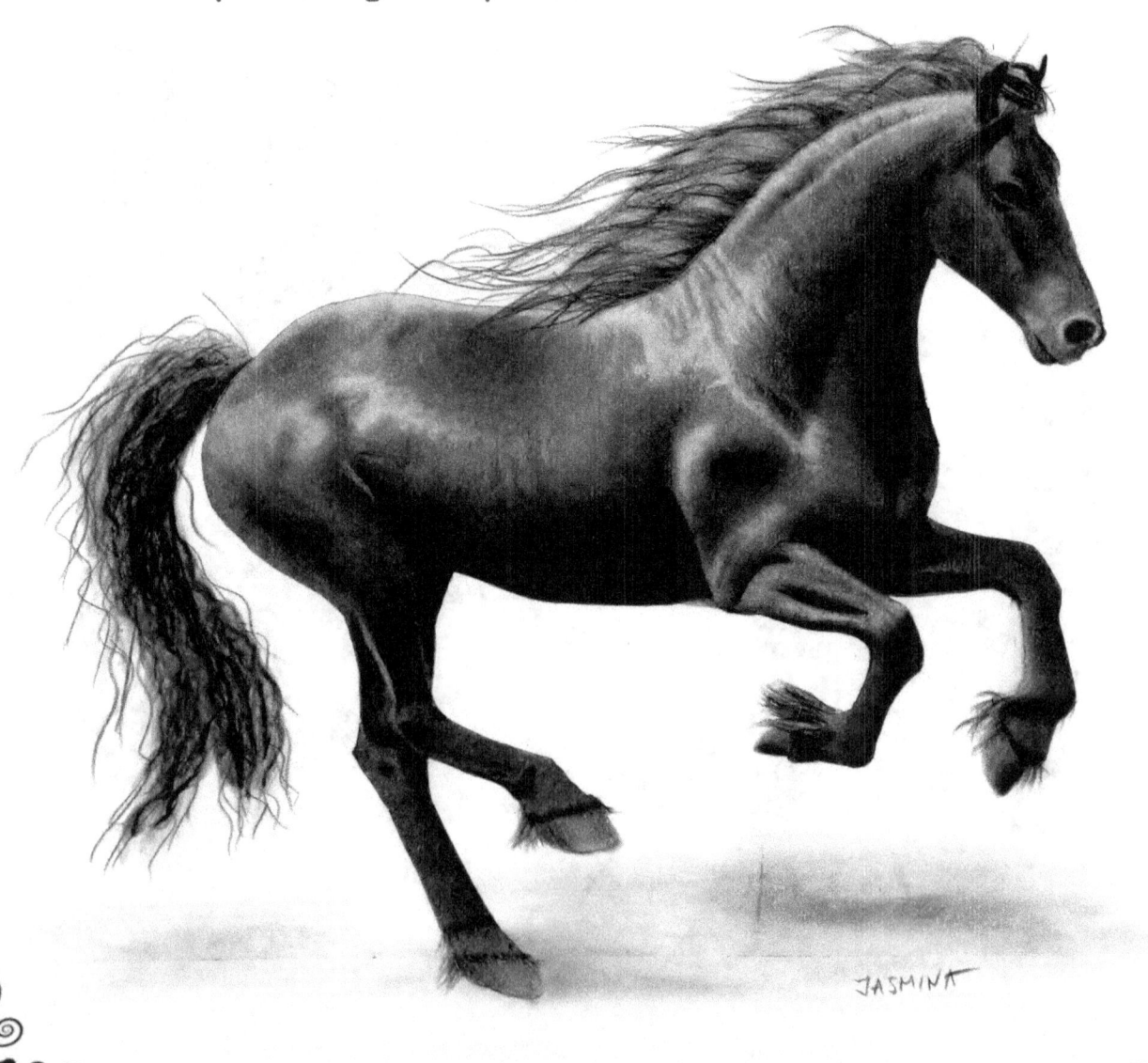

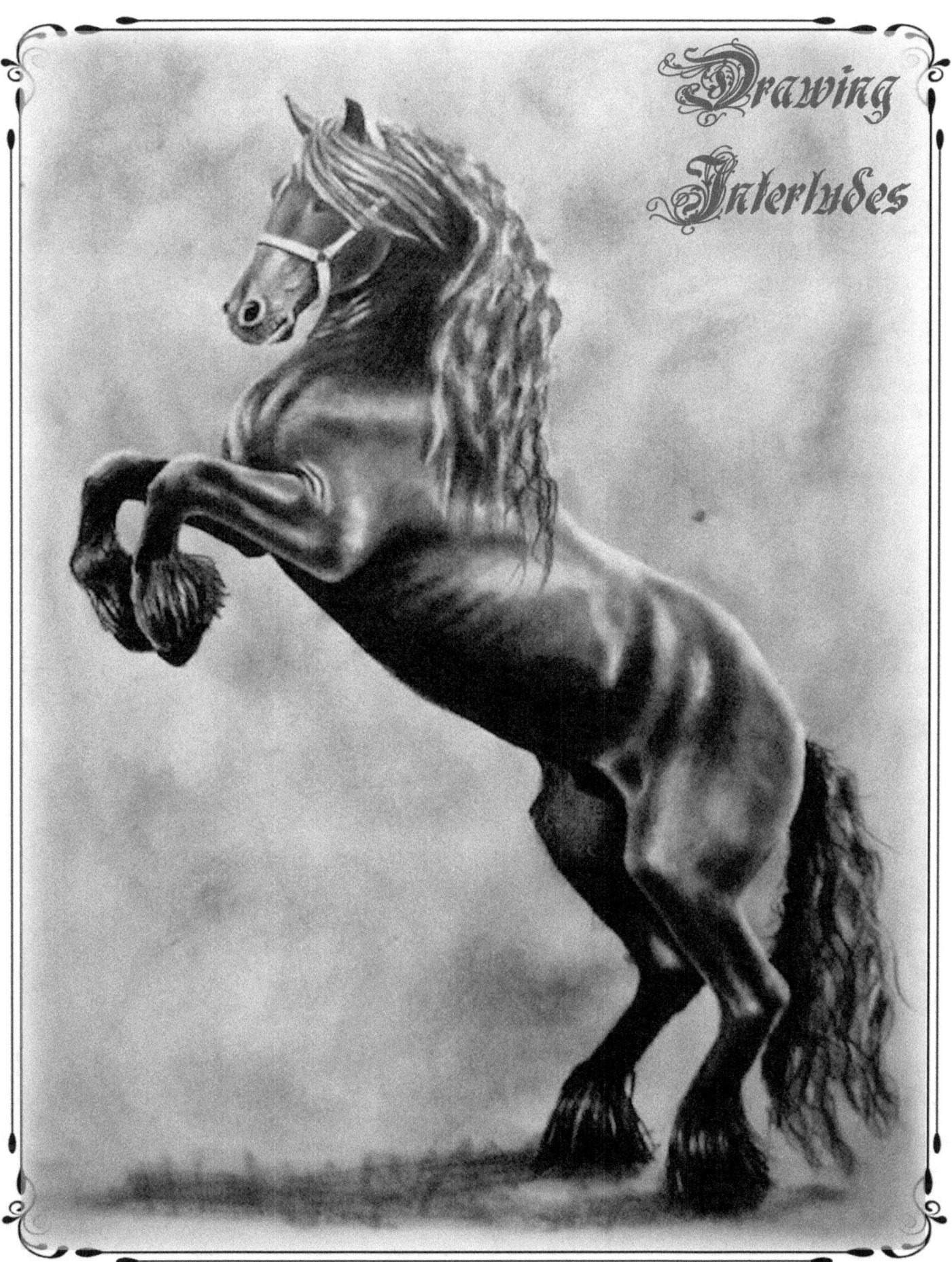

How to Draw a Husky

Drawing a husky offers a fulfilling artistic experience. These animals, known for their unique fur patterns and captivating eyes, provide an intriguing subject for artists. Capturing the challenging features of huskies, such as fur texture and facial markings, presents an opportunity for skill enhancement.

The Reference Photo

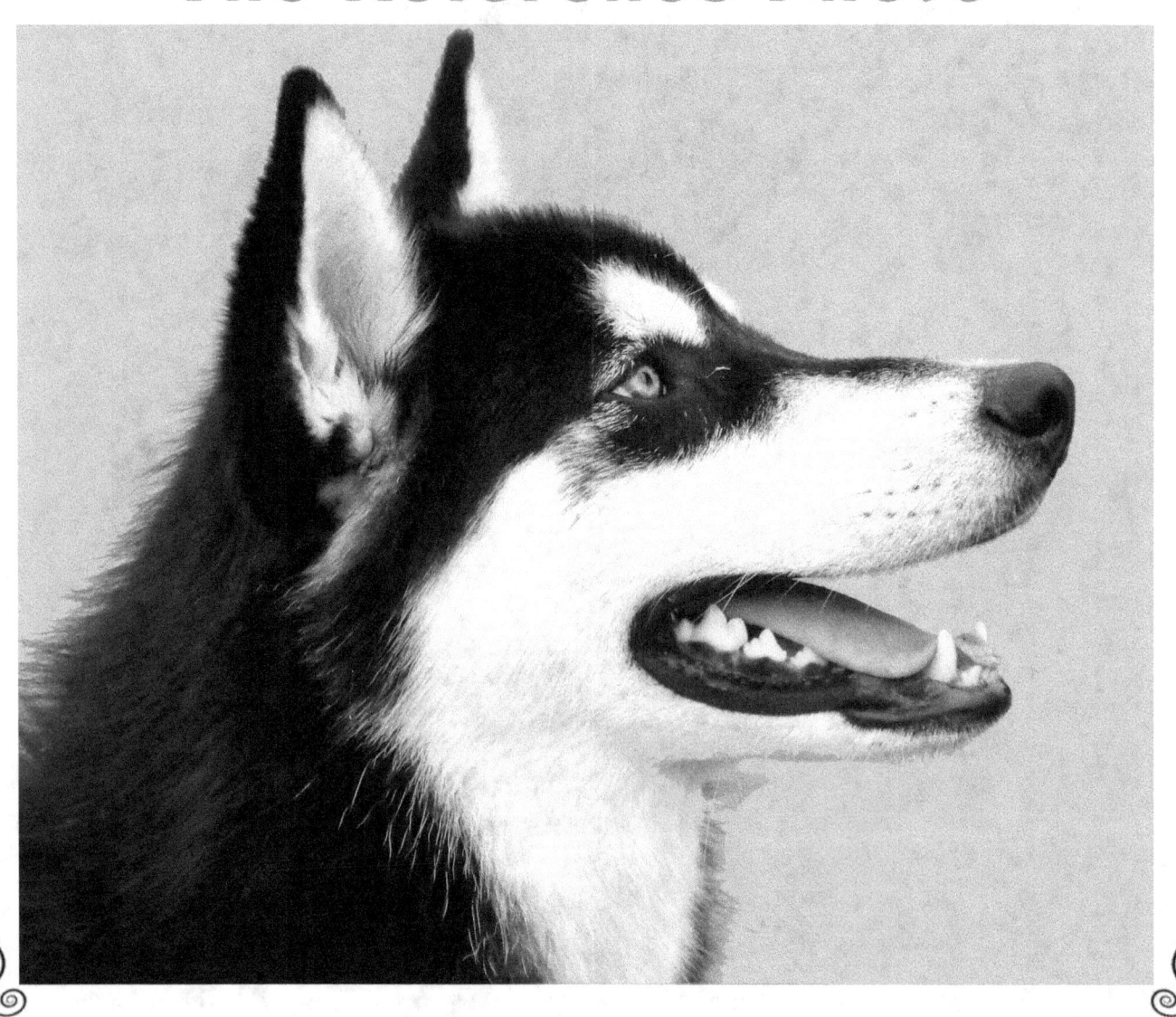

Sketching and Basic Shapes

Let's depict this husky on grey paper using graphite pencils, white charcoal, and white opaque markers to amplify the contrast between the grey background and its white fur. I opted for Clay paper by Fabriano, but alternatives like Strathmore Toned Gray or similar options can yield equally impressive results. In the image below, observe my pencil sketch lines, highlighting crucial outlines such as the boundary between the black and white fur, the primary contour of the head, and facial features. Notably, I aimed to slightly enlarge the eye for added emphasis and expression.

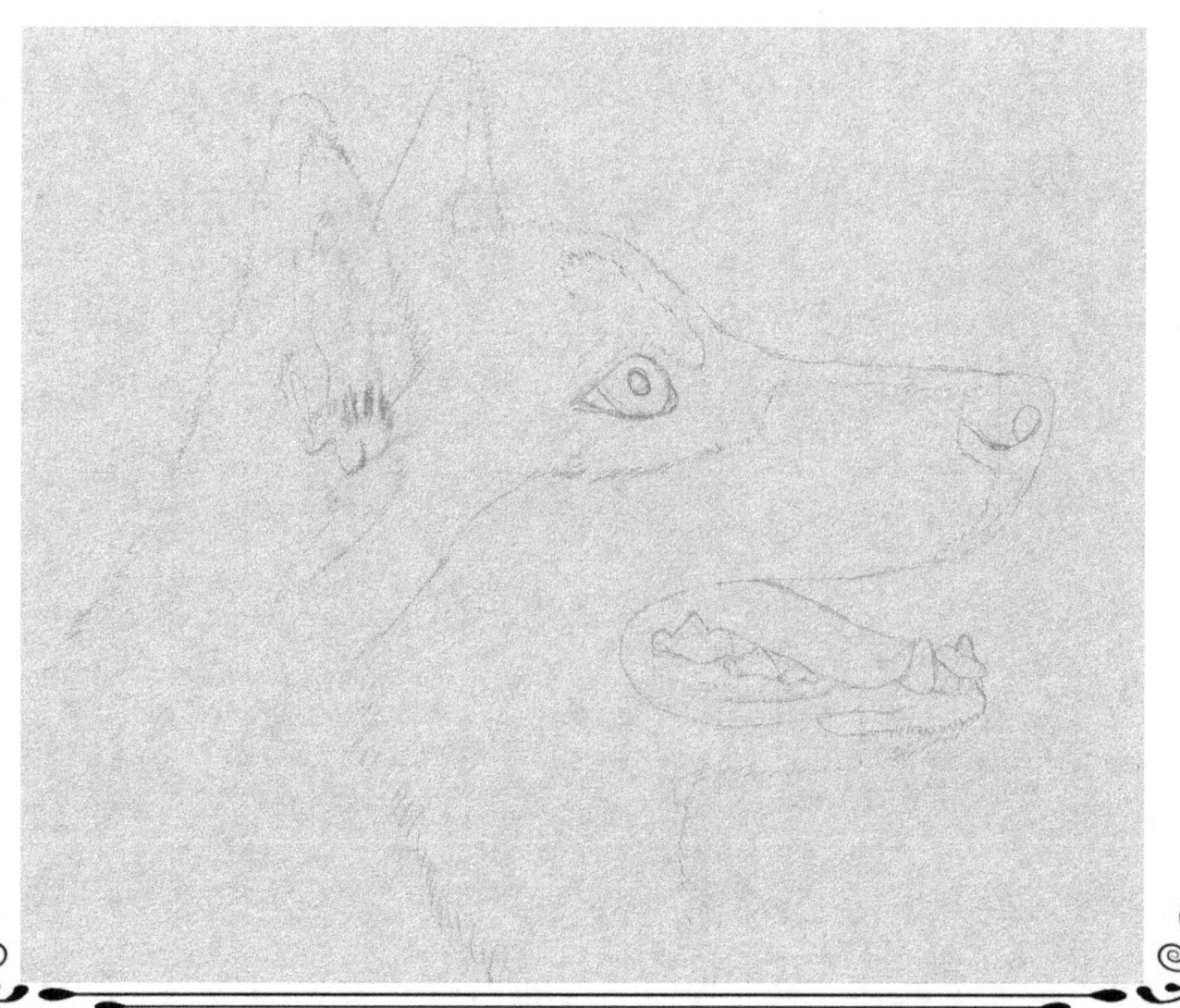

Iris Shading

Now, let's proceed with shading, and I recommend beginning with the eyes. In this case, we have only one eye to draw. I suggest using an HB pencil for the iris, prioritizing its detailed rendering. Start by using the HB pencil next to the iris boundary, creating strokes that radiate from the center of the pupil. Apply more pressure as you initiate each stroke and gradually release the pressure towards the pupil, allowing for a natural transition and depth in the shading.

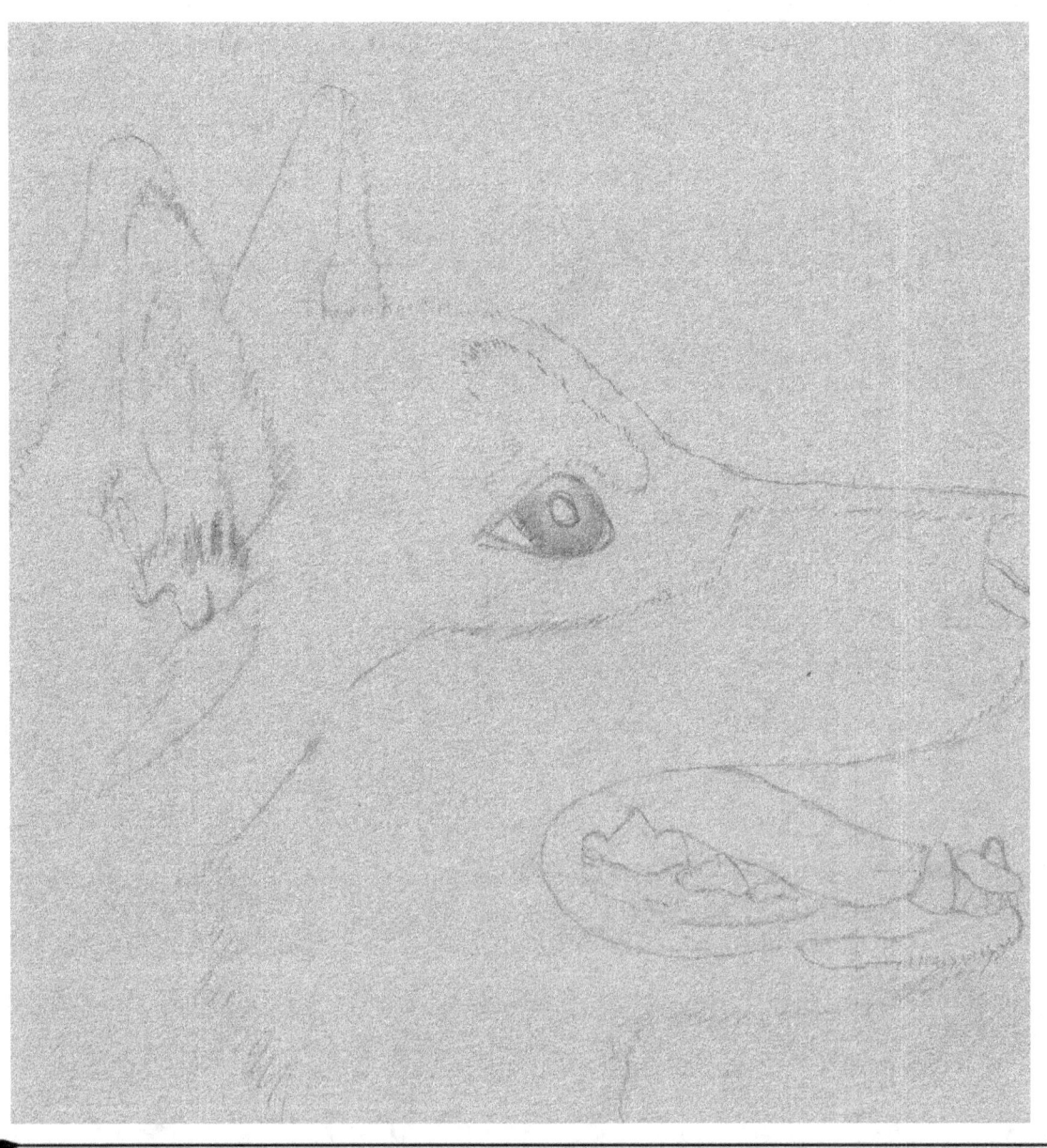

Sclera Detailing

Next, let's introduce white charcoal or a white opaque marker to depict the visible whites of the eye, known as the sclera.

Refer to the image below to see how the application of white color on grey paper creates a striking contrast, drawing attention to this area.

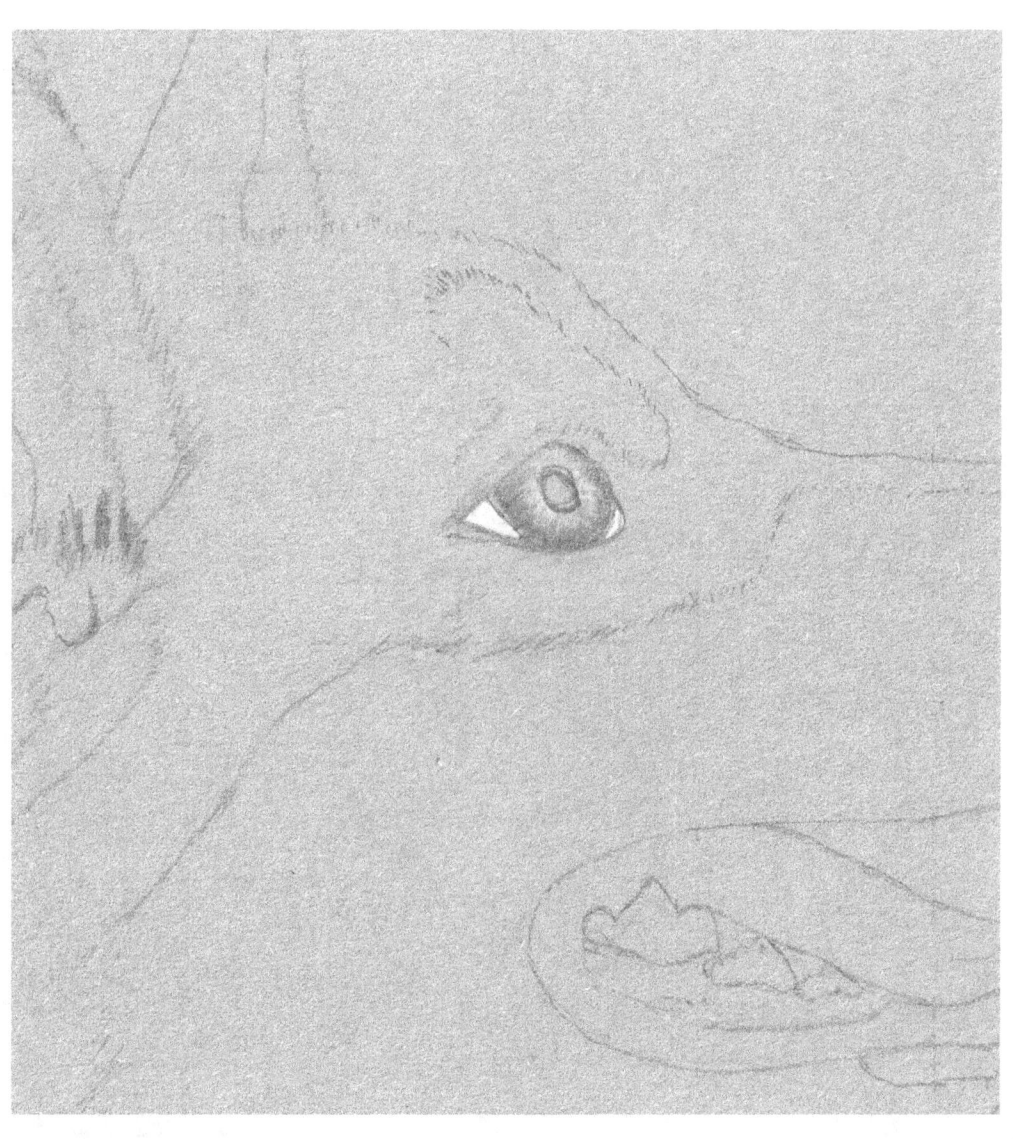

Deepening Contrast

To enhance contrast further, use a **14B** pencil to shade all around the irises, as demonstrated in the next image.

Apply firm pressure while shading the iris boundary and the pupil, aiming to create the deepest shade and achieve the blackest value.

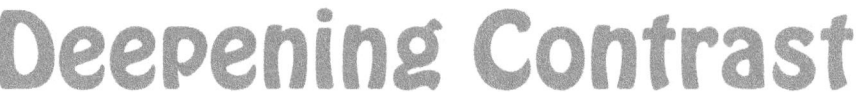

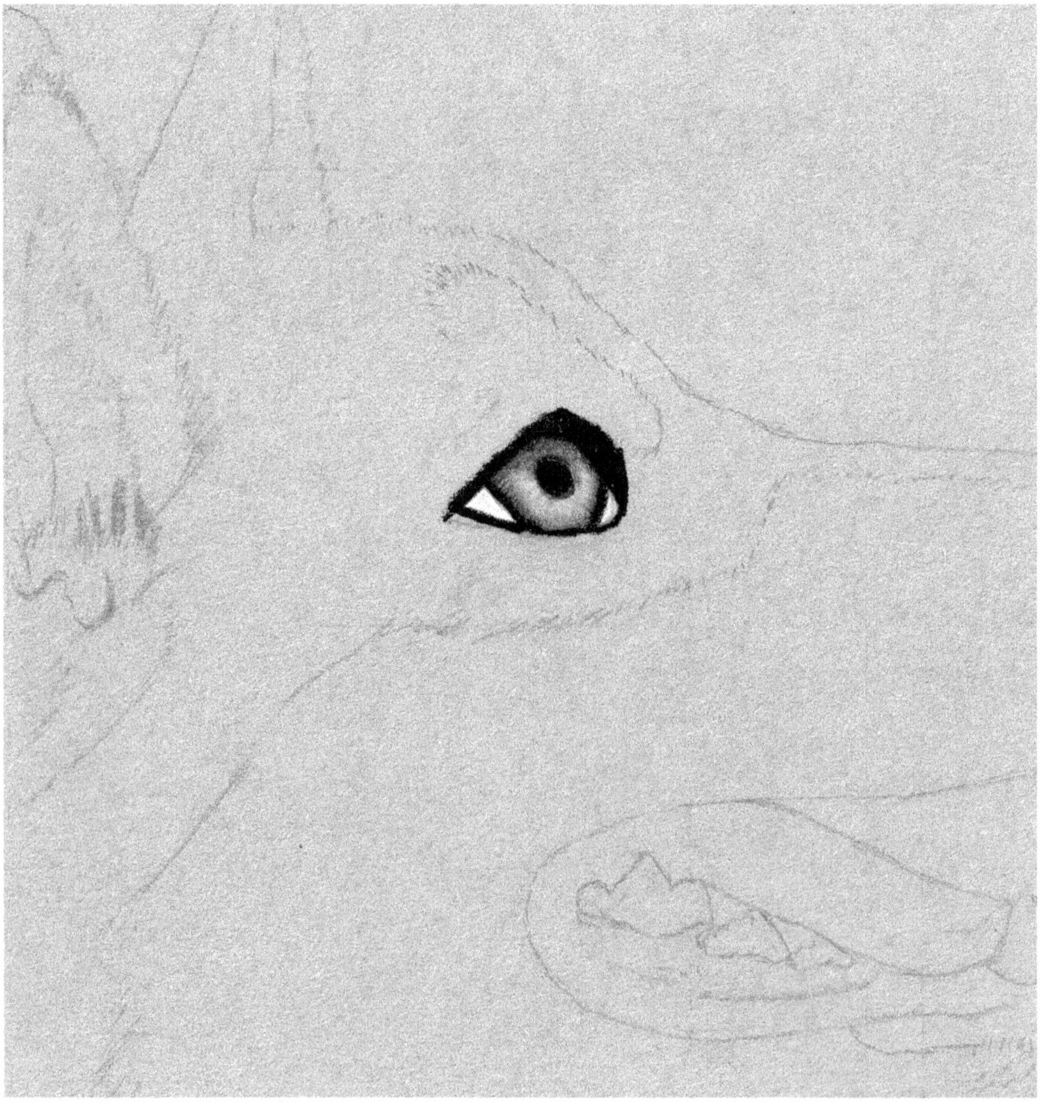

Crafting Reflected Light

To bring the eye to life and reduce its flat appearance, use an eraser to delicately create a reflected light effect over the upper part of the eyeball. Notice how this subtle touch adds depth and realism to the overall portrayal.

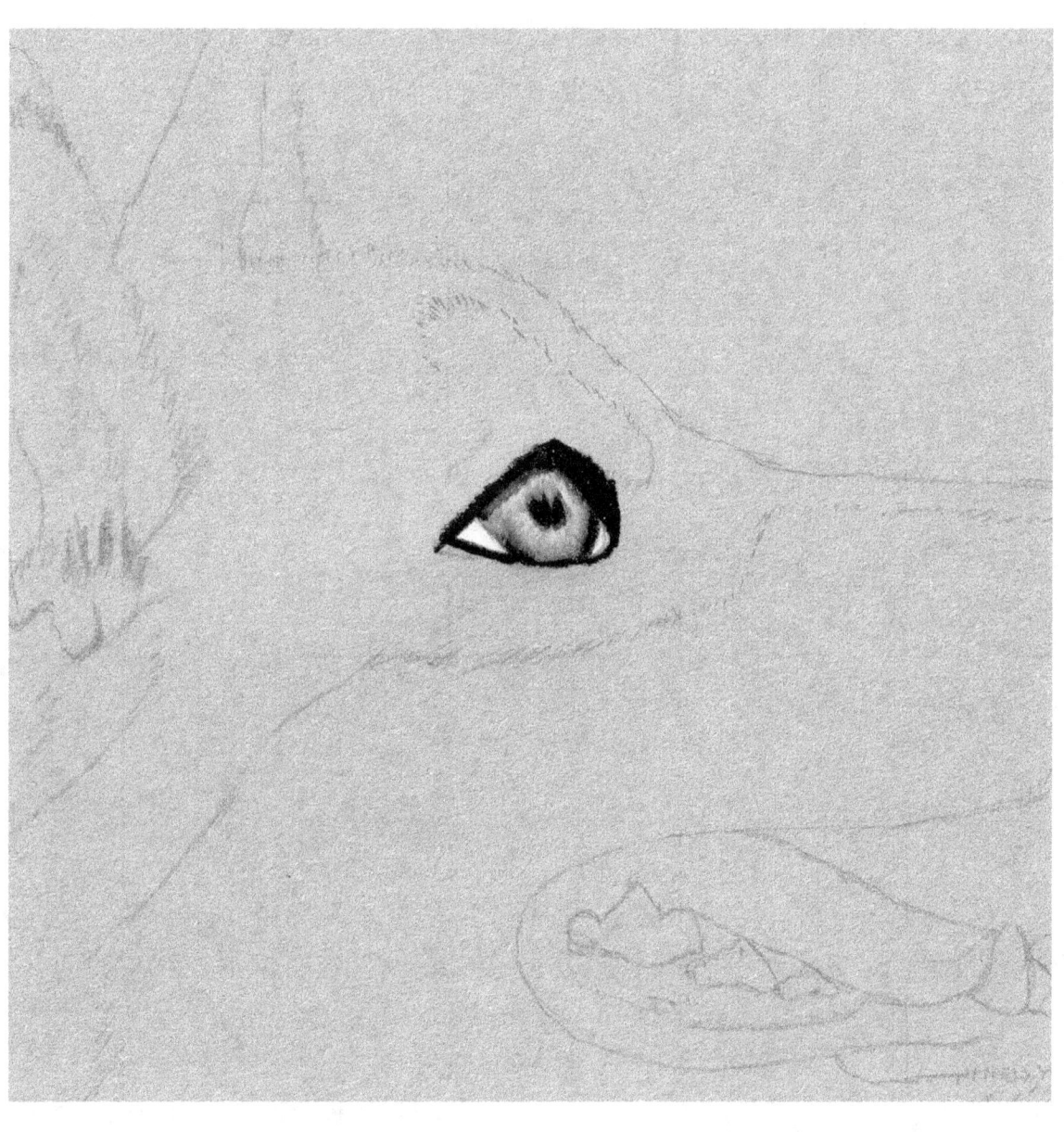

Beginning with Brilliance

To streamline the drawing process, I propose breaking it down into three phases. First, we'll focus on drawing and shading the white fur. Second, we'll tackle the black fur. Lastly, we'll refine the edges where white and black furs overlap. This segmented approach allows us to concentrate on one layer at a time for clarity and ease of explanation.

Let's commence with a bold step by coloring all the white fur using either a white charcoal or an opaque white marker.

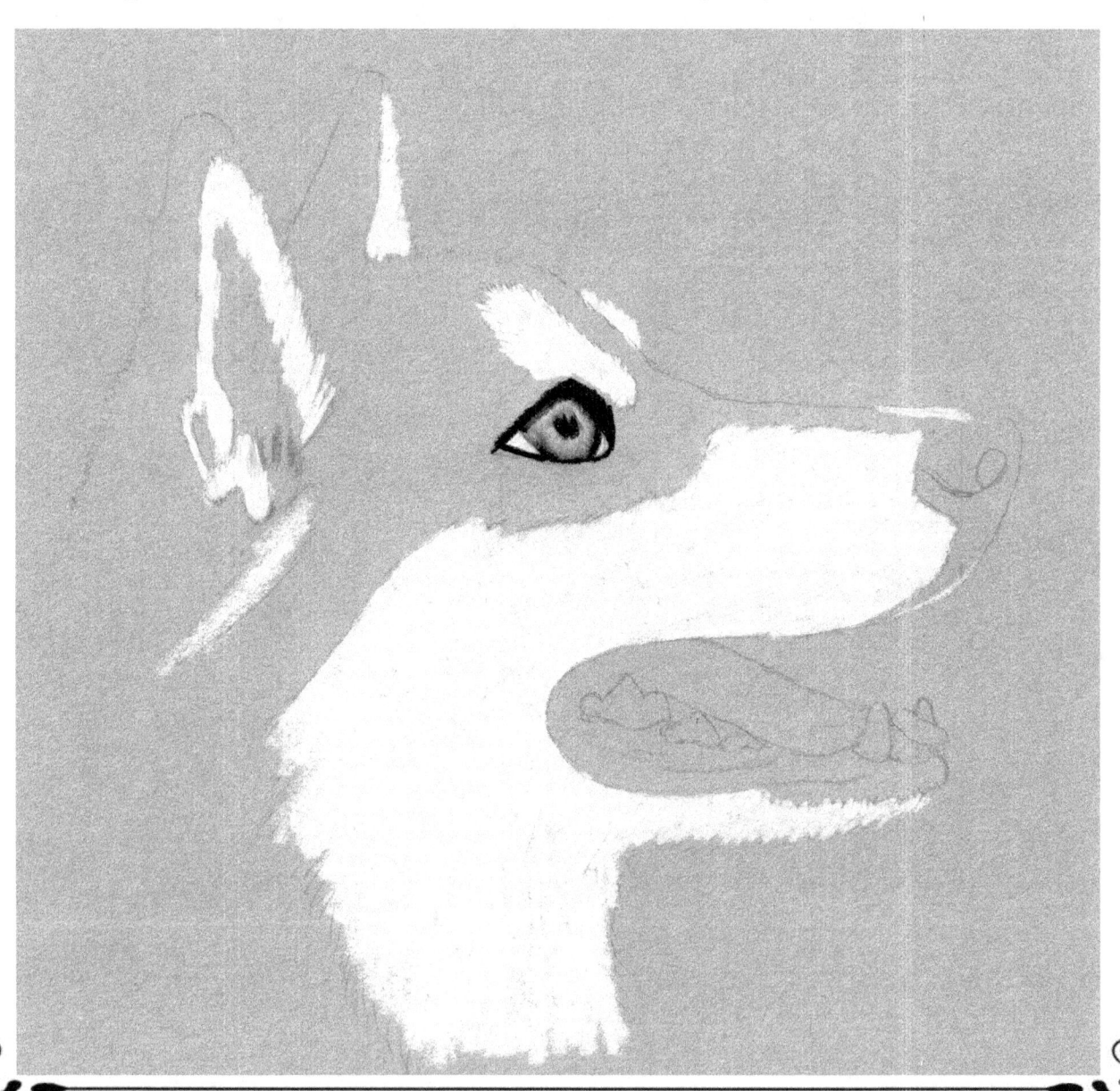

While it may appear that the entire white fur is uniformly white, our eyes can be deceiving. To determine what is truly pure white and what requires shading, it is essential to reduce the brightness in any image editor. In my screenshot, I demonstrate this process using the Highlight & Shadow Isolator Online Free Tool that I created and provide for free on my Pencil Drawing Tutor website www.pencildrawingtutor.com
After moving the scale toward Highlights, it becomes clear that only the areas above the eyes, the upper face, and the muzzle are truly pure white. Everything else requires varying degrees of shading with graphite pencils.

Drawing from reference photos simplifies the process, as it spares us from having to imagine the skull structure and other underlying details. I highly recommend printing the reference image on paper rather than viewing it on a digital screen, since screen light can exaggerate the brightness of white areas and lead to overly light shading where more subtle tones are needed.

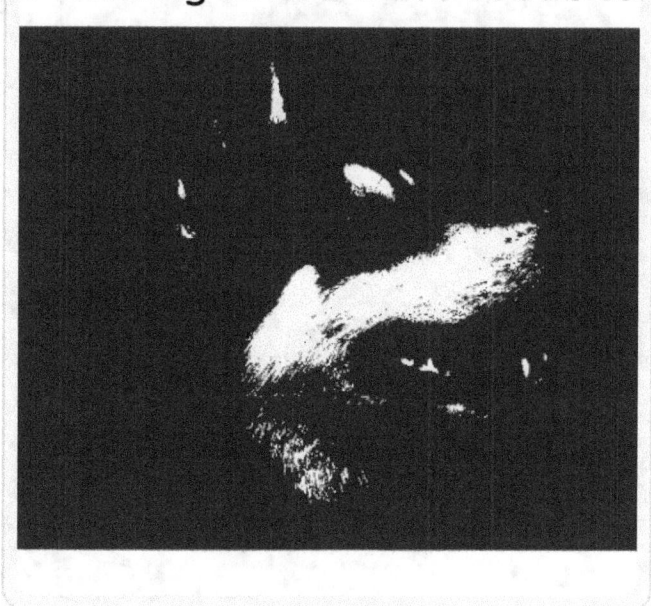

Shadows ◄ 0 ► Highlights

Value: 93

Download image

Shading White Fur

Let's begin shading the white fur, particularly under and next to the nose, using an HB pencil to introduce a slightly darker tone. This step also allows us to create the roots of the whiskers. Ensure you maintain the direction of the hair growth consistently. Shade areas where the skin underneath bends, focusing on the less illuminated parts. Refer to the reference photo and the accompanying image to better grasp the nuances of this step.

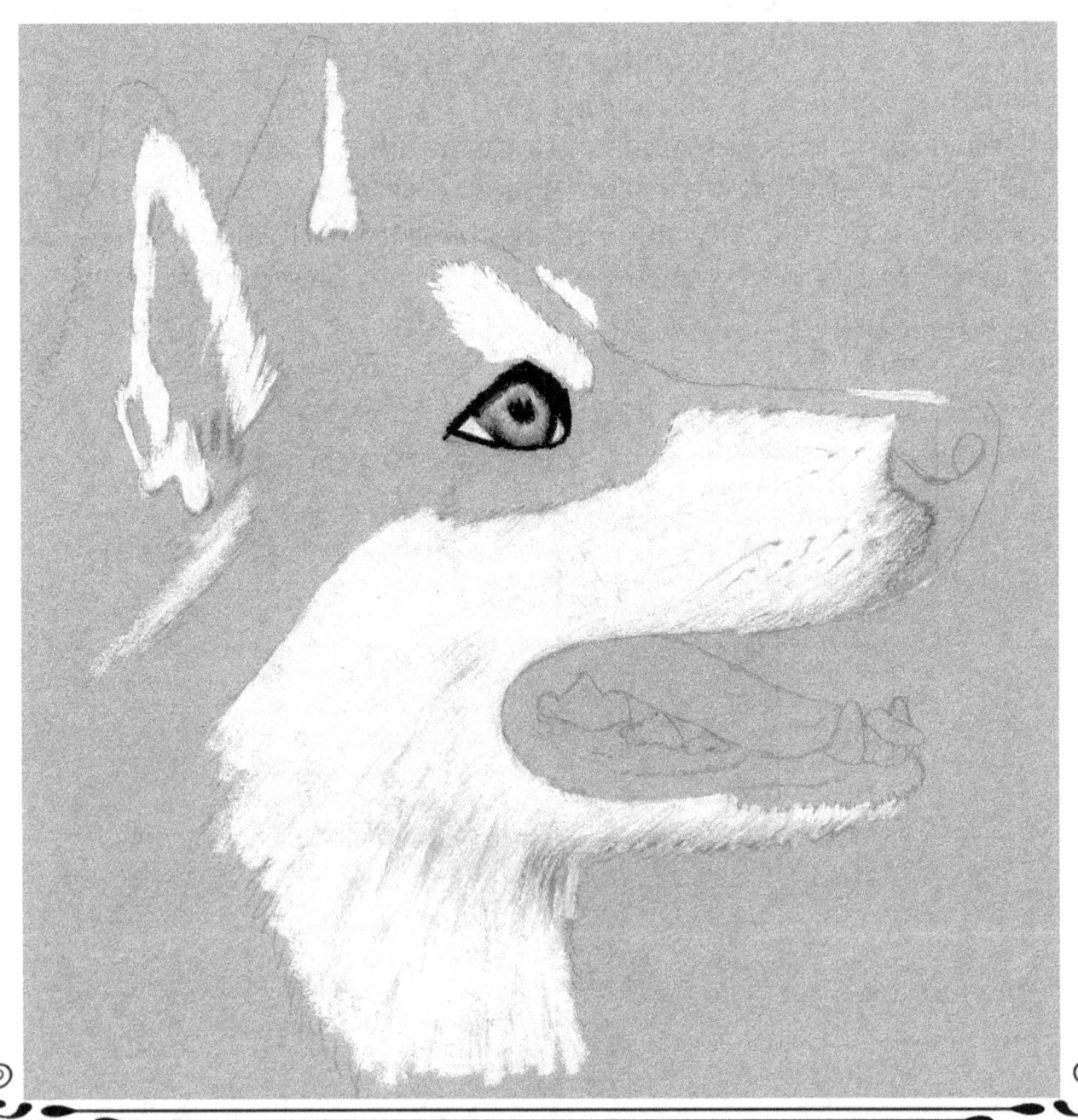

Inner Ear Detail

Proceed to draw the inner area of the ear, utilizing an HB for the deeper section and blending it lightly with white charcoal. Achieve a seamless finish by using a wax colorless blender. This concludes our work on the white fur; any further adjustments can be made as needed in later stages.

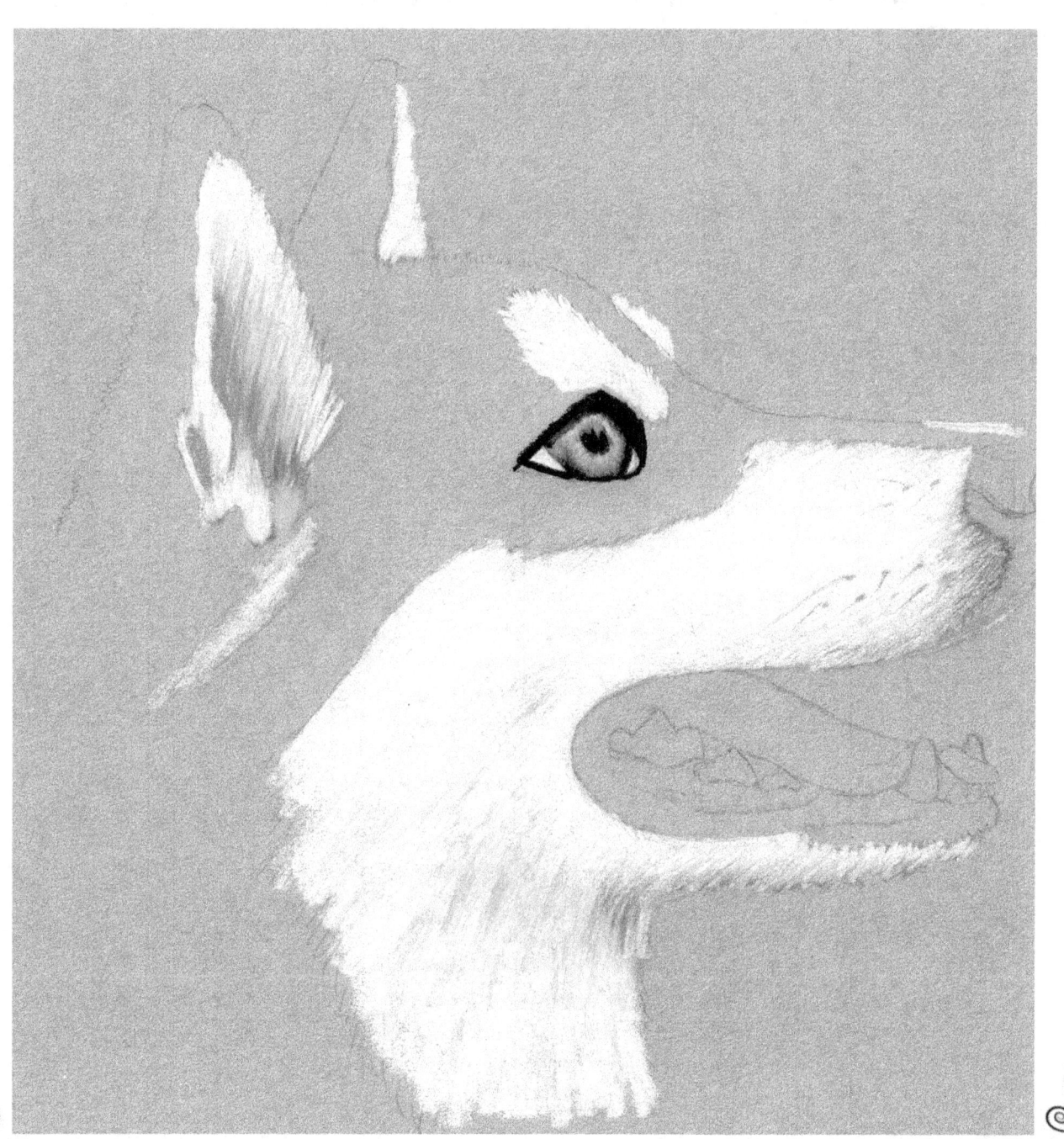

Defining Nose Shadows

Prior to tackling the black fur, let's focus on drawing the nose. Begin by using a 14B pencil to emphasize the black areas, coloring the nostril and a small channel on the side of the nose, as demonstrated in the next image. Apply firm pressure, ensuring these areas are richly dark. It's worth noting that even black skin, when highlighted, transforms into shades of grey rather than staying purely black.

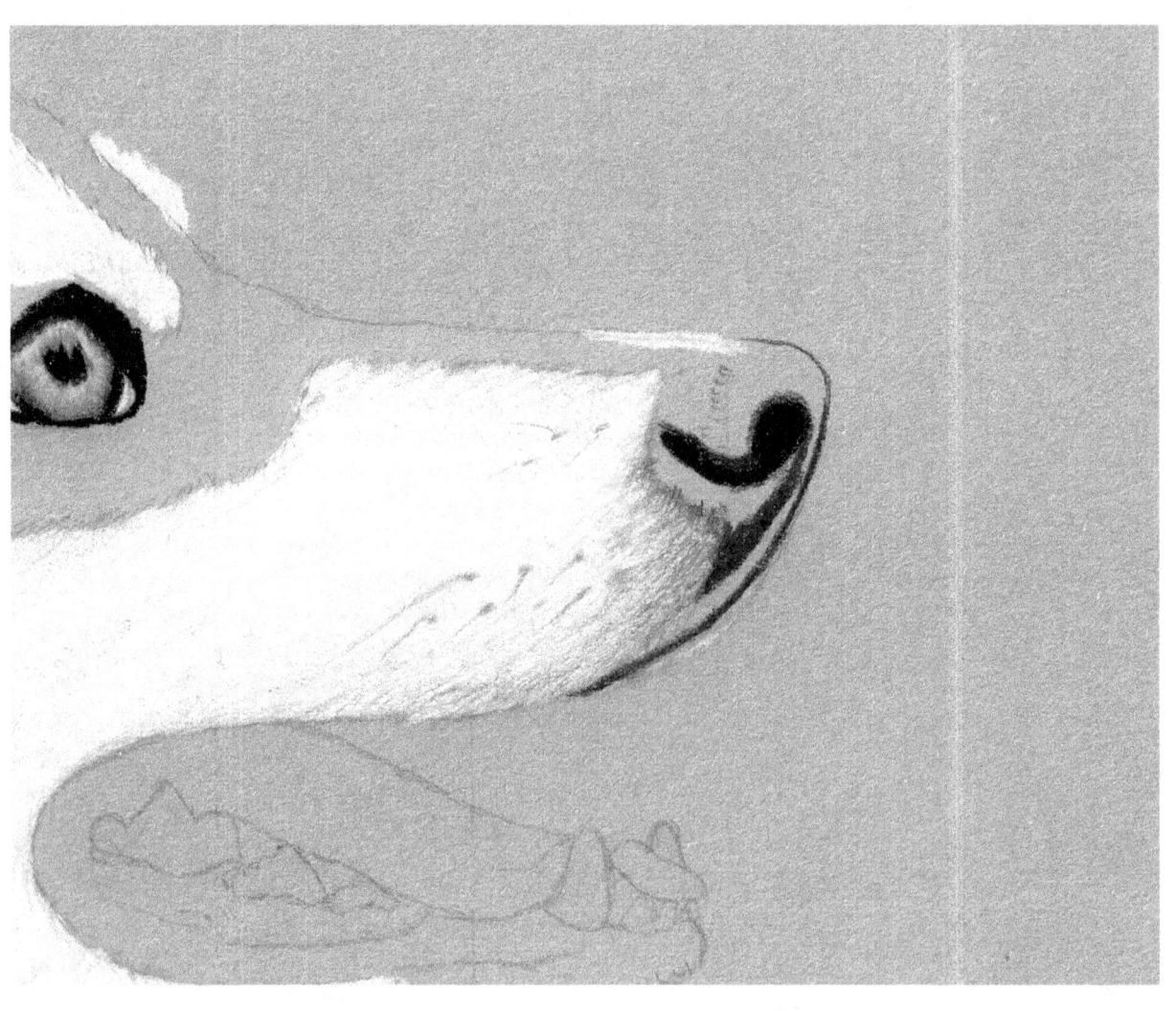

Applying Basic Shade

Now, proceed to color the remainder of the nose using an HB pencil. Apply the circulism technique instead of hatching to achieve a uniform texture.

Circulism involves drawing small, overlapping circles until the entire area is shaded evenly.

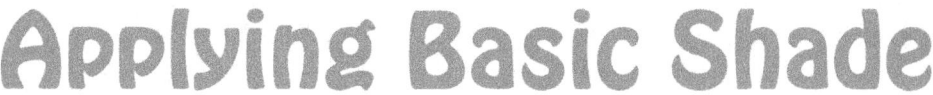

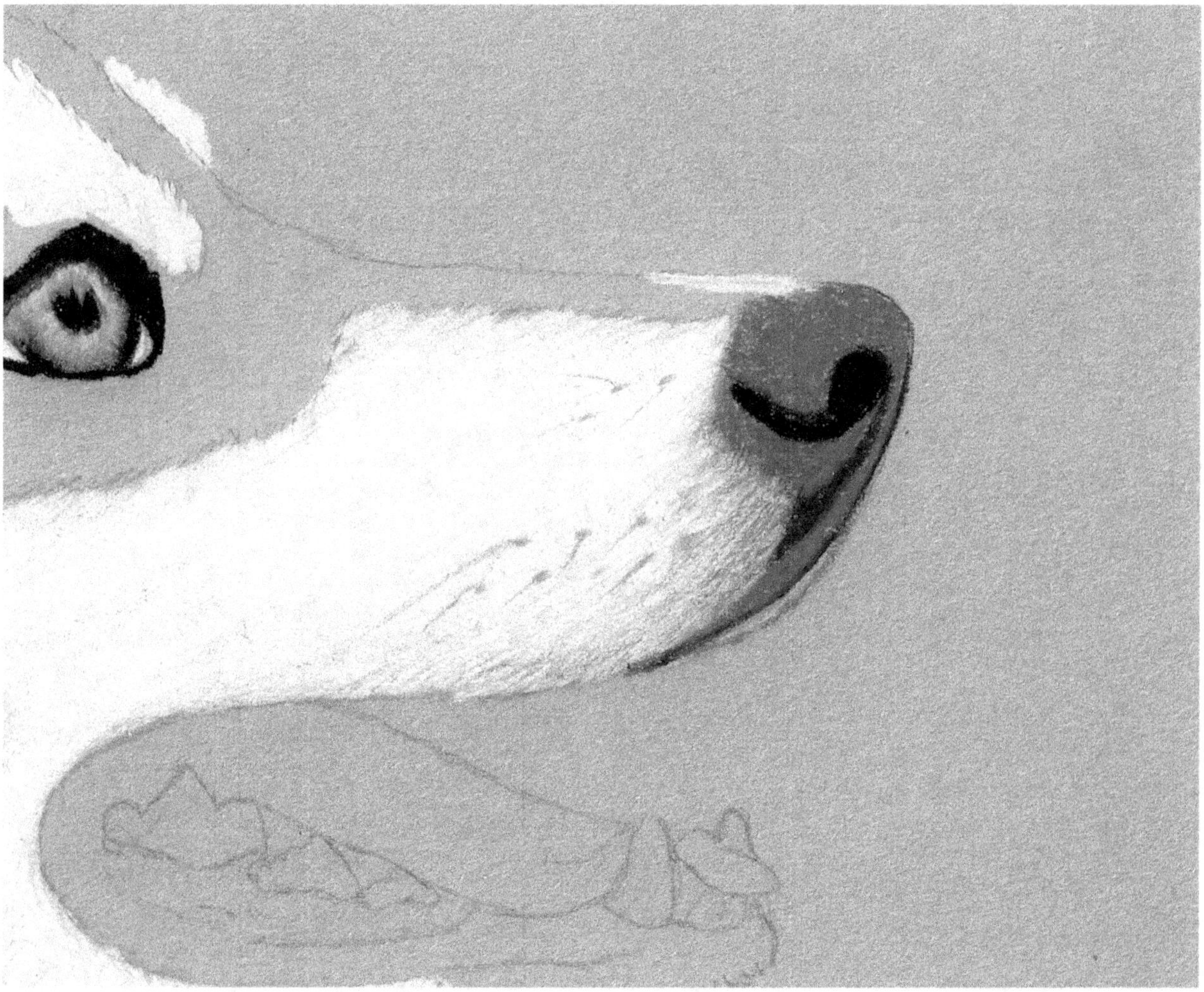

Crafting Seamless Transitions

To seamlessly blend the edges between the 14B and HB areas of the nose, employ a 4B pencil. Apply firmer pressure adjacent to the 14B regions and gradually release pressure as you move away. Aim for a smooth gradient to impart a rounded shape to the nose.

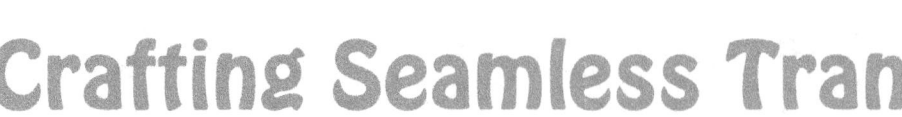

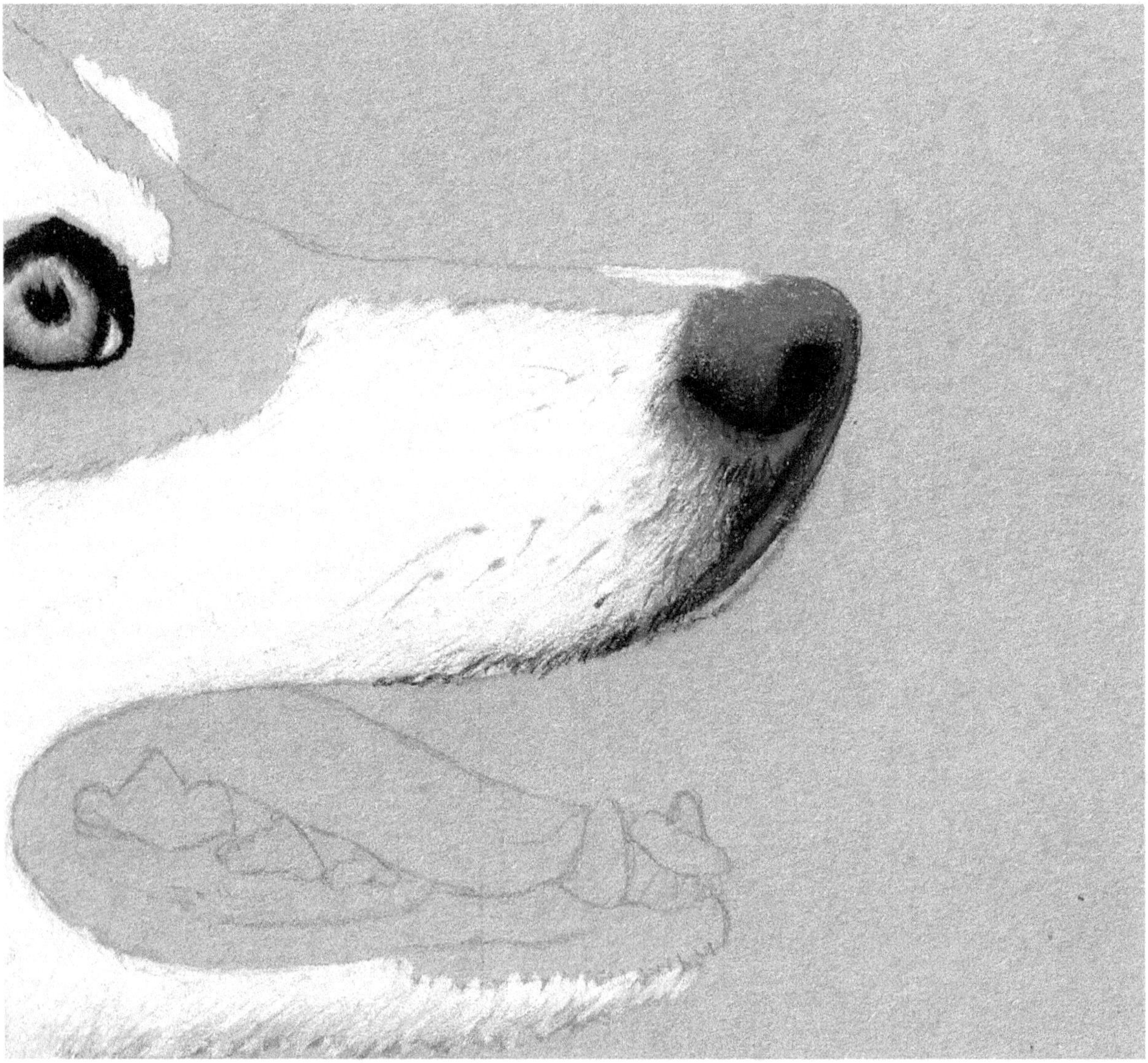

Enhancing Nose Highlights

Finally, to enhance the overall effect, delicately remove selected portions of the graphite using a kneaded eraser to create subtle highlights on the bridge of the nose.

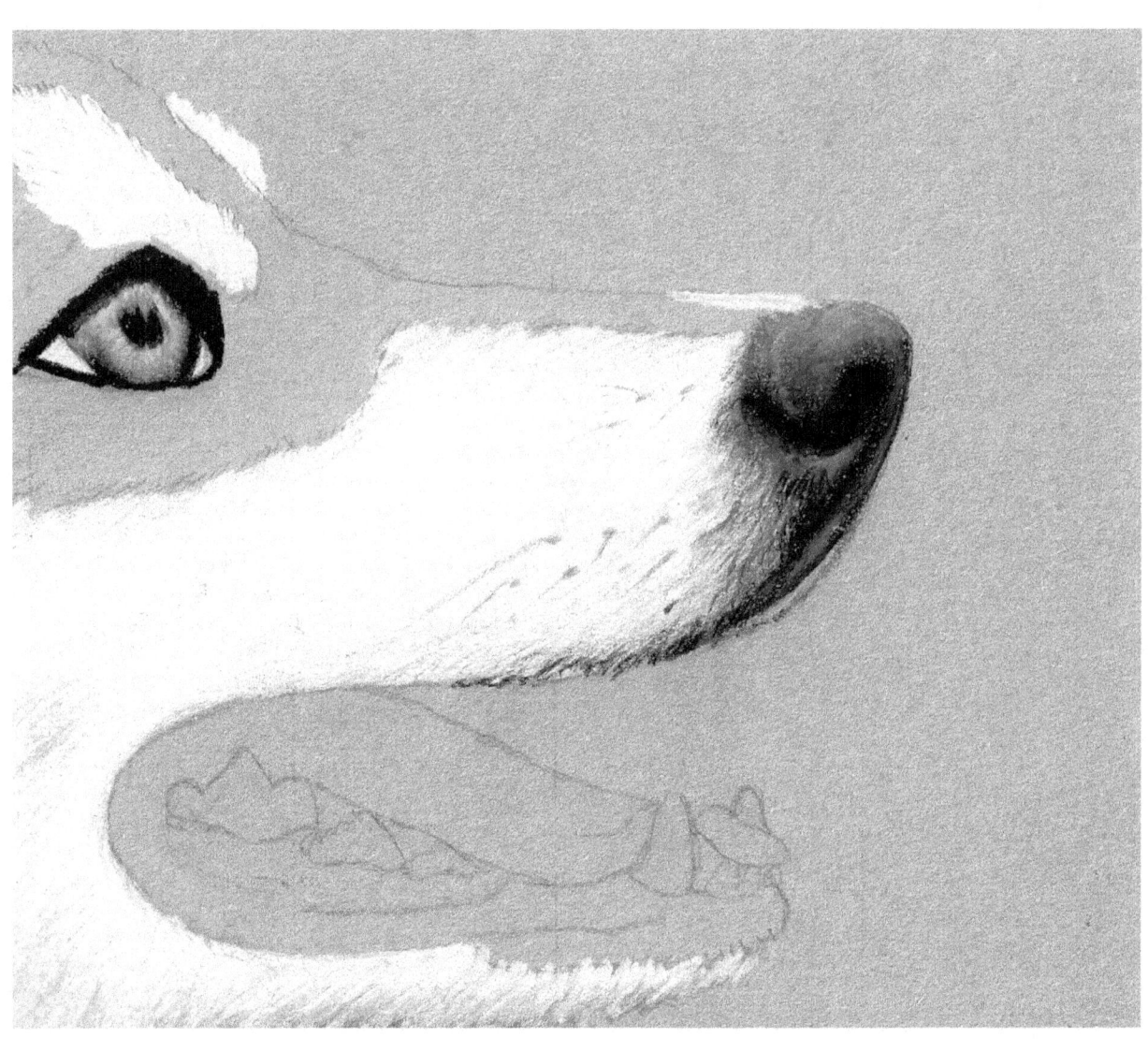

Identifying Black Highlights

Now let's move on to drawing the black parts of the fur. Remember how we moved the scale toward Highlights in the Highlight & Shadow Isolator Online Free Tool to find the pure white areas in the white fur? Now we need to do the opposite and move the scale toward Shadows to see which parts are completely black and which are gray.

In the screenshot, you can see that this tool revealed that only a few areas of the fur are truly black.

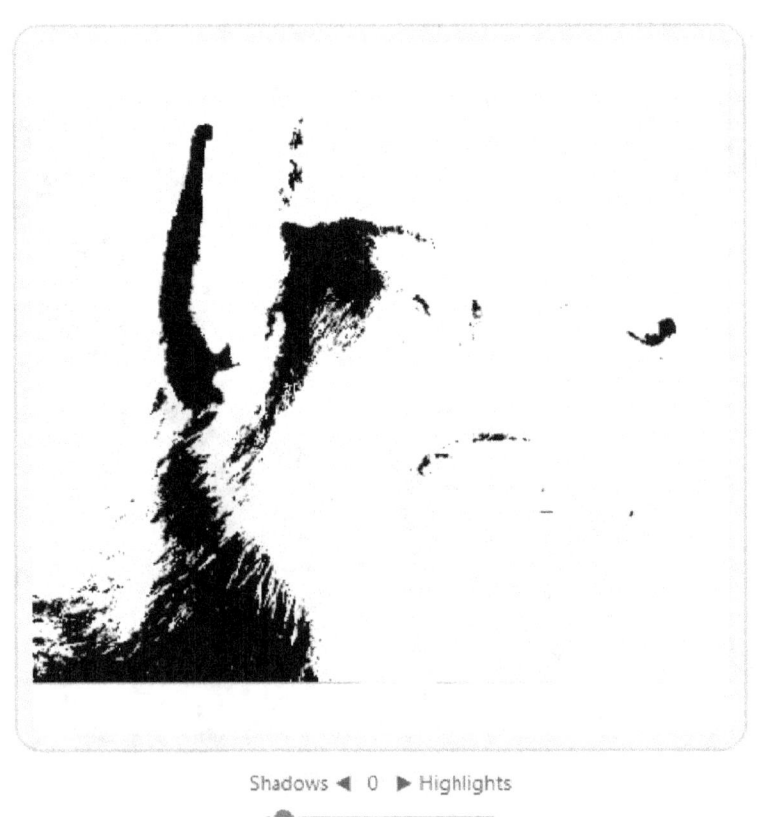

Shadows ◀ 0 ▶ Highlights

Value: -94

Download image

Drawing Darkest Fur

Now, use a 14B pencil to sketch the darkest parts, following the direction of the hair's flow. Refer to the next image to identify the specific areas I've shaded with this pencil.

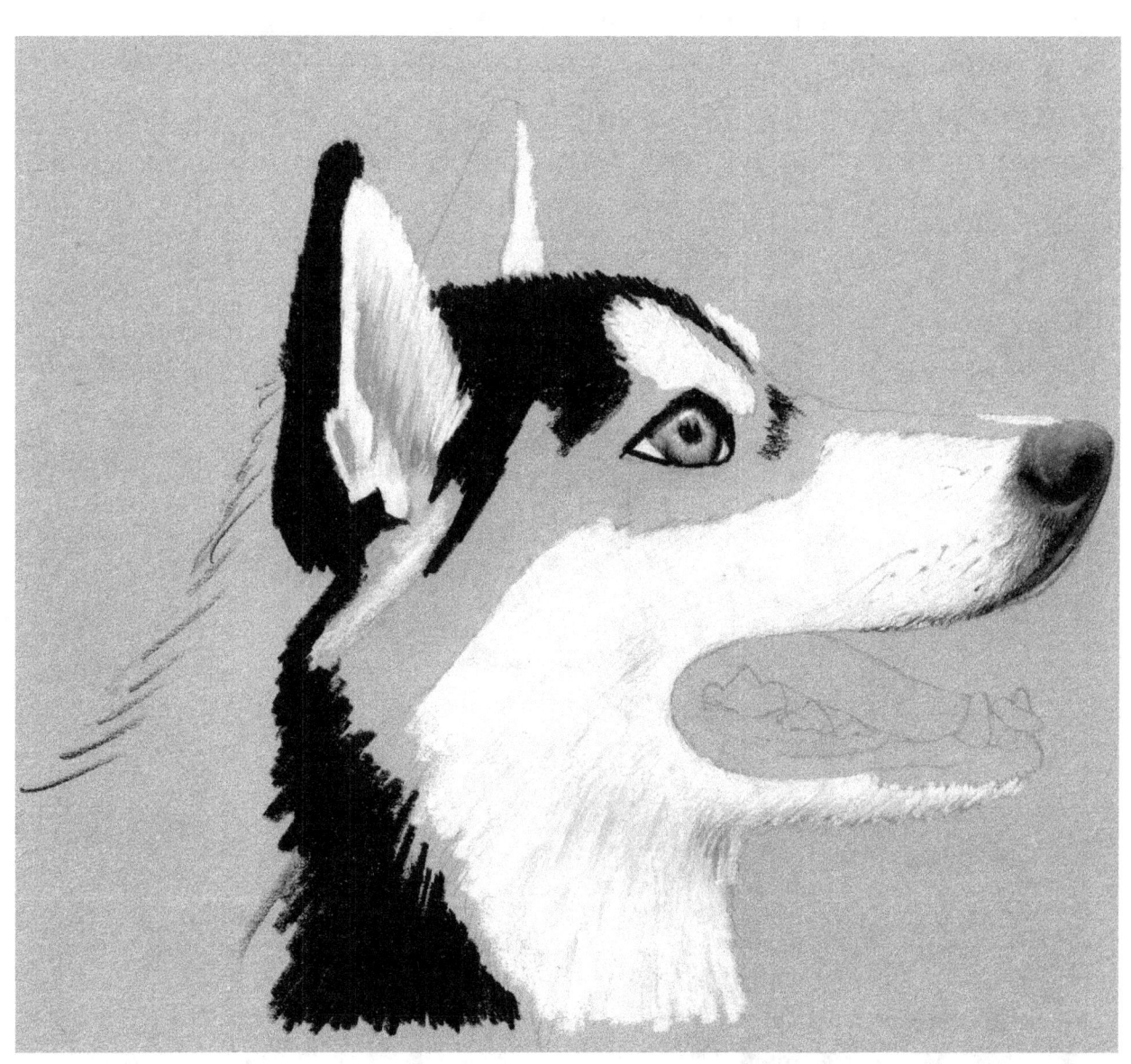

Shading with 6B Pencil

Next, proceed to shade the remaining fur using a 6B pencil, which, while still dark, is slightly brighter than the 14B. Maintain the consistent practice of following the natural direction of hair growth. Extend the shading to even cover areas where tiny white hairs may be present, such as above the eye. It's essential to note that simply because there are some white hairs doesn't categorize the entire section as white. Therefore, apply the darker pencil generously, and plan to incorporate those few white hairs later using a white marker. While the subtleties between the 14B and 6B might not be as evident in my scanned drawing, you'll notice the distinction more prominently in your own artwork.

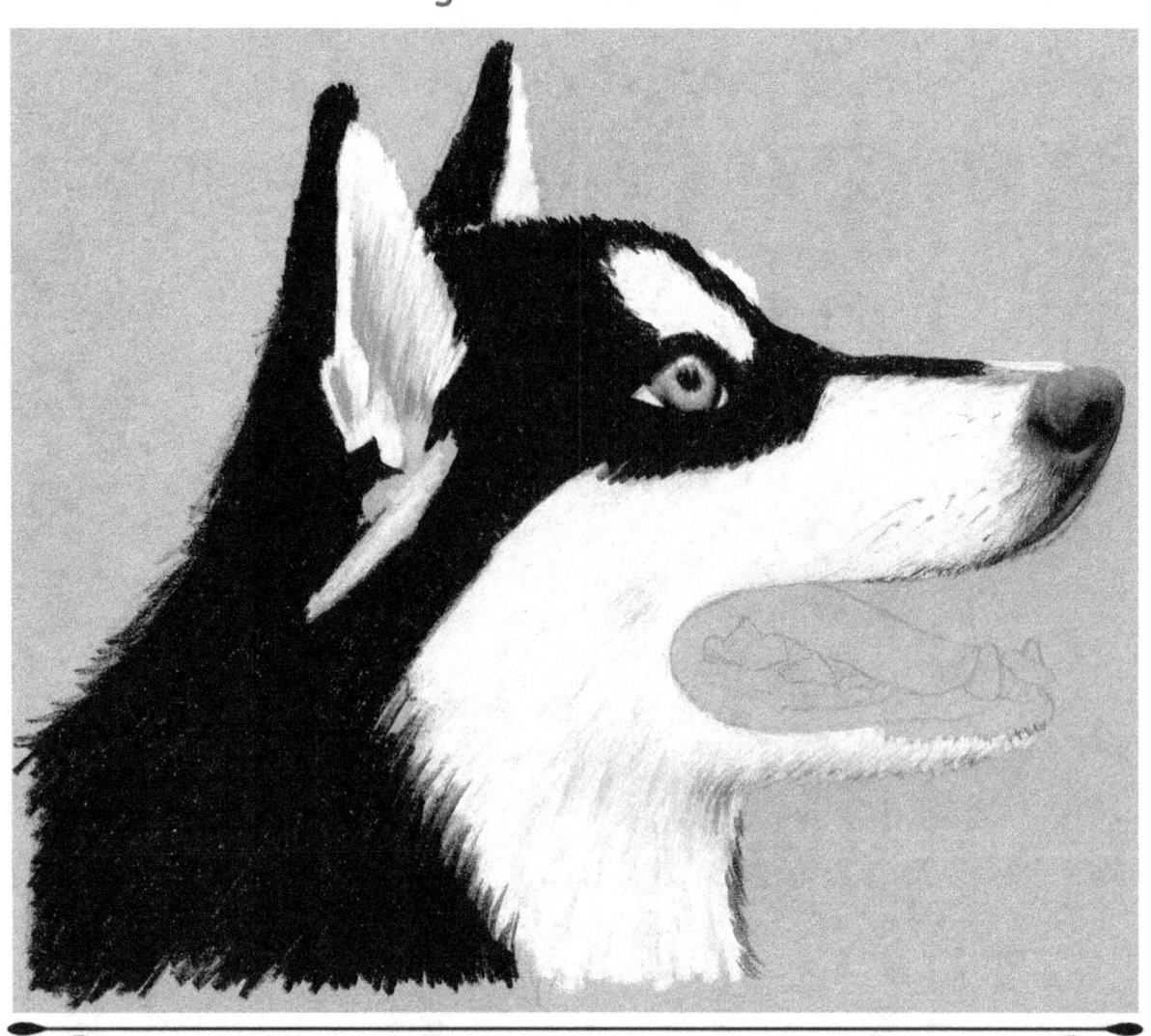

Highlighting Dark Fur

It's time to create some highlights with an eraser over the dark fur and areas such as under the eye, at the top of the muzzle, at the top of the head, and the back. Essentially, the protruding areas that receive more light have to be brightened up by eliminating some of the graphite.

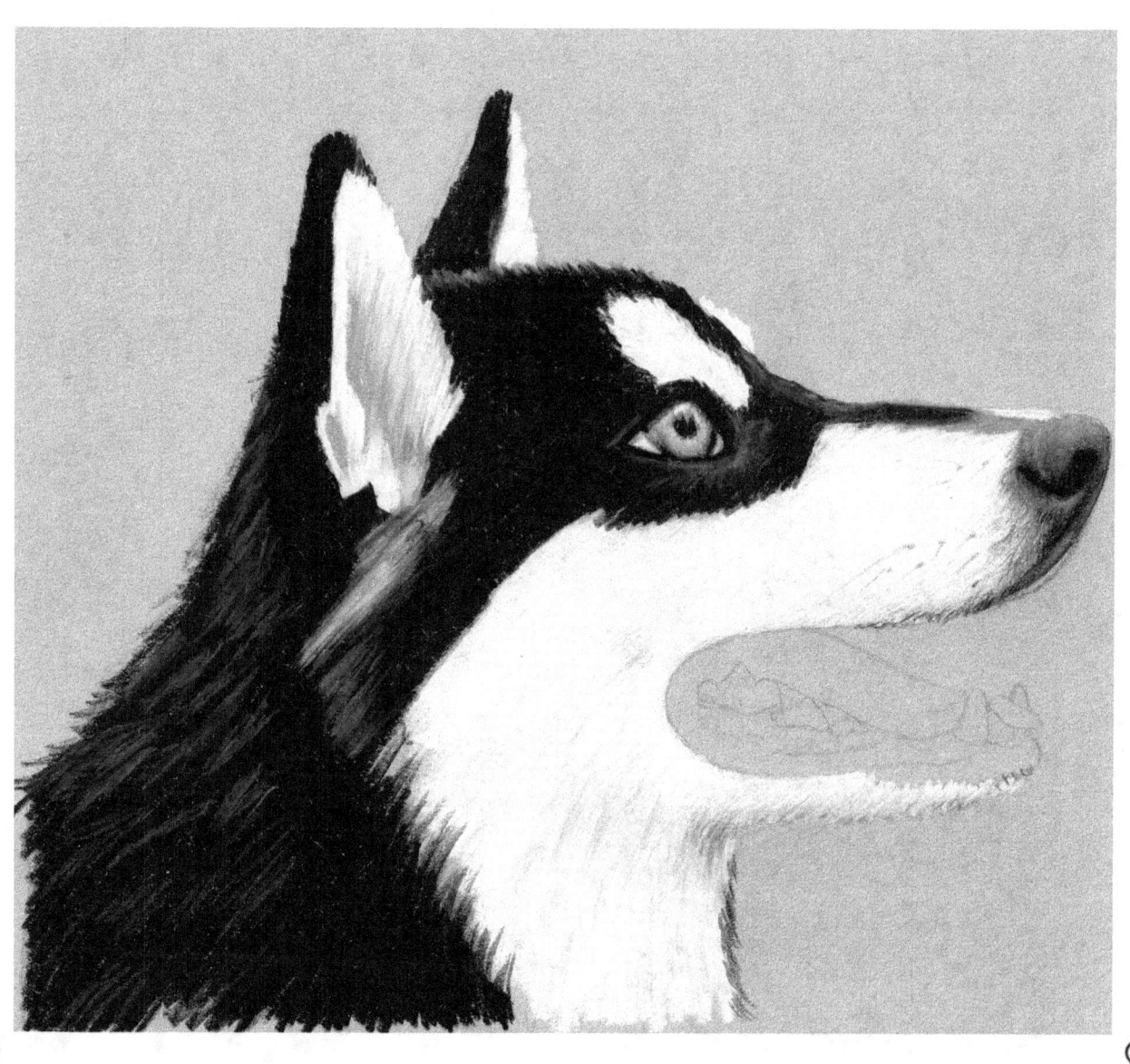

Softening the Look

As the next step, let's smooth out the outer edge of the black fur. Initially, I focused solely on applying the main color to the dark fur, neglecting the outer part. Now, the line between the fur and the background is too clear. We need to soften it up by adding tiny hairs that extend beyond the fur, and for this, I use a wax colorless blender by Prismacolor. Take the sharp tip of the colorless blender and run it along the edge of the black fur, moving it outward with quick, confident strokes. Check the image below to see how I softened the outer edges. This step will make the fur's outer edge look fluffy and soft. Some hairs should be shorter, like around the ear and forehead, and some should be longer, especially on the back. Now, you can see how it looks much more natural.

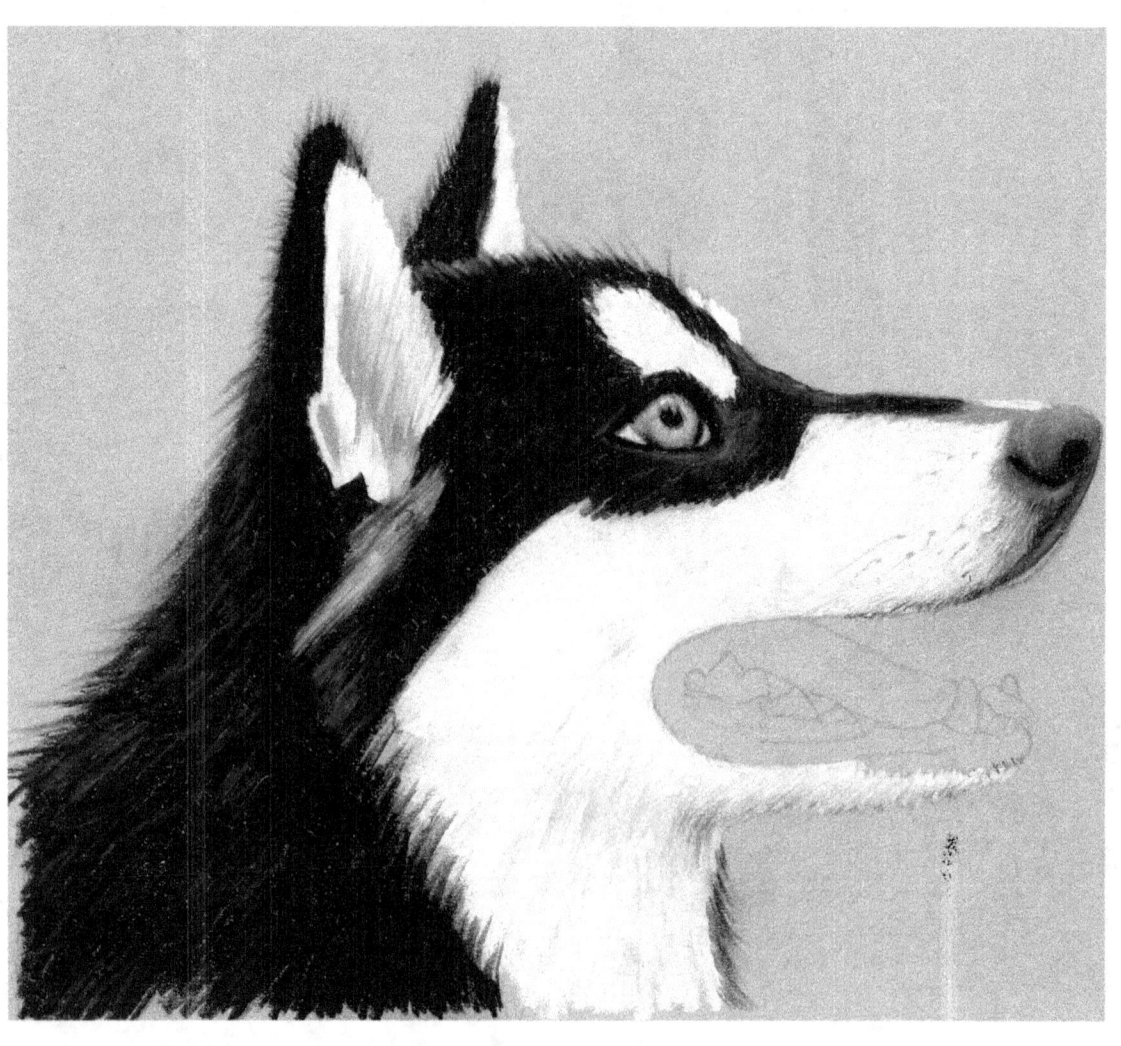

Black to White Transition

Now, let's tackle the transition between the black and white furs that we previously discussed. Similar to our approach in the previous step, we need to soften the boundary between these two colors along the outer edge. Position the tip of your wax colorless blender over the black fur, and with inward strokes, meld it into the white fur. Be mindful of the direction of hair growth for a natural look. For added depth, consider using a dark pencil like 4B to draw some hairs over the edge, blending them seamlessly. Specifically near the ear, place the pencil tip and the wax colorless blender over the black area. Draw lines inward toward the white fur of the ear, creating a harmonious blend between the two contrasting colors.

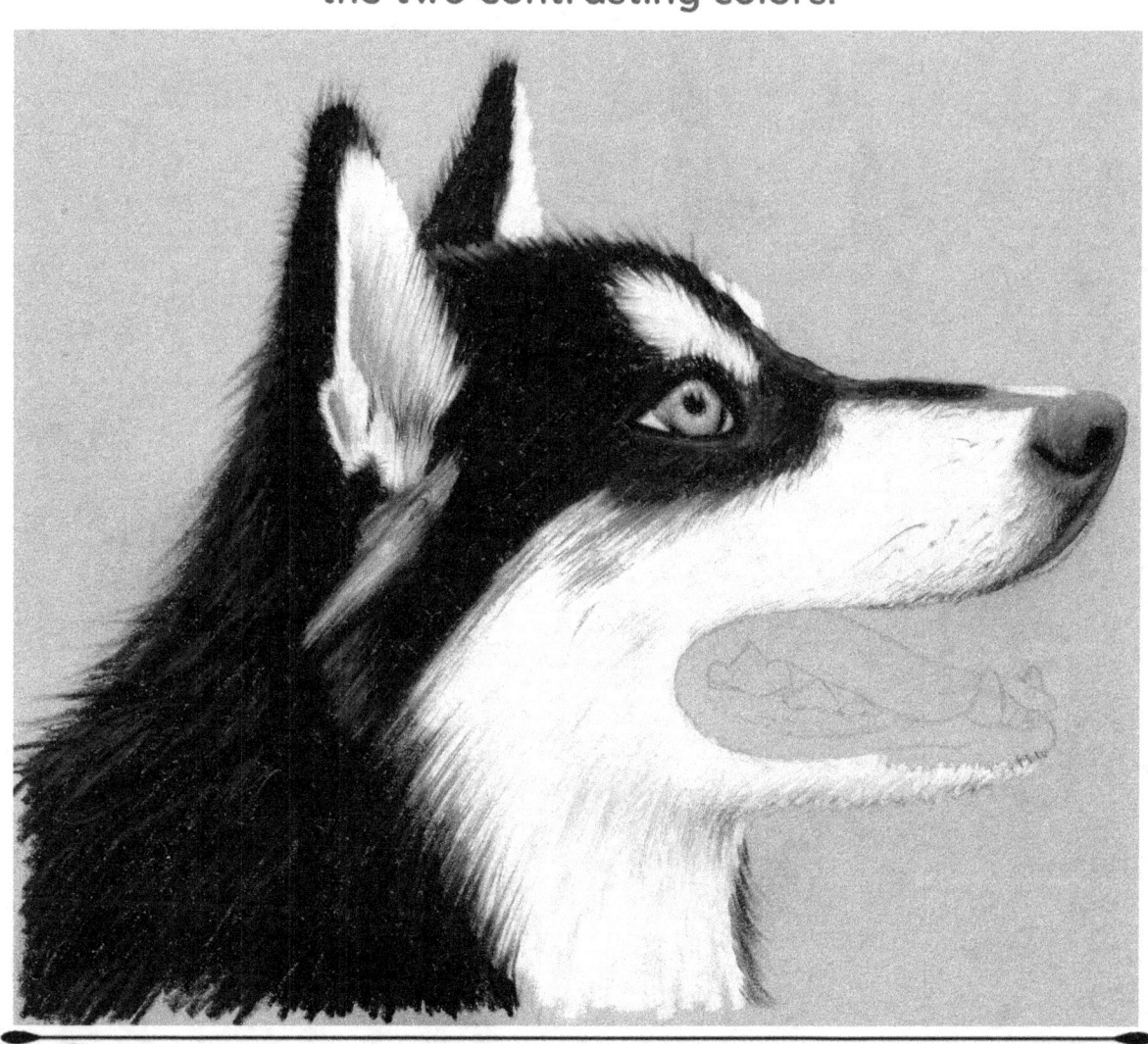

White Hairs on Dark Fur

Soften the outer white fur in a similar manner as the black fur, using a well-sharpened white charcoal for better results. Focus on areas above the eye and on the right side of the ears. Next, draw white hairs over the black ones near the color transition using an opaque white marker or a white ink gel pen. Regularly clean the pen's tip on a separate sheet to prevent it from picking up black residue. To control the brightness, gently tap the freshly drawn hairs with your finger while they're still wet. If any undesired white hairs occur, easily remove them using your nail or a precision knife. Draw the white whiskers after completing the mouth, leaving it as the final step.

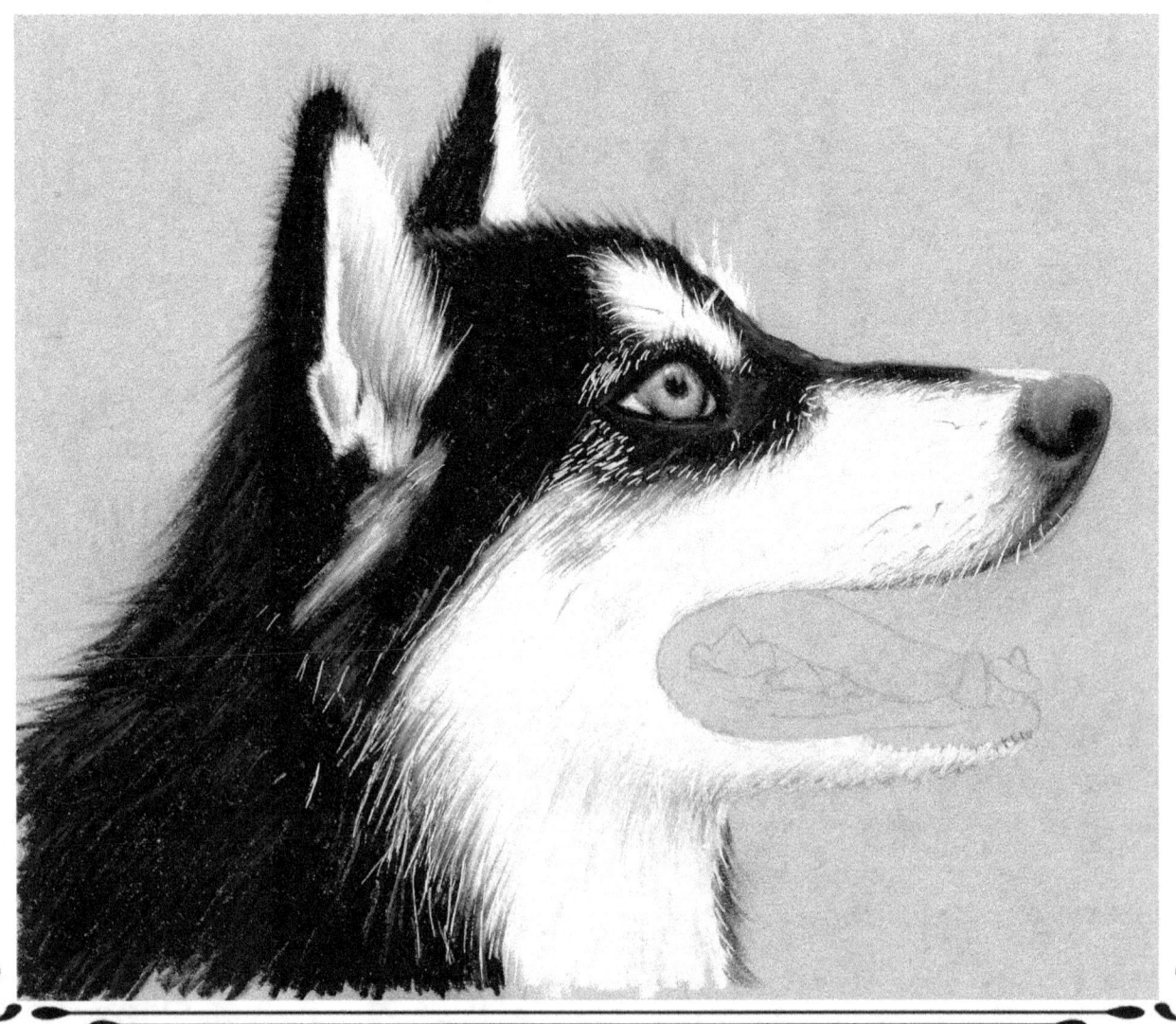

Coloring the Teeth

Now, let's focus on the finishing touch—the mouth.
Begin by carefully coloring the teeth with a white charcoal pencil or an opaque white marker. Afterward, gently go over the shaded parts of the teeth using an HB pencil, applying light pressure for subtle shading. This step brings precision to the details, completing the overall refinement of your drawing.

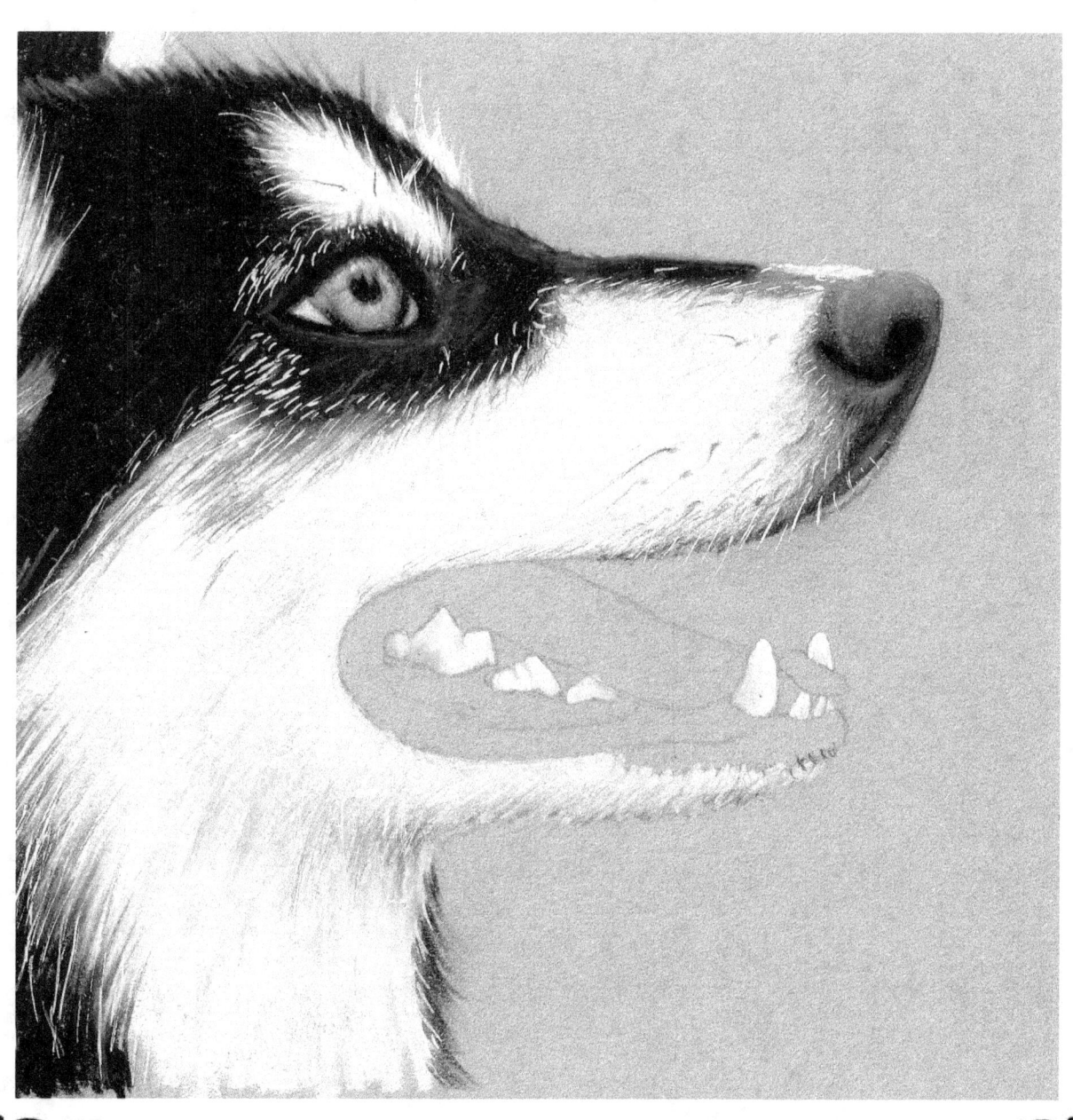

Shading the Tongue

Proceed by shading the tongue, following the visual guide in the next image. Utilize an **HB** pencil for nuanced depth and realism. The choice is yours—add more details or maintain its current simplicity. Keep in mind, a superior drawing isn't necessarily the most intricate one. Your preferred piece is typically the one that resonates with you the most. Strive to create an artwork that truly satisfies your artistic vision.

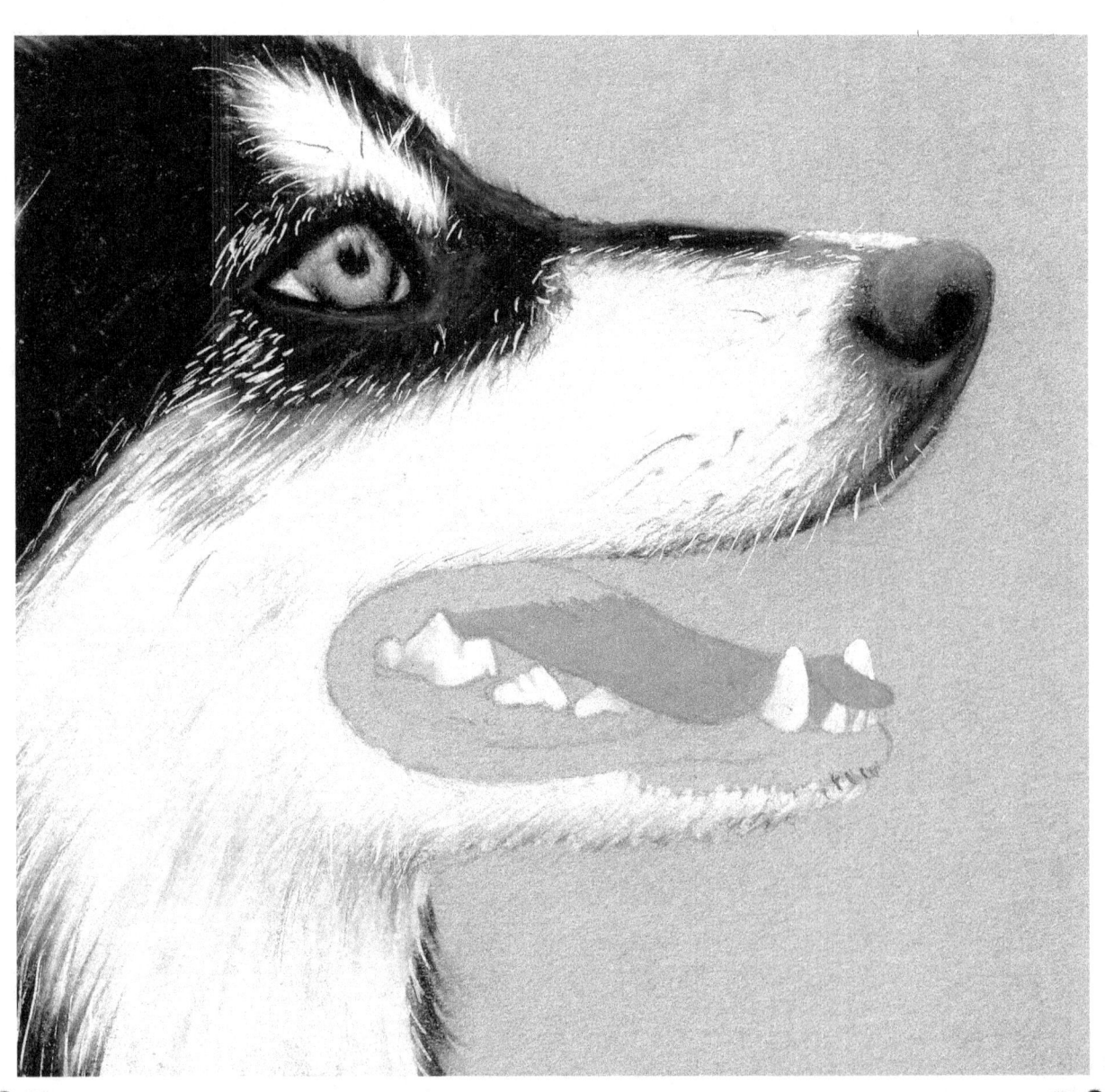

Shading the Mouth with Precision

Shade the remaining areas of the mouth, the surrounding skin, and the entirely black gum around the teeth, excluding the section next to the shaded tongue. Grab a 14B pencil and apply firm pressure for intense shadows. Exercise precision as you carefully outline around the teeth and tongue, using a well-sharpened pencil to maintain their original shapes.

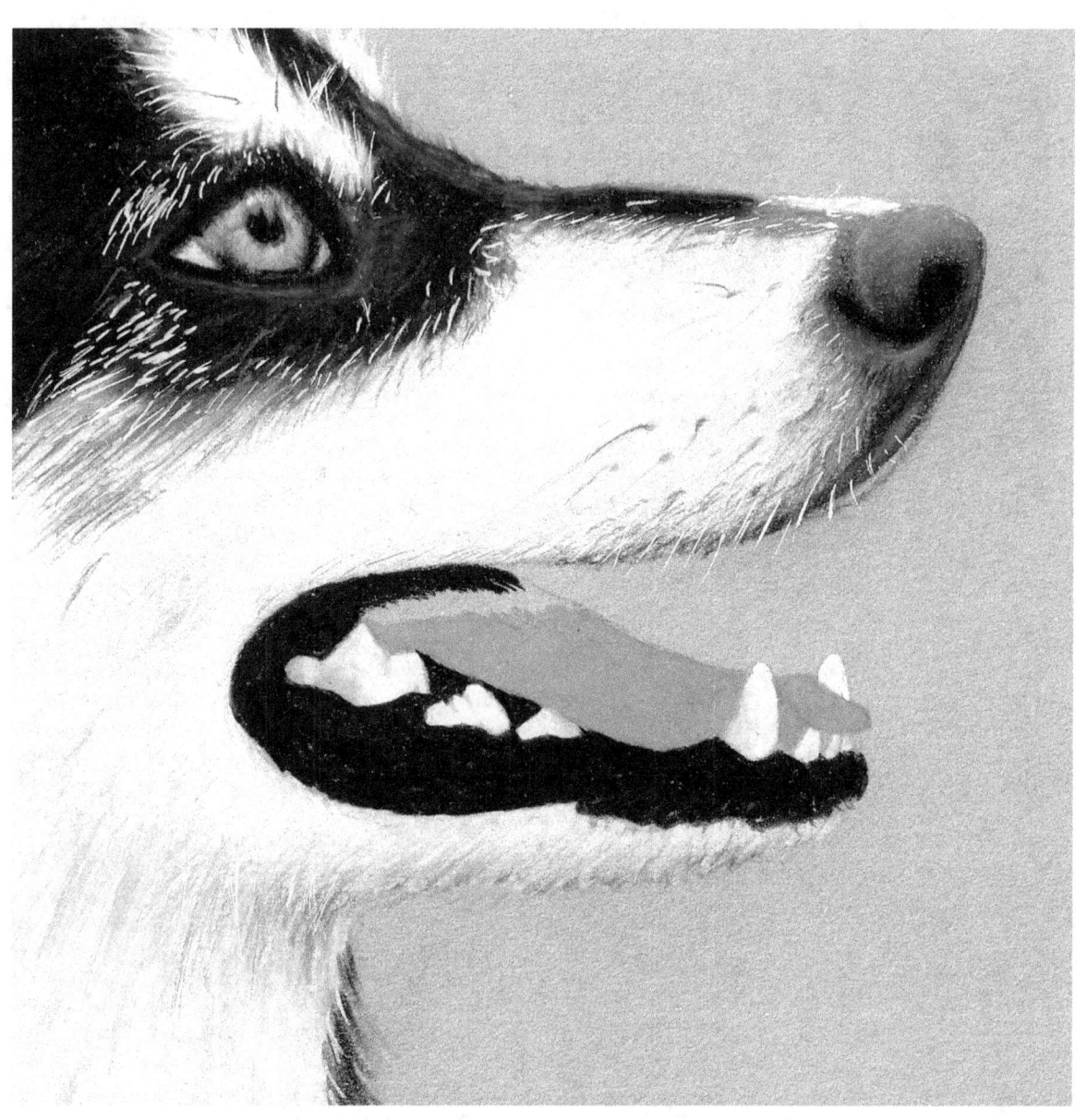

Blending the Tongue

Ensure a smooth transition as the HB area of the tongue gradually melds into the previously shaded 14B area. Use a 4B pencil to connect the HB and black regions, applying firm pressure over the black section and gradually releasing it as you reach the edge of the HB area. This technique creates a seamless gradation between the two, enhancing the overall realism. Extend your shading to the lower section of the tongue, addressing the shadow cast by the canines. Gradually intensify the shade in the lower part while keeping it lighter next to the initial HB shading. This technique enhances the roundness of the tongue edges, contributing to a more lifelike depiction.

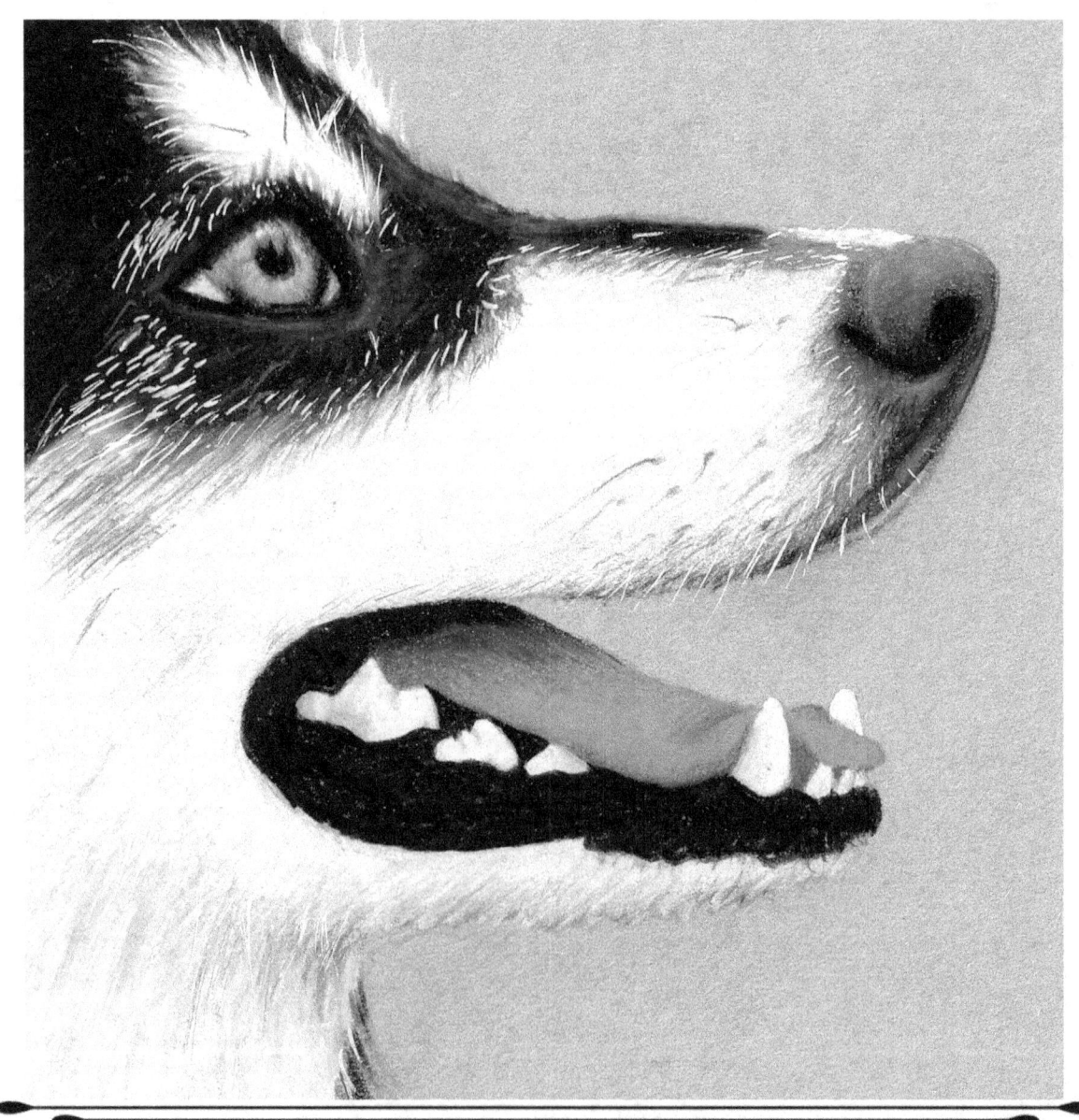

Adding Highlights and Whiskers

Finish off your drawing by adding highlights to the gums, tongue, and shaded areas using a firm touch with the eraser. Press down to make these spots stand out.
For the final touch, draw the whiskers above the mouth and outline the open mouth area, following the reference photo.
Use a white marker or a white ink gel pen for this step to give it that extra pop and make your drawing look complete.

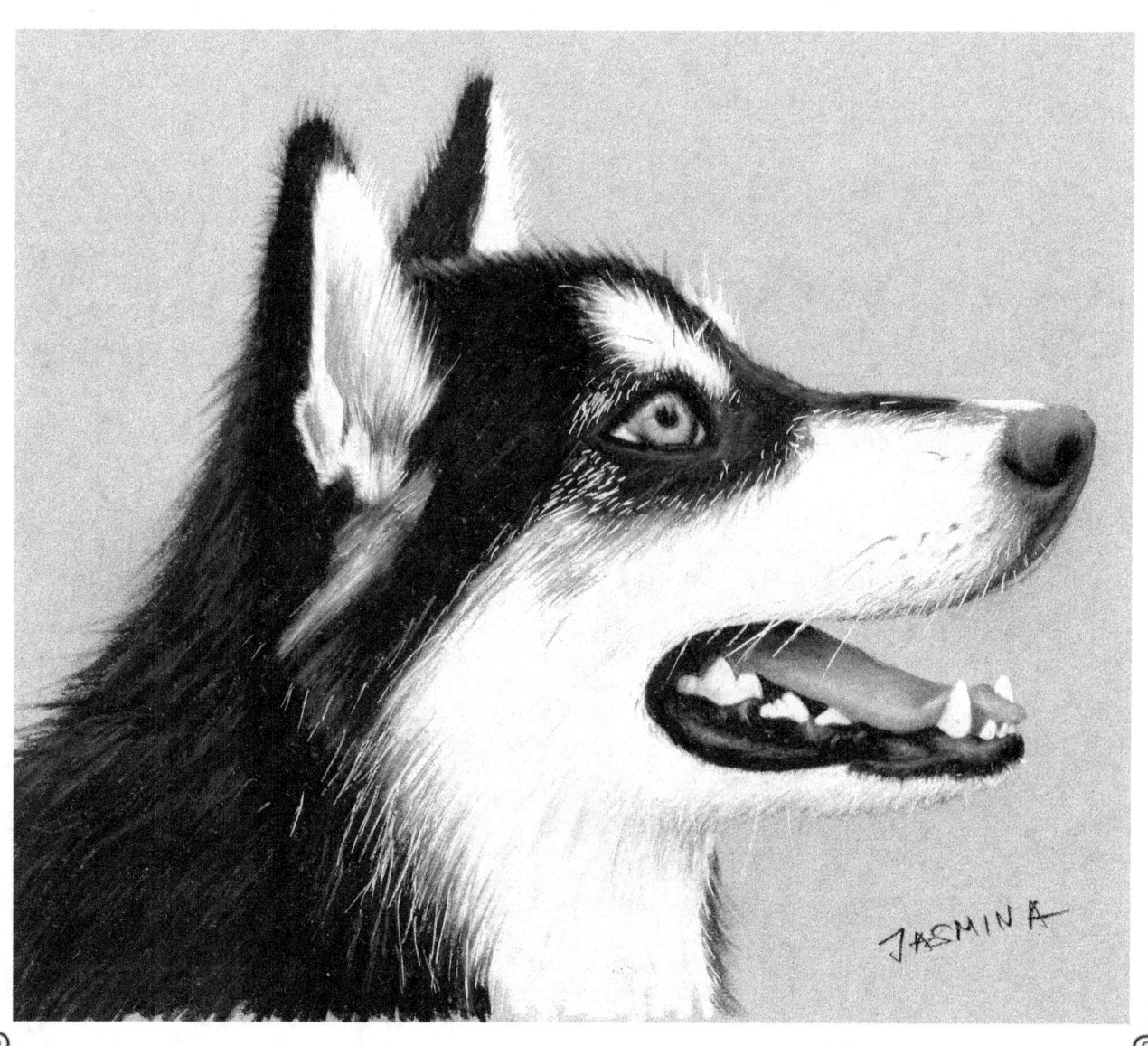

How to Draw a Tiger

Drawing a tiger from a reference photo provides a focused opportunity for skill development in observation and technical proficiency. Tigers, as subjects, offer intricate details that challenge artists to refine their abilities and enhance artistic skills by working on details, textures, and proportions. It also allows for a focused study of the animal's unique features, fostering a deeper understanding of wildlife and potentially raising awareness about the importance of conservation.

The Reference Photo

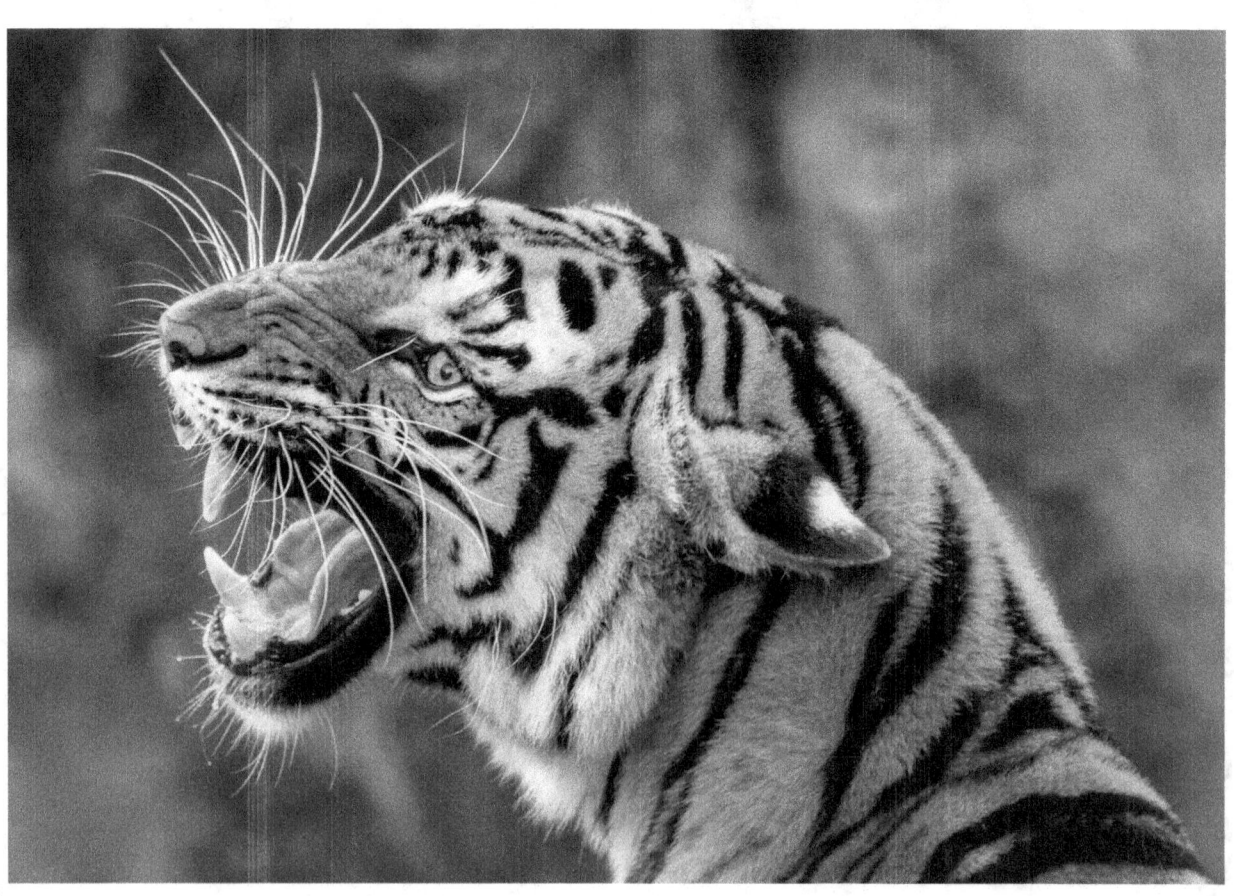

Sketching and Basic Shapes

Explore your drawing skills by depicting this tiger on grey paper, allowing the white fur and whiskers to stand out. Working on a toned background not only adds depth but also presents a unique opportunity to develop your artistic technique.

I recommend Clay by Fabriano or Strathmore Toned Gray paper for this. In the following image, you'll find my pencil sketch after removing the gridlines. To guide my shading process, I've marked the distinctive black stripes with 'X.' This serves as a helpful reference, ensuring accuracy and allowing for a focused approach when adding shading details.

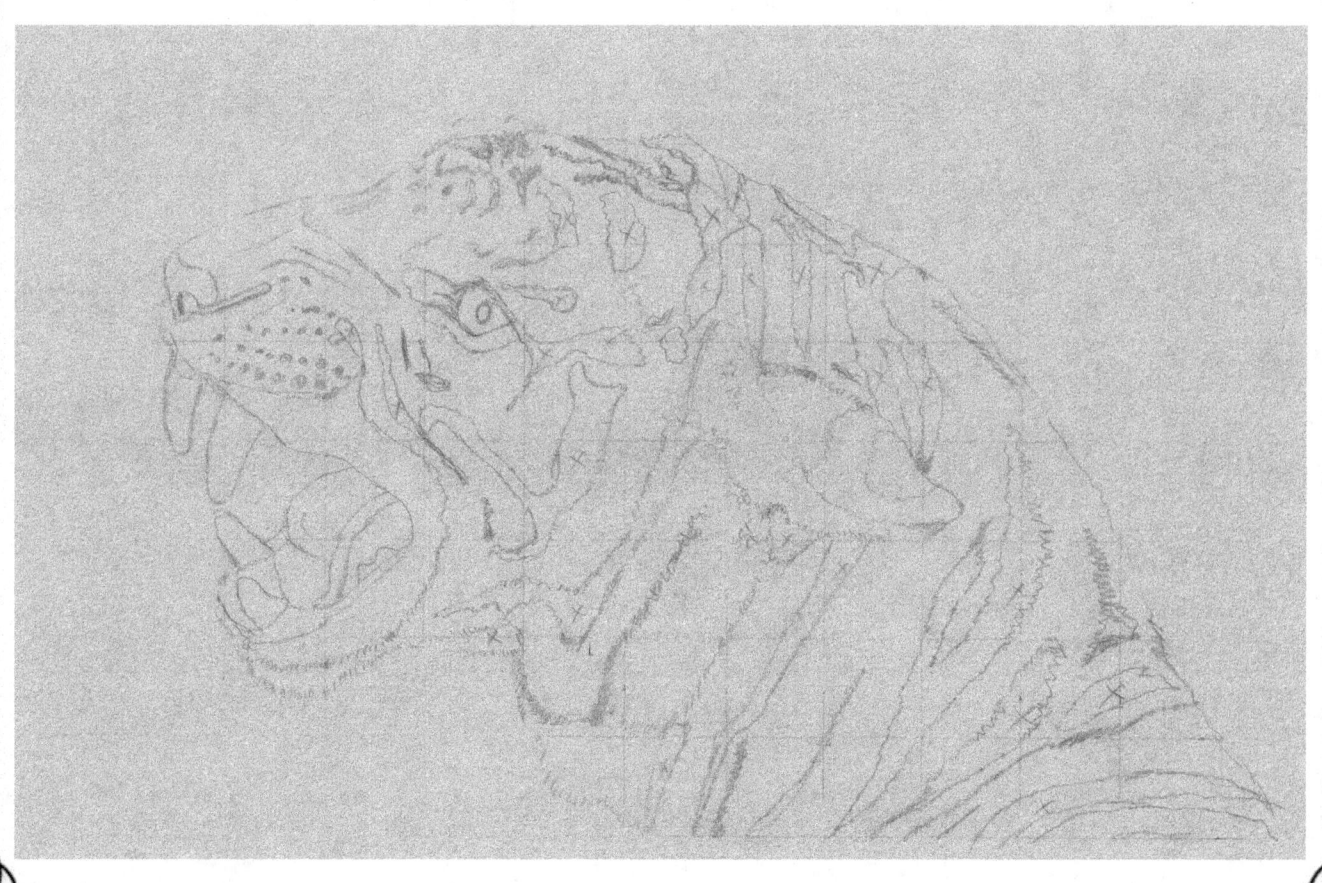

Captivating Eyes

Begin by bringing the tiger to life through its eyes.
Start by coloring the pupil with a 14B pencil for depth.
Then, add highlights over the grey paper-colored iris using
either white charcoal or opaque white markers.
This subtle contrast on grey paper will intensify the gaze and
create a captivating effect.

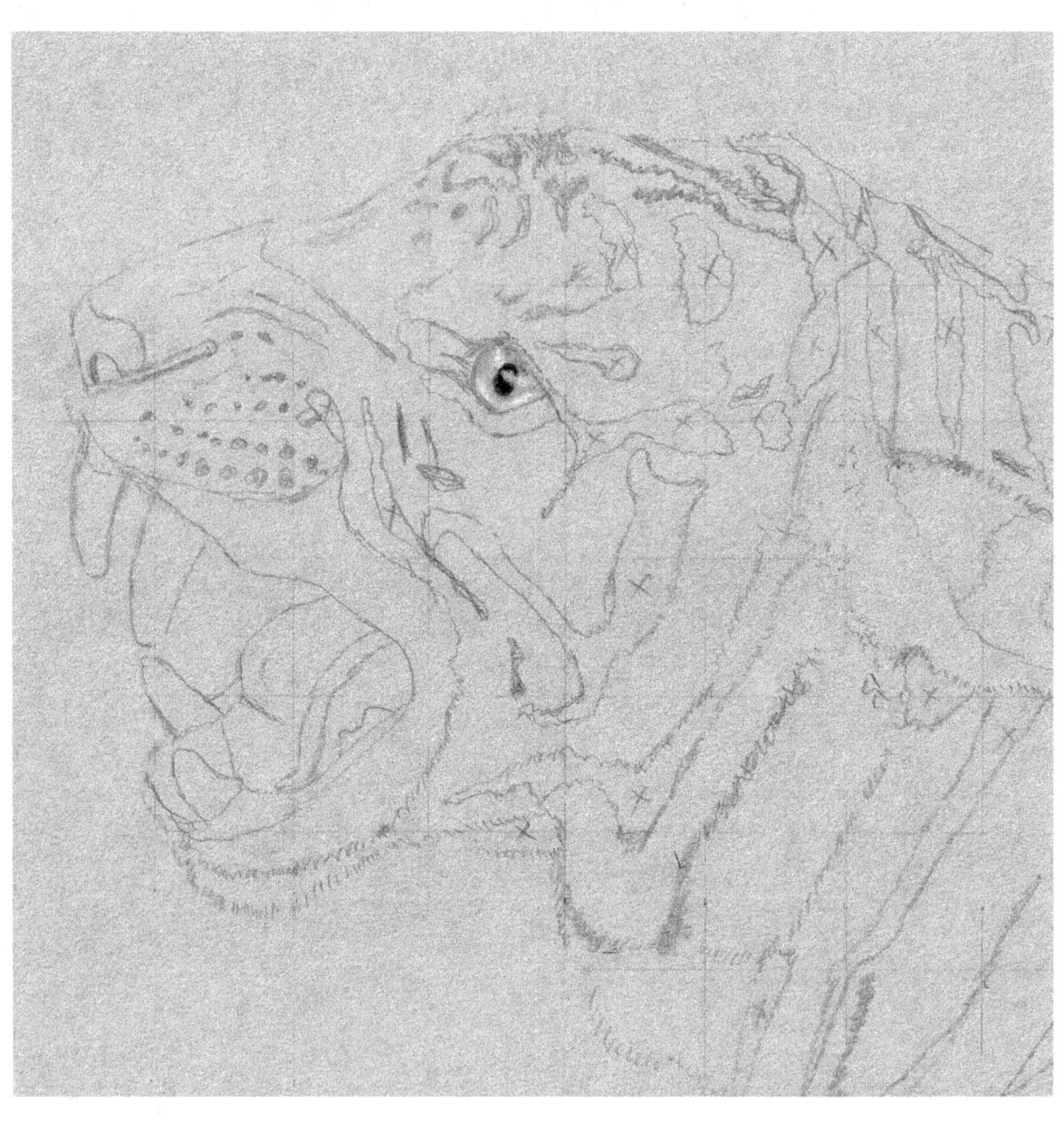

Shading Darkest Elements

Let's shade the darkest elements using a 14B pencil. This includes the black stripes and other areas such as the skin around the muzzle, tear duct, and nostrils. Apply firm pressure to achieve an intense black color, making sure to follow the direction of the hair's flow and growth. Take special care when shading over the nose and muzzle to maintain their proportional shapes. However, when coloring the stripes, feel free to relax, as they don't need to precisely match the reference photo.

This step may be time-consuming, so there's no need to rush. Pressing hard for an extended period may cause discomfort, so take breaks every 10-15 minutes. In the image below, you can observe the completed shading for the black areas.

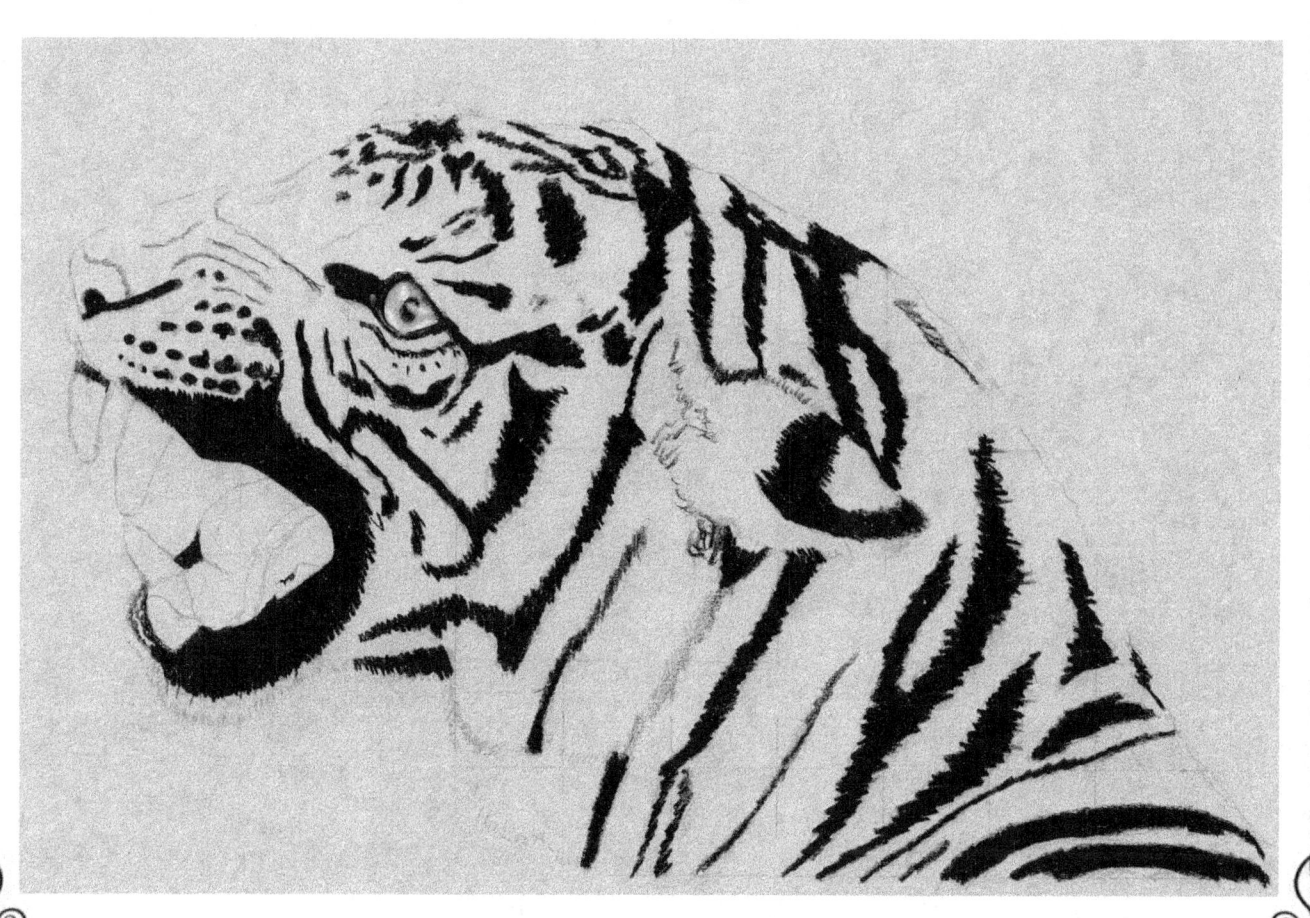

Coloring White Features

Transition to coloring the white elements like the canine, highlighted tongue parts, and the white fur using a white charcoal pencil, as demonstrated in the illustration below. Pay close attention to the direction of hair flow and growth for a natural look. Exercise care while coloring next to the black areas to maintain their intensity. Going over them might affect their absolute blackness and could pick up some black pencil residue, especially if applied over the white sections. While the world isn't just black and white, for now, let's focus on applying these primary colors, reserving detailed work on the edges for later.

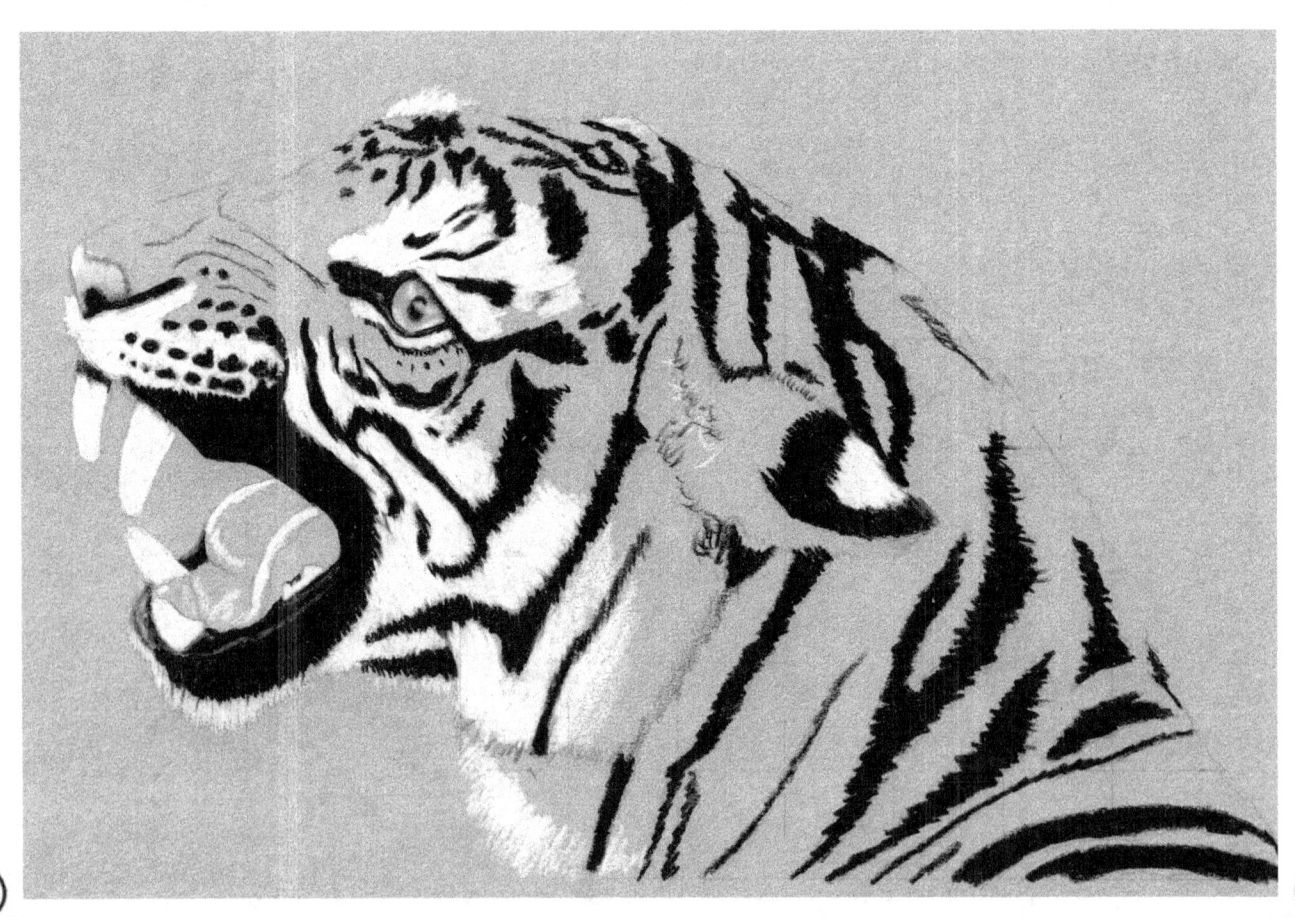

Shading Tiger's Canines

Begin shading the tiger's canines from the right side with an HB pencil. Gradually ease off the pressure as you move left, stopping in the middle for a nuanced three-dimensional effect.

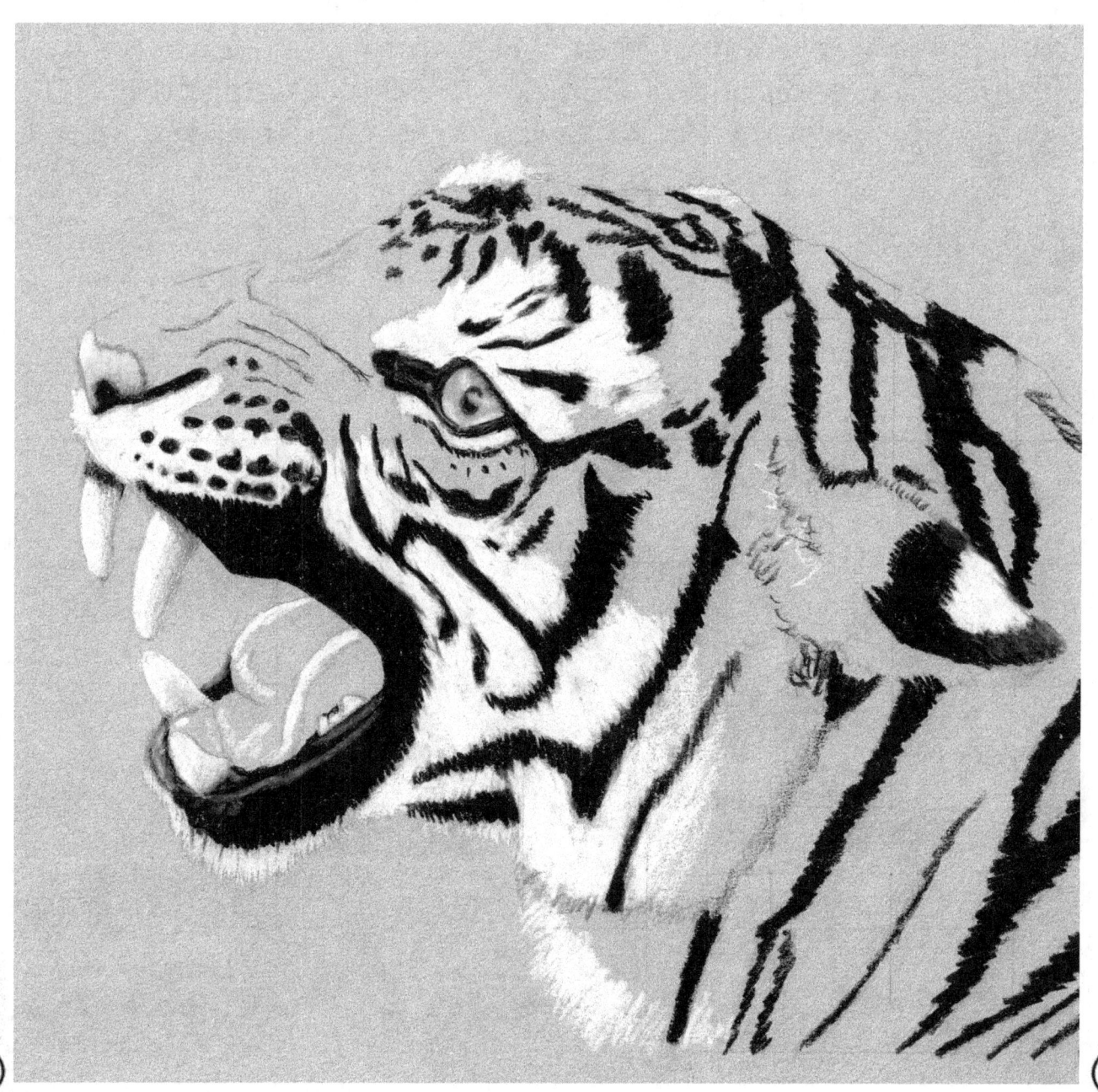

Shading the Brown Fur

Using an HB pencil with a delicate touch, apply a light pressure to shade the brown fur. Follow the natural direction of the hair's growth, making sure to mark the brown areas for future detailing. This step requires patience, as we'll later enhance the drawing with highlights and shadows over the brown fur. At this point, the drawing may appear somewhat two-dimensional, but upcoming additions of shadows, highlights, and smooth gradients will bring realism and a three-dimensional quality to the artwork.

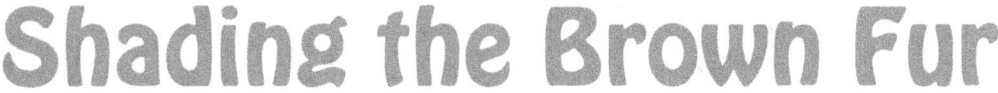

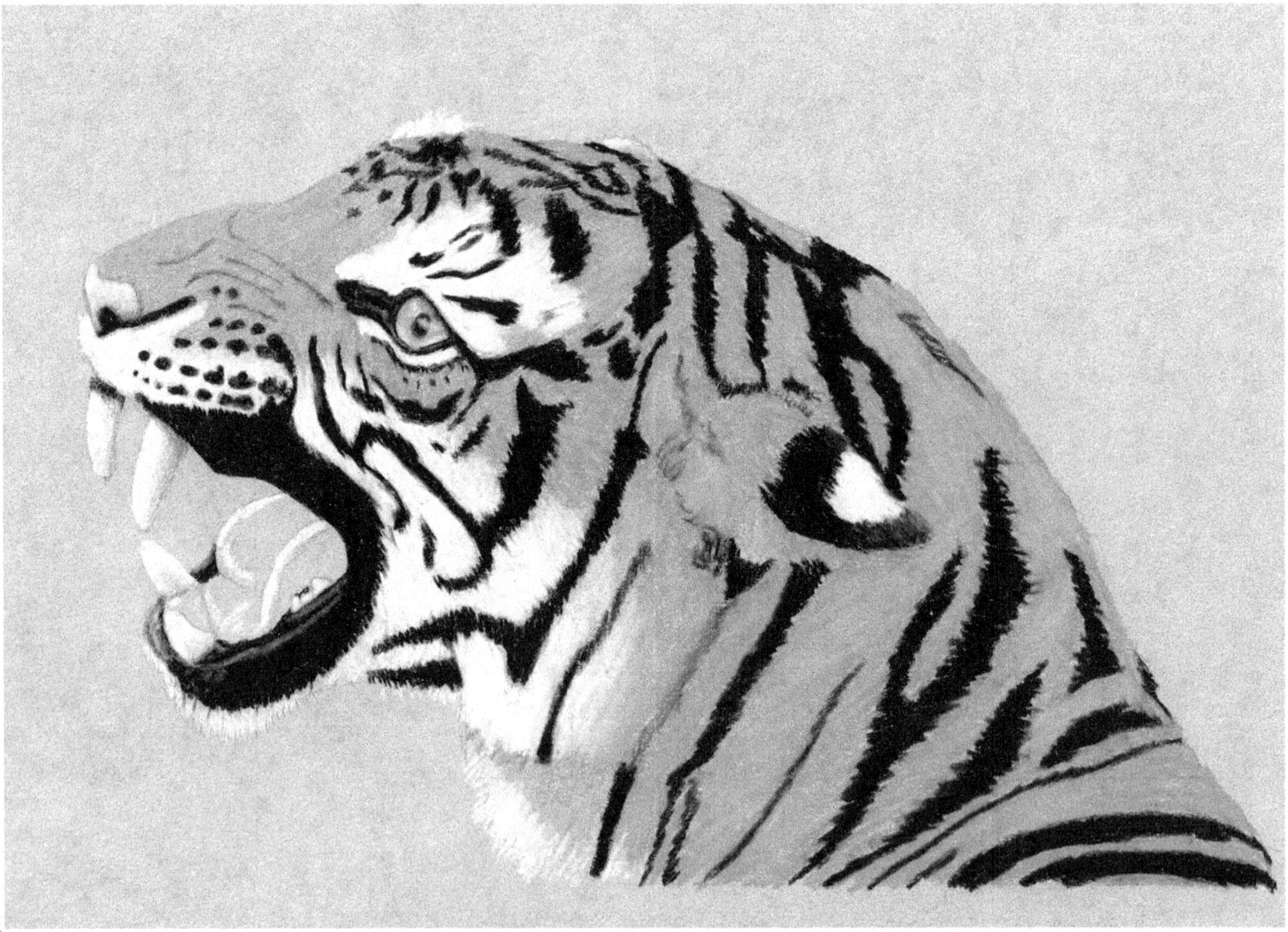

Crafting Shadows

Utilize a 2B pencil to create shadowed areas over the brown fur drawn with an HB, concentrating on the darkest regions like the shadow cast by the ear, facial wrinkles, and other relevant areas. This phase invites a closer focus on details, allowing you to draw hair by hair now that the primary shades have been established.

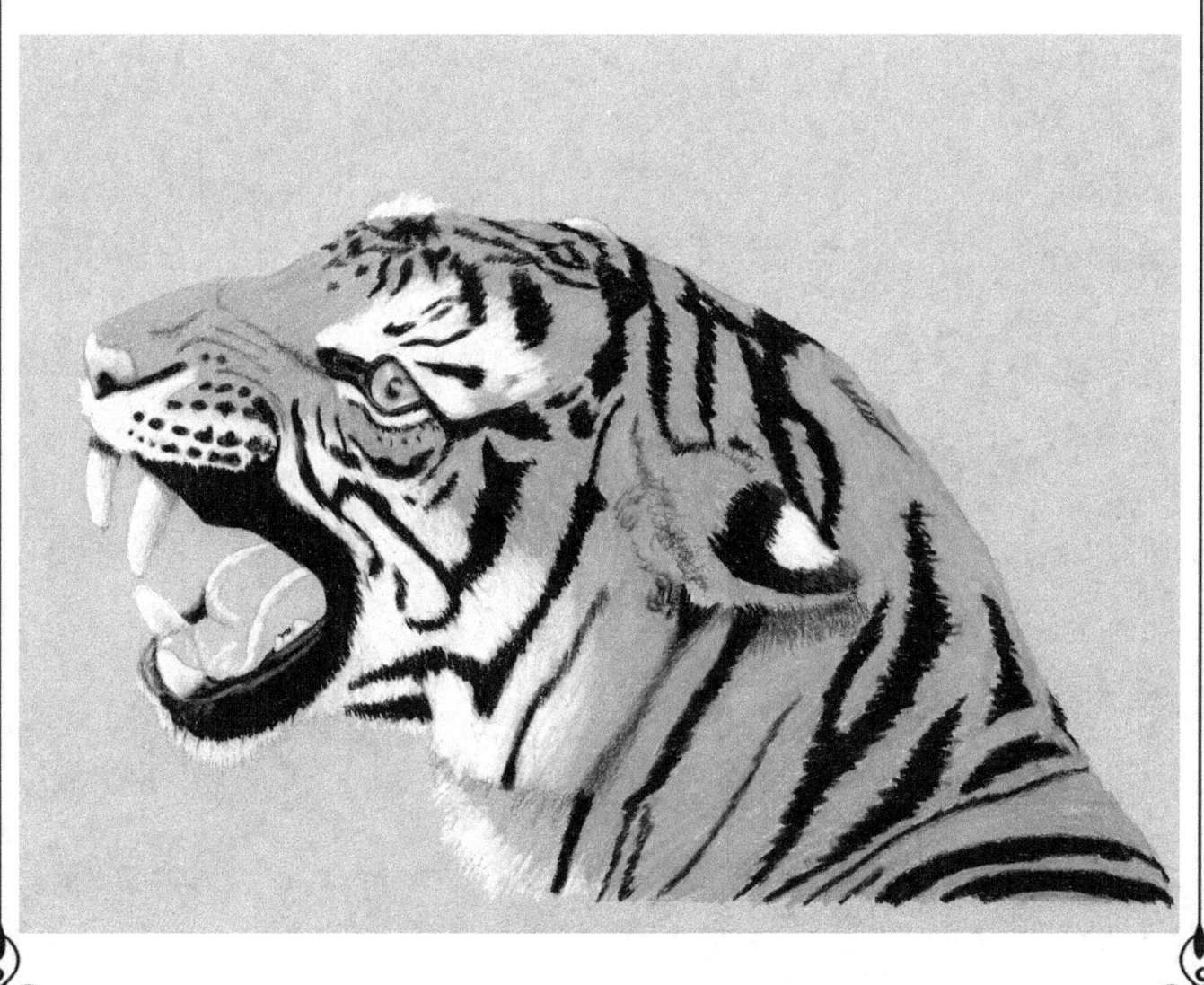

Refining Details

Extend the detailed work with a 2B pencil across the remaining shadowed brown fur. Blend the edges between the 2B-shaded areas and the basic brown fur created with an HB, using a B pencil. Focus on adding numerous tiny hairs to any areas darker than the basic fur value, creating a nuanced and realistic effect. Compare the previous and following images to observe the noticeable difference, especially in areas that have become darker.

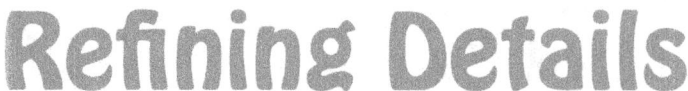

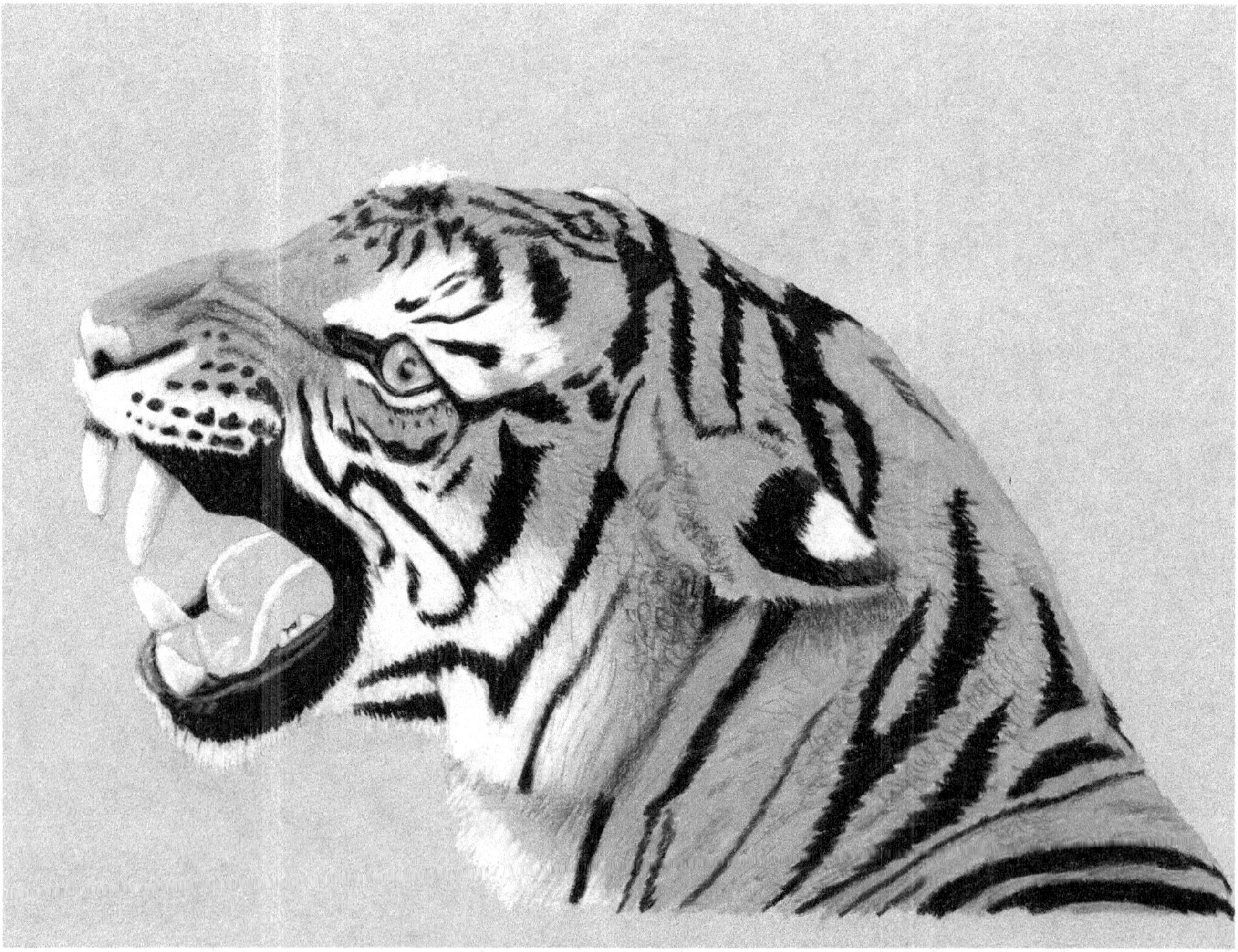

Adding Highlights and Gradients

Now, let's make those lighter parts of the brown fur pop. Take your eraser and gently work over the HB marks, especially on the top of the head and back where the fur catches more light. With a pointed eraser, carefully remove small hair-like details, adjusting the pressure for varied highlights. Pay attention to the edges—they should be a bit brighter too.

To create a seamless shift between the white and brown fur, use a 2B pencil. Just glide over both sections, and you'll achieve a nice, gradual blend. Add more shading with this pencil as needed to enrich the depth and texture.

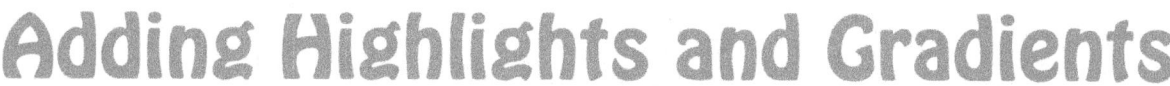

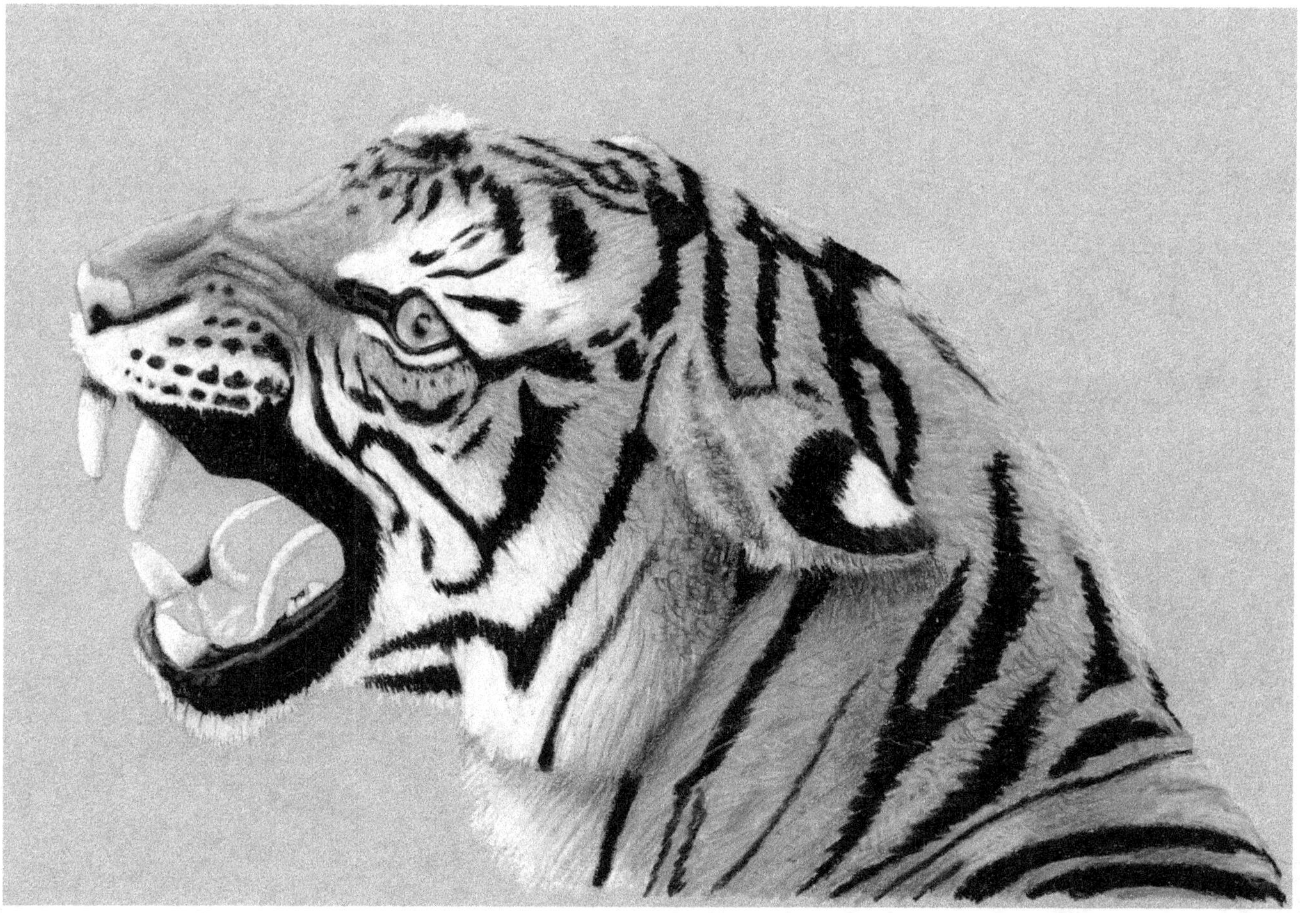

Refining Black Stripes

Using a colorless blender (such as Prismacolor Premier's PC 1077), gently place the tip over the black stripe and draw outward. This technique introduces black hairs over the white and brown hairs, resulting in a soft and fluffy texture. The goal is to create blended and blurry hairs for a more realistic look. Maintain careful attention to the direction of the hair's growth and flow during this process for a more natural and lifelike outcome.

This step may be time-consuming as you delicately navigate around each black area, but the significant transformation in texture and appearance will be well worth the effort.

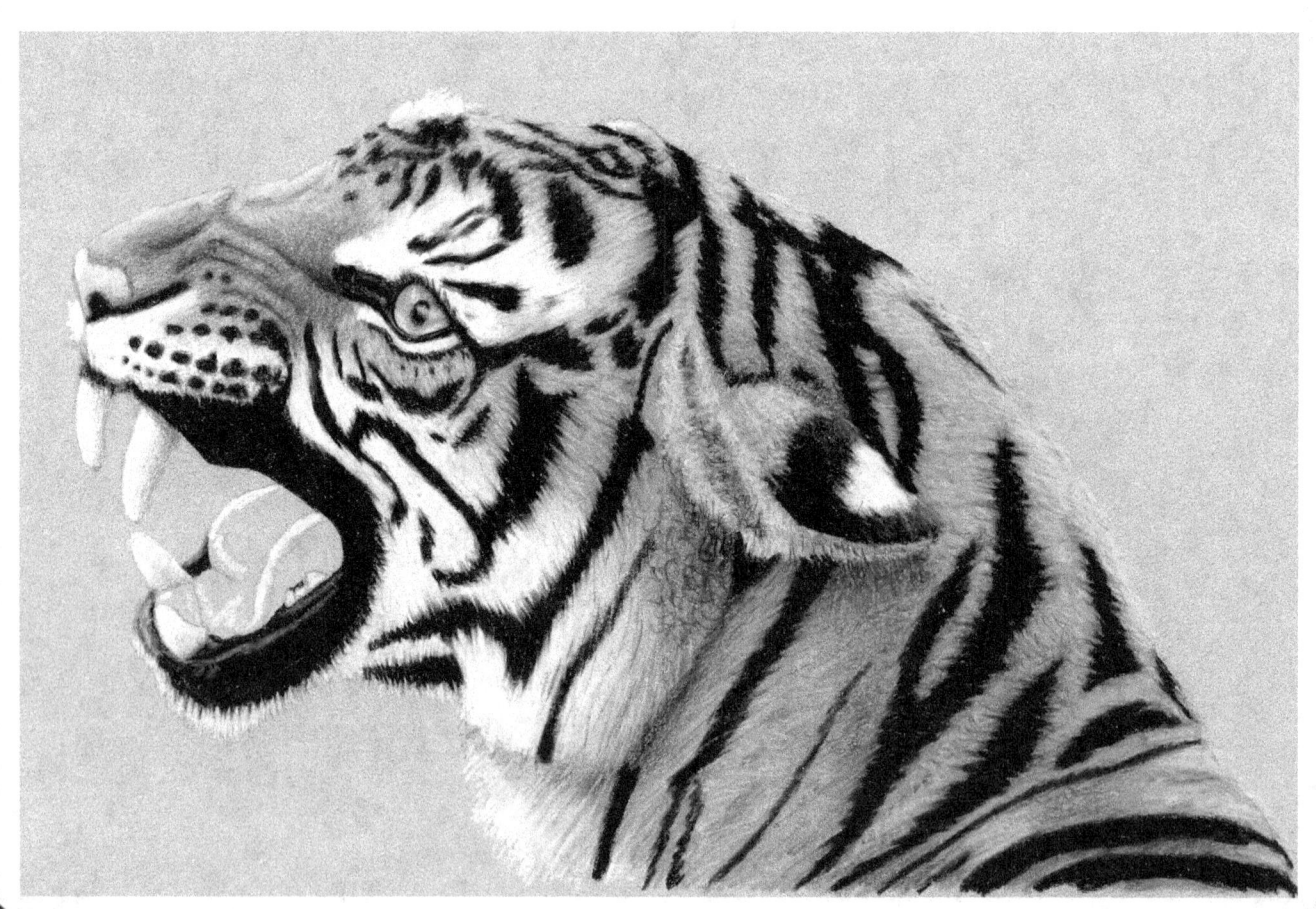

Shading Shadows on White Fur

Now, let's deepen the shadows on the white fur in areas with less light. Take an HB pencil and shade over the white sections where needed. Remember, white objects tend to turn gray in reduced light, so consider this while shading.

Highlight the slightly curved area above the tiger's eyes in the middle of the white fur by darkening it with the HB pencil. Additionally, make sure the white fur appears darkest on the right side of the muzzle, as it receives less light. This step adds dimension and realism to the tiger's features.

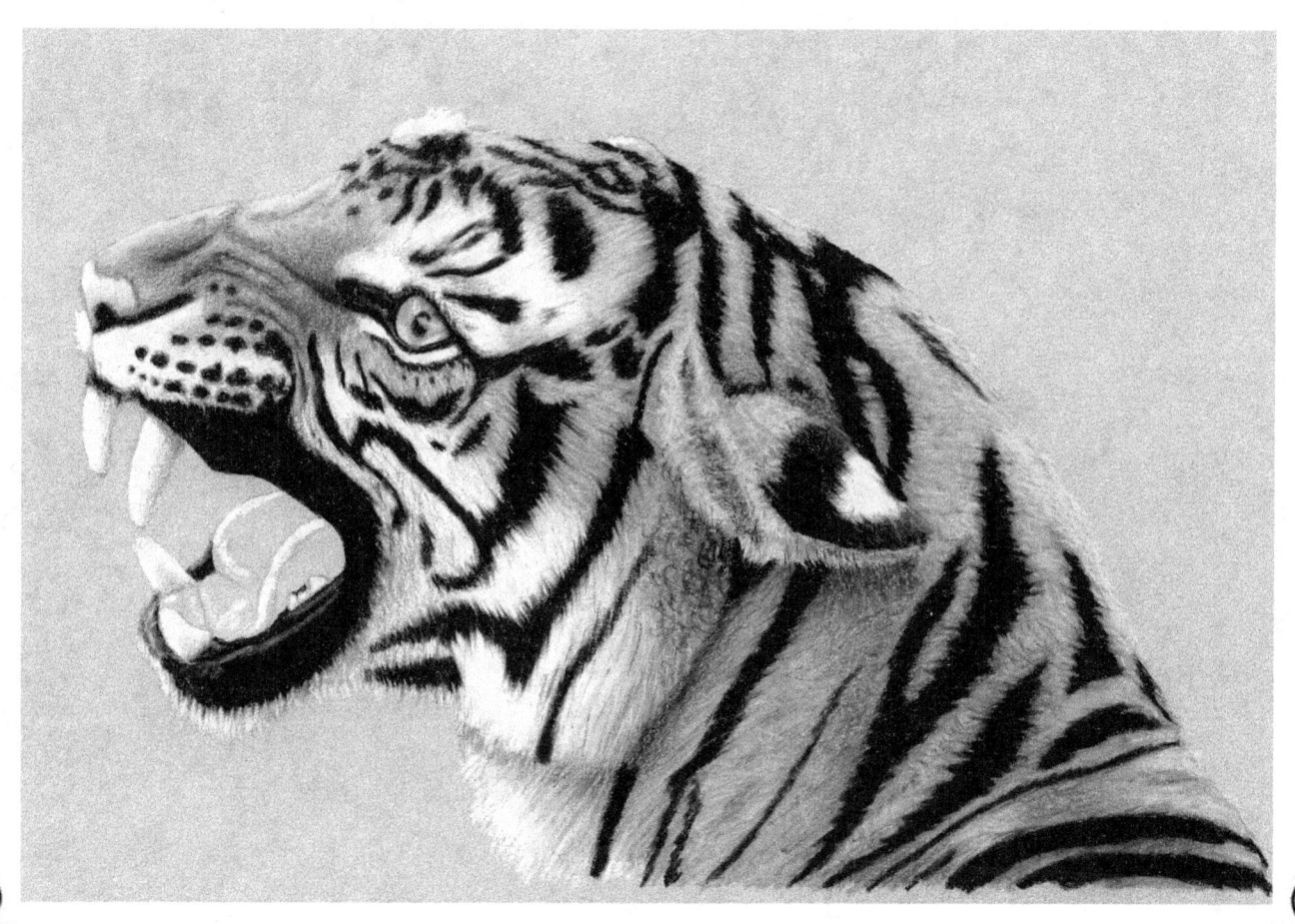

Shading the Tongue

Follow the image below to shade the tiger's nose and tongue with an HB pencil. Adjust pressure to create nuanced shaded and highlighted areas. Consider using lighter or darker pencils than HB for additional variation.

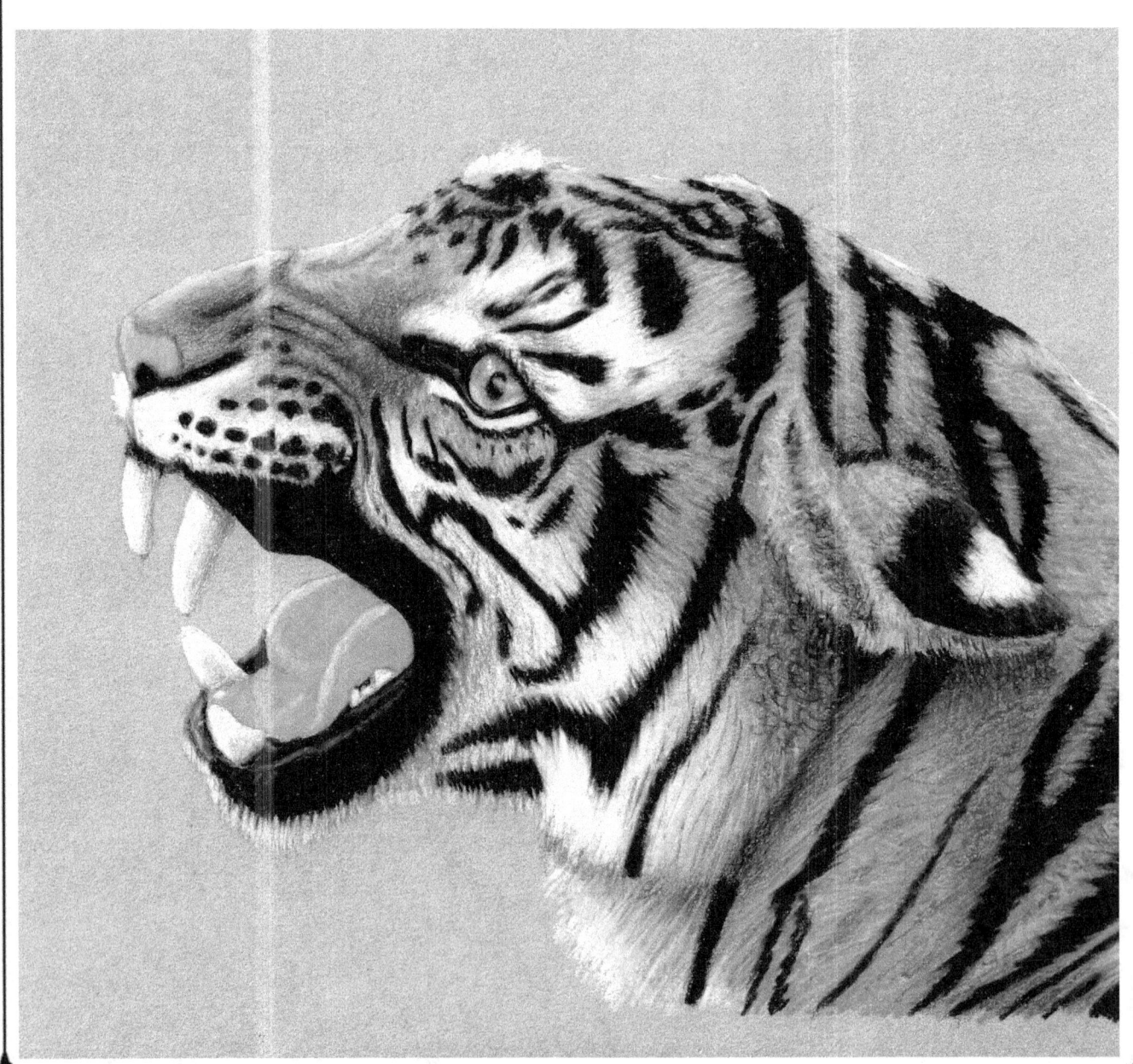

Adding Details

To add intricate details to the tongue, use an electric eraser to carefully remove graphite, creating tiny needle-like textures. This step enhances realism and brings attention to the finer aspects of the tiger's features.

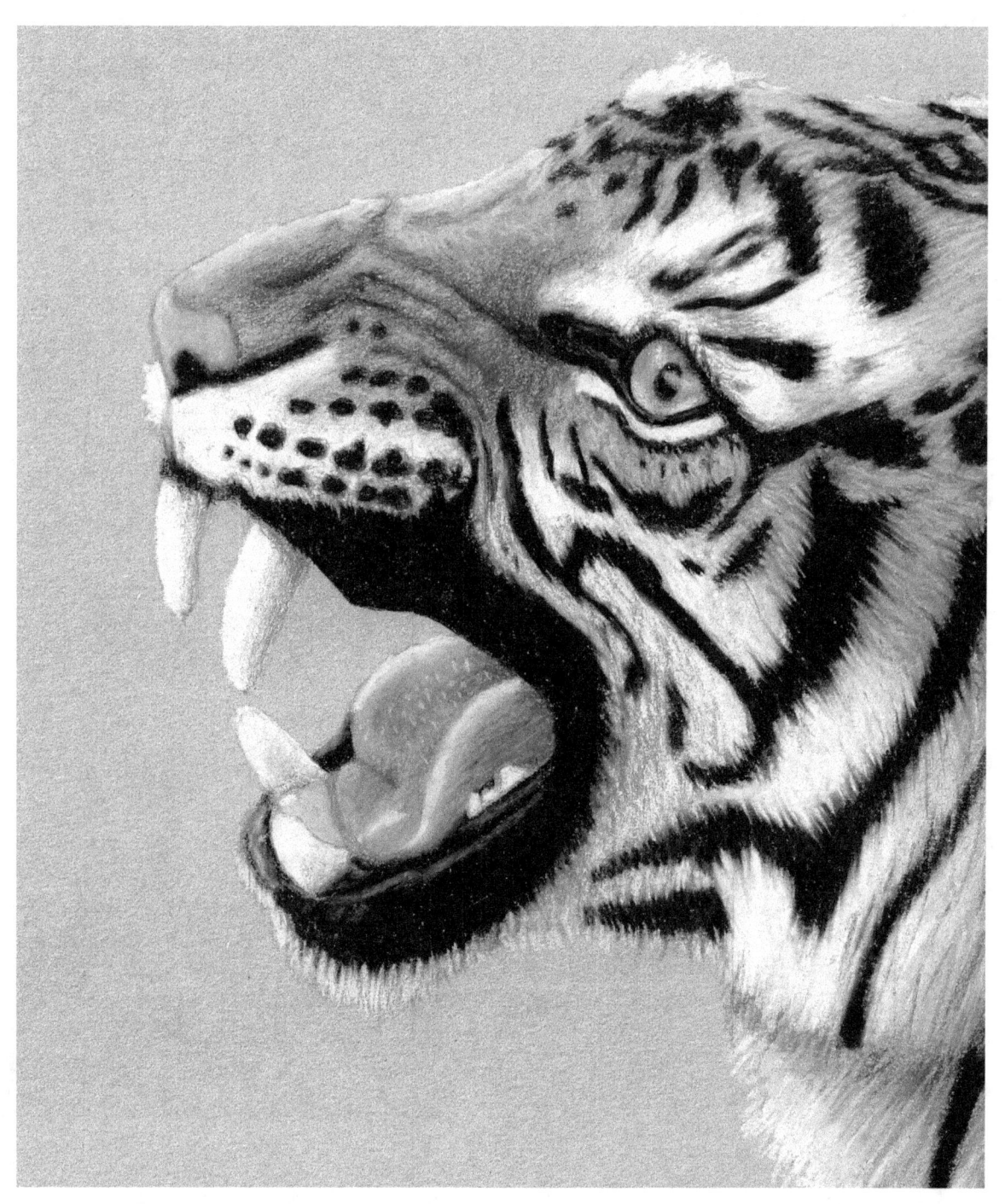

Final Touches

As a final touch, delicately draw fine lines for the whiskers using a white marker. Feel free to add as many details as desired, adjusting the shading to your preferred style. This step allows for personalization, giving you the creative freedom to refine and enhance the drawing to your satisfaction.

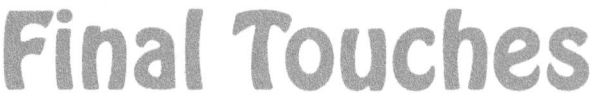

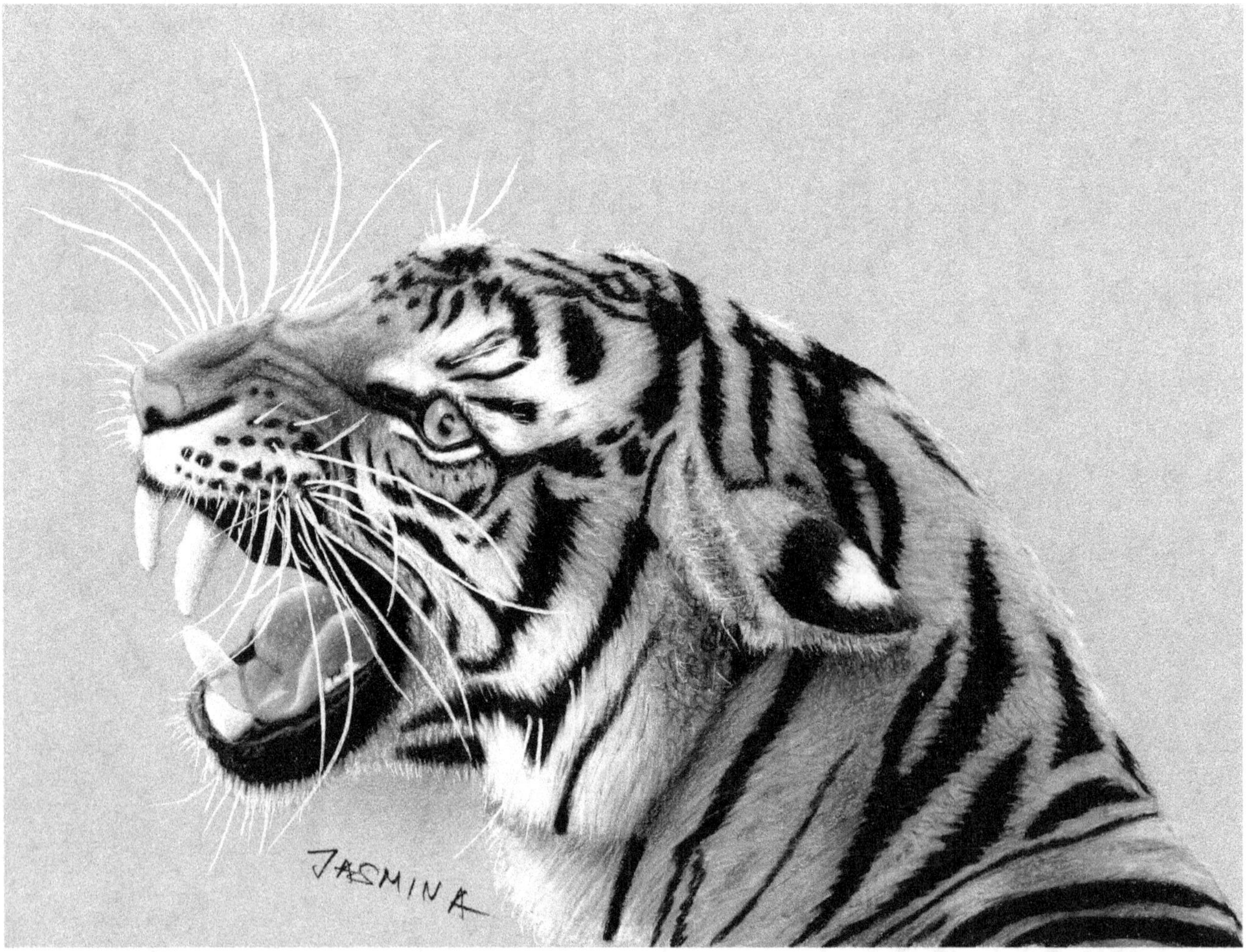

Drawing Interludes

JASMINA
2022

Editing Your Drawing

Alright, you've completed your drawing, and now it's time to showcase it online. After scanning or photographing your artwork, you might notice that it doesn't look quite the same as it does in person. To ensure your drawings shine in their true glory, displaying them in natural light becomes essential, especially if you plan to sell or take commissions.

In this tutorial, we will explore the process of editing your scanned drawing to enhance its appearance. After completing your drawing, you may notice that the scanned or photographed version appears pale and the graphite is overly shiny. To present your drawing accurately and showcase its true beauty, it is important to edit it using an image editing software.

Before and After

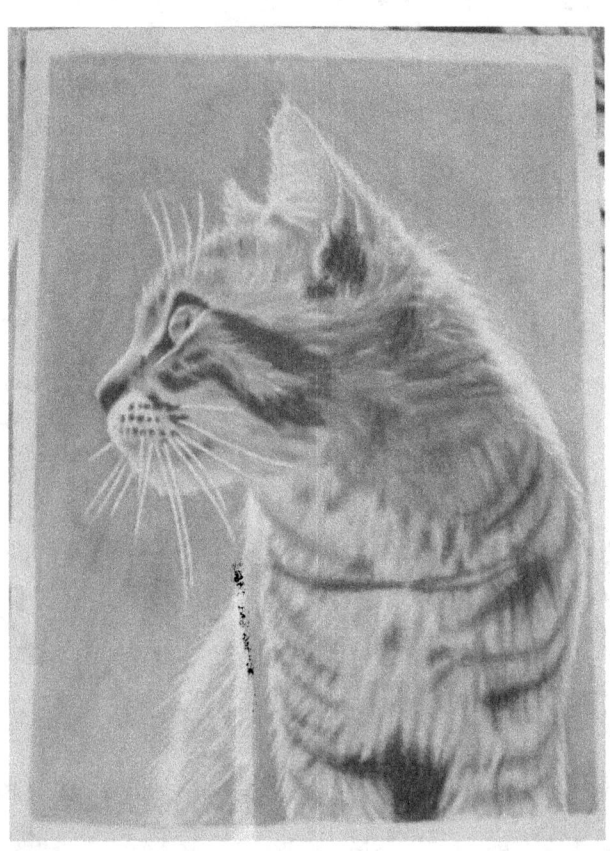 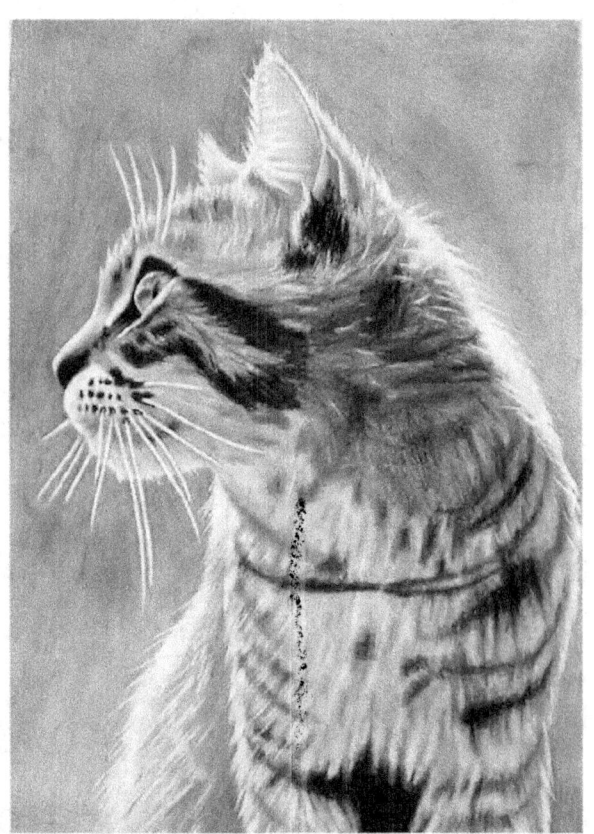

Straightening, Cropping, and Sharpening Your Drawing

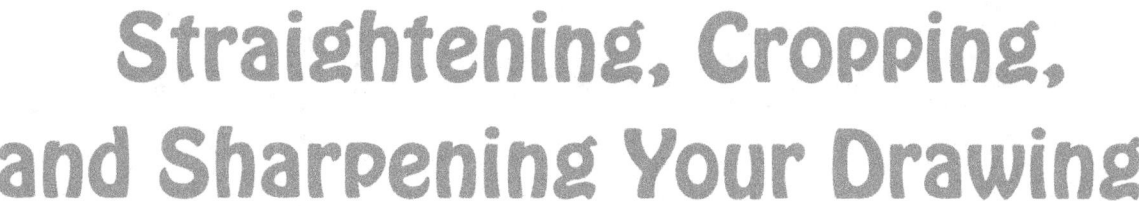

I personally use Windows Photo Gallery for editing, as demonstrated in this tutorial. However, you can use any image editing program that offers adjustment capabilities, such as PaintNET, Photoshop, or Picasa. I will guide you through my preferred method using Windows Photo Gallery, but feel free to adapt the steps to your chosen software.

Start by straightening the image if needed. This will correct any tilt or skew that may have occurred during scanning or photography, resulting in a more balanced and aligned composition.

Next, carefully crop the image to remove any unnecessary or distracting elements. By cropping strategically, you can focus the viewer's attention on the most important parts of your drawing, creating a more compelling and visually impactful presentation.

Finally, apply a sharpening filter or tool to enhance the clarity and crispness of your drawing. This will bring out the fine details and textures, making your artwork appear more defined and professional.

Adjusting Contrast and Saturation

In this step, we will focus on editing the contrast and saturation of our scanned or photographed drawing.
Start by reducing the saturation to
remove any remaining color. This will transform the image into a grayscale representation that emphasizes the graphite shades. Next, increase the contrast slightly to add depth and definition to the drawing, enhancing the lights and darks and making the details stand out. Optionally, you can also darken the shadows to create a more dramatic effect, emphasizing the depth and dimension of your artwork.

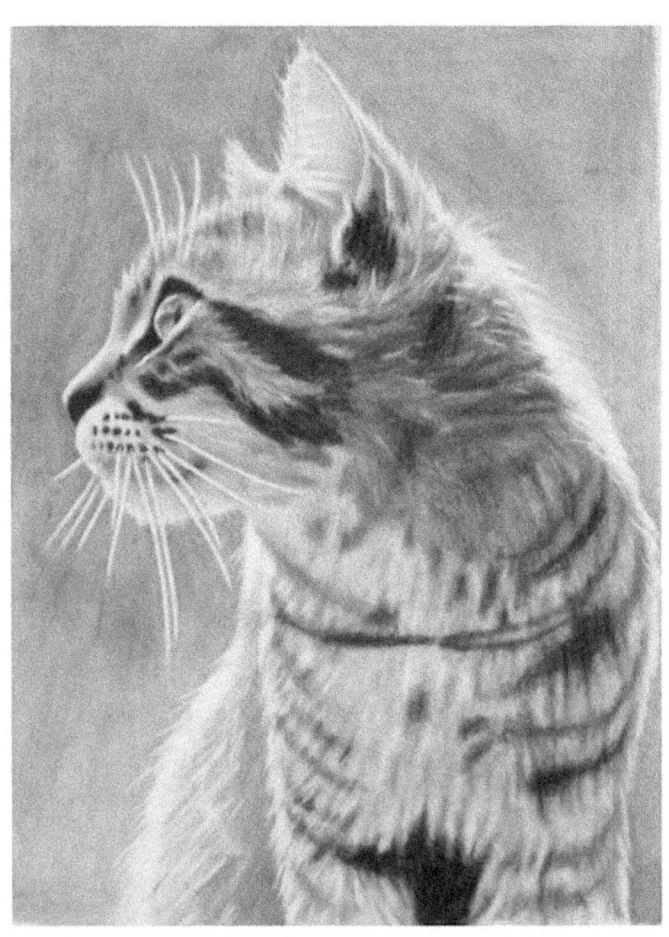

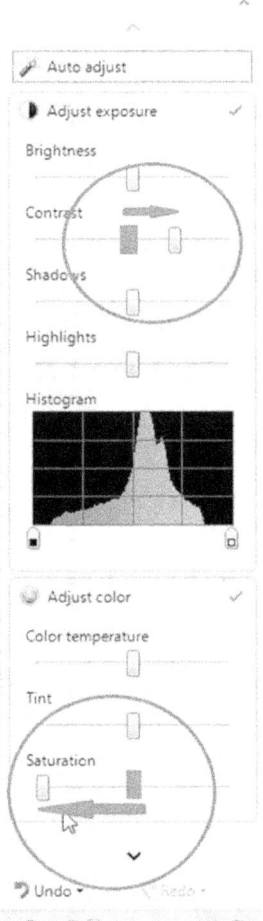

Instead of using the contrast function, you can rely on the histogram function to adjust darkness and highlights in your scanned or photographed drawing. By manipulating the sliders, you can deepen shadows and bring out brighter areas, adding richness and vibrancy to your artwork.

This alternative method not only enhances the overall appearance of your drawing but also allows you to fine-tune specific areas with precision. Once you become comfortable with this technique, you'll be amazed at how quickly you can elevate the visual impact of your artwork, giving it an extra touch of depth and life.

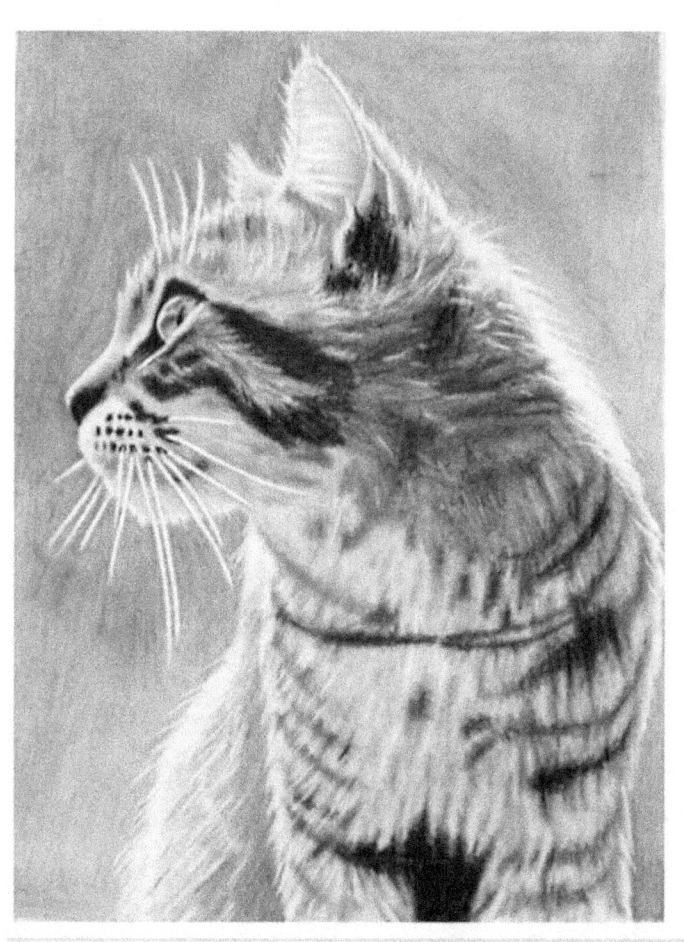
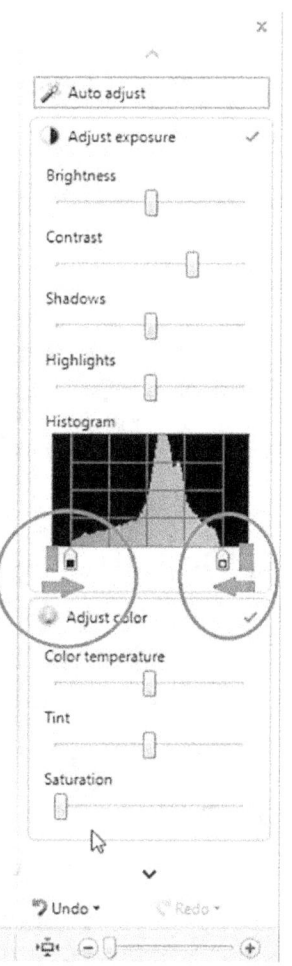

Epilogue

In closing, I want to express my sincere gratitude to each and every one of you who has embarked on this artistic journey with me. Through these tutorials, I have shared my passion for photorealistic drawing and the techniques that have shaped my own artistic style. Throughout my own artistic evolution, I have come to appreciate the endless inspiration that lies within a blank canvas or sheet of paper. Each stroke and mark made holds the potential to bring forth a captivating and awe-inspiring finished piece.

As you delve into the world of photorealistic drawing, remember the importance of building a strong foundation. Start with graphite or charcoal to master the fundamental skills of value creation, gradually transitioning into more complex techniques, such as adding colors to your drawings. Practice, dedication, and self-discipline are key to achieving the desired results in your art.

I understand that it can be discouraging when we compare ourselves to more successful artists, but it's important to remember that everyone has their own unique path and progress. Remember, those artists have invested countless hours, effort, and hard work into their craft, honing their skills and producing hundreds of drawings. It's important to recognize that everyone learns at their own pace. While some individuals may grasp concepts easily and progress quickly, others may require more time and practice to achieve the same level of proficiency. Comparison can hinder our progress, so let's appreciate the inspiration from others while staying true to our own artistic development. Remember that achieving even a slight likeness in your drawing is a testament to your hard work and dedication. Be proud of your accomplishments and let them fuel your motivation to keep pushing forward. Instead of comparing ourselves to others, let's focus on our own growth and celebrate our achievements along the way.

Drawing is not only a creative outlet but also a source of immense joy and fulfillment. It transcends age barriers and has profound benefits for your overall well-being. No matter your age, engaging in drawing promotes focus, mindfulness, and a deep sense of presence in the present moment. It allows you to escape the pressures of daily life and immerse yourself in a world of creativity and self-expression.
Beyond personal growth, I firmly believe in the power of art to inspire and make a positive impact in the world. Each drawing has the potential to spread compassion, raise awareness, or simply uplift someone's spirits. As you create your artwork, consider the messages you can convey and the difference you can make through your art.

It has been an honor to guide you through the intricate steps. Please do not hesitate to reach out to me on social media or through my website. I would be delighted to see your drawings, hear your suggestions, and answer any questions you may have.

Keep creating, keep exploring, and let your artistic journey unfold in ways you never imagined.
Thank you for joining me on this artistic adventure, and may your future drawings inspire and delight others.

Warmest regards,
Jasmina

About the Author

Jasmina Susak is a self-taught artist with a passion for creating photorealistic drawings and acrylic paintings. Specializing in colored and graphite pencil work, she has gained recognition for her ability to capture the essence and likeness of animals, portraits, movie characters, and everyday objects.

Driven by a desire to see her drawings come to life, Jasmina embarked on her artistic journey armed with nothing more than a graphite pencil, paper, and an eraser. The joy of seeing the resemblance in her portraits became a driving force in her artistic pursuits. Fans of her work encouraged her to try with colors so she delved into the realm of colored pencils, primarily focusing on their vibrant qualities while occasionally revisiting her beloved graphite medium.

Beyond her pencil work, Jasmina also finds joy in painting landscapes with acrylics. This form of artistic expression allows her to relax and embrace a sense of freedom, deviating from the strict likeness of reference photos. Both drawing and painting play a vital role in her artistic growth.

With a significant following on social media, Jasmina has connected with hundreds of thousands of art enthusiasts and aspiring artists who appreciate her work and find inspiration in her artistic journey.

In her free time, Jasmina indulges in her passion for gardening and continuously seeks opportunities to learn new things. She is a firm believer in the value of lifelong learning, recognizing it as a fundamental aspect of being human and a catalyst for personal growth, both physically and mentally.

Jasmina's passions extend far beyond the world of art. She finds joy and inspiration in the wonders of nature, the intricacies of science, the mysteries of astronomy, the advancements of technology, the creativity of web designing, the melodies of music, and the thrill of engaging in various sports activities.

Through her art and her journey as a self-taught artist, Jasmina aims to inspire others to explore their creativity, encourage self-expression, and discover the transformative power of art in their lives.

Jasmina believes in the power of a positive and optimistic outlook, emphasizing the importance of self-discipline and self-care not only in art but in all aspects of life. She recognizes that the lessons learned through drawing can deeply influence our personalities and the way we live, guiding us towards a more positive and fulfilling existence.

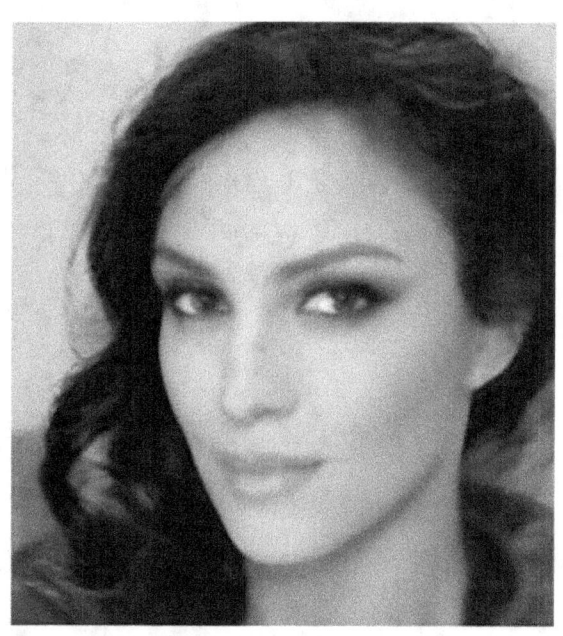

www.jasminasusak.com

Reference Photos for Skill Enhancement

Here are a collection of reference photos, thoughtfully selected to complement the tutorial strategies covered in the book. Dive into the joy of drawing as you explore these public domain images to enhance your skills. Happy drawing!

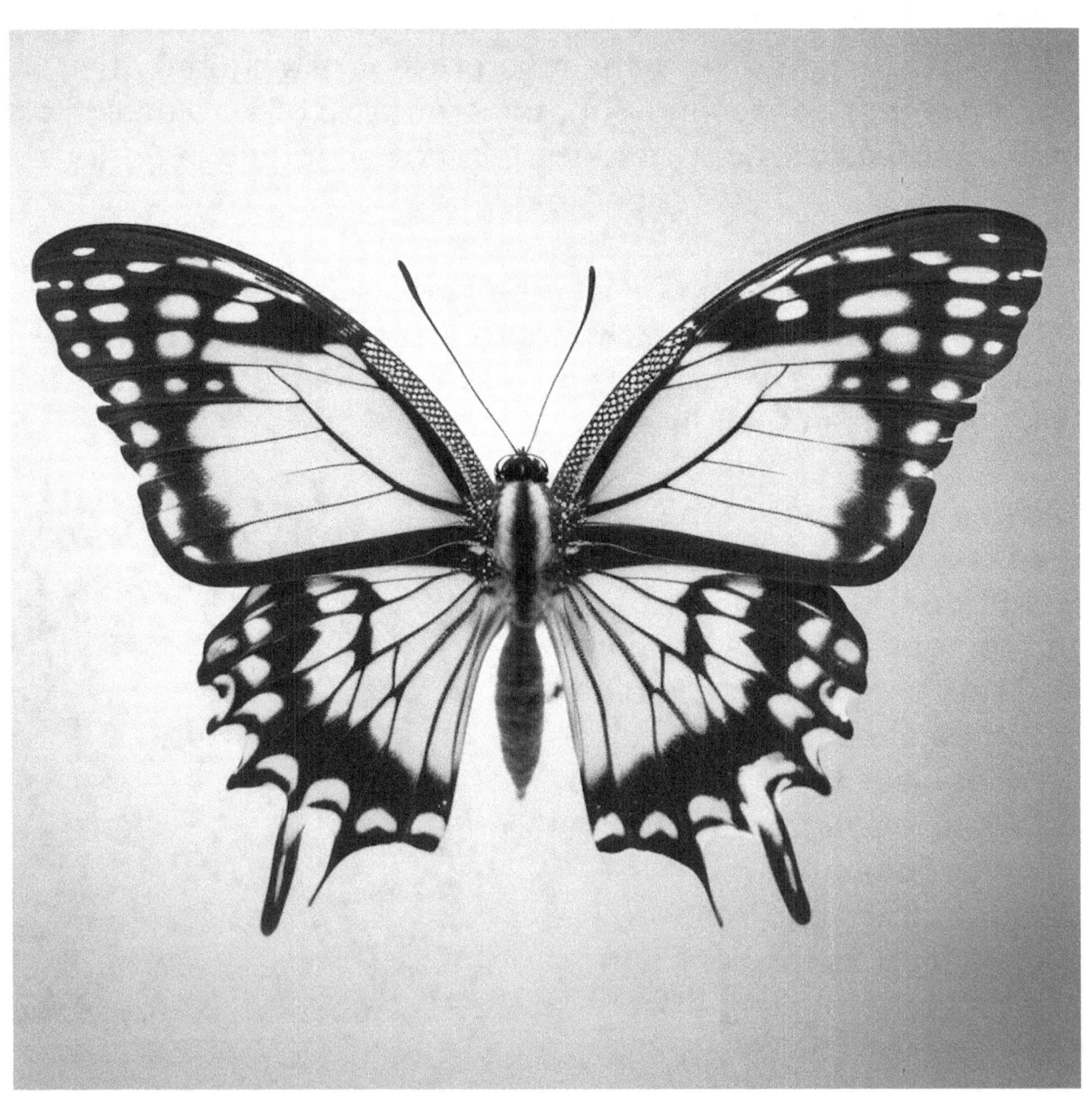

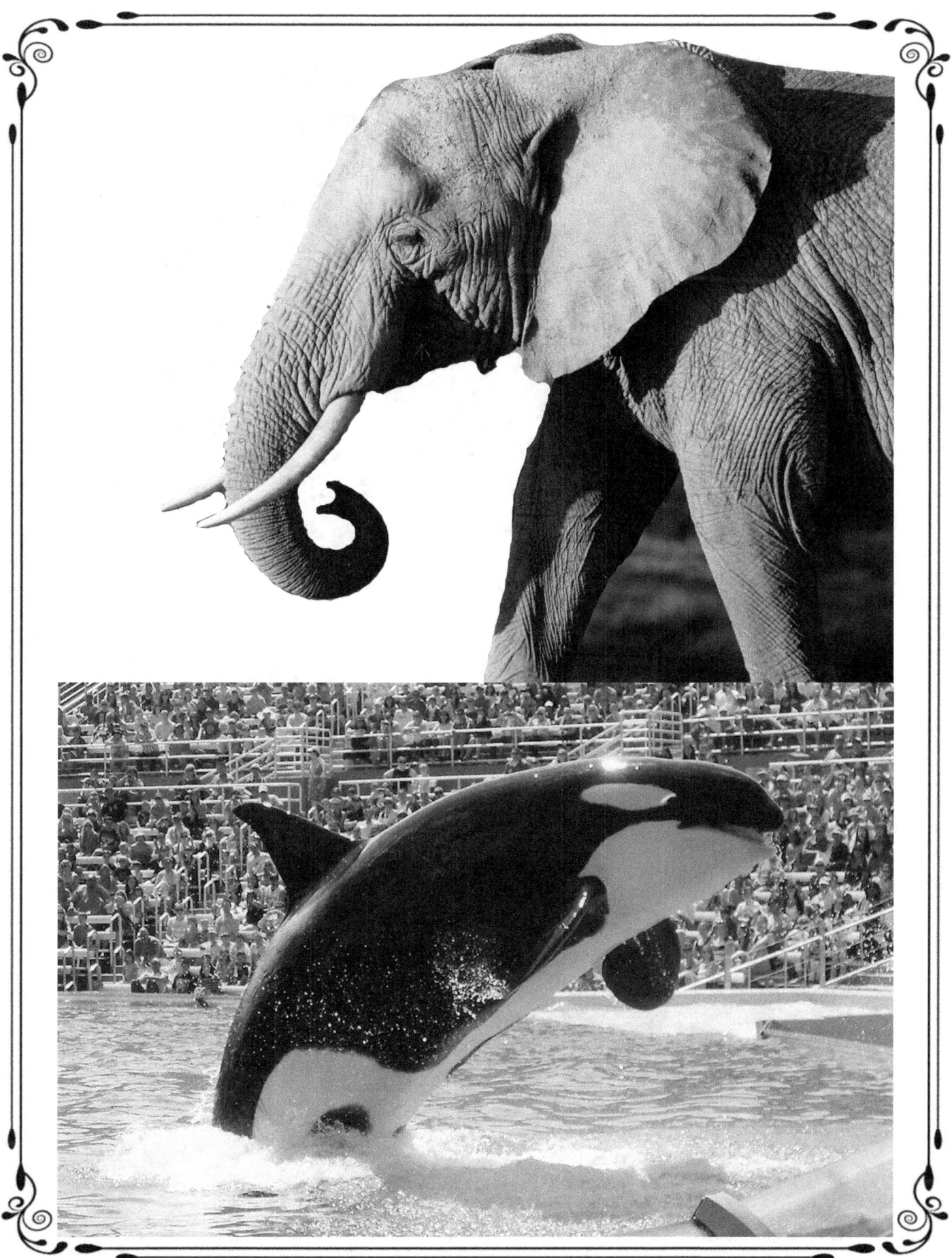

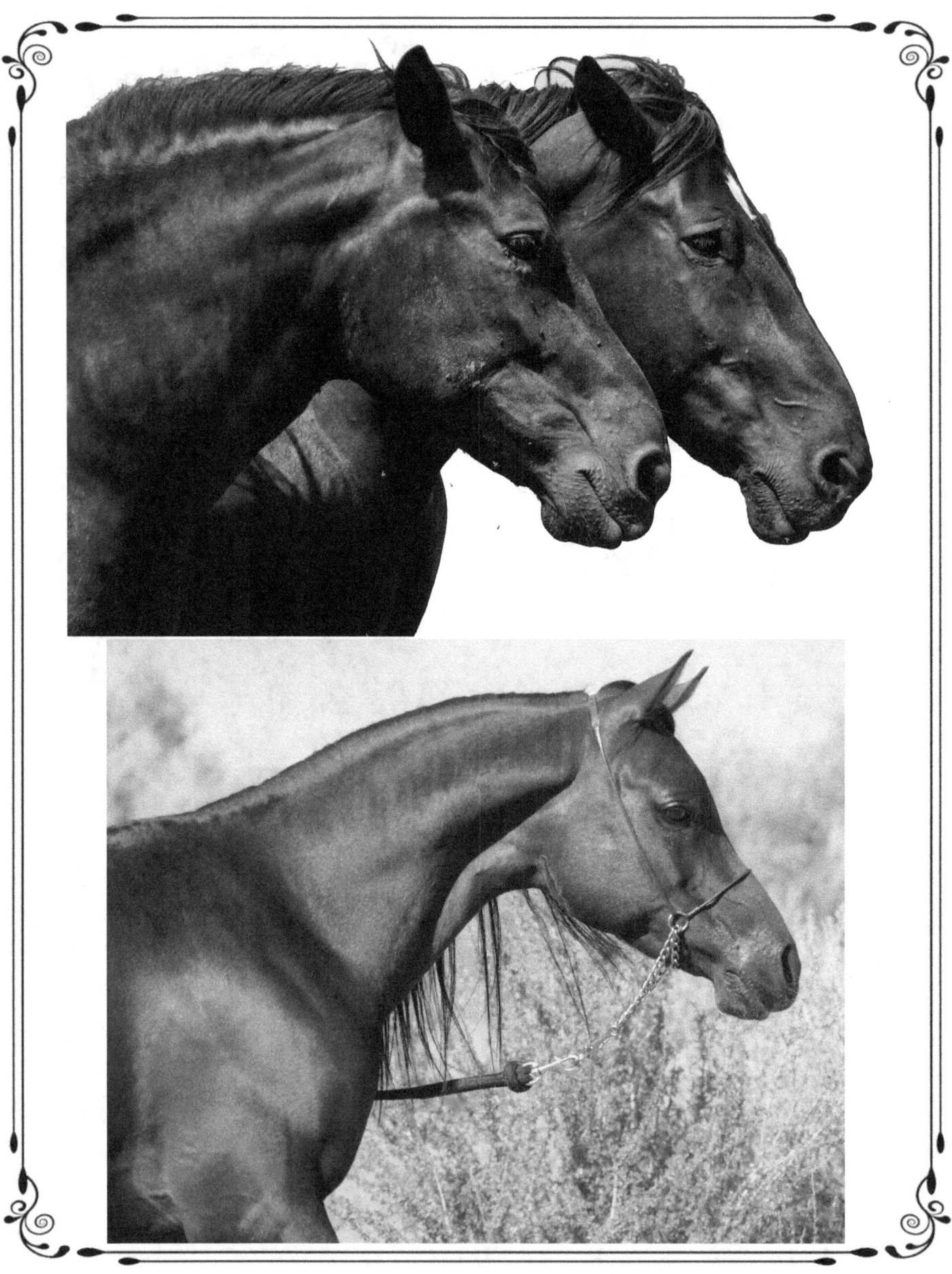

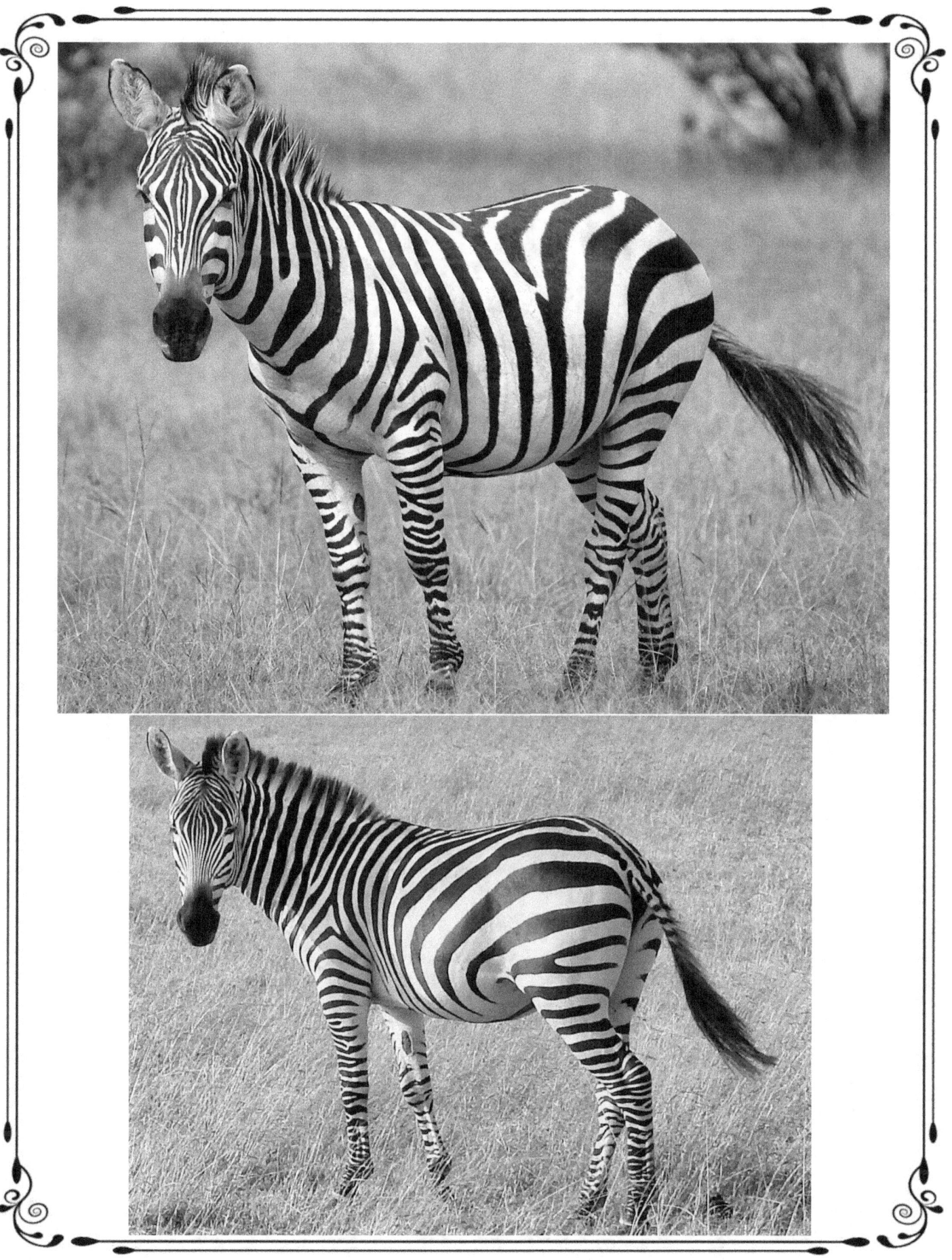

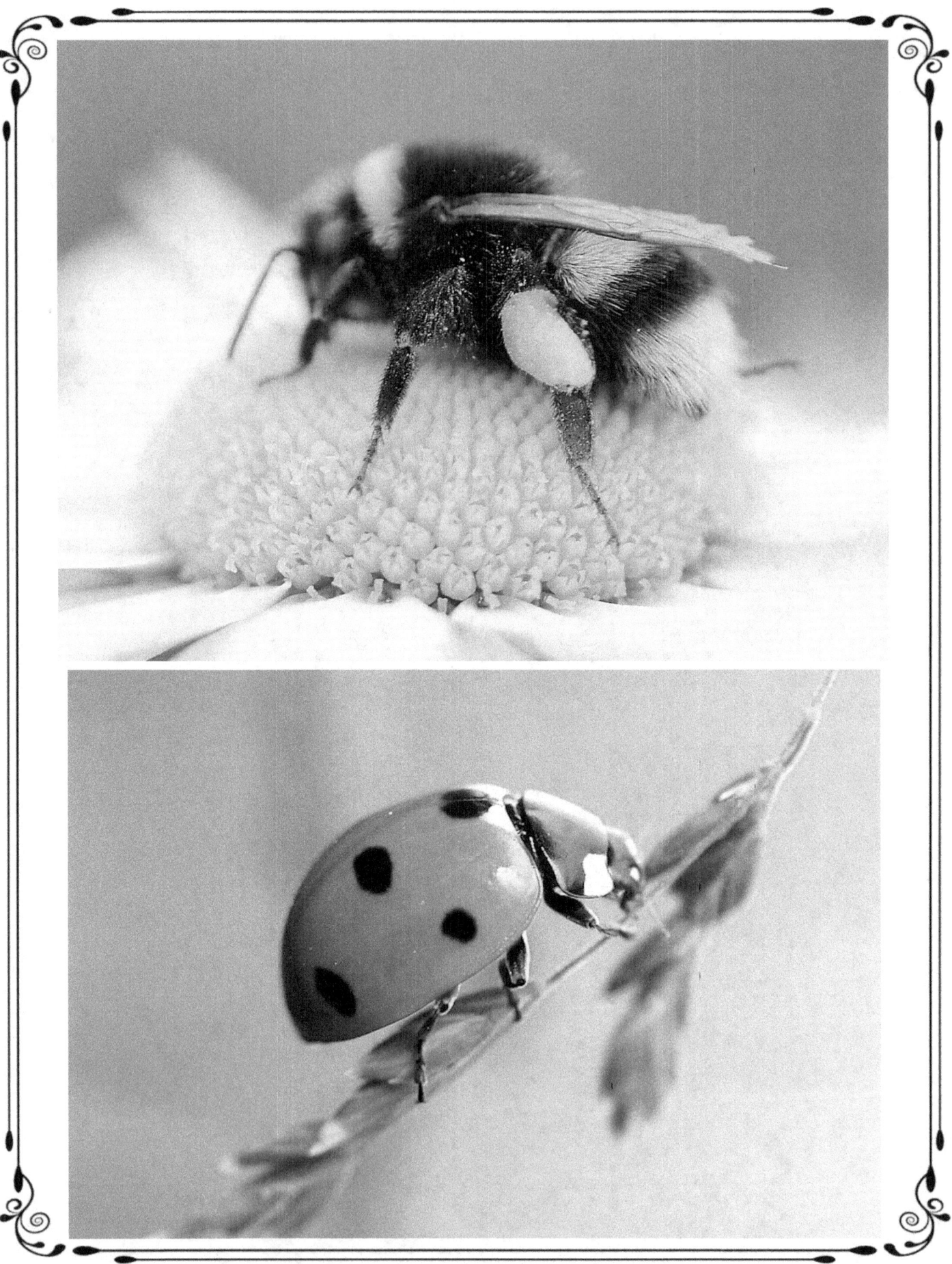

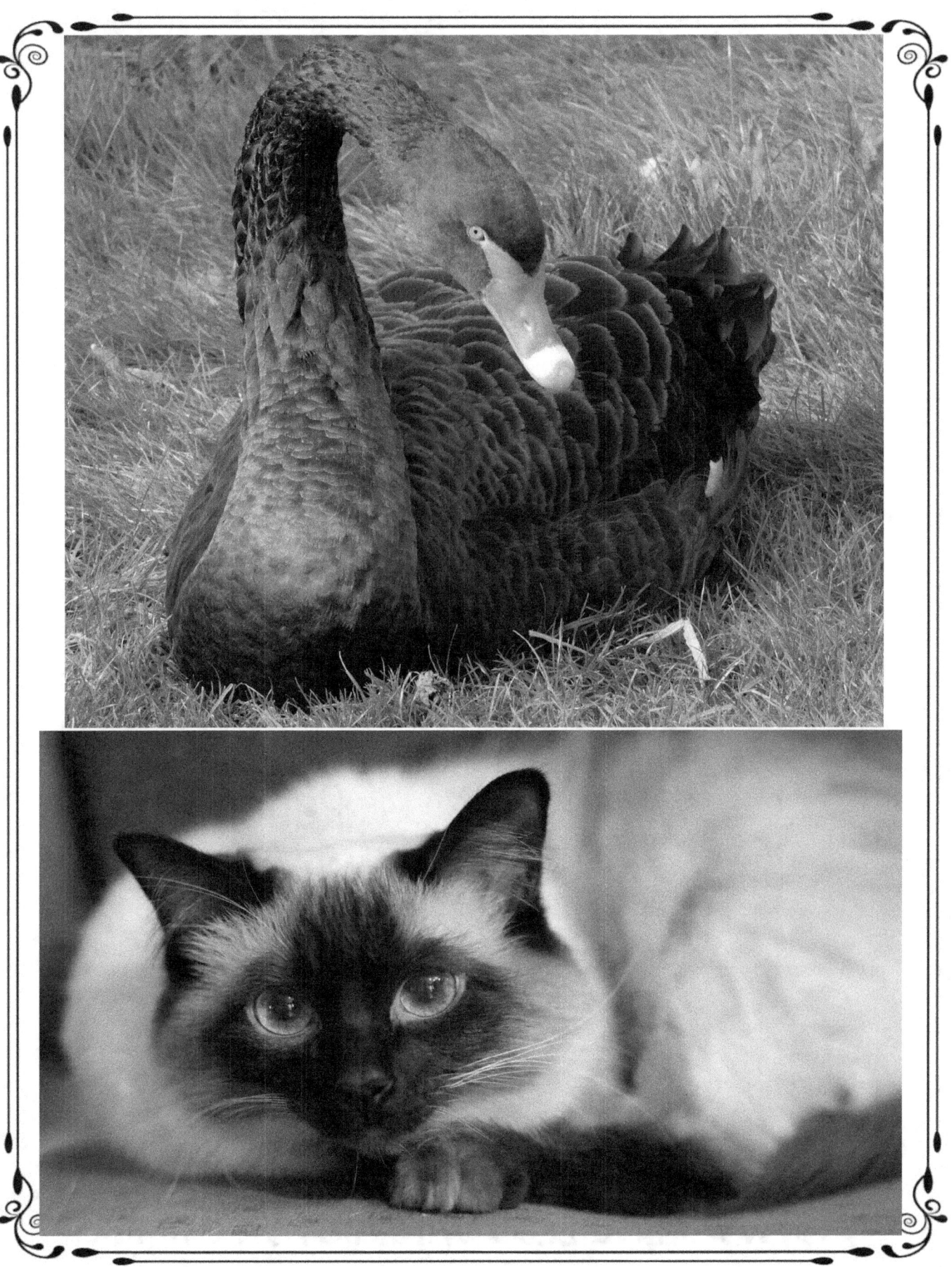

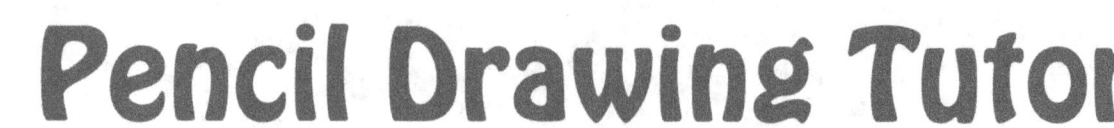

Pencil Drawing Tutor

If you want to learn faster and better, I recommend joining my website, Pencil Drawing Tutor. As a member, you'll learn through real-time narrated videos, step-by-step written tutorials with pictures, and have 24/7 access to PenPick Graphite. You can attach your drawings under any tutorial and chat with other members.

The lessons are perfect for beginners, those looking to improve, or anyone who wants inspiration and fun.

Brand new tutorial every WEEK.
Come join us!

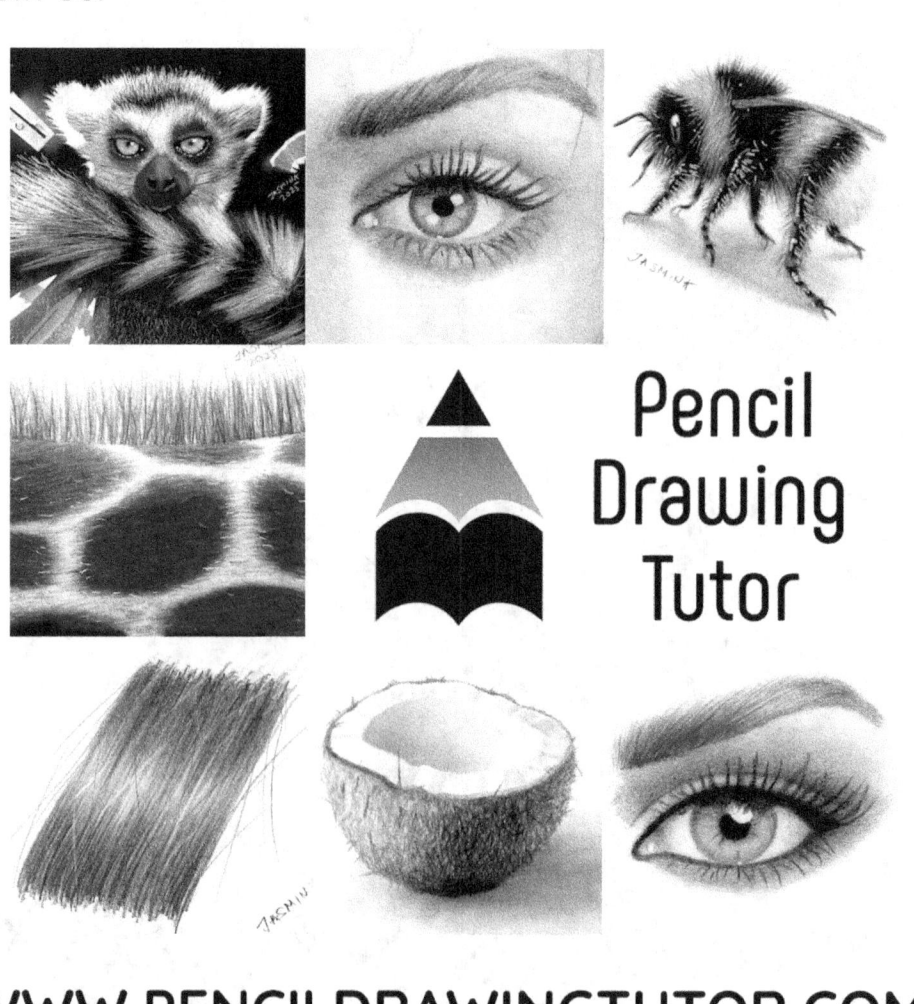

WWW.PENCILDRAWINGTUTOR.COM